Betty Crocker® ULTIMATE Bisquick® COOKBOOK

323 DELICIOUS RECIPES FOR BREAKFAST, DINNER, DESSERT & MORE!

RODALE

Front cover photograph: Impossibly Easy Chef's Salad Pie, page 327
Photography: General Mills Photography Studios and Image Library
Photographer: Chuck Nields
Food Stylists: Sue Finley, Sue Brue

Published by arrangement with Wiley Publishing, Inc., Hoboken, New Jersey

Library of Congress Cataloging-in-Publication Data
Betty Crocker ultimate Bisquick cookbook : 323 delicious recipes for breakfast, dinner, dessert & more!.
    p.   cm.
   Includes index.
   ISBN–13 978–1–60529–816–0 hardcover
   ISBN–10 1–60529–816–6 hardcover
   1. Cookery, American. 2. Quick and easy cookery. I. Crocker, Betty.
 TX715.B48883 2009
 641.5'55—dc22   2009008558

14 16 18 20 19 17 15 13   hardcover

RODALE
LIVE YOUR WHOLE LIFE™

We inspire and enable people to improve their lives and the world around them
For more of our products visit **rodalestore.com** or call 800-848-4735

Biscuits were just the beginning . . .

When Bisquick baking mix was created in 1931, it had one basic purpose: provide a fast and easy way to make homemade biscuits. More than 75 years later it has become an everyday cooking staple. Versatility and easy is the name of the game and that's what Bisquick is all about. Whip up some pancakes or a warm cinnamon streusel-topped coffee cake for brunch. Your family will love Impossibly Easy Pie for supper any night of the week. And who doesn't love strawberry shortcake?

Whether you've used Bisquick for years or are trying it for the first time, this cookbook is packed with delicious new recipes, favorite classic recipes, cooking tips, and a fun look at the history of Bisquick. Favorites like Impossibly Easy Pizza Pie, Ultimate Pancakes, Chicken and Dumplings, and Oven-Fried Chicken with Biscuits are sure to please as well as many new recipes such as Skillet Tomato Mac with Cheese Biscuits, Sour Cream-Blueberry Pancakes and Olive and Rosemary Foccacia.

For those preferring lighter recipes, look for ones using Heart Smart Bisquick such as Deluxe Turkey Cheeseburger Melt, Lemon-Pepper Baked Orange Roughy, and Buttermilk Cornbread Wedges. When it's just two of you, turn to the Cooking for Two chapter featuring smaller, tasty dishes such as Hearty Chicken-Vegetable Stew with Dumplings and Chicken Caesar Salad in Bread Bowls.

No time to cook? No problem. Bisquick makes supper a breeze. Salisbury Steak with Mushroom Gravy, Skillet Chicken Parmesan, or California Pork Tenderloin Sandwiches are just a few offerings from the 30-Minute Weeknight Dinners chapter.

With 323 recipes to choose from, you'll never have to worry about "What's for Dinner?" So let Bisquick help you serve up delicious home-made meals any night of the week.

Warmly,

Contents

Bisquick
Decades of Great Taste

The year was 1930. Carl Smith, a General Mills sales executive, was traveling by train between Portland, Oregon, and San Francisco. While dining aboard the train, Smith was served a plate of delicious, oven-hot biscuits, even though it was well past the usual meal hour. He was amazed at the cook's ability to produce fresh biscuits in such a short time. The chef's time-saving secret? He had blended lard, baking powder and salt in advance, and stored the mixture in an ice chest. From this batter, he had quickly made the biscuits to order. This was an entirely new idea.

Smith recognized the potential of a premixed baking mix, and took the idea to Charlie Kress, the chief chemist of General Mills at the time. The challenges in creating such a product were significant. Most important was creating the proper blend to make the biscuits as good as—or better than—homemade. The result was Bisquick mix, now the country's premiere convenience baking mix.

1930S: BISQUICK BEGINNINGS

Less than one year after Smith's diner-car discovery, Bisquick biscuit mix appeared on the market in 1931. It was a runaway hit! Competitors, eager to jump on the Bisquick bandwagon, worked feverishly to develop comparable products. Within a year, 95 other biscuit mixes were introduced to the marketplace. Only six survived into the following year, and they all trailed in sales behind Bisquick.

1940S AND 1950S: BISQUICK MAKES IT EASY

With America at war during the first half of the forties, families came to depend on the convenience of Bisquick. The Betty Crocker Kitchens continued to develop great-tasting recipes for every meal occasion, earning Bisquick the slogan of "a world of baking in a box."

In the fabulous fifties, the ad slogan "12 Good Things From One Good Mix!" said it all. The ad included photographs of 12 basic recipes that were easily made from Bisquick: biscuits, shortcake, pancakes and more. The most popular recipes started appearing regularly on the friendly yellow box. Many of these recipe favorites are still printed on the Bisquick package today.

1960S: SO QUICK WITH NEW BISQUICK

"Now a completely new Bisquick! Makes biscuits even lighter, fluffier than scratch!" was the headline of the fast-paced sixties, when New Bisquick was introduced. Designed to appeal to makers of southern-style biscuits, the reformulated Bisquick performed so well in test markets that it was rolled out into national distribution. Regular Bisquick was soon replaced, and the word "New" was dropped from the product name.

1970S: BISQUICK COOKBOOK TO THE RESCUE

With the dawn of the seventies came an abundance of new Bisquick recipes. Betty Crocker's Bisquick Cookbook, an updated version of a previous cookbook, was introduced in the fall of 1971 to help promote Bisquick as a multipurpose mix. The book was packed full with more than 200 creative recipes for breads, main dishes and desserts, and was a raging success. By 1979, the cookbook was in its eighth printing!

1980S: A MILESTONE IN BISQUICK HISTORY

To celebrate the fiftieth anniversary of Bisquick, a special cookbook, Betty Crocker's Creative Recipes with Bisquick, was introduced. Hundreds of thousands of enthusiastic fans joined the Bisquick Recipe Club and received The Bisquick Banner, a quarterly newsletter that featured relevant articles, recipes for family meals and entertaining ideas.

In the early 1980s, the "pie that did the impossible—formed its own crust as it baked" was heavily promoted with recipes, product advertising and booklets. "Impossible Coconut Pie," which was based on a grassroots coconut custard pie recipe, was the first Impossible Pie. Soon more than 100 sweet or savory Impossible pies were created in the Betty Crocker Kitchens. Since then, these crustless pies have been renamed Impossibly Easy Pies and they continue to be requested favorites.

1990S: BISQUICK . . . WHAT A GREAT IDEA!

A desire to return to simplicity and use trusted favorites helped Bisquick continue to be a staple in homes across America. People were drawn to the comfort of fresh-baked breads, pizzas and one-dish meals, but schedules were busier than ever. Bisquick made it easy to get great-tasting, home-made meals on the table fast.

2000 AND BEYOND: THE BEST OF BISQUICK

Today, Bisquick remains a household word. Although different formulas and box sizes have been developed over the years, cooks depend on the mix in the familiar yellow and blue box for quick, easy and delicious meal solutions. Bisquick celebrated its 75th anniversary in 2006 and remains the country's premiere convenience baking mix.

Bisquick Q&A

Bisquick is great to have on hand and a snap to use. But some questions still occasionally crop up. Here are the most frequently asked questions about Bisquick.

Q: *What's the best way to measure Bisquick mix?*

A: For best results, spoon Bisquick mix—without sifting—into a dry-ingredient measuring cup, and level with a straight-edged knife or spatula. Don't pack or tap Bisquick mix into the cup.

Q: *Can I use Bisquick mix in recipes that call for flour?*

A: Because Bisquick mix contains fat and leavening as well as flour, you can't use it as a straight substitute in baked foods, such as cookies and cakes. However, if you want to use Bisquick mix to thicken a stew or gravy, use the same amount of Bisquick mix as you would flour.

Q: *How should I store Bisquick mix?*

A: To keep Bisquick mix fresh, store it in an airtight container or plastic bag in a cool, dry place, like on your pantry shelf. If you intend to keep it for a long time, store it in the refrigerator or freezer. If frozen, bring it to room temperature before using.

Q: *Is Bisquick mix affected by humidity?*

A: Bisquick mix reacts to the environment just like any other flour-based product does. In humid conditions, you may find that doughs and batters are stickier, softer or more fluid.

You can add small amounts of Bisquick mix to make the dough or batter easier to work with.

Q: *Can I substitute Bisquick Heart Smart® mix for Original Bisquick mix in my recipes?*

A: It depends. Because the formulas are different, the products perform differently in some recipes. The biggest difference is in the amount of water absorbed when preparing doughs and batters. For that reason, we recommend using the type of Bisquick mix called for in the recipe.

Q: *Will Reduced Fat Bisquick recipes work with Bisquick Heart Smart mix?*

A: Yes, all your favorite Reduced Fat Bisquick recipes still work with Bisquick Heart Smart mix.

Q: *Can I double the recipes for Impossibly Easy Pies?*

A: Impossibly Easy Pies, the crustless pies made with Bisquick mix that have been a favorite of Bisquick users since the 1970s, can successfully be doubled. Just double the ingredients for any Impossibly Easy Pie recipe and bake in either two 9-inch pie plates or a 13 × 9 × 2-inch baking dish. If you use the baking dish, bake the pie for about 10 minutes longer than the recipe indicates.

Q: *Can Impossibly Easy Pies be made ahead?*

A: Savory Impossibly Easy Pies may be covered and refrigerated up to 24 hours before baking. You may need to bake longer than the recipe directs—and watch for doneness carefully. Premade pies will have a slightly lower volume because refrigeration decreases the strength of the leavening. We don't recommend preparing sweet Impossibly Easy Pies ahead.

Q: *What's the best way to store Impossibly Easy Pies?*

A: Cool (if warm), cover and immediately refrigerate any remaining cooked pie. It will keep in the refrigerator for up to 3 days.

Q: *Can I reheat leftover Impossibly Easy Pies?*

A: Reheat leftovers in the microwave. Place one slice on a microwavable plate, and cover with waxed paper. Microwave on Medium (50%) for 2 or 3 minutes or until hot.

High-Altitude Baking with Bisquick

The decrease in air pressure at higher altitudes changes the way foods cook and bake. High-altitude considerations that affect Bisquick mix include:

- *gases expanding more from the leavening*
- *a decrease in the boiling point of liquids*
- *a faster rate of evaporation*

In baked goods, these changes translate into longer bake times, collapse of product structure and possible overbrowning. Common high-altitude adjustments from the sea-level recipe include one or more of the following:

- *increasing oven temperature*
- *longer bake time*
- *adding more Bisquick mix*

In addition, some recipes may require adding flour or decreasing sugar or oil.

There are no hard and fast rules to follow when baking with Bisquick at high altitude. Changes to recipes depend upon the food you are baking and the proportion of ingredients. We suggest you use recipes that have been tested and adjusted for high altitude. All of the recipes in this book have been tested at high altitude.

Bisquick Basics Pancakes

Fluffy pancakes are a perfect way to start a morning. Here are some pancake pointers to get you on your way:

1. Heat your skillet over medium-high heat, or turn on your griddle to 375°F about 5 minutes before using. Grease the surface with a light coating of vegetable oil. If greasing with cooking spray, spray it before heating. To test the temperature, sprinkle it with a few drops of water. If the water bubbles skittle around before they disappear, the heat is just right.

2. Stir the batter with a wire whisk or a fork, just until the ingredients are moistened. Any small lumps in the batter will disappear during cooking.

3. Test one pancake so you can see how your pancake batter will act. If the batter is too thin, it will spread unevenly and result in flat pancakes; a too-thick pancake batter won't spread much at all. Add a little milk until the batter reaches the desired consistency.

4. Repeated cooking on both sides will toughen the pancakes. Flip the pancakes when they're puffed, covered with bubbles and dry around the edges. Cook the other side until golden brown (the second side never browns as evenly as the first).

5. Keep pancakes warm by placing them in a single layer on a wire rack or paper towel–lined cookie sheet in a 200°F oven. Don't stack warm pancakes, or they'll become limp and soggy.

Q: *Why are my pancakes raw in the center?*

A: Too little liquid or too much Bisquick mix may be reasons. Or, your griddle temperature may be too high. For best results, cook pancakes approximately 1 minute 15 seconds on the first side and 1 minute on the second side.

Q: *Can Bisquick mix pancake batter be prepared ahead of time?*

A: Yes, but not too far ahead. Make the batter, then cover and refrigerate no longer than 1 hour.

Q: *Why are my pancakes tough and leathery?*

A: If the temperature is too low, pancakes will take longer to brown and become dry and tough. If the griddle is too hot, the pancakes' edges will be overcooked and tough.

Q: *Can I use buttermilk in pancakes?*

A: Yes, just use the same amount of buttermilk as you would use milk or water for pancakes.

Q: *What's the best way to store leftover pancakes?*

A: Store them in an airtight container or plastic food-storage bag in the refrigerator no longer than 2 days, or freeze for up to 3 months. Microwave individual frozen pancakes on High for 20 to 30 seconds.

Bisquick Basics Waffles

Wow them with wonderful waffles! It's easy—here's how.

Q: *Why didn't my waffles rise?*

A: The temperature of the waffle iron may be too hot or not hot enough. Or, you may have used too much Bisquick mix and not enough liquid.

1. Prevent waffles from sticking by seasoning the waffle iron according to the manufacturer's directions. If greasing with cooking spray, remember to spray it before heating the iron. Starting with a clean waffle iron is also important. After each time you use it, remove all traces of baked-on batter or crumbs.

2. Mix the waffle batter right in a 4- or 8-cup glass measuring cup that has a handle and a spout, which makes it easy pouring onto the waffle iron.

3. The amount of batter you use depends on the model of your waffle iron. Usually it's a little less than a cupful, but every waffle iron is slightly different. Pour the batter onto the waffle iron so each section of the waffle grid gets covered and it is full but not overflowing. Close the lid and wait. When the iron stops giving off steam, the waffle should be done. Try lifting the lid—if it resists at all, the waffle needs more time to cook.

4. Lift the waffle from the iron using a fork. To keep waffles warm until serving time, place them in a single layer on a wire rack or paper towel-lined cookie sheet in a 350°F oven for up to 20 minutes. Don't stack warm waffles, or they'll become soggy.

Q: *Why are my waffles tough?*

A: You may have used too much Bisquick mix and not enough liquid. Your waffle iron may be too hot.

Q: *Why are my waffles crispy?*

A: You may have used too much liquid and not enough Bisquick mix.

Q: *Can Bisquick mix waffle batter be prepared ahead of time?*

A: Yes, but not too far ahead. Make the batter, then cover and refrigerate no longer than 1 hour.

Q: *What's the best way to store leftover waffles?*

A: Store them in an airtight container in the refrigerator no longer than 2 days, or freeze up to 3 months. Reheat by toasting them in your toaster.

Bisquick Basics Muffins

Making muffins that look and taste great doesn't involve any magic—just a few quick tips and techniques.

1. Stir the batter just until the ingredients are moistened; the batter will look a little lumpy. If you mix the batter too much, the muffins will be tough and the tops will be pointed instead of nicely rounded. Gently fold berries into the batter at the very end to keep the berries from breaking apart and coloring the batter.

2. Grease only the bottoms of the muffin cups for nicely shaped muffins with rounded tops and no overhanging edges, or use paper baking cups for easy cleanup.

3. Divide the batter evenly among the muffin cups, filling the cups about two-thirds full. Take the guesswork out of filling muffin cups; Use a No. 20 or 24 spring-handled ice cream scoop. After filling the cups, wipe up any batter that spills onto the edge of the pan so it won't stick and burn. If you have empty cups in the muffin pan, fill them half full with water so the muffins bake evenly.

4. Bake muffins for the shortest time stated in the recipe, then check for doneness. If the muffin tops aren't golden brown or don't spring back when touched lightly in the center, bake a minute or two longer. If the pan has a dark nonstick finish, you may need to lower the oven temperature by 25°F. If you're using an insulated pan, you may need to increase the baking time slightly. Also, placing the pan on the center oven rack is important so the bottoms of the muffins don't brown too much.

5. Remove muffins from the pan immediately so they don't become soggy. Loosen the muffins with a knife or metal spatula, then gently lift. Muffins baked in paper cups should lift right out. Sometimes a recipe will tell you to leave the muffins in the pan for a few minutes so they don't fall apart when you take them out of the pan.

Q: *Why are my muffins peaked and full of holes?*

A: You may have overmixed the batter or your oven temperature may be too high.

Q: *Why didn't my muffins rise?*

A: Your oven temperature may be too low or you may have undermixed the batter.

Q: *What cause muffins to be tough, heavy or rubbery?*

A: Too much egg causes this problem or overmixing.

Bisquick Basics Biscuits

It takes just minutes to stir up a batch of homemade biscuits, with these easy biscuit basics:

1. Stir the ingredients until a soft, slightly sticky dough forms. If the dough is too soft to handle, stir in 2 to 4 tablespoons of Bisquick.

Q: *Why didn't my biscuits rise?*

A: **Too much liquid or too little Bisquick mix could be reasons. Too little or too gentle kneading might also be the cause.**

2. Knead the dough on a surface sprinkled with Bisquick. Roll the dough in Bisquick to keep it from sticking to the surface. Dipping your fingers into a little Bisquick will keep the dough from sticking to your hands. Shape the dough into a ball, and knead it gently about ten times.

3. Roll the dough about ½ inch thick. Here's a trick for rolling dough to the right thickness: Use two sticks, ½ inch thick and about 14 inches long, as a guide. Place the ball of dough between the sticks, and roll the dough to the thickness of the sticks.

4. Cut the dough with a round biscuit cutter dipped in Bisquick, pushing the cutter straight down through the dough. If you twist as you cut, the biscuits may be uneven. Cut the biscuits out of the dough as close together as possible. After cutting as many biscuits as possible, lightly press the scraps of dough together. Roll or pat the remaining dough until it is ½ inch thick, then cut. These biscuits may look slightly uneven.

5. Place the biscuits about 1 inch apart on an ungreased cookie sheet. Shiny aluminum cookie sheets of good quality produce the best biscuits. If the cookie sheet is dark, the bottoms of the biscuits will be darker in color. Reducing the oven temperature to 400°F may help. Place the cookie sheet on the center oven rack so the biscuits will brown evenly on both the top and bottom.

Q: *Why are my biscuits tough and hard?*

A: **Overmixing or overkneading, oven temperature too high or too long a bake time, overmeasurement of Bisquick mix or undermeasurement of liquid.**

Q: *Why is my biscuit dough so sticky?*

A: **With the change to a trans fat–free formula, the dough has become a little softer and stickier. You can try working in a little more mix during the kneading stage.**

Bisquick Basics Dumplings

Light and tender dumplings are a welcome addition to many soups, stews and chilies. Plus, they're as easy to make as 1-2-3:

1. Stir the ingredients until a soft, slightly sticky dough forms. Be careful not to mix the dough too much or the dumplings will be tough and heavy.

Q: *Why are my dumplings tough?*
A: Make sure you're not overmixing the dough or overcooking. You also might have added the dough to the stew too soon. The stew should be gently boiling with bubbles breaking the surface continually.

Q: *Why are my dumplings heavy and raw in the center?*
A: Overmeasurement of Bisquick mix or undermeasurement of liquid are two common reasons. Or, you may have added the dough to the stew too soon or not cooked the dumplings properly. Your stew should continue to boil gently (bubbles breaking the surface gently and continually throughout the cooking time).

2. Add the dumpling dough to hot liquid. You can tell if the temperature is hot enough when the liquid is gently boiling with bubbles breaking on the surface. If you add the dough before the liquid is hot enough, the dumplings will end up soggy and undercooked.

Q: *Why do my dumplings fall apart?*
A: It's important to drop dough onto meat or vegetables rather than directly into liquid; the simmering action may force the dough apart. (See step 3.)

3. Drop the dough by spoonfuls onto the meat or vegetables in the stew, not into the gravy or liquid. If the dough is dropped right into the liquid, the simmering action may break up the dumplings. Also, the dough will soak up moisture from the liquid so the dumplings will become soft and soggy.

Bisquick Basics Shortcakes

Shortcakes, the sweet sister to biscuits, are simple to make and simply delicious. Here are some surefire shortcake secrets:

1. Stir the ingredients until a soft, slightly sticky dough forms.

Q: *Why are my shortcakes raw or doughy in the center?*

A: Undermeasurement of liquid or overmeasurement of Bisquick mix are two common reasons. Check your oven temperature; it may be too high. Also, make sure not to underbake the shortcake.

2. Drop the dough by large spoonfuls onto an ungreased cookie sheet. Shiny aluminum cookie sheets of good quality produce the best shortcakes and keep the bottoms from getting overly browned.

3. Sugar causes shortcakes to have a dark bottom crust. If your cookie sheet is dark, the bottoms of the shortcakes may burn. Reducing the oven temperature to 400°F may help.

4. Sticking slightly to the cookie sheet sometimes happens due to the sugar. Use a turner to lift the shortcakes easily off the cookie sheet.

Q: *Why is the bottom crust of my shortcake dark?*

A: Shortcakes tend to have dark bottom crusts due to their sugar content. The pan you use is important. For the same color crust, top and bottom, use shiny metal pans of good quality. If your pan is brown, black or darkened from an accumulation of fat, biscuits will be darker in color. Decreasing your oven temperature to 400°F may help. Also, shortcakes should be baked on a cookie sheet on the center oven rack.

Q: *Why did my shortcakes stick to the cookie sheet?*

A: It is typical for drop shortcakes to stick slightly to the cookie sheet. Use a turner to remove them. A clean cookie sheet is essential for successful shortcakes. Make sure to remove all grease, crumbs or baked-on dough for best results.

Q: *Why don't my shortcakes brown evenly?*

A: Be sure to place the cookie sheet on the center oven rack. That way, the shortcakes will brown evenly on both the top and bottom.

CHAPTER 1

Bisquick
through the Decades

Breakfast Pinwheels

PREP TIME: 20 MINUTES ● START TO FINISH: 40 MINUTES
12 PINWHEELS

These warm breakfast treats were based on the "Lightning Quick Biscuits" recipe from the 1930s. The original recipe included a choice of finely chopped dates, citron or figs with the raisins.

PINWHEELS

2¼ cups Original Bisquick mix

½ cup milk

1 tablespoon butter or margarine, softened

¼ cup granulated sugar

1 teaspoon ground cinnamon

½ cup finely chopped walnuts

½ cup dried currants

1 tablespoon butter or margarine, melted

GLAZE

¾ cup powdered sugar

¼ teaspoon vanilla

1 tablespoon milk

1 Heat oven to 400°F. Line cookie sheet with parchment paper. In medium bowl, stir Bisquick mix and ½ cup milk until soft dough forms. Place dough on surface generously sprinkled with Bisquick mix; roll in Bisquick mix to coat. Knead 5 times.

2 Press or roll dough into 11 × 8-inch rectangle. Spread dough with 1 tablespoon softened butter. In small bowl, mix granulated sugar, cinnamon, walnuts and currants; sprinkle over top of dough; press in slightly. Starting with an 11-inch side, roll up dough tightly; seal edge. Cut into ¾-inch slices. Place slices on cookie sheet. Brush slices with 1 tablespoon melted butter.

3 Bake 8 to 10 minutes or until golden brown. Remove from cookie sheet; cool 10 minutes. In small bowl, mix all glaze ingredients, adding milk, 1 teaspoon at a time, until glaze is thin enough to drizzle. Drizzle glaze over pinwheels. Serve warm.

High Altitude (3500–6500 ft): Bake 13 to 15 minutes.

1 PINWHEEL: Calories 210 (Calories from Fat 70); Total Fat 8g (Saturated Fat 2.5g); Cholesterol 5mg; Sodium 290mg; Total Carbohydrate 32g (Dietary Fiber 1g; Sugars 17g); Protein 3g **% DAILY VALUE:** Vitamin A 0%; Vitamin C 0%; Calcium 4%; Iron 6% **EXCHANGES:** 1 Starch, 1 Other Carbohydrate, 1½ Fat **CARBOHYDRATE CHOICES:** 2

Sweet Muffins

PREP TIME: 10 MINUTES ● START TO FINISH: 30 MINUTES
12 MUFFINS

This muffin recipe first appeared on Bisquick boxes in the 1930s and was simply called "Bisquick Muffins." To get a more tender muffin, we use granulated sugar instead of the brown sugar used in the original recipe. Serve these muffins warm, with cream cheese and your favorite fruit jam.

⅔ cup milk

2 tablespoons vegetable oil, or butter or margarine, melted

1 egg

2 cups Original Bisquick mix

⅓ cup sugar

1 Heat oven to 400°F. Spray bottoms only of 12 regular-size muffin cups with cooking spray or line with paper baking cups. In medium bowl, beat milk, oil and egg with wire whisk or fork until blended. Stir in Bisquick mix and sugar just until moistened. Spoon batter into muffin cups.

2 Bake 15 to 18 minutes or until golden brown.

High Altitude (3500–6500 ft): No change.

1 MUFFIN: Calories 140 (Calories from Fat 50); Total Fat 5g (Saturated Fat 1.5g); Cholesterol 20mg; Sodium 260mg; Total Carbohydrate 19g (Dietary Fiber 0g; Sugars 7g); Protein 2g **% DAILY VALUE:** Vitamin A 0%; Vitamin C 0%; Calcium 4%; Iron 4% **EXCHANGES:** ½ Starch, 1 Other Carbohydrate, 1 Fat **CARBOHYDRATE CHOICES:** 1

Apple-Cinnamon Muffins: Stir in 1 teaspoon ground cinnamon with the Bisquick mix. Stir ¾ cup chopped peeled all-purpose apple into batter.

Blueberry Muffins: Stir ¾ cup fresh or frozen (do not thaw) blueberries into batter.

Oatmeal-Raisin Muffins: Decrease Bisquick mix to 1½ cups. Stir ¾ cup quick-cooking oats, ½ cup raisins and 1 teaspoon ground cinnamon into batter.

Rolled Milk Biscuits

PREP TIME: 10 MINUTES ● START TO FINISH: 20 MINUTES
10 BISCUITS

These rolled biscuits were originally called "Lightning Quick Biscuits" because they could be hastily thrown together for "unexpected guests or an impromptu luncheon or supper."

2¼ cups Original Bisquick mix
⅔ cup milk

1 Heat oven to 450°F. In medium bowl, stir ingredients until soft dough forms; beat 30 seconds. If dough is sticky, gradually stir in enough Bisquick mix (up to ¼ cup) to make dough easy to handle.

2 Place dough on surface generously sprinkled with Bisquick mix; roll in Bisquick mix to coat. Shape into a ball; knead 10 times. Press or roll until ½ inch thick. Cut into rounds with 2-inch cutter dipped in Bisquick mix. On ungreased cookie sheet, place rounds.

3 Bake 8 to 10 minutes or until golden brown.

High Altitude (3500–6500 ft): No change.

1 BISCUIT: Calories 120 (Calories from Fat 35); Total Fat 3.5g (Saturated Fat 1g); Cholesterol 0mg; Sodium 340mg; Total Carbohydrate 18g (Dietary Fiber 0g; Sugars 2g); Protein 3g **% DAILY VALUE:** Vitamin A 0%; Vitamin C 0%; Calcium 4%; Iron 4% **EXCHANGES:** 1 Starch, 1 Fat **CARBOHYDRATE CHOICES:** 1

Rolled Water Biscuits: Stir 2⅓ cups Bisquick mix and ⅔ cup cold water until soft dough forms; beat 30 seconds.

Dropped Milk Biscuits: After beating, on ungreased cookie sheet, drop dough by 10 spoonfuls.

Apple Cake

PREP TIME: 15 MINUTES ● **START TO FINISH: 50 MINUTES**
9 SERVINGS

*Originally, "Bisquick Fruit Cake" required rolling out dough, fitting it into
a pan and topping with peeled sliced apples. We simplified things by adding sugar,
butter and more milk to make the batter pourable. Leaving the peel on
the apple saves time and adds color to the cake.*

2 cups Original Bisquick mix

2 tablespoons sugar

½ cup milk

2 tablespoons butter or
    margarine, softened

1 egg

1 medium unpeeled red apple,
    thinly sliced (about 1 cup)

¼ cup butter or margarine,
    melted

2 tablespoons sugar

½ teaspoon ground
    cinnamon

1 Heat oven to 400°F. Spray 9-inch square pan with cooking
spray. In medium bowl, stir Bisquick mix, 2 tablespoons
sugar, the milk, 2 tablespoons butter and egg until well
blended. Spread batter evenly in pan.

2 Arrange apple slices in 3 rows, overlapping slices slightly,
on batter. Brush ¼ cup melted butter over tops of apple slices.

3 In small bowl, mix 2 tablespoons sugar and the cinnamon;
sprinkle over apples.

4 Bake 16 to 18 minutes or until edges are golden brown.
Cool 15 minutes before serving. Cut with serrated knife into
9 squares.

High Altitude (3500–6500 ft): Bake 18 to 20 minutes.

1 SERVING: Calories 220 (Calories from Fat 110); Total Fat 12g (Saturated Fat 6g);
Cholesterol 45mg; Sodium 390mg; Total Carbohydrate 25g (Dietary Fiber 1g; Sugars 8g);
Protein 3g **% DAILY VALUE:** Vitamin A 6%; Vitamin C 0%; Calcium 4%; Iron 4% **EXCHANGES:**
1 Starch, ½ Other Carbohydrate, 2½ Fat **CARBOHYDRATE CHOICES:** 1½

Orange Biscuits

PREP TIME: 10 MINUTES ● START TO FINISH: 20 MINUTES
8 BISCUITS

"Orange or Lemon Bisquicks" was a popular recipe on Bisquick boxes in
the 1940s. The original recipe directed: "Before baking, dip ½ cube loaf sugar into
orange or lemon juice. Press into top of each Bisquick." We simplified things
by brushing with orange juice and sprinkling with sugar.

2¼ cups Original Bisquick mix
2 teaspoons grated orange peel
⅔ cup milk
1 tablespoon orange juice
2 teaspoons sugar

1 Heat oven to 400°F. Spray cookie sheet with cooking spray. In medium bowl, stir Bisquick mix, orange peel and milk until soft dough forms.

2 Place dough on surface generously sprinkled with Bisquick mix; roll in Bisquick mix to coat. Press or roll dough ½ inch thick. Cut into rounds with 2½-inch cutter. Place rounds 2 inches apart on cookie sheet. Brush with orange juice; sprinkle with sugar.

3 Bake 8 to 10 minutes or until edges begin to turn brown and tops are light golden brown. Serve warm.

High Altitude (3500–6500 ft): Bake 11 to 13 minutes.

1 BISCUIT: Calories 150 (Calories from Fat 40); Total Fat 4.5g (Saturated Fat 1.5g); Cholesterol 0mg; Sodium 420mg; Total Carbohydrate 24g (Dietary Fiber 0g; Sugars 3g); Protein 3g **% DAILY VALUE:** Vitamin A 0%; Vitamin C 0%; Calcium 6%; Iron 6%
EXCHANGES: 1 Starch, ½ Other Carbohydrate, 1 Fat **CARBOHYDRATE CHOICES:** 1½

Hot Dogs 'n' Crescents

PREP TIME: 10 MINUTES ● **START TO FINISH: 25 MINUTES**
8 SERVINGS

There were several versions of this popular "Pigs in Blankets" recipe over the years—one with sauerkraut. This one is a kid-pleaser with mustard, pickle relish and sliced American cheese.

1¾ cups Original Bisquick mix

⅓ cup milk

1 tablespoon yellow mustard

3 tablespoons pickle relish, drained

2 slices American cheese, each cut into 4 strips

8 hot dogs

1 Heat oven to 425°F. Spray cookie sheet with cooking spray. In medium bowl, stir Bisquick mix, milk and mustard until soft dough forms; beat 30 seconds. Place dough on surface sprinkled with Bisquick mix; roll in Bisquick mix to coat. Shape into a ball; knead 10 times.

2 Roll or press dough into 13-inch round; cut into 8 wedges. Place about 1 teaspoon pickle relish and 1 cheese strip on each wedge about 1 inch from rounded edge. Top with hot dog. Roll up, beginning at rounded edge. On cookie sheet, place crescents, tip sides down.

3 Bake about 12 minutes or until golden brown.

High Altitude (3500–6500 ft): Heat oven to 450°F.

1 SERVING: Calories 320 (Calories from Fat 200); Total Fat 22g (Saturated Fat 8g); Cholesterol 35mg; Sodium 1140mg; Total Carbohydrate 22g (Dietary Fiber 0g; Sugars 5g); Protein 9g **% DAILY VALUE:** Vitamin A 2%; Vitamin C 0%; Calcium 8%; Iron 8% **EXCHANGES:** 1 Starch, ½ Other Carbohydrate, 1 High-Fat Meat, 2½ Fat **CARBOHYDRATE CHOICES:** 1½

Chicken and Dumplings

PREP TIME: 20 MINUTES ● **START TO FINISH: 3 HOURS 5 MINUTES**
4 SERVINGS

This "robust, zippy-flavored stew of meat and vegetables with fluffy dumplings"
was touted as a great way to stretch food dollars in the 1940s.

1 cut-up whole chicken
(3 to 3½ lb)

2 medium stalks celery (with
leaves), cut up (about 1 cup)

1 medium carrot, sliced (½ cup)

1 small onion, sliced

2 tablespoons chopped fresh
parsley or 2 teaspoons
parsley flakes

1 teaspoon salt

⅛ teaspoon pepper

5 cups water

2½ cups Original Bisquick mix

⅔ cup milk

1 Remove and discard excess fat from chicken. In 4-quart Dutch oven, place chicken, giblets (except discard liver), neck, celery, carrot, onion, parsley, salt, pepper and water. Cover and heat to boiling; reduce heat. Simmer about 2 hours or until juice of chicken is clear when thickest part is cut to bone (170°F for breasts; 180°F for thighs and legs).

2 Remove chicken and vegetables from Dutch oven. Discard giblets and neck. Skim ½ cup fat from broth; reserve. Transfer broth to large bowl; reserve 4 cups (reserve remaining broth for another use).

3 In Dutch oven, heat reserved ½ cup fat over low heat. Stir in ½ cup of the Bisquick mix. Cook, stirring constantly, until mixture is smooth and bubbly; remove from heat. Stir in reserved 4 cups broth. Heat to boiling, stirring constantly. Boil and stir 1 minute. Add chicken and vegetables; reduce heat to low. Heat about 20 minutes or until hot.

4 In medium bowl, stir remaining 2 cups Bisquick mix and the milk with wire whisk or fork until soft dough forms. Drop dough by spoonfuls onto hot chicken mixture (do not drop directly into liquid). Cook uncovered over low heat 10 minutes. Cover and cook 10 minutes longer.

High Altitude (3500–6500 ft): Cook dumplings uncovered over low heat 12 minutes. Cover and cook 12 minutes longer.

1 SERVING: Calories 680 (Calories from Fat 270); Total Fat 30g (Saturated Fat 9g); Cholesterol 130mg; Sodium 1680mg; Total Carbohydrate 55g (Dietary Fiber 3g; Sugars 6g); Protein 47g **% DAILY VALUE:** Vitamin A 70%; Vitamin C 4%; Calcium 15%; Iron 25% **EXCHANGES:** 2½ Starch, 1 Other Carbohydrate, 5½ Lean Meat, 2½ Fat **CARBOHYDRATE CHOICES:** 3½

Old-Fashioned Chicken Pie

PREP TIME: 15 MINUTES ● START TO FINISH: 35 MINUTES
4 SERVINGS

During the war years of the 1940s "meat-stretching pies" were found on many family dinner tables. Not only were they an excellent way to use leftover cooked meat and vegetables, they helped stretch the food budget too.

2 cups cubed cooked chicken

2 cups frozen mixed
  vegetables

1 jar (12 oz) chicken gravy

¼ teaspoon dried thyme leaves

1 cup Original Bisquick mix

¼ cup milk

1 Heat oven to 400°F. Spray 1½-quart round casserole with cooking spray. In 2-quart saucepan, stir chicken, vegetables, gravy and thyme until well mixed. Cook over medium heat 6 to 8 minutes, stirring occasionally, until vegetables are thawed and mixture is hot and begins to bubble. Pour into casserole.

2 In medium bowl, stir Bisquick mix and milk until soft dough forms; beat vigorously 30 seconds. Place dough on surface sprinkled with Bisquick mix; roll in Bisquick mix to coat. Press or roll dough into 7½-inch round (or large enough round to cover top of 1½-quart casserole).

3 Place dough round on chicken mixture in casserole. Cut slits in dough to allow steam to escape.

4 Bake 15 to 20 minutes or until golden brown.

High Altitude (3500–6500 ft): No change.

1 SERVING: Calories 380 (Calories from Fat 130); Total Fat 14g (Saturated Fat 4g); Cholesterol 65mg; Sodium 950mg; Total Carbohydrate 37g (Dietary Fiber 5g; Sugars 5g); Protein 27g **% DAILY VALUE:** Vitamin A 80%; Vitamin C 2%; Calcium 10%; Iron 15% **EXCHANGES:** 2 Starch, 1 Vegetable, 2½ Lean Meat, 1 Fat **CARBOHYDRATE CHOICES:** 2½

Old-Fashioned Turkey Pot Pie: Substitute 2 cups cubed cooked turkey for the chicken.

1–2–3 Chewy Peanut Butter Cookies

PREP TIME: 45 MINUTES ● START TO FINISH: 1 HOUR
4 DOZEN COOKIES

*A 1950 Bisquick ad featured Betty Crocker's "1–2–3 Cooky" recipe.
This recipe was promoted as "thrifty" because it cost 5 1/2 cents to make a
dozen cookies and a large box of Bisquick yielded 390 cookies.*

1 cup peanut butter

1 can (14 oz) sweetened condensed milk (not evaporated)

2 cups Original Bisquick mix

1 teaspoon vanilla

2 tablespoons sugar

1 Heat oven to 375°F. In large bowl, mix peanut butter and milk until smooth. Stir in Bisquick mix and vanilla until blended.

2 Shape dough into 1¼-inch balls. Roll tops in sugar. On ungreased cookie sheet, place balls, sugar sides up, 2 inches apart. Flatten in crisscross pattern with fork dipped in additional sugar.

3 Bake 7 to 9 minutes or until centers are set and bottoms are light golden brown. Do not overbake. Remove from cookie sheet to cooling rack. Cool 15 minutes.

High Altitude (3500–6500 ft): Bake 8 to 10 minutes.

1 COOKIE: Calories 80 (Calories from Fat 35); Total Fat 4g (Saturated Fat 1g); Cholesterol 0mg; Sodium 95mg; Total Carbohydrate 9g (Dietary Fiber 0g; Sugars 5g); Protein 2g **% DAILY VALUE:** Vitamin A 0%; Vitamin C 0%; Calcium 4%; Iron 0% **EXCHANGES:** ½ Other Carbohydrate, ½ High-Fat Meat **CARBOHYDRATE CHOICES:** ½

The '50s really were fabulous with Bisquick's 3-ingredient cookies!

Velvet Crumb Cake

PREP TIME: 15 MINUTES ● START TO FINISH: 1 HOUR 10 MINUTES
8 SERVINGS

Bisquick's original "Velvet-Crumb Cake" didn't have a topping. In 1951 a broiled coconut topping was introduced, making the cake one of Bisquick's most requested recipes.

CAKE

1½ cups Original Bisquick mix

½ cup sugar

½ cup milk or water

2 tablespoons shortening

1 teaspoon vanilla

1 egg

TOPPING

½ cup flaked coconut

⅓ cup packed brown sugar

¼ cup chopped nuts

3 tablespoons butter or
  margarine, softened

2 tablespoons milk

1 Heat oven to 350°F. Grease and flour 8-inch square pan or 9-inch round cake pan, or spray with baking spray with flour. In large bowl, beat all cake ingredients with electric mixer on low speed 30 seconds, scraping bowl constantly. Beat on medium speed 4 minutes, scraping bowl occasionally. Pour into pan.

2 Bake 30 to 35 minutes or until toothpick inserted in center comes out clean. Cool slightly, about 15 minutes.

3 Set oven control to broil. In small bowl, mix all topping ingredients until crumbly. Spread topping over cake. Broil cake with top 3 inches from heat about 3 minutes or until topping is golden brown.

Which is easier, the quick-to-mix cake batter or the rich broiled coconut topping? You be the judge!

High Altitude (3500–6500 ft): Heat oven to 375°F. Decrease Bisquick mix to 1⅓ cups and add ⅓ cup all-purpose flour. Increase milk to ⅔ cup. Bake about 25 minutes.

1 SERVING: Calories 310 (Calories from Fat 140); Total Fat 15g (Saturated Fat 7g); Cholesterol 40mg; Sodium 340mg; Total Carbohydrate 40g (Dietary Fiber 1g; Sugars 25g); Protein 4g **% DAILY VALUE:** Vitamin A 4%; Vitamin C 0%; Calcium 6%; Iron 6% **EXCHANGES:** 1 Starch, 1½ Other Carbohydrate, 3 Fat **CARBOHYDRATE CHOICES:** 2½

Pineapple Upside-Down Cake

PREP TIME: 15 MINUTES ● START TO FINISH: 1 HOUR
8 SERVINGS

"Pineapple Upside-Down Cake" was created as an extension of the
"Velvet-Crumb Cake." A 1950s ad introduced this recipe as "Betty Crocker teams
nature's most refreshing flavor with Bisquick's new way to bake."

¼ cup butter or margarine

¼ cup packed brown sugar

1 can (8 oz) sliced pineapple,
   drained, slices cut in half

2 tablespoons chopped pecans,
   if desired

Maraschino cherries, if desired

1½ cups Original Bisquick mix

½ cup granulated sugar

½ cup milk or water

2 tablespoons vegetable oil

1 teaspoon vanilla

1 egg

1 Heat oven to 350°F. In 9-inch round cake pan or 8-inch square pan, melt butter in oven. Sprinkle brown sugar over butter. Arrange pineapple slices in single layer on sugar mixture. Sprinkle with pecans. Arrange cherries next to each pineapple slice.

2 In large bowl, beat all remaining ingredients with electric mixer on low speed 30 seconds, scraping bowl constantly. Beat on medium speed 4 minutes, scraping bowl occasionally. Pour batter over pineapple.

3 Bake 30 to 35 minutes or until toothpick inserted in center comes out clean. Immediately turn pan upside down onto heatproof serving plate; leave pan over cake a few minutes. Remove pan. Let cake stand at least 10 minutes before serving.

High Altitude (3500–6500 ft): Heat oven to 375°F. Decrease Bisquick mix to 1⅓ cups and add ⅓ cup all-purpose flour. Increase milk to ⅔ cup. Bake 25 to 30 minutes.

1 SERVING: Calories 280 (Calories from Fat 120); Total Fat 13g (Saturated Fat 5g); Cholesterol 45mg; Sodium 330mg; Total Carbohydrate 37g (Dietary Fiber 0g; Sugars 22g); Protein 3g **% DAILY VALUE:** Vitamin A 6%; Vitamin C 0%; Calcium 6%; Iron 6% **EXCHANGES:** 1 Starch, 1½ Other Carbohydrate, 2½ Fat **CARBOHYDRATE CHOICES:** 2½

Banana Upside-Down Cake: Omit pineapple, cherries and pecans. Sprinkle 2 tablespoons chopped walnuts over brown sugar mixture in pan. Cut 2 bananas into slices; arrange on brown sugar mixture.

Pear Upside-Down Cake: Substitute 1 large pear, thinly sliced, for the pineapple.

In the 1950s, Bisquick stood on its head for a topsy-turvy dessert—Pineapple Upside-Down Cake, one of the century's most popular desserts.

Candy Bars

PREP TIME: 15 MINUTES ● **START TO FINISH: 35 MINUTES**
16 BARS

*"Candy Bars" are based on the "Bisquick Brownie" recipe that appeared in a
1950 magazine ad that included a valuable coupon for six 5-cent Baby Ruth Candy Bars.
Other than the price of candy bars, the only change in this updated recipe is that
one candy bar is sprinkled on top before baking. And just like the success tip in the ad,
these bars do settle as they cool but are still moist and tasty.*

¾ cup packed brown sugar

1 egg

1 tablespoon water

1⅓ cups Original Bisquick mix

2 bars (2.1 oz each) milk
 chocolate-covered
 peanut, caramel and nougat
 candy, coarsely chopped
 (about ⅔ cup)

1 Heat oven to 375°F. Lightly spray bottom only of 8-inch square pan with cooking spray.

2 In medium bowl, mix brown sugar, egg, water and Bisquick mix until well blended (mixture will be very thick).

3 Reserve ⅓ cup candy; stir remaining candy into dough. With metal spatula, spread dough evenly in pan. Sprinkle with reserved candy.

4 Bake 18 to 20 minutes or until golden brown and edges begin to pull away from sides of pan (do not overbake). Bars will be puffy but will fall during cooling. Cool on cooling rack about 45 minutes. For bars, cut into 4 rows by 4 rows.

High Altitude (3500–6500 ft): Bake 22 minutes.

1 BAR: Calories 120 (Calories from Fat 30); Total Fat 3.5g (Saturated Fat 1.5g); Cholesterol 15mg; Sodium 150mg; Total Carbohydrate 21g (Dietary Fiber 0g; Sugars 14g); Protein 2g
% DAILY VALUE: Vitamin A 0%; Vitamin C 0%; Calcium 2%; Iron 4% **EXCHANGES:** ½ Starch, 1 Other Carbohydrate, ½ Fat **CARBOHYDRATE CHOICES:** 1½

Nut Bread

PREP TIME: 10 MINUTES ● START TO FINISH: 2 HOURS 20 MINUTES
1 LOAF (16 SLICES)

*This recipe was published in a 1964 Bisquick cookbook with the
following suggestion: "Moist, deliciously rich fruit and nut breads make
delightful little tea sandwiches for two, twenty or two hundred."*

2¾ cups Original Bisquick mix

½ cup sugar

1 cup milk

2 tablespoons butter or
    margarine, melted

1 teaspoon vanilla

3 eggs

1½ cups finely chopped
    walnuts

1 Heat oven to 350°F. Spray 9 × 5-inch loaf pan with
cooking spray.

2 In large bowl, beat all ingredients except walnuts with
electric mixer on low speed 30 seconds, scraping bowl
frequently. Beat on medium speed 3 minutes, scraping bowl
occasionally. Stir in walnuts. Spread batter in pan.

3 Bake 50 to 60 minutes or until toothpick inserted in center
comes out clean.

4 Cool 10 minutes. Run knife or metal spatula around sides
of pan to loosen bread; remove from pan to cooling rack.
Cool completely, about 1 hour.

High Altitude (3500–6500 ft): Heat oven to 375°F.

1 SLICE: Calories 220 (Calories from Fat 110); Total Fat 12g (Saturated Fat 3g); Cholesterol 45mg;
Sodium 280mg; Total Carbohydrate 22g (Dietary Fiber 1g; Sugars 8g); Protein 5g **% DAILY VALUE:**
Vitamin A 2%; Vitamin C 0%; Calcium 6%; Iron 6% **EXCHANGES:** 1½ Starch, 2 Fat
CARBOHYDRATE CHOICES: 1½

Fresh Peach Cobbler

PREP TIME: 25 MINUTES ● START TO FINISH: 50 MINUTES
6 SERVINGS

Cobbler comes from "cobble up," which means to mix in a hurry. More young women were entering the workplace in the 1960s and having enough time to feed their families was a concern. What could be quicker than a cobbler made with Bisquick?

⅓ cup sugar

1 tablespoon cornstarch

¼ teaspoon ground cinnamon

6 peaches, peeled, cut into ½-inch slices (6 cups)

2 tablespoons water

2 teaspoons lemon juice

1 cup Original Bisquick mix

2 tablespoons sugar

⅓ cup milk

1 tablespoon butter or margarine, melted

1 Heat oven to 400°F. In 4-quart saucepan, mix ⅓ cup sugar, the cornstarch and cinnamon. Stir in peaches, water and lemon juice. Heat to boiling, stirring constantly; boil and stir 1 minute. Pour into ungreased 8- or 9-inch square (2-quart) glass baking dish.

2 In medium bowl, stir Bisquick mix, 1 tablespoon of the sugar, the milk and butter until soft dough forms.

3 Drop dough by 6 tablespoonfuls onto hot peach mixture. Sprinkle remaining 1 tablespoon sugar over dough.

4 Bake 20 to 25 minutes or until golden brown.

High Altitude (3500–6500 ft): No change.

1 SERVING: Calories 250 (Calories from Fat 45); Total Fat 5g (Saturated Fat 2g); Cholesterol 5mg; Sodium 260mg; Total Carbohydrate 47g (Dietary Fiber 3g; Sugars 31g); Protein 4g **% DAILY VALUE:** Vitamin A 15%; Vitamin C 10%; Calcium 4%; Iron 6% **EXCHANGES:** 1 Starch, 1 Fruit, 1 Other Carbohydrate, 1 Fat **CARBOHYDRATE CHOICES:** 3

Buttons & Bows

PREP TIME: 15 MINUTES ● START TO FINISH: 25 MINUTES

8 BUTTONS AND BOWS

Betty Crocker described this recipe as "buttons and bowknots made with Bisquick for the homey satisfaction of good baking, and less work."

2 cups Original Bisquick mix

2 tablespoons sugar

1 teaspoon ground nutmeg

⅛ teaspoon ground cinnamon

⅓ cup milk

1 egg

¼ cup butter or margarine, melted

½ cup sugar

1 Heat oven to 400°F. In medium bowl, stir Bisquick mix, 2 tablespoons sugar, the nutmeg, cinnamon, milk and egg until soft dough forms.

2 Place dough on surface sprinkled with Bisquick mix. Roll dough into a ball; knead about 5 times. Press or roll dough until ½ inch thick. Cut dough with doughnut cutter dipped in Bisquick mix. To make bow shapes, hold opposite sides of each ring of dough, then twist to make a figure 8. On ungreased cookie sheet, place bows and buttons (the dough from the center of each ring).

3 Bake 8 to 10 minutes or until light golden brown. Immediately dip each bow and button in melted butter, then in ½ cup sugar. Serve warm.

High Altitude (3500–6500 ft): No change.

1 BUTTON AND BOW: Calories 250 (Calories from Fat 90); Total Fat 10g (Saturated Fat 5g); Cholesterol 45mg; Sodium 420mg; Total Carbohydrate 36g (Dietary Fiber 0g; Sugars 17g); Protein 3g **% DAILY VALUE:** Vitamin A 4%; Vitamin C 0%; Calcium 4%; Iron 6%
EXCHANGES: 1 Starch, 1½ Other Carbohydrate, 2 Fat **CARBOHYDRATE CHOICES:** 2½

The spiced sweet rolls may be twisted, but Bisquick ensured that the baking was blissfully straightforward.

Cherry-Pecan Ring

PREP TIME: 15 MINUTES ● START TO FINISH: 50 MINUTES
10 SERVINGS

This recipe appeared in a 1972 Bisquick ad that encouraged readers,
"Sit yourself down and think of all the good things you could make."

COFFEE CAKE

⅓ cup butter or margarine, melted

⅓ cup packed brown sugar

1 jar (6 oz) maraschino cherries (about 25 cherries), drained, stems removed

⅓ cup pecan halves

2 cups Original Bisquick mix

2 tablespoons granulated sugar

⅔ cup milk

2 tablespoons butter or margarine, softened

1 egg

GLAZE

1 cup powdered sugar

4 teaspoons water

½ teaspoon vanilla

1 Heat oven to 400°F. Spray 8-cup fluted tube cake pan with cooking spray. Pour ⅓ cup melted butter into pan; turn pan to coat with butter. Sprinkle brown sugar over butter. Arrange cherries and pecans on sugar mixture.

2 In medium bowl, stir Bisquick mix, granulated sugar, milk, 2 tablespoons softened butter and egg until combined; beat vigorously 30 seconds. Spoon batter evenly over cherries and pecans.

3 Bake 20 to 25 minutes or until toothpick inserted in center comes out clean. Immediately place heatproof plate upside down on pan; carefully turn plate and pan over to remove coffee cake. Cool 10 minutes.

4 In small bowl, mix all glaze ingredients until smooth and thin enough to drizzle, adding additional water, 1 teaspoon at a time, to desired consistency. Drizzle glaze over warm coffee cake.

High Altitude (3500–6500 ft): No change.

1 SERVING: Calories 320 (Calories from Fat 130); Total Fat 15g (Saturated Fat 7g); Cholesterol 45mg; Sodium 370mg; Total Carbohydrate 43g (Dietary Fiber 1g; Sugars 27g); Protein 3g **% DAILY VALUE:** Vitamin A 6%; Vitamin C 0%; Calcium 6%; Iron 6% **EXCHANGES:** 1 Starch, 2 Other Carbohydrate, 3 Fat **CARBOHYDRATE CHOICES:** 3

Chocolate Chip Pancakes

PREP TIME: 20 MINUTES ● **START TO FINISH: 20 MINUTES**
5 SERVINGS (3 PANCAKES EACH)

Pancakes were given a decadent twist in the 1970s with the addition of chocolate chips.
Topped with whipped cream and fresh berries, what's not to like?

2 cups Original Bisquick mix

1 cup milk

2 eggs

½ cup miniature semisweet chocolate chips

1 In medium bowl, stir Bisquick mix, milk and eggs with wire whisk or fork until blended. Stir in chocolate chips.

2 Brush nonstick griddle or nonstick skillet with vegetable oil; heat griddle to 350°F or heat skillet over medium-low heat.

3 For each pancake, pour slightly less than ¼ cup batter onto hot griddle. Cook until edges are dry. Turn; cook other sides until golden brown.

High Altitude (3500–6500 ft): No change.

1 SERVING: Calories 340 (Calories from Fat 130); Total Fat 14g (Saturated Fat 6g); Cholesterol 90mg; Sodium 630mg; Total Carbohydrate 44g (Dietary Fiber 2g; Sugars 13g); Protein 8g **% DAILY VALUE:** Vitamin A 4%; Vitamin C 0%; Calcium 10%; Iron 10% **EXCHANGES:** 2 Starch, 1 Other Carbohydrate, 2½ Fat **CARBOHYDRATE CHOICES:** 3

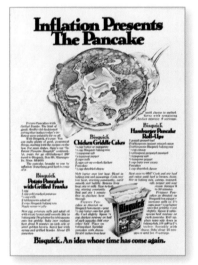

Though they never really left, pancakes make a return in 1975 in a new guise—as breakfast for dinner!

Deep-Dish Taco Squares

PREP TIME: 25 MINUTES ● **START TO FINISH: 55 MINUTES**
6 SERVINGS

*Tortillas became popular in the 1970s and tacos were a family dinner favorite.
This "one-pan" taco combines all the great ingredients of tacos but is a
snap to make and less messy to eat than regular tacos.*

½ lb lean (at least 80%) ground beef

¼ cup chopped onion

2 tablespoons taco seasoning mix (from 1.25-oz package)

1 cup Original Bisquick mix

¼ cup cold water

½ cup sour cream

⅓ cup mayonnaise or salad dressing

½ cup shredded sharp Cheddar cheese (2 oz)

1 medium tomato, chopped (¾ cup)

1 can (4.5 oz) chopped green chiles

1 Heat oven to 375°F. Spray 8-inch square (2-quart) glass baking dish with cooking spray. In 8-inch skillet, cook beef and onion over medium-high heat 5 to 7 minutes, stirring occasionally, until thoroughly cooked; drain. Stir in taco seasoning mix until blended.

2 In medium bowl, stir Bisquick mix and water until soft dough forms. Using fingers dipped in Bisquick mix, pat dough in bottom and ½ inch up sides of baking dish.

3 In same bowl, mix sour cream, mayonnaise and cheese until blended.

4 Layer beef mixture, tomato and chiles over dough; spoon sour cream mixture over top.

5 Bake 25 to 30 minutes or until edges of dough are light golden brown.

High Altitude (3500–6500 ft): Bake 28 to 33 minutes.

1 SERVING: Calories 340 (Calories from Fat 210); Total Fat 23g (Saturated Fat 8g); Cholesterol 50mg; Sodium 870mg; Total Carbohydrate 19g (Dietary Fiber 1g; Sugars 5g); Protein 12g **% DAILY VALUE:** Vitamin A 20%; Vitamin C 6%; Calcium 10%; Iron 10% **EXCHANGES:** 1 Starch, ½ Other Carbohydrate, 1 Medium-Fat Meat, 3½ Fat **CARBOHYDRATE CHOICES:** 1

Impossibly Easy Pizza Pie

PREP TIME: 10 MINUTES ● **START TO FINISH: 50 MINUTES**
6 SERVINGS

*The very first "Impossible Pie," a coconut dessert pie, was created in
the 1970s. Savory "Impossible Pies" were introduced in the '80s.*

1 medium onion, chopped
   (½ cup)

⅓ cup grated Parmesan cheese

½ cup Original Bisquick mix

1 cup milk

2 eggs

1 can (8 oz) pizza sauce

½ package (3-oz size) sliced
   pepperoni

¼ cup chopped green bell
   pepper

¾ cup shredded mozzarella
   cheese (3 oz)

1 Heat oven to 400°F. Spray 9-inch glass pie plate with cooking spray. Sprinkle onion and Parmesan cheese in pie plate.

2 In medium bowl, stir Bisquick mix, milk and eggs with wire whisk or fork until blended. Pour into pie plate.

3 Bake 20 minutes. Spread with pizza sauce; top with remaining ingredients. Bake 10 to 15 minutes longer or until cheese is light golden brown. Let stand 5 minutes before serving. Sprinkle with additional Parmesan cheese if desired.

High Altitude (3500–6500 ft): Increase first bake time to 30 minutes.

1 SERVING: Calories 210 (Calories from Fat 100); Total Fat 11g (Saturated Fat 5g); Cholesterol 95mg; Sodium 610mg; Total Carbohydrate 14g (Dietary Fiber 1g; Sugars 5g); Protein 12g **% DAILY VALUE:** Vitamin A 8%; Vitamin C 6%; Calcium 25%; Iron 8% **EXCHANGES:** ½ Starch, ½ Other Carbohydrate, 1½ Medium-Fat Meat, ½ Fat **CARBOHYDRATE CHOICES:** 1

In the 1980s, Bisquick introduced pies that "did the impossible" and made their own crust. One of the favorites was cheesy pizza pie, shown in this ad from 1983.

Easy Lasagna Squares

**PREP TIME: 20 MINUTES ● START TO FINISH: 1 HOUR 5 MINUTES
6 SERVINGS**

*"You've Got It Made with Bisquick" was the slogan for a 1986 ad featuring
this recipe. It takes only 5 minutes to assemble because there are no noodles to cook.*

1 lb lean (at least 80%)
  ground beef

½ teaspoon dried oregano
  leaves

½ teaspoon dried basil leaves

1 can (6 oz) tomato paste

2 cups shredded mozzarella
  cheese (8 oz)

½ cup small-curd cottage
  cheese

¼ cup shredded Parmesan
  cheese (1 oz)

1 cup milk

2 eggs

⅔ cup Original Bisquick mix

1 Heat oven to 400°F. In 10-inch skillet, cook beef over medium-high heat 5 to 7 minutes, stirring occasionally, until thoroughly cooked; drain. Stir in oregano, basil, tomato paste and ½ cup of the mozzarella cheese.

2 Spray 8-inch square (2-quart) glass baking dish with cooking spray. Layer cottage cheese and Parmesan cheese in baking dish. Spoon beef mixture evenly over top of cheese.

3 In medium bowl, beat milk, eggs and Bisquick mix with wire whisk or fork about 1 minute or until smooth. Pour into dish.

4 Bake 30 to 35 minutes or until knife inserted in center comes out clean.

5 Sprinkle remaining 1½ cups mozzarella cheese over top. Bake 2 to 3 minutes longer or until cheese is melted. Let stand 5 minutes before serving.

High Altitude (3500–6500 ft): Bake 33 to 38 minutes.

1 SERVING: Calories 400 (Calories from Fat 200); Total Fat 22g (Saturated Fat 11g); Cholesterol 145mg; Sodium 810mg; Total Carbohydrate 18g (Dietary Fiber 1g; Sugars 7g); Protein 33g **% DAILY VALUE:** Vitamin A 15%; Vitamin C 6%; Calcium 45%; Iron 15% **EXCHANGES:** ½ Starch, ½ Other Carbohydrate, 4½ Medium-Fat Meat **CARBOHYDRATE CHOICES:** 1

Sweet-and-Sour Chicken Stir-Fry

PREP TIME: 30 MINUTES ● START TO FINISH: 30 MINUTES
6 SERVINGS (1¼ CUPS EACH)

Chinese food was all the rage in the 1980s and chicken with sweet-and-sour sauce was at the top of the list. This stir-fry chicken recipe first appeared in a 1986 magazine ad.

1 cup Original Bisquick mix

½ teaspoon pepper

2 eggs

1 lb boneless skinless chicken breasts, cut into cubes

¼ cup vegetable oil

3 medium carrots, cut diagonally into ¼-inch slices (1½ cups)

1 medium green bell pepper, cut into strips (1 cup)

1 small onion, thinly sliced, separated into rings (⅓ cup)

1 can (20 oz) pineapple chunks, drained

½ cup sweet-and-sour sauce

1 In large resealable food-storage plastic bag, mix Bisquick mix and pepper.

2 In medium bowl, beat eggs slightly. Stir in chicken until combined. Using slotted spoon, remove chicken from eggs; place in bag with Bisquick mix. Seal bag; shake bag until chicken is coated.

3 In 12-inch skillet, heat 1 tablespoon of the oil over medium-high heat. Add carrots; cook 2 minutes, stirring frequently. Add bell pepper and onion; cook 2 minutes longer, stirring frequently. Remove from skillet.

4 In same skillet, heat remaining oil. Add chicken; cook, stirring frequently, until golden brown on outside and no longer pink in center. Add vegetables; cook about 2 minutes, stirring frequently, until thoroughly heated. Stir in pineapple and sweet-and-sour sauce; cook until thoroughly heated.

High Altitude (3500–6500 ft): No change.

1 SERVING: Calories 370 (Calories from Fat 150); Total Fat 16g (Saturated Fat 3.5g); Cholesterol 115mg; Sodium 410mg; Total Carbohydrate 34g (Dietary Fiber 3g; Sugars 17g); Protein 21g **% DAILY VALUE:** Vitamin A 110%; Vitamin C 15%; Calcium 6%; Iron 10% **EXCHANGES:** ½ Starch, 1½ Other Carbohydrate, 1 Vegetable, 2½ Very Lean Meat, 3 Fat **CARBOHYDRATE CHOICES:** 2

Extra-Easy Pizza

PREP TIME: 15 MINUTES ● START TO FINISH: 30 MINUTES
8 SERVINGS

Pizza was a popular family dinner in the 1980s and this easy-to-prepare
crust made it possible to create a homemade pizza in just 30 minutes.

1½ cups Original Bisquick mix

⅓ cup very hot water

1 can (8 oz) pizza sauce

1 package (3.5 oz) sliced
  pepperoni

½ cup sliced fresh
  mushrooms

½ cup chopped bell pepper

1½ cups shredded mozzarella
  cheese (6 oz)

1 Heat oven to 450°F. Spray 12-inch pizza pan with cooking spray. In medium bowl, stir Bisquick mix and water; beat 20 strokes until soft dough forms.

2 In pizza pan, press dough evenly. Spread pizza sauce over dough. Top with all remaining ingredients.

3 Bake 12 to 15 minutes or until crust is golden brown and cheese is bubbly.

High Altitude (3500–6500 ft): No change.

1 SERVING: Calories 230 (Calories from Fat 110); Total Fat 12g (Saturated Fat 6g); Cholesterol 25mg; Sodium 740mg; Total Carbohydrate 19g (Dietary Fiber 1g; Sugars 3g); Protein 10g **% DAILY VALUE:** Vitamin A 4%; Vitamin C 8%; Calcium 20%; Iron 8% **EXCHANGES:** 1 Starch, 1 High-Fat Meat, 1 Fat **CARBOHYDRATE CHOICES:** 1

Glazed Cinnamon Rolls

PREP TIME: 20 MINUTES ● START TO FINISH: 50 MINUTES
12 ROLLS

*Convenience was key during the 1990s and cinnamon rolls made
with Bisquick replaced time-consuming yeast rolls.*

ROLLS

2 tablespoons granulated sugar

1 teaspoon ground
    cinnamon

2½ cups Original Bisquick mix

2 tablespoons granulated sugar

⅔ cup milk

2 tablespoons butter or
    margarine, softened

¼ cup raisins

GLAZE

1⅓ cups powdered sugar

2 tablespoons milk

1 Heat oven to 375°F. Spray 13 × 9-inch pan with cooking spray. In small bowl, mix 2 tablespoons granulated sugar and the cinnamon; set aside.

2 In medium bowl, stir Bisquick mix, 2 tablespoons granulated sugar and ⅔ cup milk until soft dough forms. If dough is sticky, gradually mix in enough Bisquick mix (up to ¼ cup) to make dough easy to handle.

3 Place dough on surface sprinkled with Bisquick mix; gently roll in Bisquick mix to coat. Shape into a ball; knead 10 times. Press or roll into 15 × 9-inch rectangle. Spread rectangle with butter; sprinkle evenly with sugar mixture and raisins. Roll up tightly, starting at 15-inch side. Pinch edge of dough to seal well. Cut into 1¼-inch slices. In pan, place slices, cut sides down.

4 Bake 20 to 23 minutes or until golden brown. Cool 5 minutes. Remove from pan.

5 In small bowl, mix powdered sugar and 2 tablespoons milk until smooth. Spread glaze over warm rolls.

High Altitude (3500–6500 ft): Heat oven to 400°F. Bake about 20 minutes.

1 ROLL: Calories 210 (Calories from Fat 50); Total Fat 5g (Saturated Fat 2.5g); Cholesterol 5mg; Sodium 330mg; Total Carbohydrate 37g (Dietary Fiber 0g; Sugars 20g); Protein 3g **% DAILY VALUE:** Vitamin A 0%; Vitamin C 0%; Calcium 4%; Iron 4% **EXCHANGES:** 1 Starch, 1½ Other Carbohydrate, 1 Fat **CARBOHYDRATE CHOICES:** 2½

Ultimate Pancakes

PREP TIME: 5 MINUTES ● **START TO FINISH: 20 MINUTES**
5 SERVINGS (3 PANCAKES EACH)

When consumers requested lighter, fluffier pancakes, Bisquick complied by introducing the recipe "Ultimate Pancakes" made with lemon juice and baking powder.

2 cups Original Bisquick mix
1 tablespoon sugar
2 teaspoons baking powder
1 cup milk
2 tablespoons lemon juice
2 eggs

1 In medium bowl, stir all ingredients with wire whisk or fork until blended.

2 Brush griddle or skillet with vegetable oil or spray with cooking spray; heat griddle to 375°F or heat skillet over medium heat.

3 For each pancake, pour slightly less than ¼ cup batter onto hot griddle. Cook until edges are dry. Turn; cook other sides until golden brown.

High Altitude (3500–6500 ft): No change.

1 SERVING: Calories 260 (Calories from Fat 80); Total Fat 9g (Saturated Fat 3g); Cholesterol 90mg; Sodium 830mg; Total Carbohydrate 37g (Dietary Fiber 1g; Sugars 7g); Protein 8g **% DAILY VALUE:** Vitamin A 4%; Vitamin C 0%; Calcium 20%; Iron 10% **EXCHANGES:** 2 Starch, ½ Other Carbohydrate, 1½ Fat **CARBOHYDRATE CHOICES:** 2½

Oven-Fried Chicken with Biscuits

PREP TIME: 10 MINUTES ● **START TO FINISH: 1 HOUR**
4 SERVINGS

A 1970s version suggested topping the chicken with drained canned
peach halves after adding the biscuits to the pan.

CHICKEN

½ cup Original Bisquick mix

1 teaspoon salt

1 teaspoon paprika

¼ teaspoon pepper

1 cut-up whole chicken
    (2½ to 3 lb)

BISCUITS

2¼ cups Original Bisquick mix

⅔ cup milk

2 teaspoons chopped fresh
    parsley

1 Heat oven to 425°F. Spray 15 × 10 × 1-inch pan with cooking spray. In shallow bowl, stir ½ cup Bisquick mix, the salt, paprika and pepper. Coat chicken with Bisquick mixture; place skin sides down in pan. Bake 35 minutes.

2 In medium bowl, stir all biscuit ingredients until soft dough forms.

3 Turn chicken, pushing pieces to one side of pan. Drop dough by 8 (¼-cup) spoonfuls into pan in single layer next to chicken. Bake about 15 minutes longer or until biscuits are light golden brown and juice of chicken is clear when thickest piece is cut to bone (170°F for breasts; 180°F for thighs and legs).

High Altitude (3500–6500 ft): No change.

1 SERVING: Calories 640 (Calories from Fat 250); Total Fat 28g (Saturated Fat 8g); Cholesterol 110mg; Sodium 1720mg; Total Carbohydrate 56g (Dietary Fiber 2g; Sugars 4g); Protein 41g **% DAILY VALUE:** Vitamin A 15%; Vitamin C 0%; Calcium 15%; Iron 20% **EXCHANGES:** 3½ Starch, 4 Lean Meat, 3 Fat **CARBOHYDRATE CHOICES:** 4

"Dinner on the double" gained new meaning with the clever idea to bake biscuits and chicken in the same dish.

Salsa Chicken Fiesta

PREP TIME: 15 MINUTES ● START TO FINISH: 45 MINUTES
6 SERVINGS

This recipe was created for the Bisquick box in 2004 as part of a "Create Family Favorites with What's On Hand!" campaign.

⅔ cup Original Bisquick mix

2 tablespoons water

1 egg

1½ cups shredded Cheddar cheese (6 oz)

3 boneless skinless chicken breasts (about 1 lb), cut into ½-inch pieces

2 teaspoons vegetable oil

1¼ cups chunky-style salsa

1 Heat oven to 400°F. Spray 8- or 9-inch square pan with cooking spray. In small bowl, stir Bisquick mix, water and egg with wire whisk or fork until blended. Spread mixture evenly in pan. Sprinkle with 1¼ cups of the cheese.

2 In 10-inch skillet, cook chicken in oil over medium-high heat, stirring frequently, until chicken is no longer pink in center; drain. Stir in salsa; heat until hot, stirring occasionally. Spoon over batter in pan to within ½ inch of edges.

3 Bake 22 to 25 minutes or until edges are dark golden brown. Sprinkle with remaining ¼ cup cheese. Bake 1 to 3 minutes longer or until cheese is melted.

High Altitude (3500–6500 ft): Increase first bake time to 25 to 30 minutes.

1 SERVING: Calories 280 (Calories from Fat 140); Total Fat 15g (Saturated Fat 8g); Cholesterol 100mg; Sodium 710mg; Total Carbohydrate 13g (Dietary Fiber 1g; Sugars 3g); Protein 23g **% DAILY VALUE:** Vitamin A 10%; Vitamin C 0%; Calcium 20%; Iron 8% **EXCHANGES:** 1 Starch, 3 Lean Meat, 1 Fat **CARBOHYDRATE CHOICES:** 1

Heart Smart Deluxe Cheeseburger Melt

PREP TIME: 15 MINUTES ● **START TO FINISH: 45 MINUTES**
8 SERVINGS

We've trimmed the fat and calories from this cheeseburger melt by using Bisquick Heart Smart, fat-free egg product, reduced-fat cheese and extra-lean ground beef.

1⅓ cups Bisquick Heart Smart mix

¼ cup water

½ cup fat-free egg product or 4 egg whites

1½ cups shredded reduced-fat Cheddar cheese (6 oz)

1 lb extra-lean (at least 90%) ground beef

1 can (10.75 oz) condensed 98% fat-free cream of mushroom soup

1 cup frozen mixed vegetables

1 Heat oven to 400°F. Spray 13 × 9-inch pan with cooking spray. In medium bowl, stir Bisquick mix, water, egg product and 1 cup of the cheese. Spread mixture in pan.

2 In 10-inch skillet, cook beef over medium-high heat 5 to 7 minutes, stirring frequently, until thoroughly cooked; drain. Stir in soup and vegetables; heat until hot. Spread over batter in pan.

3 Bake 23 to 25 minutes or until edges are light golden brown. Sprinkle with remaining ½ cup cheese. Bake 1 to 3 minutes longer or until cheese is melted.

High Altitude (3500–6500 ft): No change.

1 SERVING: Calories 240 (Calories from Fat 80); Total Fat 8g (Saturated Fat 3g); Cholesterol 40mg; Sodium 770mg; Total Carbohydrate 20g (Dietary Fiber 1g; Sugars 3g); Protein 20g **% DAILY VALUE:** Vitamin A 20%; Vitamin C 0%; Calcium 25%; Iron 15% **EXCHANGES:** 1½ Starch, 2 Lean Meat **CARBOHYDRATE CHOICES:** 1

Ultimate Chicken Fingers

PREP TIME: 20 MINUTES ● **START TO FINISH: 35 MINUTES**
4 SERVINGS

*Eating more healthfully is an ongoing concern. This kid-friendly recipe
is made more healthy by baking, rather than frying, the chicken.
It appeared on the Bisquick box in 2005 as a Family Favorite.*

⅔ cup Original Bisquick mix

½ cup grated Parmesan cheese

½ teaspoon salt or garlic salt

½ teaspoon paprika

3 boneless skinless chicken
   breasts (about 1 lb), cut
   crosswise into ½-inch strips

1 egg, slightly beaten

3 tablespoons butter or
   margarine, melted

1 Heat oven to 450°F. Line cookie sheet with foil; spray with cooking spray. In 1-gallon resealable food-storage plastic bag, place Bisquick mix, cheese, salt and paprika.

2 Dip half of chicken strips into egg; place in bag of Bisquick mixture. Seal bag; shake to coat. On cookie sheet, place chicken. Repeat with remaining chicken. Drizzle butter over chicken.

3 Bake 12 to 14 minutes, turning after 6 minutes with pancake turner, until no longer pink in center.

High Altitude (3500–6500 ft): No change.

1 SERVING: Calories 340 (Calories from Fat 170); Total Fat 19g (Saturated Fat 10g); Cholesterol 140mg; Sodium 860mg; Total Carbohydrate 14g (Dietary Fiber 0g; Sugars 0g); Protein 28g **% DAILY VALUE:** Vitamin A 10%; Vitamin C 0%; Calcium 20%; Iron 8% **EXCHANGES:** 1 Starch, 3½ Lean Meat, 1½ Fat **CARBOHYDRATE CHOICES:** 1

Microwave Apple Crisp

PREP TIME: 15 MINUTES ● START TO FINISH: 25 MINUTES
6 SERVINGS

With the start of the millennium, convenience and saving time have become even more important in people's busy lives. Here, we combined two kitchen timesavers—Bisquick and the microwave oven—to create a warm, tasty dessert.

4 medium tart cooking apples, peeled, sliced (4 cups)

⅔ cup packed brown sugar

⅔ cup quick-cooking or old-fashioned oats

½ cup Original Bisquick mix

3 tablespoons butter or margarine, softened

¾ teaspoon ground cinnamon

¾ teaspoon ground nutmeg

1 In ungreased 2-quart microwavable casserole or 8-inch square microwavable dish, arrange apple slices. In small bowl, stir remaining ingredients until crumbly. Sprinkle over apples.

2 Microwave uncovered on High 7 to 10 minutes, rotating dish ½ turn after 5 minutes, until apples are tender. Serve warm.

High Altitude (3500–6500 ft): Microwave 10 to 13 minutes, rotating dish ½ turn after 5 minutes.

1 SERVING: Calories 260 (Calories from Fat 70); Total Fat 8g (Saturated Fat 4g); Cholesterol 15mg; Sodium 170mg; Total Carbohydrate 46g (Dietary Fiber 2g; Sugars 31g); Protein 2g **% DAILY VALUE:** Vitamin A 4%; Vitamin C 2%; Calcium 4%; Iron 8% **EXCHANGES:** ½ Starch, ½ Fruit, 2 Other Carbohydrate, 1½ Fat **CARBOHYDRATE CHOICES:** 3

Baked Apple Crisp: Heat oven to 375°F. Spray an 8-inch square pan or glass baking dish with cooking spray. Decrease oats to ½ cup; increase butter to ⅓ cup. Bake about 30 minutes or until topping is golden brown and apples are tender.

CHAPTER 2

Day Brighter Breakfasts

Applesauce Pancakes

PREP TIME: 15 MINUTES ● START TO FINISH: 15 MINUTES
5 SERVINGS (3 PANCAKES EACH)

2 cups Original Bisquick mix

1 cup sweetened applesauce

½ cup milk

1 teaspoon ground
    cinnamon

2 eggs

1 In medium bowl, stir all ingredients with wire whisk or fork until blended.

2 Brush griddle or skillet with vegetable oil or spray with cooking spray; heat griddle to 375°F or heat skillet over medium heat.

3 For each pancake, pour slightly less than ¼ cup batter onto hot griddle. Cook until edges are dry. Turn; cook other sides until golden brown.

High Altitude (3500–6500 ft): No change.

1 SERVING: Calories 280 (Calories from Fat 80); Total Fat 9g (Saturated Fat 3g); Cholesterol 85mg; Sodium 620mg; Total Carbohydrate 43g (Dietary Fiber 2g; Sugars 11g); Protein 7g **% DAILY VALUE:** Vitamin A 4%; Vitamin C 0%; Calcium 10%; Iron 10% **EXCHANGES:** 2 Starch, 1 Other Carbohydrate, 1½ Fat **CARBOHYDRATE CHOICES:** 3

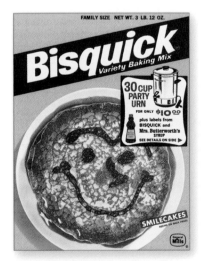

The Bisquick box puts a smile on the face of 1960s kids—and anyone else who's young at heart.

Sour Cream–Blueberry Pancakes

PREP TIME: 15 MINUTES ● START TO FINISH: 15 MINUTES
5 SERVINGS (3 PANCAKES EACH)

2 cups Original Bisquick mix

1 cup sour cream

½ cup milk

2 eggs

1 cup fresh or frozen (thawed and drained) blueberries

Maple syrup, if desired

1 In medium bowl, stir all ingredients except blueberries and syrup with wire whisk or fork until blended. Stir in blueberries.

2 Brush griddle or skillet with vegetable oil or spray with cooking spray; heat griddle to 375°F or heat skillet over medium heat.

3 For each pancake, pour slightly less than ¼ cup batter onto hot griddle. Cook until edges are dry. Turn; cook other sides until golden brown. Serve with syrup.

High Altitude (3500–6500 ft): Increase milk to ¾ cup. Makes 20 pancakes.

1 SERVING: Calories 350 (Calories from Fat 160); Total Fat 18g (Saturated Fat 8g); Cholesterol 115mg; Sodium 640mg; Total Carbohydrate 38g (Dietary Fiber 2g; Sugars 7g); Protein 8g **% DAILY VALUE:** Vitamin A 10%; Vitamin C 2%; Calcium 15%; Iron 10% **EXCHANGES:** 2 Starch, ½ Other Carbohydrate, 3½ Fat **CARBOHYDRATE CHOICES:** 2½

Banana Split Pancakes

PREP TIME: 15 MINUTES ● **START TO FINISH: 15 MINUTES**
5 SERVINGS (3 PANCAKES EACH)

2 cups Original Bisquick mix

1¼ cups milk

¼ cup chocolate-flavor syrup

1 egg

2 medium bananas, sliced

2 cups sliced strawberries

Whipped topping, if desired

Chopped peanuts, if desired

Additional chocolate-flavor
   syrup, if desired

Maraschino cherries, if desired

1 In medium bowl, stir Bisquick mix, milk, ¼ cup chocolate-flavor syrup and the egg with wire whisk or fork until blended (batter may be thin).

2 Brush griddle or skillet with vegetable oil or spray with cooking spray; heat griddle to 375°F or heat skillet over medium heat.

3 For each pancake, pour slightly less than ¼ cup batter onto hot griddle. Cook until edges are dry. Turn; cook other sides until golden brown.

4 Serve with bananas, strawberries, whipped topping, peanuts, chocolate-flavor syrup and maraschino cherries.

High Altitude (3500–6500 ft): No change.

1 SERVING: Calories 350 (Calories from Fat 80); Total Fat 9g (Saturated Fat 3g); Cholesterol 45mg; Sodium 640mg; Total Carbohydrate 60g (Dietary Fiber 4g; Sugars 21g); Protein 8g **% DAILY VALUE:** Vitamin A 4%; Vitamin C 35%; Calcium 15%; Iron 10% **EXCHANGES:** 2½ Starch, ½ Fruit, 1 Other Carbohydrate, 1½ Fat **CARBOHYDRATE CHOICES:** 4

Quick Tip Love turtle sundaes? You'll love turtle banana split pancakes too. Use 4 bananas instead of the strawberries. Top the pancakes with sliced bananas and drizzle with warm caramel sauce and warm hot fudge ice cream topping. Sprinkle generously with chopped pecans and top off with a dollop of whipped topping. Enjoy!

Spicy Pumpkin Pancakes

PREP TIME: 15 MINUTES ● START TO FINISH: 15 MINUTES
6 SERVINGS (3 PANCAKES EACH)

MAPLE-PECAN SYRUP

1 cup maple-flavored syrup

1 tablespoon butter or margarine

¼ cup chopped pecans

PANCAKES

2⅓ cups Original Bisquick mix

2 tablespoons sugar

¼ teaspoon ground cinnamon

¼ teaspoon ground nutmeg

¼ teaspoon ground ginger

1¼ cups milk

⅓ cup canned pumpkin (not pumpkin pie mix)

¼ cup vegetable oil

2 eggs

1 In 1-quart saucepan, heat syrup and butter until butter is melted, stirring constantly. Remove from heat; stir in pecans.

2 In large bowl, stir all pancake ingredients with wire whisk or fork until blended.

3 Brush griddle or skillet with vegetable oil or spray with cooking spray; heat griddle to 375°F or heat skillet over medium heat.

4 For each pancake, pour slightly less than ¼ cup batter onto hot griddle. Cook until edges are dry. Turn; cook other sides until golden brown. Serve with syrup.

High Altitude (3500–6500 ft): No change.

1 SERVING: Calories 560 (Calories from Fat 210); Total Fat 23g (Saturated Fat 6g); Cholesterol 80mg; Sodium 660mg; Total Carbohydrate 79g (Dietary Fiber 2g; Sugars 29g); Protein 8g **% DAILY VALUE:** Vitamin A 45%; Vitamin C 0%; Calcium 15%; Iron 10% **EXCHANGES:** 2½ Starch, 2½ Other Carbohydrate, 4½ Fat **CARBOHYDRATE CHOICES:** 5

Quick Tip Love nuts? Boost the nutty flavor and texture of these pancakes by stirring ½ cup chopped pecans or walnuts into the batter.

Strawberries and Cream Pancakes

PREP TIME: 15 MINUTES ● START TO FINISH: 15 MINUTES
4 SERVINGS (3 PANCAKES EACH)

2 cups Original Bisquick mix

1 cup milk

2 eggs

1 pint (2 cups) fresh
strawberries, sliced

½ cup whipped cream topping
in aerosol can

1 In medium bowl, stir Bisquick mix, milk and eggs with wire whisk or fork until blended.

2 Brush griddle or skillet with vegetable oil or spray with cooking spray; heat griddle to 375°F or heat skillet over medium heat.

3 For each pancake, pour slightly less than ¼ cup batter onto hot griddle. Cook until edges are dry. Turn; cook other sides until golden brown.

4 Spoon strawberries over pancakes. Top with whipped cream.

High Altitude (3500–6500 ft): No change.

1 SERVING: Calories 360 (Calories from Fat 120); Total Fat 13g (Saturated Fat 5g); Cholesterol 115mg; Sodium 800mg; Total Carbohydrate 49g (Dietary Fiber 3g; Sugars 9g); Protein 10g **% DAILY VALUE:** Vitamin A 6%; Vitamin C 35%; Calcium 15%; Iron 10% **EXCHANGES:** 3 Starch, ½ Other Carbohydrate, 2 Fat **CARBOHYDRATE CHOICES:** 3

Apricot-Almond Pancakes

PREP TIME: 30 MINUTES ● **START TO FINISH: 30 MINUTES**
4 SERVINGS (3 PANCAKES EACH)

1 cup apricot jam or spreadable fruit

2 cups Bisquick Heart Smart mix

1 cup fat-free (skim) milk

½ teaspoon almond extract

2 eggs, 4 egg whites or ½ cup fat-free egg product

¼ cup chopped almonds

1 In 1-quart saucepan, heat jam over low heat until melted, stirring constantly. Keep warm while making pancakes.

2 In medium bowl, stir all remaining ingredients with wire whisk or fork until blended.

3 Brush griddle or skillet with vegetable oil or spray with cooking spray; heat griddle to 375°F or heat skillet over medium heat.

4 For each pancake, pour slightly less than ¼ cup batter onto hot griddle. Cook until edges are dry. Turn; cook other sides until golden brown. Serve with warm apricot jam.

High Altitude (3500–6500 ft): No change.

1 SERVING: Calories 550 (Calories from Fat 100); Total Fat 11g (Saturated Fat 1g); Cholesterol 105mg; Sodium 730mg; Total Carbohydrate 101g (Dietary Fiber 1g; Sugars 47g); Protein 12g **% DAILY VALUE:** Vitamin A 6%; Vitamin C 6%; Calcium 35%; Iron 20% **EXCHANGES:** 4 Starch, 2½ Other Carbohydrate, 2 Fat **CARBOHYDRATE CHOICES:** 7

Ginger Pancakes with Lemon Sauce

PREP TIME: 30 MINUTES ● START TO FINISH: 30 MINUTES
6 SERVINGS (2 PANCAKES EACH)

SAUCE

1 egg

1 cup sugar

½ cup butter or margarine

¼ cup water

1 tablespoon grated lemon peel

3 tablespoons lemon juice

PANCAKES

2 cups Original Bisquick mix

1½ teaspoons ground ginger

1 teaspoon ground cinnamon

½ teaspoon ground cloves

1⅓ cups milk

¼ cup light molasses

1 egg

1 In medium bowl, beat 1 egg with wire whisk; set aside. In 2-quart saucepan, heat remaining sauce ingredients to boiling over medium heat, stirring constantly. Pour ½ cup of sauce mixture into beaten egg, then stir egg mixture back into saucepan. Boil and stir 1 minute; remove from heat. Cover to keep warm while making pancakes.

2 In medium bowl, stir Bisquick mix, ginger, cinnamon, cloves, milk, molasses and 1 egg with wire whisk or fork until blended.

3 Heat nonstick griddle to 350°F or nonstick skillet over medium-low heat.

4 For each pancake, pour slightly less than ¼ cup batter onto hot griddle. Cook until edges are dry. Turn; cook other sides until golden brown. Serve pancakes topped with sauce.

High Altitude (3500–6500 ft): No change.

1 SERVING: Calories 530 (Calories from Fat 210); Total Fat 23g (Saturated Fat 12g); Cholesterol 115mg; Sodium 650mg; Total Carbohydrate 74g (Dietary Fiber 1g; Sugars 45g); Protein 7g **% DAILY VALUE:** Vitamin A 15%; Vitamin C 2%; Calcium 15%; Iron 10% **EXCHANGES:** 2 Starch, 3 Other Carbohydrate, 4½ Fat **CARBOHYDRATE CHOICES:** 5

Quick Tip Short on time? Use store-bought lemon curd instead of making the lemon sauce. Look for it near the jams and jellies in the supermarket.

Oatmeal Pancakes
with Banana-Walnut Syrup

PREP TIME: 30 MINUTES ● **START TO FINISH: 30 MINUTES**
6 SERVINGS (3 PANCAKES EACH)

BANANA-WALNUT SYRUP

2 tablespoons butter or margarine

¼ cup chopped walnuts

2 bananas, sliced

1 cup maple-flavored syrup

PANCAKES

2 cups Original Bisquick mix

½ cup old-fashioned or quick-cooking oats

2 tablespoons packed brown sugar

1¼ cups milk

2 eggs

1 In 1½-quart saucepan, melt butter over medium heat. Cook walnuts in butter, stirring occasionally, until walnuts and butter just begin to brown. Add bananas; stir to coat with butter. Stir in syrup; reduce heat to low. Cook until warm. Keep warm while making pancakes.

2 In medium bowl, stir all pancake ingredients with wire whisk or fork until blended.

3 Brush griddle or skillet with vegetable oil or spray with cooking spray; heat griddle to 375°F or heat skillet over medium heat.

4 For each pancake, pour slightly less than ¼ cup batter onto hot griddle. Cook until edges are dry. Turn; cook other sides until golden brown. Serve with warm syrup.

High Altitude (3500–6500 ft): No change.

1 SERVING: Calories 520 (Calories from Fat 140); Total Fat 15g (Saturated Fat 6g); Cholesterol 85mg; Sodium 590mg; Total Carbohydrate 87g (Dietary Fiber 3g; Sugars 33g); Protein 9g **% DAILY VALUE:** Vitamin A 6%; Vitamin C 2%; Calcium 15%; Iron 10% **EXCHANGES:** 3 Starch, ½ Fruit, 2½ Other Carbohydrate, 2½ Fat **CARBOHYDRATE CHOICES:** 6

Quick Tip Butter can burn quickly so watch it carefully when it's browning. It should be an even golden brown color and just begin to smell toasty.

Lemon–Poppy Seed Pancakes

PREP TIME: 20 MINUTES ● START TO FINISH: 20 MINUTES
5 SERVINGS (3 PANCAKES EACH)

LEMON-SCENTED HONEY

1 cup honey
½ lemon, thinly sliced

PANCAKES

2 cups Original Bisquick mix
1 tablespoon poppy seed
1 cup sour cream
½ cup milk
2 teaspoons grated lemon peel
2 teaspoons fresh lemon juice
2 eggs

1 In 1-quart saucepan, cook honey and lemon over medium heat, stirring occasionally, until hot. Keep warm while making pancakes.

2 In medium bowl, stir all pancake ingredients with wire whisk or fork until blended.

3 Brush griddle or skillet with vegetable oil or spray with cooking spray; heat griddle to 375°F or heat skillet over medium heat.

4 For each pancake, pour slightly less than ¼ cup batter onto hot griddle. Cook until edges are dry. Turn; cook other sides until golden brown. Remove lemon slices from honey; discard. Serve pancakes with honey.

High Altitude (3500–6500 ft): Decrease sour cream to ½ cup; increase milk to 1 cup.

1 SERVING: Calories 570 (Calories from Fat 160); Total Fat 18g (Saturated Fat 8g); Cholesterol 115mg; Sodium 640mg; Total Carbohydrate 91g (Dietary Fiber 2g; Sugars 60g); Protein 9g **% DAILY VALUE:** Vitamin A 10%; Vitamin C 4%; Calcium 15%; Iron 10% **EXCHANGES:** 3 Starch, 3 Other Carbohydrate, 3½ Fat **CARBOHYDRATE CHOICES:** 6

From 1974—Light, fluffy pancakes is one of the seven basic recipes made the easy way, with Bisquick.

Cornmeal Pancakes 'n' Sausage Syrup

PREP TIME: 20 MINUTES ● START TO FINISH: 20 MINUTES
5 SERVINGS (3 PANCAKES EACH)

SAUSAGE SYRUP

1 package (8 oz) frozen
  brown-and-serve sausages

1 cup maple-flavored syrup

PANCAKES

1½ cups Original Bisquick mix

1 cup shredded Cheddar
  cheese (4 oz)

½ cup yellow cornmeal

2 eggs

1 cup milk

1 Cut sausage links into ½-inch pieces. In 1½-quart saucepan, cook sausage pieces over medium heat, stirring frequently, until golden brown. Add syrup; heat to boiling, stirring constantly. Keep warm while making pancakes.

2 In medium bowl, stir Bisquick mix, cheese, cornmeal, eggs and milk with wire whisk or fork until blended.

3 Brush griddle or skillet with vegetable oil or spray with cooking spray; heat griddle to 375°F or heat skillet over medium heat.

4 For each pancake, pour slightly less than ¼ cup batter onto hot griddle. Cook until edges are dry. Turn; cook other sides until golden brown. Serve with syrup.

High Altitude (3500–6500 ft): No change.

1 SERVING: Calories 700 (Calories from Fat 280); Total Fat 31g (Saturated Fat 13g); Cholesterol 145mg; Sodium 1010mg; Total Carbohydrate 85g (Dietary Fiber 1g; Sugars 28g); Protein 20g **% DAILY VALUE:** Vitamin A 10%; Vitamin C 0%; Calcium 30%; Iron 15% **EXCHANGES:** 2 Starch, 3½ Other Carbohydrate, 2 High-Fat Meat, 3 Fat **CARBOHYDRATE CHOICES:** 5½

Granola Pancakes

PREP TIME: 15 MINUTES ● START TO FINISH: 15 MINUTES
6 SERVINGS (3 PANCAKES EACH)

2 cups Original Bisquick mix

1 cup milk

2 eggs

⅓ cup granola

Flavored yogurt, if desired

Additional granola, if desired

1 In medium bowl, stir Bisquick mix, milk and eggs with wire whisk or fork until blended. Stir in granola.

2 Brush griddle or skillet with vegetable oil or spray with cooking spray; heat griddle to 375°F or heat skillet over medium heat.

3 For each pancake, pour slightly less than ¼ cup batter onto hot griddle. Cook until edges are dry. Turn; cook other sides until golden brown. To serve, top pancakes with a dollop of yogurt and sprinkle with granola.

High Altitude (3500–6500 ft): No change.

1 SERVING: Calories 230 (Calories from Fat 70); Total Fat 8g (Saturated Fat 2.5g); Cholesterol 75mg; Sodium 540mg; Total Carbohydrate 32g (Dietary Fiber 1g; Sugars 5g); Protein 7g **% DAILY VALUE:** Vitamin A 6%; Vitamin C 0%; Calcium 10%; Iron 8% **EXCHANGES:** 2 Starch, 1½ Fat **CARBOHYDRATE CHOICES:** 2

Quick Tip Any type of granola will work fine in this recipe, whether you like it loaded with crunchy nuts or filled with dried fruit and spices.

Bacon Pancakes
with Maple–Peanut Butter Syrup

PREP TIME: 35 MINUTES ● START TO FINISH: 35 MINUTES
5 SERVINGS (3 PANCAKES EACH)

MAPLE–PEANUT BUTTER SYRUP

3 tablespoons peanut butter

1 tablespoon butter or margarine, softened

½ cup maple-flavored syrup

PANCAKES

2 cups Original Bisquick mix

¾ cup milk

¼ cup maple-flavored syrup

2 eggs

½ cup real bacon pieces (from 3-oz package)

1 In small bowl, beat peanut butter and butter with electric mixer on low speed until smooth. Beat in ½ cup syrup until well mixed.

2 Heat nonstick griddle to 350°F or heat 12-inch nonstick skillet over medium-low heat.

3 In medium bowl, stir all pancake ingredients except bacon with wire whisk or fork until blended. Stir in bacon.

4 For each pancake, pour slightly less than ¼ cup batter onto hot griddle. Cook 2 to 3 minutes or until edges are dry. Turn; cook other sides until golden brown. Serve pancakes with syrup.

High Altitude (3500–6500 ft): No change.

1 SERVING: Calories 510 (Calories from Fat 180); Total Fat 19g (Saturated Fat 6g); Cholesterol 105mg; Sodium 900mg; Total Carbohydrate 71g (Dietary Fiber 2g; Sugars 22g); Protein 13g **% DAILY VALUE:** Vitamin A 6%; Vitamin C 0%; Calcium 10%; Iron 10% **EXCHANGES:** 2 Starch, 2½ Other Carbohydrate, 1 High-Fat Meat, 2 Fat **CARBOHYDRATE CHOICES:** 5

Quick Tip To save time (and dishes), purchase precooked bacon, found at the supermarket alongside the regular bacon.

Ham and Apple Pancakes

PREP TIME: 30 MINUTES ● **START TO FINISH: 30 MINUTES**
4 SERVINGS (3 PANCAKES EACH)

1 can (21 oz) apple pie filling

2 cups Original Bisquick mix

1 cup milk

2 eggs

¾ cup diced cooked ham

½ cup shredded Cheddar
cheese (2 oz)

2 medium green onions, sliced
(2 tablespoons), if desired

Ground cinnamon, if desired

1 In 1-quart saucepan, heat pie filling over low heat, stirring occasionally, until hot. Keep warm while making pancakes.

2 In large bowl, stir Bisquick mix, milk and eggs with wire whisk or fork until blended. Stir in ham, cheese and onions.

3 Brush griddle or skillet with vegetable oil or spray with cooking spray; heat griddle to 375°F or heat skillet over medium heat.

4 For each pancake, pour slightly less than ¼ cup batter onto hot griddle. Cook until edges are dry. Turn; cook other sides until golden brown. Serve with warm pie filling; sprinkle with cinnamon.

High Altitude (3500–6500 ft): No change.

1 SERVING: Calories 570 (Calories from Fat 170); Total Fat 18g (Saturated Fat 8g); Cholesterol 140mg; Sodium 1260mg; Total Carbohydrate 82g (Dietary Fiber 3g; Sugars 40g); Protein 19g **% DAILY VALUE:** Vitamin A 8%; Vitamin C 0%; Calcium 25%; Iron 15% **EXCHANGES:** 2 Starch, 3½ Other Carbohydrate, 2 Lean Meat, 2 Fat **CARBOHYDRATE CHOICES:** 5½

Quick Tip Liven up these pancakes by stirring 1 tablespoon Dijon mustard in with the milk and eggs.

Apple and Sausage Oven Pancake

PREP TIME: 15 MINUTES ● **START TO FINISH: 40 MINUTES**
4 SERVINGS

1 package (8 oz) frozen brown-and-serve sausage links

1 cup Original Bisquick mix

½ teaspoon ground cinnamon

½ cup milk

1 egg

½ cup chopped peeled apple

Maple-flavored syrup, if desired

1 Heat oven to 450°F. Spray 8-inch square (2-quart) glass baking dish with cooking spray. Cook sausage links as directed on package.

2 In medium bowl, stir Bisquick mix, cinnamon, milk and egg with wire whisk or fork, until smooth. Stir in apple. Pour into baking dish. Arrange sausage links on top.

3 Bake uncovered 20 to 25 minutes or until pancake is light golden brown. Serve with syrup.

High Altitude (3500–6500 ft): Heat oven to 475°F.

1 SERVING: Calories 380 (Calories from Fat 230); Total Fat 26g (Saturated Fat 9g); Cholesterol 95mg; Sodium 820mg; Total Carbohydrate 23g (Dietary Fiber 1g; Sugars 4g); Protein 13g **% DAILY VALUE:** Vitamin A 4%; Vitamin C 0%; Calcium 15%; Iron 8% **EXCHANGES:** 1 Starch, ½ Other Carbohydrate, 1½ High-Fat Meat, 2½ Fat **CARBOHYDRATE CHOICES:** 1½

Polka Dot Sausage Pancakes

PREP TIME: 20 MINUTES ● START TO FINISH: 20 MINUTES
6 SERVINGS (3 PANCAKES EACH)

1 package (8 oz) frozen brown-and-serve sausage links

2 cups Original Bisquick mix

1½ cups milk

1 egg

1 Cut sausage links into ⅛-inch slices. In 10-inch skillet, cook sausage until brown; drain and set aside.

2 In medium bowl, stir remaining ingredients with wire whisk or fork until blended.

3 Brush griddle or skillet with vegetable oil or spray with cooking spray; heat griddle to 375°F or heat skillet over medium heat.

4 For each pancake, place about 10 sausage slices randomly within a 3-inch circle on hot griddle. Pour slightly less than ¼ cup batter over sausage slices. Cook until edges are dry. Turn; cook other sides until golden brown.

High Altitude (3500–6500 ft): No change.

1 SERVING: Calories 340 (Calories from Fat 180); Total Fat 20g (Saturated Fat 7g); Cholesterol 70mg; Sodium 810mg; Total Carbohydrate 29g (Dietary Fiber 1g; Sugars 4g); Protein 12g **% DAILY VALUE:** Vitamin A 4%; Vitamin C 0%; Calcium 15%; Iron 8% **EXCHANGES:** 1½ Starch, ½ Other Carbohydrate, 1 High-Fat Meat, 2 Fat **CARBOHYDRATE CHOICES:** 2

Wearing a syrupy smile, the Jack-o'-Lantern pancake in this 1951 ad was easy to make, thanks to foolproof batter made with Bisquick.

Caramel Apple–Topped Waffles

PREP TIME: 20 MINUTES ● START TO FINISH: 20 MINUTES
6 SERVINGS (TWO 4-INCH WAFFLES EACH)

CARAMEL APPLE TOPPING

2 tablespoons butter or margarine

3 medium apples, peeled, sliced (about 3½ cups)

¼ cup caramel topping

WAFFLES

2 cups Original Bisquick mix

1⅓ cups milk

2 tablespoons vegetable oil

1 egg

1 In 10-inch skillet, melt butter over medium heat. Cook apples in butter about 3 minutes, stirring frequently, until tender. Pour caramel topping over apples. Cook, stirring frequently, until warm. Keep warm while making waffles.

2 Heat waffle iron. (Waffle irons without a nonstick coating may need to be brushed with vegetable oil or sprayed with cooking spray.) In medium bowl, stir all waffle ingredients with wire whisk or fork until blended.

3 For each waffle, pour batter onto center of hot waffle iron. (Check manufacturer's directions for recommended amount of batter.) Close lid of waffle iron. Bake 3 to 5 minutes or until steaming stops. Carefully remove waffle. Serve waffles with topping.

High Altitude (3500–6500 ft): No change.

1 SERVING: Calories 350 (Calories from Fat 140); Total Fat 15g (Saturated Fat 6g); Cholesterol 50mg; Sodium 600mg; Total Carbohydrate 46g (Dietary Fiber 2g; Sugars 17g); Protein 6g **% DAILY VALUE:** Vitamin A 6%; Vitamin C 2%; Calcium 10%; Iron 8% **EXCHANGES:** 2 Starch, ½ Fruit, ½ Other Carbohydrate, 3 Fat **CARBOHYDRATE CHOICES:** 3

Quick Tip Freeze any leftover waffles, then reheat in the microwave or pop 'em in the toaster for another breakfast.

Banana-Nut Waffles

PREP TIME: 20 MINUTES ● **START TO FINISH: 20 MINUTES**
6 SERVINGS (TWO 4-INCH WAFFLES EACH)

2 cups Original Bisquick mix

¼ cup finely chopped
   walnuts or pecans

1 cup mashed very ripe
   bananas (2 medium)

1 cup milk

2 tablespoons vegetable oil

1 egg

Sliced bananas, if desired

Chopped walnuts or pecans,
   if desired

Maple-flavored syrup, if desired

1 Heat waffle iron. (Waffle irons without a nonstick coating may need to be brushed with vegetable oil or sprayed with cooking spray.) In medium bowl, stir Bisquick mix, finely chopped walnuts, mashed bananas, milk, oil and egg with wire whisk or fork until blended.

2 For each waffle, pour batter onto center of hot waffle iron. (Check manufacturer's directions for recommended amount of batter.) Close lid of waffle iron. Bake 3 to 5 minutes or until steaming stops. Carefully remove waffle.

3 Serve waffles with sliced bananas, chopped walnuts and syrup.

High Altitude (3500–6500 ft): No change.

1 SERVING: Calories 310 (Calories from Fat 130); Total Fat 15g (Saturated Fat 3.5g); Cholesterol 40mg; Sodium 520mg; Total Carbohydrate 37g (Dietary Fiber 2g; Sugars 8g); Protein 7g **% DAILY VALUE:** Vitamin A 4%; Vitamin C 2%; Calcium 10%; Iron 8% **EXCHANGES:** 1½ Starch, 1 Other Carbohydrate, 3 Fat **CARBOHYDRATE CHOICES:** 2½

Dreamy Orange Waffles

PREP TIME: 35 MINUTES ● START TO FINISH: 35 MINUTES
6 SERVINGS (TWO 4-INCH WAFFLES EACH)

ORANGE SYRUP

1 cup packed brown sugar

2 tablespoons cornstarch

1 cup orange juice

1 can (11 oz) mandarin orange
    segments, drained

WAFFLES

2 cups Original Bisquick mix

1¼ cups milk

2 tablespoons butter or
    margarine, melted

1 tablespoon grated orange
    peel

1 egg

TOPPING

1 cup frozen (thawed) whipped
    topping

1 In 1-quart saucepan, heat brown sugar, cornstarch and orange juice to boiling over medium-high heat, stirring frequently. Boil and stir 1 to 2 minutes or until syrup is slightly thickened and mixture is clear. Remove from heat; stir in orange segments. Keep warm while making waffles.

2 Heat waffle iron. (Waffle irons without a nonstick coating may need to be brushed with vegetable oil or sprayed with cooking spray.) In medium bowl, stir all waffle ingredients with wire whisk or fork until blended.

3 For each waffle, pour batter onto center of hot waffle iron. (Check manufacturer's directions for recommended amount of batter.) Close lid of waffle iron. Bake 3 to 5 minutes or until steaming stops. Carefully remove waffle.

4 Spoon syrup over waffles; top with whipped topping.

High Altitude (3500–6500 ft): No change.

1 SERVING: Calories 460 (Calories from Fat 120); Total Fat 13g (Saturated Fat 7g); Cholesterol 50mg; Sodium 570mg; Total Carbohydrate 78g (Dietary Fiber 2g; Sugars 49g); Protein 7g **% DAILY VALUE:** Vitamin A 15%; Vitamin C 25%; Calcium 15%; Iron 10% **EXCHANGES:** 2 Starch, 3 Other Carbohydrate, 2½ Fat **CARBOHYDRATE CHOICES:** 5

Quick Tip Use a fork as a tool to lift the waffle from the iron. It helps prevent the hot waffle from breaking and you won't burn your fingers.

Orange Waffles
with Maple-Orange Syrup

PREP TIME: 30 MINUTES ● START TO FINISH: 30 MINUTES
6 SERVINGS (TWO 4-INCH WAFFLES EACH)

MAPLE-ORANGE SYRUP

1 cup maple-flavored syrup

3 tablespoons orange juice

3 tablespoons butter or
  margarine

WAFFLES

2 cups Original Bisquick mix

⅔ cup milk

⅔ cup orange juice

2 tablespoons vegetable oil

1 egg

1 In 1-quart saucepan, heat all syrup ingredients just until hot. Keep warm while making waffles.

2 Heat waffle iron. (Waffle irons without a nonstick coating may need to be brushed with vegetable oil or sprayed with cooking spray.) In large bowl, stir all waffle ingredients with wire whisk or fork until blended.

3 For each waffle, pour batter onto center of hot waffle iron. (Check manufacturer's directions for recommended amount of batter.) Close lid of waffle iron. Bake 3 to 5 minutes or until steaming stops. Carefully remove waffle. Serve waffles with syrup.

High Altitude (3500–6500 ft): No change.

1 SERVING: Calories 460 (Calories from Fat 150); Total Fat 17g (Saturated Fat 6g); Cholesterol 55mg; Sodium 590mg; Total Carbohydrate 71g (Dietary Fiber 1g; Sugars 26g); Protein 5g **% DAILY VALUE:** Vitamin A 6%; Vitamin C 10%; Calcium 8%; Iron 6% **EXCHANGES:** 1½ Starch, 3 Other Carbohydrate, 3½ Fat **CARBOHYDRATE CHOICES:** 5

Waffle magic from 1940—a dinner so easy, it could have come on Santa's sleigh.

Pear 'n' Ginger–Topped Waffles

PREP TIME: 25 MINUTES ● START TO FINISH: 25 MINUTES
6 SERVINGS (TWO 4-INCH WAFFLES EACH)

PEAR 'N' GINGER TOPPING

¼ cup sugar

1 tablespoon finely chopped crystallized ginger

2 teaspoons cornstarch

½ cup water

2 teaspoons butter or margarine

1½ teaspoons lemon juice

2 medium pears, peeled, sliced (about 1⅔ cups)

½ cup fresh raspberries

WAFFLES

2 cups Original Bisquick mix

1⅓ cups milk

2 tablespoons vegetable oil

1 egg

1 In 1½-quart saucepan, heat all topping ingredients except pears and raspberries over medium heat, stirring frequently, until mixture thickens and boils. Boil and stir 1 minute. Stir in pears; cook until pears are hot, stirring occasionally. Remove from heat. Stir in raspberries; set aside.

2 Heat waffle iron. (Waffle irons without a nonstick coating may need to be brushed with vegetable oil or sprayed with cooking spray.) In medium bowl, stir all waffle ingredients with wire whisk or fork until blended.

3 For each waffle, pour batter onto center of hot waffle iron. (Check manufacturer's directions for recommended amount of batter.) Close lid of waffle iron. Bake 3 to 5 minutes or until steaming stops. Carefully remove waffle. Serve waffles with topping.

High Altitude (3500–6500 ft): No change.

1 SERVING: Calories 330 (Calories from Fat 120); Total Fat 13g (Saturated Fat 4g); Cholesterol 45mg; Sodium 530mg; Total Carbohydrate 47g (Dietary Fiber 3g; Sugars 17g); Protein 6g **% DAILY VALUE:** Vitamin A 4%; Vitamin C 4%; Calcium 10%; Iron 8% **EXCHANGES:** 2 Starch, 1 Other Carbohydrate, 2½ Fat **CARBOHYDRATE CHOICES:** 3

Quick Tip Mix the waffle batter in a 4-cup glass measuring cup with a handle and spout. The batter will be easy to pour onto the waffle iron.

Lemon-Almond Waffles
with Lemon Cream

PREP TIME: 30 MINUTES ● START TO FINISH: 30 MINUTES
6 SERVINGS (TWO 4-INCH WAFFLES EACH)

LEMON CREAM

¾ cup whipping cream

3 tablespoons powdered sugar

1 teaspoon grated lemon peel

1 package (3 oz) cream cheese, softened

WAFFLES

2 cups Original Bisquick mix

2 tablespoons powdered sugar

2 teaspoons grated lemon peel

1⅓ cups milk

2 tablespoons vegetable oil

1 egg

½ cup chopped slivered almonds

Additional powdered sugar, if desired

Toasted slivered almonds, if desired

1 In chilled small bowl, beat all lemon cream ingredients with electric mixer on high speed just until soft and fluffy. Refrigerate while making waffles.

2 Heat Belgian or regular waffle iron. (Waffle irons without a nonstick coating may need to be brushed with vegetable oil or sprayed with cooking spray.) In large bowl, stir Bisquick mix, 2 tablespoons powdered sugar, the lemon peel, milk, oil and egg with wire whisk or fork until blended. Stir in ½ cup chopped almonds.

3 For each waffle, pour batter onto center of hot waffle iron. (Check manufacturer's directions for recommended amount of batter.) Close lid of waffle iron. Bake 3 to 5 minutes or until steaming stops. Carefully remove waffle.

4 Sprinkle waffles with additional powdered sugar and toasted almonds. Serve waffles with lemon cream.

High Altitude (3500–6500 ft): No change.

1 SERVING: Calories 470 (Calories from Fat 280); Total Fat 31g (Saturated Fat 12g); Cholesterol 90mg; Sodium 580mg; Total Carbohydrate 38g (Dietary Fiber 2g; Sugars 12g); Protein 10g **% DAILY VALUE:** Vitamin A 15%; Vitamin C 0%; Calcium 15%; Iron 10% **EXCHANGES:** 2½ Starch, 6 Fat **CARBOHYDRATE CHOICES:** 2½

Macadamia Nut Waffles with Coconut Syrup

PREP TIME: 25 MINUTES ● START TO FINISH: 25 MINUTES
6 SERVINGS (TWO 4-INCH WAFFLES EACH)

COCONUT SYRUP

¾ cup cream of coconut

1 cup white corn syrup

WAFFLES

2 cups Original Bisquick mix

2 tablespoons sugar

1 cup milk

2 tablespoons vegetable oil

2 eggs

½ cup coarsely chopped macadamia nuts

½ cup whole macadamia nuts

1 In 1-quart saucepan, heat syrup ingredients over low heat, stirring constantly, until hot. Keep warm while making waffles.

2 Heat waffle iron. (Waffle irons without a nonstick coating may need to be brushed with vegetable oil or sprayed with cooking spray.) In large bowl, stir all waffle ingredients except nuts with wire whisk or fork until blended. Stir in chopped and whole nuts.

3 For each waffle, pour batter onto center of hot waffle iron. (Check manufacturer's directions for recommended amount of batter.) Close lid of waffle iron. Bake 3 to 5 minutes or until steaming stops. Carefully remove waffle. Serve waffles with syrup.

High Altitude (3500–6500 ft): No change.

1 SERVING: Calories 700 (Calories from Fat 340); Total Fat 38g (Saturated Fat 15g); Cholesterol 75mg; Sodium 620mg; Total Carbohydrate 81g (Dietary Fiber 3g; Sugars 32g); Protein 9g **% DAILY VALUE:** Vitamin A 4%; Vitamin C 0%; Calcium 10%; Iron 15% **EXCHANGES:** 3 Starch, 2½ Other Carbohydrate, 7 Fat **CARBOHYDRATE CHOICES:** 5½

Quick Tip These nutty waffles are also delicious when served with fresh fruit rather than the coconut syrup. Chunks of fresh pineapple, slices of juicy peaches or fresh strawberries or raspberries piled on top are excellent choices.

Chocolate Waffles
with Caramel-Banana Topping

PREP TIME: 15 MINUTES ● START TO FINISH: 15 MINUTES
6 SERVINGS (TWO 4-INCH WAFFLES EACH)

CARAMEL-BANANA TOPPING

½ cup packed brown sugar

¼ cup whipping (heavy) cream

¼ cup light corn syrup

2 tablespoons margarine or butter

1 teaspoon vanilla

3 medium bananas, sliced

WAFFLES

1½ cups Original Bisquick

1 cup sugar

⅓ cup baking cocoa

¾ cup water

2 tablespoons vegetable oil

2 eggs

1 Mix all topping ingredients except bananas in 1-quart saucepan. Heat to boiling, stirring occasionally; remove from heat. Add bananas; stir gently until well coated. Keep warm while making waffles.

2 Heat waffle iron. (Waffle irons without a nonstick coating may need to be brushed with vegetable oil or sprayed with cooking spray.) In medium bowl, stir all waffle ingredients with wire whisk or fork until blended.

3 For each waffle, pour batter onto center of hot waffle iron. (Check manufacturer's directions for recommended amount of batter.) Close lid of waffle iron. Bake 3 to 5 minutes or until steaming stops. Carefully remove waffles. Serve waffles with topping.

High Altitude (3500–6500 ft): No change.

1 SERVING: Calories 560 (Calories from Fat 170); Total Fat 19g (Saturated Fat 6g); Cholesterol 84mg; Sodium 466mg; Total Carbohydrate 19g (Dietary Fiber 3g; Sugars 63g); Protein 6g **% DAILY VALUE:** Vitamin A 8%; Vitamin C 4%; Calcium 8%; Iron 12% **EXCHANGES:** 2 Starch, 4 Fruit, 3½ Fat **CARBOHYDRATE CHOICES:** 6½

Quick Tip These warm and wonderful waffles are not just for breakfast. For a truly decadent dessert, try these scrumptious squares topped with a scoop of vanilla or chocolate chip ice cream.

Whole Wheat–Granola Waffles

PREP TIME: 55 MINUTES ● START TO FINISH: 55 MINUTES
6 SERVINGS (TWO 4-INCH WAFFLES EACH)

2 cups Original Bisquick mix

½ cup whole wheat flour

½ cup granola

1½ cups milk

2 tablespoons packed
   brown sugar

2 tablespoons vegetable oil

1 egg

1½ cups fresh berries
   (raspberries, blueberries,
   sliced strawberries)

¾ cup maple-flavored syrup

1 Heat waffle iron. (Waffle irons without a nonstick coating may need to be brushed with vegetable oil or sprayed with cooking spray.) In medium bowl, stir all ingredients except berries and syrup with wire whisk or fork until blended.

2 For each waffle, pour batter onto center of hot waffle iron. (Check manufacturer's directions for recommended amount of batter.) Close lid of waffle iron. Bake 3 to 5 minutes or until steaming stops. Carefully remove waffle.

3 Serve waffles with berries and syrup.

High Altitude (3500–6500 ft): No change.

1 SERVING: Calories 480 (Calories from Fat 120); Total Fat 13g (Saturated Fat 3.5g); Cholesterol 40mg; Sodium 560mg; Total Carbohydrate 81g (Dietary Fiber 4g; Sugars 28g); Protein 9g **% DAILY VALUE:** Vitamin A 4%; Vitamin C 6%; Calcium 15%; Iron 10% **EXCHANGES:** 3 Starch, 2½ Other Carbohydrate, 2 Fat **CARBOHYDRATE CHOICES:** 5½

Quick Tip Get a head start by making a batch of waffles for the freezer. Wrap cooled waffles in aluminum foil or in a resealable plastic freezer bag and freeze up to 1 month. To serve, place frozen waffles on a cookie sheet and reheat in a 350°F oven for 10 minutes or pop them in a toaster.

Chocolate Chip Waffles with Orange Cream

PREP TIME: 30 MINUTES ● START TO FINISH: 30 MINUTES
6 SERVINGS (TWO 4-INCH WAFFLES EACH)

ORANGE CREAM

¾ cup whipping cream

2 tablespoons powdered sugar

2 tablespoons frozen orange juice concentrate, thawed

WAFFLES

2 cups Original Bisquick mix

2 tablespoons powdered sugar

2 tablespoons grated orange peel

1⅓ cups milk

2 tablespoons vegetable oil

1 egg

½ cup miniature semisweet chocolate chips

1 In chilled small bowl, beat whipping cream and 2 tablespoons powdered sugar with electric mixer on high speed just until soft and fluffy. Beat in juice concentrate until blended. Refrigerate while making waffles.

2 Heat waffle iron. (Waffle irons without a nonstick coating may need to be brushed with vegetable oil or sprayed with cooking spray.) In medium bowl, mix all waffle ingredients except chocolate chips with wire whisk or fork until blended. Stir in chocolate chips.

3 For each waffle, pour batter onto center of hot waffle iron. (Check manufacturer's directions for recommended amount of batter.) Close lid of waffle iron. Bake 3 to 5 minutes or until steaming stops. Carefully remove waffle. Serve waffles with orange cream.

High Altitude (3500–6500 ft): No change.

1 SERVING: Calories 440 (Calories from Fat 220); Total Fat 25g (Saturated Fat 11g); Cholesterol 75mg; Sodium 530mg; Total Carbohydrate 46g (Dietary Fiber 2g; Sugars 19g); Protein 7g **% DAILY VALUE:** Vitamin A 10%; Vitamin C 10%; Calcium 15%; Iron 10% **EXCHANGES:** 2 Starch, 1 Other Carbohydrate, 5 Fat **CARBOHYDRATE CHOICES:** 3

Quick Tip To keep waffles warm until serving time, place them in a single layer on a wire rack or paper towel–lined cookie sheet in a 350°F oven for up to 20 minutes. Just make sure you don't stack warm waffles because they will become soggy.

Cheddar and Sausage Waffles

PREP TIME: 25 MINUTES ● START TO FINISH: 25 MINUTES
6 SERVINGS (TWO 4-INCH WAFFLES EACH)

⅓ lb bulk pork sausage

2 cups Original Bisquick mix

1 cup shredded Cheddar
    cheese (4 oz)

1⅓ cups milk

2 tablespoons vegetable oil

1 egg

1 In 8-inch skillet, cook sausage over medium-high heat 5 to 7 minutes, stirring frequently, until thoroughly cooked; drain.

2 Heat waffle iron. (Waffle irons without a nonstick coating may need to be brushed with vegetable oil or sprayed with cooking spray.) In medium bowl, stir Bisquick mix, cheese, milk, oil and egg with wire whisk or fork until blended. Stir in sausage.

3 For each waffle, pour batter onto center of hot waffle iron. (Check manufacturer's directions for recommended amount of batter.) Close lid of waffle iron. Bake 3 to 5 minutes or until steaming stops. Carefully remove waffle.

High Altitude (3500–6500 ft): No change.

1 SERVING: Calories 360 (Calories from Fat 190); Total Fat 21g (Saturated Fat 8g); Cholesterol 70mg; Sodium 730mg; Total Carbohydrate 29g (Dietary Fiber 1g; Sugars 4g); Protein 13g **% DAILY VALUE:** Vitamin A 6%; Vitamin C 0%; Calcium 20%; Iron 8%
EXCHANGES: 1½ Starch, ½ Other Carbohydrate, 1 High-Fat Meat, 2½ Fat
CARBOHYDRATE CHOICES: 2

Quick Tip Apples in any form will taste delicious with these waffles. Try fresh apple slices, chunky apple sauce, apple butter, hot apple pie filling or fried apples with cinnamon. So simple, so good!

Banana-Nut Bread

PREP TIME: 10 MINUTES ● START TO FINISH: 1 HOUR 20 MINUTES
1 LOAF (16 SLICES)

1⅓ cups mashed very ripe bananas (about 2 large)

⅔ cup sugar

¼ cup milk

3 tablespoons vegetable oil

½ teaspoon vanilla

3 eggs

2⅔ cups Original Bisquick mix

½ cup chopped nuts

1 Heat oven to 350°F. Spray bottom only of 9 × 5-inch loaf pan with cooking spray. In large bowl, stir bananas, sugar, milk, oil, vanilla and eggs until blended. Stir in Bisquick mix and nuts. Pour into pan.

2 Bake 50 to 60 minutes or until toothpick inserted in center comes out clean. Cool 10 minutes. Run knife or metal spatula around sides of pan to loosen loaf. Remove from pan to cooling rack. Cool completely.

High Altitude (3500–6500 ft): Heat oven to 375°F. Decrease sugar to ⅓ cup. Bake 45 to 55 minutes.

1 SLICE: Calories 200 (Calories from Fat 80); Total Fat 9g (Saturated Fat 1.5g); Cholesterol 40mg; Sodium 260mg; Total Carbohydrate 26g (Dietary Fiber 1g; Sugars 12g); Protein 4g **% DAILY VALUE:** Vitamin A 0%; Vitamin C 0%; Calcium 4%; Iron 4% **EXCHANGES:** 1 Starch, 1 Other Carbohydrate, 1½ Fat **CARBOHYDRATE CHOICES:** 2

Quick Tip This banana bread makes terrific French toast. Dip slices of bread into an egg and milk mixture. Cook in a skillet sprayed with cooking spray for 2 to 3 minutes on each side or until golden brown. Serve with maple-flavored syrup.

In 1953—or any other year—people are crazy for Bisquick's easy, delicious bread. You wouldn't want to make it any other way.

Left: Blueberry-Banana
Bread (page 74)
Right: Banana-Nut Bread

Blueberry-Banana Bread

PREP TIME: 15 MINUTES ● START TO FINISH: 3 HOURS 20 MINUTES
1 LOAF (24 SLICES)

2 cups Original Bisquick mix

¾ cup quick-cooking oats

⅔ cup sugar

1 cup mashed very ripe
    bananas (2 medium)

¼ cup milk

2 eggs

1 cup fresh or frozen (thawed
    and drained) blueberries

1 Heat oven to 350°F. Spray bottom only of 9-inch loaf pan. In large bowl, stir Bisquick mix, oats, sugar, bananas, milk and eggs with wire whisk or fork until moistened. Beat vigorously 30 seconds. Gently stir in blueberries. Pour into pan.

2 Bake 45 to 55 minutes or until toothpick inserted in center comes out clean. Cool 10 minutes. Run knife around sides of pan to loosen loaf. Remove from pan to cooling rack. Cool completely, about 2 hours.

High Altitude (3500–6500 ft): Heat oven to 375°F. Decrease Bisquick mix to 1¾ cups, sugar to ½ cup and bananas to ⅔ cup; stir ⅓ cup all-purpose flour into Bisquick mix. Increase milk to ⅓ cup and eggs to 3.

1 SLICE: Calories 90 (Calories from Fat 20); Total Fat 2g (Saturated Fat 0.5g); Cholesterol 20mg; Sodium 130mg; Total Carbohydrate 17g (Dietary Fiber 0g; Sugars 8g); Protein 2g **% DAILY VALUE:** Vitamin A 0%; Vitamin C 0%; Calcium 0%; Iron 2% **EXCHANGES:** ½ Starch, ½ Other Carbohydrate, ½ Fat **CARBOHYDRATE CHOICES:** 1

Raspberry-Banana Bread: Substitute 1 cup fresh or frozen (thawed and drained) raspberries for the blueberries.

Heart Smart Banana Bread

PREP TIME: 10 MINUTES ● START TO FINISH: 2 HOURS 50 MINUTES
1 LOAF (16 SLICES)

1⅓ cups mashed very ripe bananas (about 2 large)

⅔ cup sugar

¾ cup fat-free egg product

¼ cup fat-free (skim) milk

2 tablespoons vegetable oil

½ teaspoon vanilla

3 cups Bisquick Heart Smart mix

1 Heat oven to 350°F. Spray bottom only of 9 × 5-inch loaf pan with cooking spray. In large bowl, stir bananas, sugar, egg product, milk, oil and vanilla until blended. Stir in Bisquick mix. Pour into pan.

2 Bake 55 to 60 minutes or until toothpick inserted in center comes out clean.

3 Cool 10 minutes. Run knife or metal spatula around sides of pan to loosen bread; remove from pan to cooling rack. Cool completely, about 1 hour 30 minutes, before slicing.

High Altitude (3500–6500 ft): Heat oven to 375°F.

1 SLICE: Calories 150 (Calories from Fat 30); Total Fat 3g (Saturated Fat 0g); Cholesterol 0mg; Sodium 270mg; Total Carbohydrate 28g (Dietary Fiber 0g; Sugars 13g); Protein 3g **% DAILY VALUE:** Vitamin A 0%; Vitamin C 0%; Calcium 10%; Iron 6% **EXCHANGES:** 1 Starch, 1 Other Carbohydrate, ½ Fat **CARBOHYDRATE CHOICES:** 2

Quick Tip They may not look pretty, but the best bananas for baking have skins turning brown with black spots and are soft to the touch. Overripe bananas can be frozen (unpeeled) for later use. When you're ready to use them, just thaw them, cut off the top of the peel and squeeze the banana into your measuring cup.

Cinnamon Chip–Oatmeal Muffins

PREP TIME: 15 MINUTES ● START TO FINISH: 35 MINUTES
12 MUFFINS

1½ cups Original Bisquick mix

¾ cup old-fashioned or quick-cooking oats

⅓ cup packed brown sugar

⅔ cup milk

2 tablespoons vegetable oil

1 egg

½ cup cinnamon-flavored baking chips

¼ cup old-fashioned or quick-cooking oats

1 Heat oven to 400°F. Line 12 medium muffin cups, 2½ × 1¼ inches, with paper baking cups; or grease bottoms only of muffin cups with shortening.

2 Stir all ingredients except cinnamon chips and ¼ cup oats in medium bowl just until moistened. Fold in cinnamon chips. Divide batter evenly among muffin cups. Sprinkle with ¼ cup oats.

3 Bake 15 to 18 minutes or until toothpick inserted in center of muffin comes out clean.

High Altitude (3500–6500 ft): Use paper baking cups.

1 MUFFIN: Calories 199 (Calories from Fat 76); Total Fat 9g (Saturated Fat 3g); Cholesterol 19mg; Sodium 225mg; Total Carbohydrate 26g (Dietary Fiber 1g; Sugars 13g); Protein 4g **% DAILY VALUE:** Vitamin A 0%; Vitamin C 0%; Calcium 8%; Iron 6% **EXCHANGES:** 1 Starch, 1 Other Carbohydrate, 1 Fat **CARBOHYDRATE CHOICES:** 2

Quick Tip: For muffins with nicely rounded tops, mix ingredients only until moistened and batter is slightly lumpy, and be sure your oven is preheated. Buttermilk lovers, you will be glad to know you can substitute buttermilk for the milk in these "oaty" muffins; it adds great flavor and moistness.

Crumble-Topped Cranberry Muffins

PREP TIME: 15 MINUTES ● START TO FINISH: 35 MINUTES
12 MUFFINS

2 tablespoons packed brown sugar

1 tablespoon Original Bisquick mix

⅓ cup milk

1 egg

½ cup whole berry cranberry sauce

2 cups Original Bisquick

2 tablespoons granulated sugar

1 Heat oven to 400°F. Grease bottoms only of 12 medium muffin cups, 2½ × 1¼ inches, or line with paper baking cups. Mix brown sugar and 1 tablespoon Bisquick mix; set aside.

2 Stir milk, egg and cranberry sauce in medium bowl until well blended. Stir in 2 cups Bisquick mix and the granulated sugar just until moistened. Divide batter evenly among cups. Sprinkle with brown sugar mixture.

3 Bake about 18 minutes or until golden brown. Cool slightly; remove from pan to wire rack.

High Altitude (3500–6500 ft): No change.

1 MUFFIN: Calories 125 (Calories from Fat 25); Total Fat 3g (Saturated Fat 1g); Cholesterol 20mg; Sodium 300mg; Total Carbohydrate 22g (Dietary Fiber 0g; Sugars 8g); Protein 2g **% DAILY VALUE:** Vitamin A 0%; Vitamin C 0%; Calcium 4%; Iron 4% **EXCHANGES:** 1 Starch, ½ Fruit, ½ Fat **CARBOHYDRATE CHOICES:** 1½

Quick Tip For a simple twist to these easy muffins, try applesauce in place of the cranberry sauce.

Maple-Nut-Raisin Muffins

PREP TIME: 20 MINUTES ● **START TO FINISH: 45 MINUTES**
12 MUFFINS

TOPPING

2 tablespoons packed brown sugar

1 tablespoon Original Bisquick mix

1 teaspoon butter or margarine, softened

MUFFINS

2 cups Original Bisquick mix

⅓ cup raisins

⅓ cup chopped pecans

¼ cup packed brown sugar

⅔ cup milk

2 tablespoons vegetable oil

1 teaspoon maple flavor

1 egg

1 Heat oven to 400°F. Line 12 regular-size muffin cups with paper baking cups or grease bottoms only with shortening or cooking spray. In small bowl, mix all topping ingredients until crumbly; set aside.

2 In large bowl, stir all muffin ingredients just until moistened. Spoon batter evenly into muffin cups. Sprinkle evenly with topping.

3 Bake 15 to 18 minutes or until golden brown. Cool slightly; remove from pan to cooling rack. Serve warm.

High Altitude (3500–6500 ft): No change.

1 MUFFIN: Calories 180 (Calories from Fat 70); Total Fat 8g (Saturated Fat 2g); Cholesterol 20mg; Sodium 270mg; Total Carbohydrate 24g (Dietary Fiber 0g; Sugars 10g); Protein 3g **% DAILY VALUE:** Vitamin A 0%; Vitamin C 0%; Calcium 4%; Iron 6% **EXCHANGES:** 1 Starch, ½ Other Carbohydrate, 1½ Fat **CARBOHYDRATE CHOICES:** 1½

Rise 'n' Shine Muffins

PREP TIME: 15 MINUTES ● **START TO FINISH: 35 MINUTES**
12 MUFFINS

MUFFINS

⅔ cup orange juice

⅓ cup honey

2 tablespoons vegetable oil

1 egg

1½ cups Original Bisquick mix

1 cup Fiber One cereal®, crushed

½ teaspoon baking soda

½ cup plus 2 tablespoons salted sunflower nuts, toasted

CREAMY ORANGE SPREAD

3 oz ⅓-less-fat cream cheese (Neufchâtel), softened

2 tablespoons orange marmalade

1 Heat oven to 400°F. Spray bottoms only of 12 regular-size muffin cups with cooking spray or line with paper baking cups. In medium bowl, mix orange juice, honey, oil and egg.

2 In large bowl, stir Bisquick mix, cereal, baking soda and ½ cup of the nuts. Stir orange juice mixture into cereal mixture just until moistened. Spoon batter into muffin cups. Sprinkle with remaining nuts.

3 Bake about 20 minutes or until golden brown. Immediately remove from pan.

4 In small bowl, mix cream cheese and marmalade until well blended. Serve muffins with spread.

High Altitude (3500–6500 ft): Increase orange juice to ¾ cup and Bisquick mix to 1¾ cups. Bake about 18 minutes.

1 MUFFIN: Calories 220 (Calories from Fat 90); Total Fat 10g (Saturated Fat 2.5g); Cholesterol 25mg; Sodium 330mg; Total Carbohydrate 27g (Dietary Fiber 3g; Sugars 12g); Protein 4g **% DAILY VALUE:** Vitamin A 2%; Vitamin C 6%; Calcium 4%; Iron 8% **EXCHANGES:** 1 Starch, 1 Other Carbohydrate, 2 Fat **CARBOHYDRATE CHOICES:** 2

Quick Tip To crush the cereal without making a mess, place it in a plastic bag and crush with rolling pin or mallet. Or just throw into the blender or food processor and give it a few quick pulses.

Apricot-Orange Scones

PREP TIME: 15 MINUTES ● START TO FINISH: 35 MINUTES
8 SCONES

2 cups Original Bisquick mix

¼ cup sugar

½ cup finely chopped dried apricots

2 teaspoons grated orange peel

1 egg, beaten

½ cup whipping cream

2 tablespoons sugar

2 tablespoons sliced almonds

1 Heat oven to 425°F. Spray cookie sheet with cooking spray. In large bowl, stir Bisquick mix, ¼ cup sugar, the apricots and orange peel until mixed. Reserve 1 tablespoon of the egg. Stir in remaining egg and the whipping cream until soft dough forms.

2 Place dough on surface sprinkled with Bisquick mix; roll in Bisquick mix to coat. Shape into a ball; knead 10 times. On cookie sheet, press or roll dough into 8-inch round. Brush with reserved egg. Sprinkle with 2 tablespoons sugar and the almonds. Cut into 8 wedges, but do not separate.

3 Bake 12 to 15 minutes or until edges are golden brown. Let stand 5 minutes. Carefully separate wedges. Serve warm.

High Altitude (3500–6500 ft): No change.

1 SCONE: Calories 240 (Calories from Fat 90); Total Fat 10g (Saturated Fat 4.5g); Cholesterol 45mg; Sodium 380mg; Total Carbohydrate 35g (Dietary Fiber 1g; Sugars 15g); Protein 4g **% DAILY VALUE:** Vitamin A 10%; Vitamin C 0%; Calcium 6%; Iron 6% **EXCHANGES:** 1 Starch, 1 Other Carbohydrate, 2 Fat **CARBOHYDRATE CHOICES:** 2

It all "B"egins with Bisquick in this 1988 recipe booklet that lets you start your day in a "B"eautiful way.

Quick Tip For a nice flavor change, use other chopped dried fruits, such as peaches, pears or apples.

Coconut, Pineapple and Macadamia Scones

PREP TIME: 15 MINUTES ● START TO FINISH: 30 MINUTES
12 SCONES

2½ cups Original Bisquick mix

¼ cup sugar

¼ cup firm butter or margarine

½ cup flaked coconut

½ cup chopped macadamia nuts

¼ cup whipping cream

1 egg

1 can (8 oz) pineapple tidbits, well drained

1 Heat oven to 425°F. Spray cookie sheet with cooking spray. In large bowl, mix Bisquick mix and sugar. With fork or pastry blender, cut in butter until crumbly. Stir in remaining ingredients.

2 Pat dough into 10 × 7-inch rectangle on cookie sheet (if dough is sticky, dip fingers in Bisquick mix). Cut into 12 rectangles, but do not separate. Sprinkle with additional sugar and coconut if desired.

3 Bake 12 to 14 minutes or until golden brown; carefully separate rectangles. Serve warm.

High Altitude (3500–6500 ft): Bake 14 to 16 minutes.

1 SCONE: Calories 230 (Calories from Fat 120); Total Fat 14g (Saturated Fat 6g); Cholesterol 35mg; Sodium 400mg; Total Carbohydrate 24g (Dietary Fiber 1g; Sugars 10g); Protein 3g **% DAILY VALUE:** Vitamin A 4%; Vitamin C 0%; Calcium 6%; Iron 6% **EXCHANGES:** 1 Starch, ½ Other Carbohydrate, 2½ Fat **CARBOHYDRATE CHOICES:** 1½

Quick Tip Check scones for doneness at the minimum baking time. They're perfectly done when the top and bottom crusts are an even golden brown.

Strawberry–Cream Cheese Biscuits

PREP TIME: 15 MINUTES ● START TO FINISH: 25 MINUTES
15 BISCUITS

3 cups Original Bisquick mix

2 teaspoons grated orange peel

¾ cup orange juice

1 package (3 oz) cream cheese, softened

2 tablespoons strawberry preserves

Sugar, if desired

1 Heat oven to 450°F. Stir Bisquick mix, orange peel and orange juice until soft dough forms; beat vigorously 30 seconds.

2 Place dough on surface sprinkled with Bisquick mix; roll in Bisquick to coat. Shape into a ball; knead 10 times. Roll dough ½ inch thick. Cut with 2½-inch round cutter dipped in Bisquick. Place on ungreased cookie sheet.

3 Mix cream cheese and preserves. Spoon about 1 teaspoon cream cheese mixture onto center of each dough circle. Sprinkle with sugar. Bake 8 to 10 minutes or until golden brown.

High Altitude (3500–6500 ft): Not Recommended.

1 BISCUIT: Calories 127 (Calories from Fat 51); Total Fat 6g (Saturated Fat 2g); Cholesterol 6mg; Sodium 319mg; Total Carbohydrate 17g (Dietary Fiber 0g; Sugars 2g); Protein 2g **% DAILY VALUE:** Vitamin A 2%; Vitamin C 4%; Calcium 4%; Iron 6% **EXCHANGES:** 1 Starch, ½ Fat **CARBOHYDRATE CHOICES:** 1

Cheese and Rosemary Biscuits

PREP TIME: 10 MINUTES ● START TO FINISH: 20 MINUTES

9 BISCUITS

2 cups Original Bisquick mix

½ cup shredded Italian five-cheese blend (2 oz)

⅔ cup milk

1 teaspoon dried rosemary leaves, crushed

2 tablespoons butter or margarine, melted

⅛ teaspoon garlic powder

1 Heat oven to 450°F. In medium bowl, stir Bisquick mix, cheese, milk and ½ teaspoon of the rosemary leaves until soft dough forms. On ungreased cookie sheet, drop dough by 9 spoonfuls.

2 Bake 8 to 10 minutes or until golden brown. In small bowl, mix butter, garlic powder and remaining ½ teaspoon rosemary leaves; brush over warm biscuits.

High Altitude (3500–6500 ft): Bake 9 to 11 minutes.

1 BISCUIT: Calories 160 (Calories from Fat 70); Total Fat 8g (Saturated Fat 4g); Cholesterol 15mg; Sodium 440mg; Total Carbohydrate 18g (Dietary Fiber 0g; Sugars 2g); Protein 4g **% DAILY VALUE:** Vitamin A 4%; Vitamin C 0%; Calcium 10%; Iron 4% **EXCHANGES:** 1 Starch, 1½ Fat **CARBOHYDRATE CHOICES:** 1

The creation of Bisquick in the 1930s celebrated the convenience of home-baked goodness starting with hot, steaming biscuits.

Streusel-Topped Peach Coffee Cake

PREP TIME: 10 MINUTES ● **START TO FINISH: 1 HOUR 25 MINUTES**
12 SERVINGS

STREUSEL

1 cup Original Bisquick mix

⅔ cup packed brown sugar

1½ teaspoons ground cinnamon

3 tablespoons firm butter or margarine

COFFEE CAKE

1 can (15 oz) sliced peaches in 100% juice, drained, ¼ cup juice reserved

3 cups Original Bisquick mix

¼ cup granulated sugar

1 teaspoon vanilla

¼ teaspoon ground nutmeg

1 egg

1 Heat oven to 350°F. Spray bottom and sides of 13 × 9-inch pan with cooking spray. In small bowl, stir 1 cup Bisquick mix, the brown sugar and cinnamon. Cut in butter, using pastry blender (or pulling 2 table knives through ingredients in opposite directions), until crumbly; set aside.

2 Add enough water to ¼ cup reserved peach juice to measure ⅔ cup. In large bowl, beat juice mixture, 3 cups Bisquick mix, the granulated sugar, vanilla, nutmeg and egg with electric mixer on low speed until blended. Pour batter into pan; spread evenly. Place peach slices on batter. Sprinkle streusel over top.

3 Bake 25 to 30 minutes or until toothpick inserted in center comes out clean. Cool 45 minutes. Serve warm or cool.

High Altitude (3500–6500 ft): Bake 30 to 35 minutes.

1 SERVING: Calories 280 (Calories from Fat 80); Total Fat 8g (Saturated Fat 3.5g); Cholesterol 25mg; Sodium 520mg; Total Carbohydrate 48g (Dietary Fiber 1g; Sugars 22g); Protein 4g **% DAILY VALUE:** Vitamin A 4%; Vitamin C 0%; Calcium 6%; Iron 8% **EXCHANGES:** 1 Starch, 2 Other Carbohydrate, 1½ Fat **CARBOHYDRATE CHOICES:** 3

Banana–Chocolate Chip Coffee Cake

PREP TIME: 15 MINUTES ● START TO FINISH: 1 HOUR 15 MINUTES
9 SERVINGS

COFFEE CAKE

2¼ cups Original Bisquick mix

1 cup mashed ripe bananas (about 2 medium)

½ cup miniature semisweet chocolate chips

¼ cup granulated sugar

⅓ cup milk

2 tablespoons butter or margarine, softened

½ teaspoon ground cinnamon

1 egg

GLAZE

1 cup powdered sugar

1 tablespoon milk

½ teaspoon vanilla

1 Heat oven to 375°F. Spray 8-inch square pan with cooking spray. In medium bowl, stir all coffee cake ingredients with wire whisk or fork until blended. Spread in pan.

2 Bake 26 to 30 minutes or until golden brown and toothpick inserted in center comes out clean. Cool 30 minutes.

3 In small bowl, mix all glaze ingredients until smooth. If necessary, add additional milk, 1 teaspoon at a time, for desired consistency. Drizzle glaze over warm coffee cake. Serve warm.

High Altitude (3500–6500 ft): Bake 30 to 34 minutes.

1 SERVING: Calories 310 (Calories from Fat 90); Total Fat 10g (Saturated Fat 5g); Cholesterol 30mg; Sodium 400mg; Total Carbohydrate 51g (Dietary Fiber 2g; Sugars 28g); Protein 4g **% DAILY VALUE:** Vitamin A 2%; Vitamin C 0%; Calcium 6%; Iron 8% **EXCHANGES:** 1 Starch, 2½ Other Carbohydrate, 2 Fat **CARBOHYDRATE CHOICES:** 3½

Double-Streusel Coffee Cake

PREP TIME: 15 MINUTES ● **START TO FINISH: 1 HOUR 15 MINUTES**
6 SERVINGS

STREUSEL

⅔ cup Original Bisquick mix

⅔ cup packed brown sugar

1 teaspoon ground cinnamon

3 tablespoons firm butter or margarine

COFFEE CAKE

2 cups Original Bisquick mix

½ cup milk or water

2 tablespoons granulated sugar

1½ teaspoons vanilla

1 egg

1 Heat oven to 375°F. Spray bottom and side of 9-inch round cake pan with cooking spray. In small bowl, mix ⅔ cup Bisquick mix, the brown sugar and cinnamon. Cut in butter, using pastry blender (or pulling 2 table knives through ingredients in opposite directions), until crumbly; set aside.

2 In medium bowl, stir all coffee cake ingredients until blended. Spread about 1 cup of the batter in pan. Sprinkle with about ¾ cup of the streusel. Drop remaining batter over top of streusel; spread carefully over streusel. Sprinkle remaining streusel over top.

3 Bake 20 to 24 minutes or until golden brown. Let stand 30 minutes before serving. Serve warm or cool.

High Altitude (3500–6500 ft): No change.

1 SERVING: Calories 410 (Calories from Fat 120); Total Fat 14g (Saturated Fat 6g); Cholesterol 50mg; Sodium 720mg; Total Carbohydrate 64g (Dietary Fiber 1g; Sugars 30g); Protein 6g **% DAILY VALUE:** Vitamin A 6%; Vitamin C 0%; Calcium 10%; Iron 10% **EXCHANGES:** 2 Starch, 2 Other Carbohydrate, 2½ Fat **CARBOHYDRATE CHOICES:** 4

Quick Tip A drizzle of almond glaze adds a nice finishing touch. Stir together ¾ cup powdered sugar, 1 tablespoon milk and ½ teaspoon almond extract until thin enough to drizzle. Drizzle glaze over warm coffee cake.

Carrot-Walnut Coffee Cake

PREP TIME: 15 MINUTES ● **START TO FINISH: 1 HOUR 20 MINUTES**
9 SERVINGS

STREUSEL

½ cup Original Bisquick mix

⅓ cup packed brown sugar

2 tablespoons firm butter or margarine

COFFEE CAKE

2 cups Original Bisquick mix

2 tablespoons granulated sugar

1½ teaspoons pumpkin pie spice

½ cup chopped walnuts

½ cup shredded carrots

½ cup raisins

⅔ cup milk

2 tablespoons vegetable oil

1 egg

1 Heat oven to 375°F. In small bowl, mix ½ cup Bisquick mix and the brown sugar until well blended. Cut in butter, using pastry blender (or pulling 2 table knives through ingredients in opposite directions), until mixture is crumbly; set aside.

2 In large bowl, stir 2 cups Bisquick mix, the sugar, pumpkin pie spice, walnuts, carrots and raisins. Stir in milk, oil and egg with wire whisk or fork until blended. Pour into ungreased 8-inch square pan. Sprinkle with streusel.

3 Bake 30 to 35 minutes or until toothpick inserted in center comes out clean. Cool 30 minutes before serving. Serve warm.

High Altitude (3500–6500 ft): Increase eggs to 2. Bake 38 to 43 minutes.

1 SERVING: Calories 320 (Calories from Fat 140); Total Fat 15g (Saturated Fat 4g); Cholesterol 30mg; Sodium 450mg; Total Carbohydrate 41g (Dietary Fiber 2g; Sugars 18g); Protein 5g **% DAILY VALUE:** Vitamin A 25%; Vitamin C 0%; Calcium 8%; Iron 8% **EXCHANGES:** 1½ Starch, 1 Other Carbohydrate, 3 Fat **CARBOHYDRATE CHOICES:** 3

Quick Tip If you don't have pumpkin pie spice, use 1 teaspoon cinnamon, ¼ teaspoon ground ginger, ¼ teaspoon nutmeg and ⅛ teaspoon allspice instead.

Rancher's Egg Bake

PREP TIME: 10 MINUTES ● START TO FINISH: 2 HOURS 10 MINUTES
8 SERVINGS

1⅔ cups Original Bisquick mix

1 tablespoon taco seasoning mix (from 1.25-oz package)

⅓ cup milk

8 eggs, slightly beaten

3 cups milk

½ cup chopped drained roasted red bell peppers (from a jar)

1 can (4.5 oz) chopped green chiles, drained

1 cup shredded Mexican cheese blend (4 oz)

1 Heat oven to 450°F. Spray 13 × 9-inch (3-quart) glass baking dish with cooking spray. In medium bowl, stir Bisquick mix, taco seasoning mix and ⅓ cup milk until soft dough forms. Press dough in bottom of baking dish.

2 Bake 8 minutes. Cool 10 minutes. Reduce oven temperature to 350°F.

3 In large bowl, beat eggs, 3 cups milk, the bell peppers and chiles with wire whisk or fork until blended. Pour over crust.

4 Cover; bake 30 minutes. Uncover dish; bake 40 to 50 minutes longer or until knife inserted in center comes out clean. Sprinkle with cheese. Let stand 10 minutes before serving.

High Altitude (3500–6500 ft): No change.

1 SERVING: Calories 290 (Calories from Fat 130); Total Fat 15g (Saturated Fat 7g); Cholesterol 235mg; Sodium 610mg; Total Carbohydrate 24g (Dietary Fiber 1g; Sugars 8g); Protein 15g **% DAILY VALUE:** Vitamin A 30%; Vitamin C 20%; Calcium 30%; Iron 10% **EXCHANGES:** 1 Starch, ½ Other Carbohydrate, 1½ Medium-Fat Meat, 1½ Fat **CARBOHYDRATE CHOICES:** 1½

Quick Tip Garnish this egg bake with sour cream, cherry tomato quarters and avocado slices, then sprinkle a little taco seasoning mix over the sour cream.

Baked Puffy Cheese Omelet
with Peach Salsa

PREP TIME: 10 MINUTES ● START TO FINISH: 55 MINUTES
6 SERVINGS

OMELET

1¼ cups shredded Mexican
   cheese blend (5 oz)

3 medium green onions, thinly
   sliced (3 tablespoons)

⅓ cup Original Bisquick mix

1 cup milk

4 eggs

PEACH SALSA

¼ cup chunky-style salsa

¼ cup peach preserves

1 Heat oven to 350°F. Spray 9-inch glass pie plate with cooking spray. Sprinkle 1 cup of the cheese and the onions in pie plate.

2 In medium bowl, stir Bisquick mix, milk and eggs with wire whisk or fork until well blended. Pour into pie plate.

3 Bake 30 to 35 minutes or until knife inserted in center comes out clean. Sprinkle with remaining ¼ cup cheese; bake 3 to 5 minutes longer or until melted. Let stand 5 minutes before serving.

4 In small bowl, mix salsa and preserves. Serve omelet with salsa.

High Altitude (3500–6500 ft): Bake 33 to 38 minutes.

1 SERVING: Calories 230 (Calories from Fat 110); Total Fat 12g (Saturated Fat 6g); Cholesterol 165mg; Sodium 360mg; Total Carbohydrate 17g (Dietary Fiber 0g; Sugars 10g); Protein 12g **% DAILY VALUE:** Vitamin A 10%; Vitamin C 2%; Calcium 25%; Iron 6% **EXCHANGES:** ½ Starch, ½ Other Carbohydrate, 1½ Medium-Fat Meat, 1 Fat **CARBOHYDRATE CHOICES:** 1

Quick Tip Spicy and sweet flavors complement each other, so you may want to use a medium or hot salsa for this topping due to the sweetness of the peach preserves.

Overnight Blintz Bake

PREP TIME: 15 MINUTES ● **START TO FINISH: 9 HOURS 25 MINUTES**
12 SERVINGS

FILLING

1 container (15 oz) ricotta cheese

1 container (8 oz) pineapple cream cheese spread

2 tablespoons sugar

1 teaspoon vanilla

2 eggs

BATTER

1 cup Original Bisquick mix

1 cup sour cream

½ cup sugar

¼ cup butter or margarine, softened

½ cup pineapple juice

6 eggs

TOPPINGS

½ cup sour cream

¾ cup strawberry preserves

1 Spray 13 × 9-inch (3-quart) glass baking dish with cooking spray. In medium bowl, stir all filling ingredients until well blended; set aside.

2 In medium bowl, stir all batter ingredients with wire whisk or fork until well blended. Pour batter into baking dish. Pour filling evenly over batter. Cover; refrigerate at least 8 hours or overnight.

3 Heat oven to 325°F. Uncover baking dish; bake 55 to 60 minutes or until golden brown and center is set. Let stand 10 minutes before serving. Top servings with sour cream and strawberry preserves.

High Altitude (3500–6500 ft): Increase Bisquick mix to 1¼ cups. Bake 1 hour to 1 hour 5 minutes.

1 SERVING: Calories 390 (Calories from Fat 200); Total Fat 22g (Saturated Fat 13g); Cholesterol 200mg; Sodium 380mg; Total Carbohydrate 36g (Dietary Fiber 0g; Sugars 24g); Protein 11g **% DAILY VALUE:** Vitamin A 15%; Vitamin C 2%; Calcium 15%; Iron 6% **EXCHANGES:** 1 Starch, 1½ Other Carbohydrate, 1 Medium-Fat Meat, 3 Fat **CARBOHYDRATE CHOICES:** 2½

Quick Tip When strawberries are flavorful and juicy, top each serving with sliced fresh strawberries instead of the strawberry preserves.

Asparagus and Swiss Bake

PREP TIME: 20 MINUTES ● **START TO FINISH: 1 HOUR**
6 SERVINGS

2 cups 1-inch pieces asparagus

½ cup chopped red bell pepper

8 medium green onions, sliced (½ cup)

2 cups shredded Swiss cheese (8 oz)

¾ cup Original Bisquick mix

1 teaspoon lemon-pepper seasoning

1½ cups milk

3 eggs

1 Heat oven to 350°F. Spray 8-inch square (2-quart) glass baking dish with cooking spray. In 1-quart saucepan, heat 1 inch water to boiling. Add asparagus; cook uncovered 2 minutes. Drain well.

2 In baking dish, mix asparagus, bell pepper and onions. In medium bowl, stir 1½ cups of the cheese and all remaining ingredients with wire whisk or fork until blended. Pour into baking dish.

3 Bake uncovered 35 minutes. Sprinkle with remaining ½ cup cheese. Bake about 5 minutes longer or until knife inserted between center and edge comes out clean.

High Altitude (3500–6500 ft): Heat oven to 375°F. Increase Bisquick mix to 1 cup. Bake 40 minutes. Sprinkle with remaining ½ cup cheese. Bake about 5 minutes longer.

1 SERVING: Calories 290 (Calories from Fat 150); Total Fat 16g (Saturated Fat 9g); Cholesterol 145mg; Sodium 370mg; Total Carbohydrate 18g (Dietary Fiber 2g; Sugars 6g); Protein 18g **% DAILY VALUE:** Vitamin A 30%; Vitamin C 25%; Calcium 40%; Iron 10% **EXCHANGES:** 1 Starch, 2 High-Fat Meat **CARBOHYDRATE CHOICES:** 1

Quick Tip If you don't have fresh asparagus on hand, use a 9-ounce box of frozen asparagus cuts, thawed and drained. No need to cook the asparagus in boiling water; just add to the casserole.

Created in 1931, Bisquick mix combined flour, baking powder and other ingredients in advance—home cooks just had to add water for light, fluffy biscuit dough.

Heart Smart Cheddar and Potatoes Breakfast Bake

PREP TIME: 10 MINUTES ● **START TO FINISH: 55 MINUTES**
12 SERVINGS

4 cups frozen potatoes O'Brien with onions and peppers (from 28-oz bag), thawed

1½ cups shredded reduced-fat Cheddar cheese (6 oz)

5 slices fully cooked turkey bacon, chopped

1 cup Bisquick Heart Smart mix

3 cups fat-free (skim) milk

1 cup fat-free egg product

½ teaspoon pepper

1 Heat oven to 375°F. Spray 13 × 9-inch (3-quart) glass baking dish with cooking spray. In medium bowl, mix uncooked potatoes, 1 cup of the cheese and the bacon. Spread in baking dish.

2 In same bowl, stir Bisquick mix, milk, egg product and pepper until blended. Pour over potato mixture. Sprinkle with remaining ½ cup cheese.

3 Bake 30 to 35 minutes or until light golden brown around edges and cheese is melted. Let stand 10 minutes before serving.

High Altitude (3500–6500 ft): Bake 35 to 40 minutes.

1 SERVING: Calories 170 (Calories from Fat 30); Total Fat 3.5g (Saturated Fat 1g); Cholesterol 10mg; Sodium 460mg; Total Carbohydrate 23g (Dietary Fiber 1g; Sugars 4g); Protein 11g **% DAILY VALUE:** Vitamin A 8%; Vitamin C 6%; Calcium 25%; Iron 10% **EXCHANGES:** 1½ Starch, 1 Lean Meat **CARBOHYDRATE CHOICES:** 1½

Cheesy Chile and Egg Bake

PREP TIME: 15 MINUTES ● **START TO FINISH: 1 HOUR 5 MINUTES**
12 SERVINGS

1 package (12 oz) bulk pork sausage

1 bag (28 oz) frozen O'Brien potatoes with peppers and onions, thawed, drained

1 can (4.5 oz) chopped green chiles, drained

2 cups shredded Monterey Jack cheese with jalapeño peppers (8 oz)

½ cup Original Bisquick mix

1 teaspoon salt

1¼ cups milk

1 container (8 oz) sour cream

8 eggs, slightly beaten

1 cup tortilla chips, crushed (½ cup)

1 Heat oven to 350°F. In 10-inch skillet, cook sausage over medium-high heat 8 to 10 minutes, stirring occasionally, until thoroughly cooked; drain.

2 In ungreased 13 × 9-inch (3-quart) glass baking dish, mix sausage, uncooked potatoes, chiles and 1 cup of the cheese.

3 In large bowl, beat Bisquick mix, salt, milk, sour cream and eggs with wire whisk or fork until blended. Pour over potato mixture.

4 Bake uncovered 35 to 45 minutes or until knife inserted in center comes out clean. Sprinkle with crushed chips and remaining 1 cup cheese. Bake about 5 minutes longer or until cheese is melted.

High Altitude (3500–6500 ft): Bake 45 to 55 minutes.

1 SERVING: Calories 300 (Calories from Fat 160); Total Fat 18g (Saturated Fat 8g); Cholesterol 185mg; Sodium 640mg; Total Carbohydrate 20g (Dietary Fiber 1g; Sugars 3g); Protein 14g **% DAILY VALUE:** Vitamin A 15%; Vitamin C 10%; Calcium 20%; Iron 10% **EXCHANGES:** 1½ Starch, 1½ High-Fat Meat, 1 Fat **CARBOHYDRATE CHOICES:** 1

Pepperoni Breakfast Pizza

PREP TIME: 20 MINUTES ● START TO FINISH: 25 MINUTES
8 SERVINGS

1½ cups Original Bisquick mix

⅓ cup hot water

8 eggs

¼ cup milk

⅛ teaspoon pepper

1 cup diced pepperoni
(from 6-oz package)

2 medium green onions, sliced
(2 tablespoons)

1 tablespoon butter or
margarine

½ cup pizza sauce
(from 8-oz can)

1½ cups finely shredded Italian
cheese blend (6 oz)

1 tablespoon sliced fresh basil
leaves, if desired

1 Heat oven to 425°F. Spray 12-inch pizza pan with cooking spray. In medium bowl, stir Bisquick mix and hot water until soft dough forms. Press dough in bottom and up side of pan, using fingers dipped in Bisquick mix, forming rim at edge.

2 Bake 10 to 15 minutes or until golden brown.

3 Meanwhile, in large bowl, beat eggs, milk and pepper with wire whisk until well blended. Stir in pepperoni and onions.

4 In 12-inch nonstick skillet, melt butter over medium heat. Add egg mixture; cook 3 to 5 minutes, stirring occasionally, until firm but still moist.

5 Spread pizza sauce over baked crust. Top evenly with egg mixture. Sprinkle with cheese. Bake 3 to 5 minutes or until cheese is melted and pizza is hot. Sprinkle with basil.

High Altitude (3500–6500 ft): No change.

1 SERVING: Calories 320 (Calories from Fat 180); Total Fat 20g (Saturated Fat 9g); Cholesterol 250mg; Sodium 940mg; Total Carbohydrate 18g (Dietary Fiber 1g; Sugars 3g); Protein 16g **% DAILY VALUE:** Vitamin A 15%; Vitamin C 0%; Calcium 25%; Iron 10% **EXCHANGES:** ½ Starch, ½ Other Carbohydrate, 2 High-Fat Meat, 1 Fat **CARBOHYDRATE CHOICES:** 1

Quick Tip Cutting basil leaves into thin strips is called chiffonade. Stack the leaves on top of each other, then roll up like a cigar. Slice across the roll to form long shreds.

Apple-Sausage-Cheddar Breakfast Bake

**PREP TIME: 25 MINUTES ● START TO FINISH: 1 HOUR 10 MINUTES
12 SERVINGS**

1½ lb bulk pork sausage

1 can (21 oz) apple pie filling with more fruit

2 medium apples, peeled, chopped (about 2 cups)

2 cups shredded sharp Cheddar cheese (8 oz)

1½ cups Original Bisquick mix

1½ cups milk

¼ teaspoon salt

⅛ teaspoon pepper

6 eggs

1 Heat oven to 375°F. Spray 13 × 9-inch (3-quart) glass baking dish with cooking spray. In 12-inch skillet, cook sausage over medium-high heat 5 to 7 minutes, stirring occasionally, until thoroughly cooked; drain. Stir in pie filling and apples. Spread mixture evenly in baking dish. Top with 1 cup of the cheese.

2 In large bowl, stir Bisquick mix, milk, salt, pepper and eggs with wire whisk or fork until well blended. Pour evenly over cheese.

3 Bake 30 to 35 minutes or until knife inserted in center comes out clean. Top with remaining 1 cup cheese. Bake 3 to 5 minutes longer or until cheese is melted. Let stand 5 minutes before serving.

High Altitude (3500–6500 ft): Very finely chop apples if using firm ones.

1 SERVING: Calories 340 (Calories from Fat 170); Total Fat 19g (Saturated Fat 8g); Cholesterol 150mg; Sodium 590mg; Total Carbohydrate 28g (Dietary Fiber 1g; Sugars 16g); Protein 15g **% DAILY VALUE:** Vitamin A 8%; Vitamin C 0%; Calcium 15%; Iron 8% **EXCHANGES:** 1 Starch, 1 Other Carbohydrate, 1½ Medium-Fat Meat, 2 Fat **CARBOHYDRATE CHOICES:** 2

Do-Ahead Breakfast Bake

PREP TIME: 15 MINUTES ● START TO FINISH: 5 HOURS
12 SERVINGS

1 cup diced cooked ham

2 boxes (5.2 oz each) hash brown potatoes

1 medium green bell pepper, chopped (1 cup)

1 tablespoon dried chopped onion

2 cups shredded Cheddar cheese (8 oz)

1 cup Original Bisquick mix

½ teaspoon pepper

3 cups milk

4 eggs

1 Spray 13 × 9-inch (3-quart) glass baking dish with cooking spray. In baking dish, mix ham, uncooked potatoes, bell pepper, onion and 1 cup of the cheese; spread evenly.

2 In medium bowl, stir Bisquick mix, pepper, milk and eggs with wire whisk or fork until blended. Pour over potato mixture. Sprinkle with remaining cheese. Cover; refrigerate at least 4 hours but no longer than 24 hours.

3 Heat oven to 375°F. Uncover and bake 30 to 35 minutes or until light golden brown around edges and cheese is melted. Let stand 10 minutes before serving.

High Altitude (3500–6500 ft): No change.

1 SERVING: Calories 280 (Calories from Fat 110); Total Fat 12g (Saturated Fat 6g); Cholesterol 100mg; Sodium 870mg; Total Carbohydrate 29g (Dietary Fiber 2g; Sugars 4g); Protein 14g **% DAILY VALUE:** Vitamin A 8%; Vitamin C 8%; Calcium 20%; Iron 6% **EXCHANGES:** 2 Starch, 1 Medium-Fat Meat, 1 Fat **CARBOHYDRATE CHOICES:** 2

Do-Ahead Sausage Breakfast Bake

PREP TIME: 20 MINUTES ● **START TO FINISH: 9 HOURS 25 MINUTES**
12 SERVINGS

1 lb bulk pork sausage

2 boxes (5.2 oz each) seasoned shredded hash brown potatoes

1 medium red bell pepper, chopped (1 cup)

1 tablespoon dried chopped onion

2 cups shredded Cheddar cheese (8 oz)

1 cup Original Bisquick mix

½ teaspoon pepper

3½ cups milk

6 eggs

1 Heat oven to 375°F. Spray 13 × 9-inch (3-quart) glass baking dish with cooking spray. In 12-inch skillet, cook sausage over medium-high heat 5 to 7 minutes, stirring occasionally, until sausage is thoroughly cooked; drain.

2 In large bowl, mix cooked sausage, uncooked potatoes, bell pepper, onion and 1 cup of the cheese. Spread in baking dish.

3 In medium bowl, stir Bisquick mix, pepper, milk and eggs until blended. Pour over potato mixture. Sprinkle with remaining 1 cup cheese. Cover with foil; refrigerate at least 8 hours but no longer than 24 hours.

4 Bake covered 30 minutes. Uncover; bake 18 to 22 minutes longer or until light golden brown around edges. Let stand 10 minutes before serving.

High Altitude (3500–6500 ft): No change.

1 SERVING: Calories 340 (Calories from Fat 150); Total Fat 17g (Saturated Fat 8g); Cholesterol 145mg; Sodium 850mg; Total Carbohydrate 30g (Dietary Fiber 2g; Sugars 5g); Protein 17g **% DAILY VALUE:** Vitamin A 15%; Vitamin C 20%; Calcium 20%; Iron 8% **EXCHANGES:** 2 Starch, 1½ Medium-Fat Meat, 1½ Fat **CARBOHYDRATE CHOICES:** 2

Crunchy Ham Breakfast Bake

PREP TIME: 15 MINUTES ● START TO FINISH: 45 MINUTES
12 SERVINGS

2 cups chopped cooked ham

1 medium green bell
pepper, chopped (1 cup),
if desired

2 tablespoons dried chopped
onion

1 can (4 oz) mushroom pieces
and stems, drained

5 cups Chex cereal (any variety)

1 cup shredded Cheddar
cheese (4 oz)

1 cup Original Bisquick mix

2 cups milk

4 eggs

1 Heat oven to 375°F. Spray 13 × 9-inch (3-quart) glass baking dish with cooking spray. In 10-inch nonstick skillet, cook ham, bell pepper, onion and mushrooms 3 minutes, stirring frequently.

2 Spread 3 cups of the cereal in baking dish. Sprinkle with ham mixture; top with cheese.

3 In medium bowl, stir Bisquick mix, milk and eggs with wire whisk or fork until blended. Pour evenly over cheese. Sprinkle with remaining cereal.

4 Bake uncovered 25 to 30 minutes or until knife inserted in center comes out clean.

High Altitude (3500–6500 ft): Bake 30 to 35 minutes.

1 SERVING: Calories 220 (Calories from Fat 80); Total Fat 9g (Saturated Fat 4g); Cholesterol 95mg; Sodium 710mg; Total Carbohydrate 21g (Dietary Fiber 0g; Sugars 4g); Protein 13g **% DAILY VALUE:** Vitamin A 10%; Vitamin C 2%; Calcium 15%; Iron 25% **EXCHANGES:** 1 Starch, ½ Other Carbohydrate, 1½ Medium-Fat Meat **CARBOHYDRATE CHOICES:** 1½

Crunchy Sausage Breakfast Bake: Substitute a 12-ounce package of bulk pork sausage for the ham. Cook and crumble the sausage and add to the vegetable mixture in step 1.

Cheesy Vegetable Quiche

PREP TIME: 20 MINUTES ● **START TO FINISH: 1 HOUR 20 MINUTES**
6 SERVINGS

CRUST

1¼ cups Original Bisquick mix

¼ teaspoon dried thyme leaves

3 tablespoons butter or margarine, softened

2 tablespoons boiling water

FILLING

1 box (9 oz) frozen broccoli cuts

1 cup shredded Colby-Monterey Jack cheese blend (4 oz)

½ cup diced red bell pepper

2 tablespoons finely chopped onion

3 eggs

¾ cup half-and-half

⅛ teaspoon pepper

1 Heat oven to 350°F. Spray 9-inch glass pie plate with cooking spray. In medium bowl, mix Bisquick mix and thyme. Cut in butter, using pastry blender (or pulling 2 table knives through ingredients in opposite directions), until crumbly. Add boiling water; stir vigorously until soft dough forms. Press dough on bottom and up side of pie plate, using fingers dipped in Bisquick mix, forming edge on rim of pie plate.

2 Cook broccoli as directed on box, using minimum cook time. Drain well; pat dry with several layers of paper towels. Sprinkle cheese, broccoli, bell pepper and onion in crust.

3 In medium bowl, beat eggs, half-and-half and pepper. Pour into crust.

4 Bake 45 to 50 minutes or until knife inserted in center comes out clean. Let stand 10 minutes before serving.

High Altitude (3500–6500 ft): No change.

1 SERVING: Calories 320 (Calories from Fat 190); Total Fat 21g (Saturated Fat 11g); Cholesterol 150mg; Sodium 500mg; Total Carbohydrate 21g (Dietary Fiber 2g; Sugars 4g); Protein 12g **% DAILY VALUE:** Vitamin A 30%; Vitamin C 35%; Calcium 20%; Iron 8%
EXCHANGES: 1 Starch, ½ Other Carbohydrate, 1 Medium-Fat Meat, 3 Fat
CARBOHYDRATE CHOICES: 1½

Ham, Pineapple and Cheddar Quiche

PREP TIME: 20 MINUTES ● **START TO FINISH: 1 HOUR 15 MINUTES**
6 SERVINGS

CRUST

3 tablespoons butter or margarine, softened

1¼ cups Original Bisquick mix

2 tablespoons boiling water

FILLING

1½ cups shredded sharp Cheddar cheese (6 oz)

¾ cup finely chopped cooked ham (4 oz)

3 medium green onions, sliced (3 tablespoons)

1 can (8 oz) pineapple tidbits in juice, well drained

3 eggs

¾ cup half-and-half

¼ teaspoon white pepper

1 Heat oven to 350°F. Spray 9-inch glass pie plate with cooking spray. In medium bowl, cut butter into Bisquick mix, using pastry blender (or pulling 2 table knives through ingredients in opposite directions), until crumbly. Add boiling water; stir vigorously until soft dough forms. Press dough on bottom and up side of pie plate, using fingers dipped in Bisquick mix, forming edge on rim of pie plate.

2 Sprinkle cheese, ham, onions and pineapple in crust. In medium bowl, beat eggs, half-and-half and pepper until blended. Pour into crust.

3 Bake 40 to 45 minutes or until knife inserted in center comes out clean. Let stand 10 minutes before serving.

High Altitude (3500–6500 ft): In step 2, stir 2 tablespoons Bisquick mix into egg mixture before pouring into crust. Bake 45 to 50 minutes.

1 SERVING: Calories 390 (Calories from Fat 240); Total Fat 26g (Saturated Fat 14g); Cholesterol 175mg; Sodium 850mg; Total Carbohydrate 22g (Dietary Fiber 1g; Sugars 6g); Protein 18g **% DAILY VALUE:** Vitamin A 15%; Vitamin C 2%; Calcium 25%; Iron 8% **EXCHANGES:** 1 Starch, ½ Other Carbohydrate, 2 Medium-Fat Meat, 3 Fat **CARBOHYDRATE CHOICES:** 1½

Scrambled Egg Biscuit Cups

PREP TIME: 30 MINUTES ● START TO FINISH: 30 MINUTES
12 BISCUIT CUPS

2 cups Original Bisquick mix

⅓ cup shredded Cheddar cheese (1.5 oz)

¾ cup milk

8 eggs

⅛ teaspoon pepper

1 tablespoon butter or margarine, softened

½ cup Parmesan and mozzarella cheese pasta sauce (from 1-lb jar)

3 tablespoons real bacon bits (from 3-oz package)

1 tablespoon chopped fresh chives

Additional real bacon bits, if desired

1 Heat oven to 425°F. Spray bottoms only of 12 regular-size muffin cups with cooking spray. In medium bowl, mix Bisquick mix, cheese and ½ cup of the milk until soft dough forms.

2 Place dough on surface sprinkled with Bisquick mix. Shape into a ball; knead 4 or 5 times. Shape into 10-inch roll. Cut roll into 12 pieces. Press each piece in bottom and up side of each muffin cup, forming edge at rim.

3 Bake 8 to 10 minutes or until golden brown. Remove from oven. With back of spoon, press puffed crust in each cup to make indentation.

4 In large bowl, beat eggs, remaining ¼ cup milk and the pepper until well blended. In 10-inch nonstick skillet, melt butter over medium heat. Add egg mixture. Cook 3 to 4 minutes, stirring occasionally, until firm but still moist. Fold in pasta sauce and bacon until blended.

5 To remove biscuit cups from pan, run knife around edge of cups. Spoon egg mixture into biscuit cups. Sprinkle tops with chives and bacon.

High Altitude (3500–6500 ft): Bake 10 to 12 minutes.

1 BISCUIT CUP: Calories 180 (Calories from Fat 80); Total Fat 9g (Saturated Fat 3.5g); Cholesterol 150mg; Sodium 420mg; Total Carbohydrate 15g (Dietary Fiber 0g; Sugars 2g); Protein 8g **% DAILY VALUE:** Vitamin A 6%; Vitamin C 0%; Calcium 8%; Iron 6% **EXCHANGES:** 1 Starch, 1 Medium-Fat Meat, ½ Fat **CARBOHYDRATE CHOICES:** 1

Quick Tip Biscuit cups can be baked the day before and stored in an airtight container at room temperature. Just fill with scrambled eggs and serve.

CHAPTER 3

Savory
Appetizers, Snacks and Breads

Creamy Garden Squares

PREP TIME: 20 MINUTES ● START TO FINISH: 2 HOURS
40 APPETIZERS

1½ cups Original Bisquick mix

⅓ cup boiling water

2 tablespoons sliced green onions (2 medium)

1 package (8 oz) cream cheese, softened

½ cup sour cream

1 teaspoon dried dill weed

⅛ teaspoon garlic powder

Assorted fresh vegetables (sliced mushrooms, cherry tomato halves, chopped broccoli) and/or shredded cheeses

1 Heat oven to 450°F. In medium bowl, stir Bisquick mix, water and onions until soft dough forms; beat vigorously 20 strokes. With floured hands, press dough in ungreased 13 × 9-inch pan.

2 Bake about 10 minutes or until light golden brown. Cool 10 minutes.

3 In medium bowl, mix cream cheese, sour cream, dill weed and garlic powder until smooth; spread evenly over crust. Refrigerate 1 to 2 hours or until chilled. Just before serving, cut into 8 rows by 5 rows; top each piece with vegetables or cheese. Store in refrigerator.

High Altitude (3500–6500 ft): Heat oven to 450°F. Bake about 11 minutes.

1 APPETIZER: Calories 50 (Calories from Fat 30); Total Fat 3g (Saturated Fat 2g); Cholesterol 10mg; Sodium 75mg; Total Carbohydrate 4g (Dietary Fiber 0g; Sugars 0g); Protein 1g **% DAILY VALUE:** Vitamin A 4%; Vitamin C 6%; Calcium 0%; Iron 0% **EXCHANGES:** ½ Other Carbohydrate, ½ Fat **CARBOHYDRATE CHOICES:** 0

Quick Tip Soften cream cheese quickly in the microwave—just make sure to remove the foil wrapper first! Microwave uncovered on Medium (50%) for 1 to 1½ minutes.

Mushroom and Walnut Appetizers

PREP TIME: 15 MINUTES ● START TO FINISH: 1 HOUR 15 MINUTES
27 APPETIZERS

1 package (8 oz) fresh whole mushrooms, sliced (3 cups)

1 cup chopped onion

1 clove garlic, finely chopped

2 tablespoons butter or margarine

2 cups shredded Swiss cheese (8 oz)

1½ cups coarsely chopped walnuts

1 box (9 oz) frozen spinach, thawed, squeezed to drain

1⅓ cups milk

3 eggs

¾ cup Original Bisquick mix

1½ teaspoons salt

1 Heat oven to 400°F. Spray 13 × 9-inch pan with cooking spray. In 10-inch skillet, cook mushrooms, onion and garlic in butter over medium heat about 5 minutes or until onion is tender; drain.

2 In pan, mix mushroom mixture, cheese, walnuts and spinach; spread evenly. In medium bowl, stir all remaining ingredients with wire whisk or fork until blended. Pour into pan.

3 Bake 25 to 30 minutes or until knife inserted in center comes out clean. Cool 30 minutes. To serve, cut into 9 rows by 3 rows.

High Altitude (3500–6500 ft): No change.

1 APPETIZER: Calories 120 (Calories from Fat 80); Total Fat 9g (Saturated Fat 3g); Cholesterol 35mg; Sodium 210mg; Total Carbohydrate 5g (Dietary Fiber 0g; Sugars 1g); Protein 5g **% DAILY VALUE:** Vitamin A 20%; Vitamin C 0%; Calcium 10%; Iron 4% **EXCHANGES:** ½ Starch, ½ High-Fat Meat, 1 Fat **CARBOHYDRATE CHOICES:** ½

Quick Tip Place the thawed spinach between several layers of paper towels. Then roll and squeeze the paper towels to remove excess moisture from the spinach.

Broccoli-Cheddar Appetizers

PREP TIME: 15 MINUTES ● START TO FINISH: 1 HOUR 10 MINUTES
30 APPETIZERS

1 box (10 oz) frozen chopped broccoli, thawed, drained

1 can (7 oz) vacuum-packed whole kernel corn, drained

1 small onion, chopped (about ¼ cup)

½ cup coarsely chopped walnuts

½ cup Original Bisquick mix

¼ teaspoon garlic salt

½ cup milk

¼ cup butter or margarine, melted

2 eggs

1 cup shredded Cheddar cheese (4 oz)

1 Heat oven to 375°F. Spray 9-inch square pan with cooking spray. In pan, mix broccoli, corn, onion and walnuts.

2 In medium bowl, stir all remaining ingredients except cheese with wire whisk or fork until blended. Pour into pan.

3 Bake 23 to 25 minutes or until knife inserted in center comes out clean. Sprinkle with cheese. Bake 2 to 3 minutes longer or until cheese is melted. Cool 30 minutes. To serve, cut into 5 rows by 3 rows; cut each rectangle diagonally in half.

High Altitude (3500–6500 ft): No change.

1 APPETIZER: Calories 70 (Calories from Fat 45); Total Fat 5g (Saturated Fat 2g); Cholesterol 20mg; Sodium 90mg; Total Carbohydrate 4g (Dietary Fiber 0g; Sugars 0g); Protein 2g **% DAILY VALUE:** Vitamin A 4%; Vitamin C 4%; Calcium 4%; Iron 0% **EXCHANGES:** ½ Other Carbohydrate, 1 Fat **CARBOHYDRATE CHOICES:** 0

Far East Canapés

PREP TIME: 15 MINUTES ● START TO FINISH: 35 MINUTES
16 CANAPÉS

1 cup Original Bisquick mix

¼ cup water

½ cup finely chopped shaved turkey (3 oz)

½ cup finely chopped shaved honey ham (3 oz)

⅓ cup chutney

3 to 4 tablespoons whipping (heavy) cream

½ teaspoon curry powder

¼ cup finely shredded Parmesan cheese

¼ cup chopped dry-roasted peanuts

Sliced green onions or fresh chives, if desired

1 Heat oven to 425°F. Spray bottom and sides of 8 × 8-inch pan with cooking spray.

2 Stir Bisquick mix and water until soft dough forms; beat vigorously with spoon 20 seconds. Pat dough in pan, using fingers dipped in Bisquick mix. Bake 6 to 8 minutes or until crust begins to brown around edges.

3 Mix remaining ingredients except cheese, peanuts and green onions. Spread mixture over baked crust. Sprinkle with cheese. Bake 7 to 9 minutes or until cheese is melted. For canapés, cut into 4 rows by 4 rows. Sprinkle with peanuts; garnish with green onions. Serve warm.

High Altitude (3500–6500 ft): Bake crust 7 to 9 minutes. Bake canapés 8 to 10 minutes.

1 APPETIZER: Calories 80 (Calories from Fat 35); Total Fat 4g (Saturated Fat 2g); Cholesterol 10mg; Sodium 270mg; Total Carbohydrate 10g (Dietary Fiber 0g; Sugars 4g); Protein 4g **% DAILY VALUE:** Vitamin A 0%; Vitamin C 0%; Calcium 4%; Iron 2% **EXCHANGES:** ½ Starch, ½ Very Lean Meat, ½ Fat **CARBOHYDRATE CHOICES:** 1

Quick Tip Keep things simple by buying shaved turkey and ham from the deli when you want to whip up these super-easy appetizers. The chutney, curry and peanuts team up to give you the exotic flavors of Asia in one small bite.

Quesadilla Appetizers

PREP TIME: 10 MINUTES ● START TO FINISH: 50 MINUTES
36 APPETIZERS

1 can (4.5 oz) chopped green chiles, drained

2 cups shredded Monterey Jack or Cheddar cheese (8 oz)

1 cup Original Bisquick mix

1 cup half-and-half

⅛ teaspoon red pepper sauce, if desired

4 eggs

¾ cup chunky-style salsa

1 Heat oven to 375°F. Spray 9-inch square pan with cooking spray. Sprinkle chiles and cheese in pan.

2 In medium bowl, stir all remaining ingredients except salsa with wire whisk or fork until blended. Pour into pan.

3 Bake about 30 minutes or until golden brown and knife inserted in center comes out clean. Let stand 10 minutes. Cut into 6 rows by 6 rows. Serve with salsa.

High Altitude (3500–6500 ft): Bake 30 to 35 minutes.

1 APPETIZER (WITH 1 TEASPOON SALSA): Calories 60 (Calories from Fat 35); Total Fat 3.5g (Saturated Fat 2g); Cholesterol 30mg; Sodium 130mg; Total Carbohydrate 3g (Dietary Fiber 0g; Sugars 0g); Protein 3g **% DAILY VALUE:** Vitamin A 2%; Vitamin C 0%; Calcium 6%; Iron 0% **EXCHANGES:** ½ Starch, ½ Fat **CARBOHYDRATE CHOICES:** 0

No-Bake Cheddar Cheesecake

PREP TIME: 30 MINUTES ● START TO FINISH: 1 HOUR 30 MINUTES
32 SERVINGS (2 TABLESPOONS SPREAD AND 3 CRACKERS EACH)

1 cup Original Bisquick mix

1 teaspoon onion powder

¼ cup butter or margarine, softened

2 tablespoons boiling water

1 tablespoon water

1 teaspoon unflavored gelatin

2 packages (8 oz each) cream cheese, softened

¼ cup whipping cream

1 tablespoon Worcestershire sauce

½ teaspoon ground mustard

2 cups shredded sharp Cheddar cheese (8 oz)

2 tablespoons chopped fresh chives

1 box (13 oz) assorted crackers (about 96 crackers)

1 Heat oven to 400°F. Spray 9-inch springform pan with cooking spray. In medium bowl, stir Bisquick mix, onion powder and butter until crumbly. Add boiling water; stir vigorously until very soft dough forms. Press dough firmly in bottom and 1 inch up side of pan, using fingers coated with Bisquick mix.

2 Bake crust 8 to 10 minutes or until light golden brown. Cool on cooling rack, about 15 minutes.

3 Meanwhile, in medium microwavable bowl, place 1 table-spoon water. Sprinkle with gelatin; let stand 5 minutes. Microwave uncovered on High 30 seconds; stir until gelatin is dissolved.

4 Add cream cheese, whipping cream, Worcestershire sauce and mustard to gelatin. Beat with electric mixer on medium speed until smooth. Add Cheddar cheese; beat until well combined. Spoon into cooled crust; spread evenly. Refrigerate 1 hour.

5 To serve, carefully remove side of pan. Place cheesecake on serving platter. Garnish top with chives. Serve with crackers.

High Altitude (3500–6500 ft): Bake crust 10 to 12 minutes.

1 SERVING: Calories 170 (Calories from Fat 120); Total Fat 13g (Saturated Fat 7g); Cholesterol 30mg; Sodium 250mg; Total Carbohydrate 10g (Dietary Fiber 0g; Sugars 1g); Protein 4g
% DAILY VALUE: Vitamin A 6%; Vitamin C 0%; Calcium 6%; Iron 4% **EXCHANGES:** ½ Other Carbohydrate, ½ High-Fat Meat, 2 Fat **CARBOHYDRATE CHOICES:** ½

Pear and Blue Cheese Tart

PREP TIME: 20 MINUTES ● START TO FINISH: 1 HOUR 10 MINUTES
12 SERVINGS

CRUST

1½ cups Original Bisquick mix

⅓ cup very hot water

FILLING

2 tablespoons butter or margarine

2 shallots, finely chopped (about ⅓ cup)

2 medium pears, peeled, cut into ¼-inch slices (about 2 cups)

¼ cup chopped walnuts

½ cup crumbled blue cheese (2 oz)

2 tablespoons chopped fresh parsley

1 Heat oven to 425°F. Spray 9-inch tart pan with removable bottom with cooking spray.

2 In medium bowl, stir Bisquick mix and hot water until soft dough forms. Press dough in bottom and up side of tart pan, using fingers coated with Bisquick mix. Bake 10 minutes.

3 Meanwhile, in 8-inch skillet, melt butter over medium heat. Add shallots; cook 2 to 4 minutes, stirring occasionally, until tender; remove from heat.

4 Arrange pear slices on crust. Spread butter mixture over pears. Bake 20 minutes.

5 Sprinkle walnuts over pears. Bake about 10 minutes longer or until tart is golden brown.

6 Remove from oven; sprinkle with cheese. Cool 10 minutes on cooling rack. Sprinkle with parsley. Serve warm or at room temperature.

High Altitude (3500–6500 ft): No change.

1 SERVING: Calories 130 (Calories from Fat 60); Total Fat 7g (Saturated Fat 3g); Cholesterol 10mg; Sodium 260mg; Total Carbohydrate 15g (Dietary Fiber 1g; Sugars 3g); Protein 3g **% DAILY VALUE:** Vitamin A 4%; Vitamin C 0%; Calcium 4%; Iron 4% **EXCHANGES:** 1 Starch, 1 Fat **CARBOHYDRATE CHOICES:** 1

Apple and Blue Cheese Tart: Substitute 2 medium cooking apples for the pears.

Quick Tip Other blue-veined cheese, such as Gorgonzola or Stilton, can also complement the fruit on this tart.

Olive and Rosemary Focaccia

PREP TIME: 15 MINUTES ● START TO FINISH: 40 MINUTES
16 APPETIZERS

2 cups Original Bisquick mix

2 teaspoons garlic powder

½ cup hot water

½ cup pitted kalamata olives

2 teaspoons chopped fresh or
  ½ teaspoon dried rosemary
  leaves, crushed

1 teaspoon olive oil

1 Heat oven to 400°F. In medium bowl, stir Bisquick mix, garlic powder and water until stiff dough forms. Let stand 5 minutes.

2 Place dough on surface sprinkled with Bisquick mix; gently roll in Bisquick mix to coat. Shape into a ball; knead 50 times.

3 On ungreased cookie sheet, press or roll dough into 8-inch round. Sprinkle olives over dough; press lightly into dough. Sprinkle with rosemary.

4 Bake 12 to 14 minutes or until light golden brown. Brush oil over top. Cool 10 minutes. Cut into 16 wedges with serrated knife.

High Altitude (3500–6500 ft): Heat oven to 425°F. Bake 16 to 18 minutes.

1 APPETIZER: Calories 70 (Calories from Fat 25); Total Fat 2.5g (Saturated Fat 0.5g); Cholesterol 0mg; Sodium 220mg; Total Carbohydrate 10g (Dietary Fiber 0g; Sugars 0g); Protein 1g **% DAILY VALUE:** Vitamin A 0%; Vitamin C 0%; Calcium 0%; Iron 4% **EXCHANGES:** ½ Starch, ½ Fat **CARBOHYDRATE CHOICES:** ½

Quick Tip This makes an excellent bread to serve with an Italian dinner. Cut it into 8 wedges and, if you like, serve with olive oil for dipping.

New to cooking? Whether in the 1960s or today, young brides—and grooms— can turn to Bisquick for easy, foolproof ideas in the kitchen.

Onion Pretzels

PREP TIME: 10 MINUTES ● START TO FINISH: 30 MINUTES
32 APPETIZERS

2½ cups Original Bisquick mix

1 tablespoon onion powder

½ cup milk

2 tablespoons vegetable oil

1 egg, beaten

1 teaspoon coarse salt
(kosher or sea salt)

1 Heat oven to 425°F. Spray cookie sheets with cooking spray. In medium bowl, stir Bisquick mix, onion powder, milk and oil until well blended.

2 Gently smooth dough into a ball. Place dough on surface generously sprinkled with Bisquick mix; gently roll in Bisquick mix to coat; knead 5 times.

3 Divide dough into 32 equal portions. Roll each portion into pencil-like strip, about 12 inches long. Twist each strip into pretzel shape on cookie sheets. Brush with egg; sprinkle with salt.

4 Bake 5 to 7 minutes or until light golden brown.

High Altitude (3500–6500 ft): Bake 7 to 9 minutes.

1 APPETIZER: Calories 50 (Calories from Fat 20); Total Fat 2.5g (Saturated Fat 0.5g); Cholesterol 5mg; Sodium 170mg; Total Carbohydrate 6g (Dietary Fiber 0g; Sugars 0g); Protein 1g **% DAILY VALUE:** Vitamin A 0%; Vitamin C 0%; Calcium 0%; Iron 0% **EXCHANGES:** ½ Starch, ½ Fat **CARBOHYDRATE CHOICES:** ½

Garlic Pretzels: Substitute 1 tablespoon garlic powder for the onion powder.

Beer-Cheese Triangles

PREP TIME: 25 MINUTES ● START TO FINISH: 35 MINUTES
80 APPETIZERS

2 cups Original Bisquick mix

½ cup shredded Cheddar cheese (2 oz)

½ cup beer or apple juice

2 tablespoons butter or margarine, melted

¼ cup sesame seed

Bean dip, if desired

1 Heat oven to 450°F. Spray large cookie sheets with cooking spray. In medium bowl, stir Bisquick mix, cheese and beer until soft dough forms; beat vigorously 20 strokes.

2 On surface sprinkled with Bisquick mix, roll dough in Bisquick mix to coat. Shape into a ball; knead 5 times. Press or roll dough into 16 × 10-inch rectangle.

3 Cut rectangle into 2-inch squares (do not separate); cut squares diagonally in half. Spread melted butter over dough; sprinkle with sesame seed. Separate triangles; place on cookie sheets.

4 Bake 8 to 10 minutes or until golden brown. Serve with dip.

High Altitude (3500–6500 ft): Bake 6 to 8 minutes.

1 APPETIZER: Calories 20 (Calories from Fat 10); Total Fat 1g (Saturated Fat 0g); Cholesterol 0mg; Sodium 45mg; Total Carbohydrate 2g (Dietary Fiber 0g; Sugars 0g); Protein 0g **% DAILY VALUE:** Vitamin A 0%; Vitamin C 0%; Calcium 0%; Iron 0% **EXCHANGES:** Free **CARBOHYDRATE CHOICES:** 0

Quick Tip For a flavor twist, use ½ cup shredded Swiss cheese for the Cheddar cheese and sprinkle with poppy seed.

Cheese- and Onion-Topped Appetizer Rounds

PREP TIME: 25 MINUTES ● START TO FINISH: 50 MINUTES
40 APPETIZERS

2 cups Original Bisquick mix

¼ teaspoon garlic powder

½ cup boiling water

⅓ cup mayonnaise or salad dressing

⅓ cup shredded Cheddar cheese

⅓ cup shredded mozzarella cheese

3 tablespoons chopped green onions (3 medium)

1 Heat oven to 400°F. In medium bowl, stir Bisquick mix, garlic powder and water until soft dough forms. Let stand about 10 minutes or until cool.

2 Meanwhile, in small bowl, mix mayonnaise, Cheddar and mozzarella cheeses, and onions until blended.

3 Place dough on surface sprinkled with Bisquick mix; roll in Bisquick mix to coat. Shape into a ball; knead 12 to 15 times or until smooth. Press or roll dough until ⅛ inch thick. Cut with 2-inch round cutter dipped in Bisquick mix. On ungreased cookie sheet, place rounds about 1 inch apart. Spoon cheese mixture on each round.

4 Bake 12 to 15 minutes or until topping is golden brown. Immediately remove from cookie sheet. Serve warm.

High Altitude (3500–6500 ft): No change.

1 APPETIZER: Calories 45 (Calories from Fat 25); Total Fat 2.5g (Saturated Fat 1g); Cholesterol 0mg; Sodium 95mg; Total Carbohydrate 4g (Dietary Fiber 0g; Sugars 0g); Protein 0g **% DAILY VALUE:** Vitamin A 0%; Vitamin C 0%; Calcium 0%; Iron 0% **EXCHANGES:** 1 Fat **CARBOHYDRATE CHOICES:** 0

Quick Tip Make these appetizers even more special by adding 1 tablespoon finely chopped red bell pepper to the topping mixture.

Two-Cheese Straws

PREP TIME: 15 MINUTES ● **START TO FINISH: 35 MINUTES**
36 APPETIZERS

2½ cups Original Bisquick mix

⅔ cup milk

½ cup shredded Cheddar cheese (2 oz)

1 tablespoon butter or margarine, softened

2 tablespoons grated Parmesan cheese

Tomato pasta sauce, if desired, heated

1 Heat oven to 400°F. Spray cookie sheets with cooking spray. In large bowl, stir Bisquick mix, milk and Cheddar cheese until soft dough forms.

2 Divide dough in half. On surface lightly sprinkled with Bisquick mix, roll 1 half into 9 × 6-inch rectangle. Spread with half of the butter. Sprinkle 1 tablespoon of the Parmesan cheese over top. Cut dough lengthwise into 18 (½-inch) strips. Repeat with remaining dough.

3 Twist each dough strip as many times as possible; place on cookie sheets. Bake 6 to 8 minutes or until light golden brown. Serve with pasta sauce.

High Altitude (3500–6500 ft): Heat oven to 425°F. Bake 8 to 10 minutes.

1 APPETIZER: Calories 45 (Calories from Fat 20); Total Fat 2g (Saturated Fat 1g); Cholesterol 0mg; Sodium 120mg; Total Carbohydrate 6g (Dietary Fiber 0g; Sugars 0g); Protein 1g **% DAILY VALUE:** Vitamin A 0%; Vitamin C 0%; Calcium 2%; Iron 0% **EXCHANGES:** ½ Other Carbohydrate, ½ Fat **CARBOHYDRATE CHOICES:** ½

Quick Tip For a little added crunch, sprinkle tops with sesame seed and/or poppy seed before baking.

Sausage-Cheese Balls

PREP TIME: 20 MINUTES ● **START TO FINISH: 45 MINUTES**
ABOUT 8½ DOZEN CHEESE BALLS

3 cups Original Bisquick mix

1 lb bulk pork sausage

4 cups shredded Cheddar cheese (1 lb)

½ cup grated Parmesan cheese

½ cup milk

½ teaspoon dried rosemary leaves, crushed

1½ teaspoons chopped fresh parsley or ½ teaspoon parsley flakes

1 Heat oven to 350°F. Spray 15 × 10 × 1-inch pan with cooking spray. In large bowl, stir all ingredients until well mixed. Shape mixture into 1-inch balls. Place in pan.

2 Bake half of balls uncovered 20 to 25 minutes or until no longer pink in center. Repeat with other half. Immediately remove from pan. Serve warm.

High Altitude (3500–6500 ft): Heat oven to 375°F. Decrease Bisquick mix to 2½ cups and add ½ cup all-purpose flour. Bake half of balls 25 to 30 minutes; repeat with other half.

1 CHEESE BALL: Calories 40 (Calories from Fat 25); Total Fat 2.5g (Saturated Fat 1.5g); Cholesterol 5mg; Sodium 95mg; Total Carbohydrate 2g (Dietary Fiber 0g; Sugars 0g); Protein 2g **% DAILY VALUE:** Vitamin A 0%; Vitamin C 0%; Calcium 4%; Iron 0% **EXCHANGES:** ½ High-Fat Meat **CARBOHYDRATE CHOICES:** 0

Ham-Cheese Balls: Substitute 1½ cups finely chopped fully cooked ham for the sausage. Use 2 tablespoons parsley flakes and ⅔ cup milk. Omit rosemary. Mix and bake as directed.

Quick Tip These tasty nibbles are one of our most requested recipes, and they can be prepared up to 1 day ahead. Cover and refrigerate unbaked balls; bake as directed. Or cover and freeze unbaked balls up to 1 month. Bake frozen balls 25 to 30 minutes or until brown.

Front: Spinach-Cheese Balls
Back: Sausage-Cheese Balls (page 123)

Spinach-Cheese Balls

PREP TIME: 10 MINUTES ● START TO FINISH: 25 MINUTES
30 CHEESE BALLS

1 box (9 oz) frozen spinach, thawed, squeezed to drain

1 cup Original Bisquick mix

2 cups shredded mozzarella cheese (8 oz)

1 egg

2 teaspoons Italian seasoning

1 teaspoon garlic salt

1 cup tomato pasta sauce, if desired

1 Heat oven to 400°F. Spray cookie sheet with cooking spray. In large bowl, mix all ingredients, except pasta sauce. Shape mixture into 1-inch balls; place on cookie sheet.

2 Bake 10 to 15 minutes or until golden brown. Immediately remove from pan. Serve with pasta sauce.

High Altitude (3500–6500 ft): Make 36 balls. Bake 8 to 10 minutes.

1 CHEESE BALL: Calories 45 (Calories from Fat 20); Total Fat 2g (Saturated Fat 1g); Cholesterol 10mg; Sodium 130mg; Total Carbohydrate 3g (Dietary Fiber 0g; Sugars 0g); Protein 3g **% DAILY VALUE:** Vitamin A 15%; Vitamin C 0%; Calcium 8%; Iron 0% **EXCHANGES:** ½ High-Fat Meat **CARBOHYDRATE CHOICES:** 0

Spicy Biscuit Poppers

PREP TIME: 15 MINUTES ● START TO FINISH: 35 MINUTES
25 APPETIZERS

3 cups Original Bisquick mix

⅔ cup water

2 medium green onions, finely chopped (2 tablespoons)

¼ teaspoon chili powder

8 oz pepper Jack cheese, cut into ¾-inch cubes

1 tablespoon butter or margarine, melted

1 Heat oven to 450°F. Spray 9-inch square pan with cooking spray. In medium bowl, stir Bisquick mix, water, onions and chili powder until soft dough forms.

2 On surface generously sprinkled with Bisquick mix, gently roll dough in Bisquick mix to coat. Shape dough into ball; knead 10 times. Roll into 10 × 10-inch square. Cut 5 rows by 5 rows to make 25 (2-inch) squares.

3 Wrap 1 dough square around 1 cheese cube; roll into ball. Place in pan. Repeat with remaining dough and cheese cubes, placing 5 balls in each row. Brush butter over tops.

4 Bake 10 to 12 minutes or until light golden brown. Cool 5 minutes. Serve warm.

High Altitude (3500–6500 ft): Bake 15 to 20 minutes.

1 APPETIZER: Calories 90 (Calories from Fat 50); Total Fat 6g (Saturated Fat 3g); Cholesterol 10mg; Sodium 270mg; Total Carbohydrate 8g (Dietary Fiber 0g; Sugars 1g); Protein 0g **% DAILY VALUE:** Vitamin A 2%; Vitamin C 0%; Calcium 0%; Iron 0% **EXCHANGES:** ½ Other Carbohydrate, 1 Fat **CARBOHYDRATE CHOICES:** ½

Quick Tip For a little "stringy" fun, substitute 8 ounces mozzarella cheese cut into ¾-inch cubes for the pepper Jack cheese.

Olive Balls

PREP TIME: 25 MINUTES ● **START TO FINISH: 35 MINUTES**
ABOUT 40 APPETIZERS

1 cup shredded Cheddar cheese (4 oz)

¼ cup butter or margarine, softened

¼ teaspoon Worcestershire sauce

1 cup Original Bisquick mix

1 jar (5 oz) pimiento-stuffed olives

1 Heat oven to 400°F. In medium bowl, mix cheese, butter and Worcestershire sauce. Stir in Bisquick mix until dough forms (use hands if necessary).

2 On paper towel, pat olives completely dry. Shape 1 teaspoon dough around each olive. On ungreased cookie sheet, place about 1 inch apart.

3 Bake about 10 minutes or until light golden brown. Serve warm.

High Altitude (3500–6500 ft): Heat oven to 425°F. Decrease Bisquick mix to ¾ cup and add ¼ cup all-purpose flour.

1 APPETIZER: Calories 40 (Calories from Fat 25); Total Fat 3g (Saturated Fat 1.5g); Cholesterol 5mg; Sodium 120mg; Total Carbohydrate 2g (Dietary Fiber 0g; Sugars 0g); Protein 0g **% DAILY VALUE:** Vitamin A 0%; Vitamin C 0%; Calcium 2%; Iron 0% **EXCHANGES:** 1 Fat **CARBOHYDRATE CHOICES:** 0

Quick Tip Bake these fun party appetizers a day ahead and refrigerate. They reheat easily; just warm them on a cookie sheet in a 200°F oven before serving.

Mini Corn Cakes

PREP TIME: 25 MINUTES ● START TO FINISH: 25 MINUTES
24 APPETIZERS

1 tablespoon butter or margarine

⅓ cup chopped green onions (about 5 medium)

⅓ cup chopped celery

⅓ cup chopped red bell pepper

1 cup soft white bread crumbs (about 1½ slices bread)

½ cup Original Bisquick mix

1 teaspoon sugar

½ teaspoon salt

⅛ teaspoon ground red pepper (cayenne)

2 eggs, slightly beaten

1 can (11 oz) whole kernel corn, drained

2 tablespoons vegetable oil

½ cup chive-and-onion sour cream

1 In 12-inch nonstick skillet, melt butter over medium heat. Add onions, celery and bell pepper; cook 3 minutes, stirring occasionally.

2 In medium bowl, stir vegetable mixture and remaining ingredients except oil and sour cream until well blended.

3 In same skillet, heat 2 teaspoons of the oil over medium heat. Cooking 8 corn cakes at a time, drop corn mixture into oil by tablespoonfuls, spreading each into 1½-inch round. Cook 1 minute to 1 minute 30 seconds on each side, carefully turning once, until golden brown. Cook remaining corn cakes, using 2 teaspoons oil for each batch of 8 corn cakes. Serve with sour cream.

High Altitude (3500–6500 ft): In step 3, use medium-high heat.

1 APPETIZER (WITH 1 TEASPOON SOUR CREAM): Calories 60 (Calories from Fat 30); Total Fat 3.5g (Saturated Fat 1.5g); Cholesterol 20mg; Sodium 135mg; Total Carbohydrate 6g (Dietary Fiber 0g; Sugars 1g); Protein 1g **% DAILY VALUE:** Vitamin A 4%; Vitamin C 4%; Calcium 0%; Iron 0% **EXCHANGES:** ½ Starch, ½ Fat **CARBOHYDRATE CHOICES:** ½

Quick Tip These mini corn cakes can be baked rather than fried. Heat oven to 400°F. Spray 2 cookie sheets with cooking spray. Make corn cakes as directed except omit vegetable oil. Drop corn mixture by tablespoonfuls onto the cookie sheets; press each into 1½-inch round. Bake about 12 minutes, turning once, until golden brown.

Mini Quiches

PREP TIME: 35 MINUTES ● START TO FINISH: 55 MINUTES
24 APPETIZERS

1¼ cups Original Bisquick mix

¼ cup butter or margarine, softened

2 tablespoons boiling water

6 slices bacon, crisply cooked, crumbled

½ cup half-and-half

1 egg

2 tablespoons thinly sliced green onions (2 medium)

¼ teaspoon salt

¼ teaspoon ground red pepper (cayenne)

½ cup shredded Swiss cheese (2 oz)

1 Heat oven to 375°F. Spray 24 mini muffin cups with cooking spray. In medium bowl, stir Bisquick mix and butter. Add boiling water; stir vigorously until soft dough forms. Press rounded teaspoonful dough on bottom and up side of each muffin cup. Divide bacon evenly among muffin cups.

2 In small bowl, beat half-and-half and egg until well blended. Beat in onions, salt and red pepper. Spoon 1½ teaspoons into each muffin cup; sprinkle cheese over tops.

3 Bake about 20 minutes or until edges are golden brown and centers are set. Store any remaining quiches in the refrigerator.

High Altitude (3500–6500 ft): No change.

1 APPETIZER: Calories 70 (Calories from Fat 45); Total Fat 5g (Saturated Fat 2.5g); Cholesterol 20mg; Sodium 170mg; Total Carbohydrate 5g (Dietary Fiber 0g; Sugars 0g); Protein 2g **% DAILY VALUE:** Vitamin A 2%; Vitamin C 0%; Calcium 4%; Iron 0% **EXCHANGES:** ½ Other Carbohydrate, 1 Fat **CARBOHYDRATE CHOICES:** ½

Quick Tip These bite-size quiches can be made one day ahead. Remove the baked quiches from the muffin pan and cool completely on a wire rack. Cover tightly and store in the refrigerator. To serve, place on cookie sheet and cover loosely with aluminum foil. Reheat at 375°F about 10 minutes or until hot.

Italian Sausage Cups

PREP TIME: 30 MINUTES ● START TO FINISH: 50 MINUTES
24 APPETIZERS

1½ cups Original Bisquick mix

½ teaspoon Italian seasoning

2 tablespoons boiling water

1 egg

½ lb bulk mild Italian sausage

¼ cup chopped onion

⅓ cup tomato pasta sauce

½ cup shredded mozzarella cheese (2 oz)

1 Heat oven to 375°F. Spray 24 mini muffin cups with cooking spray. In medium bowl, stir Bisquick mix, Italian seasoning and boiling water until well blended. Stir in egg until soft dough forms. Press rounded teaspoonful of dough on bottom and up side of each muffin cup.

2 In 10-inch skillet, cook sausage and onion over medium-high heat 5 to 7 minutes, stirring occasionally, until thoroughly cooked; drain. Stir in pasta sauce.

3 Spoon sausage mixture into dough-lined muffin cups. Sprinkle with cheese.

4 Bake 15 to 20 minutes or until golden brown.

High Altitude (3500–6500 ft): No change.

1 APPETIZER: Calories 70 (Calories from Fat 35); Total Fat 3.5g (Saturated Fat 1.5g); Cholesterol 15mg; Sodium 210mg; Total Carbohydrate 6g (Dietary Fiber 0g; Sugars 0g); Protein 3g **% DAILY VALUE:** Vitamin A 0%; Vitamin C 0%; Calcium 2%; Iron 2% **EXCHANGES:** ½ Other Carbohydrate, ½ High-Fat Meat **CARBOHYDRATE CHOICES:** ½

Quick Tip These appetizers can be prepared one day ahead. Make as directed—except do not top with cheese. After baking, remove from muffin pan and cool completely on a wire cooling rack. Cover tightly and refrigerate. To serve, place on cookie sheet, top with cheese and bake at 350°F for 4 to 6 minutes or until hot.

Mini Chinese Chicken Snacks

PREP TIME: 20 MINUTES ● START TO FINISH: 45 MINUTES
2 DOZEN APPETIZERS

1¼ cups Original Bisquick mix

¼ cup margarine or butter, softened

2 tablespoons boiling water

½ cup half-and-half

1 egg

⅓ cup finely shredded carrot

⅓ cup drained sliced water chestnuts (from 8-oz can), chopped

1 tablespoon grated lemon peel

½ teaspoon salt

½ teaspoon garlic powder

½ teaspoon five-spice powder

1 medium green onion, thinly sliced (1 tablespoon)

1 can (5 oz) chunk chicken, drained

1 Heat oven to 375°. Generously grease 24 small muffin cups, 1¾ x 1 inch. Stir Bisquick mix and margarine until blended. Add boiling water; stir vigorously until soft dough forms. Press rounded teaspoonful of dough on bottom and up side of each cup.

2 Beat half-and-half and egg in medium bowl. Stir in remaining ingredients. Spoon about 1 tablespoon mixture into each cup.

3 Bake 20 to 25 minutes or until edges are golden brown and centers are set. Serve warm. Store covered in refrigerator.

High Altitude (3500–6500 ft): No change.

1 APPETIZER: Calories 65 (Calories from Fat 35); Total Fat 4g (Saturated Fat 1g); Cholesterol 15mg; Sodium 190mg; Total Carbohydrate 5g (Dietary Fiber 0g; Sugars ½g); Protein 2g **% DAILY VALUE:** Vitamin A 6%; Vitamin C 0%; Calcium 2%; Iron 2% **EXCHANGES:** ½ Starch, ½ Fat **CARBOHYDRATE CHOICES:** ½

Quick Tip Dress up these picture-perfect party bits by garnishing with shredded carrot, sliced radish, sliced green onion, chopped fresh parsley, red pepper strips or celery leaves.

Steamed Beef Dumplings

PREP TIME: 35 MINUTES ● START TO FINISH: 55 MINUTES
30 APPETIZERS

SOY DIPPING SAUCE

¼ cup rice vinegar

¼ cup soy sauce

1 medium green onion
(1 tablespoon), thinly sliced

DUMPLINGS

2 tablespoons soy sauce

1 teaspoon cornstarch

2 medium carrots, shredded
(1 cup)

2 medium green onions, thinly
sliced (2 tablespoons)

2 tablespoons chopped fresh
cilantro

¼ teaspoon salt

¾ lb ground beef

2 cups Original Bisquick mix

¼ cup boiling water

2 tablespoons cold water

1 Make Soy Dipping Sauce by mixing vinegar and soy sauce. Sprinkle with onion and set aside.

2 Mix soy sauce and cornstarch in large bowl. Stir in carrots, onions, cilantro and salt. Add beef; mix well. Shape mixture into 30 meatballs, using about 1 tablespoon for each; set aside.

3 Stir Bisquick mix and boiling water in medium bowl until soft dough forms. Stir in cold water until dough forms a ball (dough will be sticky). Divide dough in half. Return one-half of dough to bowl; cover and set aside. Divide other half of dough into 15 balls. Roll each ball into 3-inch circle on surface sprinkled with Bisquick mix. Place 1 meatball in center of each dough circle. Fold dough up and around meatball, allowing meatball to show at the top. Press dough firmly around meatball, pleating to fit. Gently flatten bottom of each dumpling. Repeat with remaining dough and meatballs.

4 Place steamer basket in ½ inch water in 3-quart saucepan (water should not touch bottom of basket). Place dumplings, open side up, in basket so edges don't touch. (If all dumplings won't fit in basket, refrigerate remainder until ready to steam.) Cover tightly and heat to boiling; reduce heat to low. Cover and steam dumplings 16 to 18 minutes or until beef is no longer pink in center. Remove dumplings from steamer. Press dough firmly around meatballs. Serve warm with sauce.

High Altitude (3500–6500 ft): No change.

1 APPETIZER: Calories 53 (Calories from Fat 16); Total Fat 2g (Saturated Fat 1g); Cholesterol 394mg; Sodium 320mg; Total Carbohydrate 6g (Dietary Fiber 0g; Sugars 1g); Protein 3g **% DAILY VALUE:** Vitamin A 15%; Vitamin C 0%; Calcium 2%; Iron 4%. **EXCHANGES:** ½ Starch, ½ Fat, ½ Lean Meat **CARBOHYDRATE CHOICES:** ½

Sesame Pork Strips

PREP TIME: 20 MINUTES ● **START TO FINISH: 55 MINUTES**
ABOUT 3 DOZEN APPETIZERS

1 tablespoon margarine or butter, melted

1 lb pork boneless loin chops, 1 inch thick

1¼ cups Original Bisquick mix

⅓ cup sesame seed

1 teaspoon salt

1 teaspoon paprika

1 teaspoon ground mustard

2 eggs

2 tablespoons milk

2 tablespoons margarine or butter, melted

Sweet-and-sour sauce or mustard, if desired

1 Heat oven to 400°F. Spread 1 tablespoon melted margarine in jelly roll pan, 15½ × 10½ × 1 inch. Remove fat from pork. Cut pork into ¼-inch slices; cut slices into ½-inch-wide strips.

2 Stir Bisquick mix, sesame seed, salt, paprika and mustard. Beat eggs and milk with fork. Dip pork strips into egg mixture, then coat with sesame seed mixture. Place in single layer in pan. Drizzle 2 tablespoons melted margarine over pork.

3 Bake 25 to 30 minutes or until brown and crisp. Serve with sweet-and-sour sauce.

High Altitude (3500–6500 ft): No change.

1 APPETIZER: Calories 50 (Calories from Fat 25); Total Fat 3g (Saturated Fat 1g); Cholesterol 18mg; Sodium 138mg; Total Carbohydrate 3g (Dietary Fiber 0g; Sugars 0g); Protein 3g **% DAILY VALUE:** Vitamin A 2%; Vitamin C 0%; Calcium 2%; Iron 2% **EXCHANGES:** ½ Lean Meat, ½ Fat **CARBOHYDRATE CHOICES:** 0

Quick Tip This sesame coating is equally delicious on chicken. To make Sesame Chicken Strips, substitute 4 boneless skinless chicken breast halves (about 1¼ pounds) for the pork.

Left: Steamed Beef
Dumplings (page 133)
Right: Sesame Pork Strips

Crab Cakes

PREP TIME: 20 MINUTES ● START TO FINISH: 35 MINUTES
ABOUT 2 DOZEN APPETIZERS

1 tablespoon margarine or butter

⅓ cup chopped onion

⅓ cup chopped celery

⅓ cup chopped bell pepper

1 cup soft bread crumbs

½ cup Original Bisquick mix

2 teaspoons Worcestershire sauce

¼ teaspoon pepper

¼ teaspoon salt

2 eggs, slightly beaten

1 package (14 oz) imitation crabmeat flakes, chopped

Cocktail sauce, if desired

1 Heat oven to 400°F. Generously grease 2 cookie sheets. Melt margarine in 10-inch skillet over medium heat. Cook onion, celery and bell pepper in margarine about 3 minutes, stirring occasionally, until crisp-tender.

2 Mix vegetable mixture and remaining ingredients except cocktail sauce. Shape mixture into 1½-inch patties. Place on cookie sheets.

3 Bake about 12 minutes, turning once, until golden brown. Serve with cocktail sauce.

High Altitude (3500–6500 ft): No change.

1 APPETIZER: Calories 43 (Calories from Fat 13); Total Fat 1g (Saturated Fat 0g); Cholesterol 20mg; Sodium 224mg; Total Carbohydrate 5g (Dietary Fiber 0g; Sugars 1g); Protein 2g **% DAILY VALUE:** Vitamin A 4%; Vitamin C 2%; Calcium 2%; Iron 2% **EXCHANGES:** 1 Lean Meat **CARBOHYDRATE CHOICES:** ½

Quick Tip You don't have to turn on your oven to enjoy these savory cakes—use a skillet instead. Heat 1 tablespoon vegetable oil in a 10-inch skillet over medium-high heat. Cook patties in oil 4 to 5 minutes, turning once, until golden.

Pesto Appetizer Squares

PREP TIME: 5 MINUTES ● START TO FINISH: 35 MINUTES
4 DOZEN APPETIZERS

4 cups Original Bisquick mix

1 cup milk

2 eggs

⅓ cup basil pesto

½ cup spaghetti sauce, heated

Chopped fresh basil, if desired

Grated Parmesan cheese,
  if desired

1 Heat oven to 375°F. Grease 13 × 9-inch pan.

2 Stir Bisquick mix, milk, eggs and pesto. Spread in pan.

3 Bake 25 to 30 minutes or until golden brown; cool slightly. For squares, cut into 8 rows by 6 rows. Top each square with about ½ teaspoon spaghetti sauce. Sprinkle with basil and cheese.

High Altitude (3500–6500 ft): No change.

1 APPETIZER: Calories 55 (Calories from Fat 30); Total Fat 3g (Saturated Fat 1g); Cholesterol 10mg; Sodium 160mg; Total Carbohydrate 7g (Dietary Fiber 0g; Sugars 1g); Protein 1g **% DAILY VALUE:** Vitamin A 2%; Vitamin C 0%; Calcium 2%; Iron 2% **EXCHANGES:** ½ Starch **CARBOHYDRATE CHOICES:** ½

Crab Mini Quiches

PREP TIME: 15 MINUTES ● START TO FINISH: 35 MINUTES
24 MINI QUICHES

1¼ cups Original Bisquick mix

¼ cup butter or margarine, softened

2 tablespoons boiling water

⅓ cup canned crabmeat, finely chopped cooked crabmeat or finely chopped imitation crabmeat

½ cup half-and-half

1 egg

2 medium green onions, thinly sliced (2 tablespoons)

¼ teaspoon salt

¼ teaspoon ground red pepper (cayenne)

½ cup shredded Parmesan cheese

1 Heat oven to 375°F. Spray 24 small muffin cups, 1¾ × 1 inch, with cooking spray. Stir Bisquick mix and butter in small bowl until blended. Add boiling water; stir vigorously until soft dough forms. Press rounded teaspoonful of dough on bottom and up side of each muffin cup. Divide crabmeat evenly among muffin cups.

2 Beat half-and-half and egg in small bowl with spoon until blended. Stir in onions, salt and red pepper. Spoon 1½ teaspoons egg mixture into each muffin cup. Sprinkle cheese over tops.

3 Bake about 20 minutes or until edges are golden brown and centers are set. Cool 5 minutes. Loosen sides of quiches from pan; remove from pan.

High Altitude (3500–6500 ft): No change.

1 MINI QUICHE: Calories 60 (Calories from Fat 35); Total Fat 4g (Saturated Fat 2g); Cholesterol 20mg; Sodium 150mg; Total Carbohydrate 4g (Dietary Fiber 0g; Sugars 0g); Protein 2g **% DAILY VALUE:** Vitamin A 2%; Vitamin C 0%; Calcium 4%; Iron 2% **EXCHANGES:** 1 Fat **CARBOHYDRATE CHOICES:** 0

Quick Tip These bite-size quiches are great-tasting appetizers. To make one day ahead, remove quiches from muffin pan and place on wire rack to cool, then store tightly covered in the refrigerator. To serve, place on cookie sheet and cover loosely with aluminum foil. Reheat in 375°F oven about 10 minutes or until hot.

Ranch Veggie Bites

PREP TIME: 15 MINUTES ● START TO FINISH: 35 MINUTES
6 SERVINGS

Vegetable oil

¾ cup Original Bisquick mix

1 teaspoon paprika

1 envelope (1 oz) ranch dressing mix

1 tablespoon water

1 egg, slightly beaten

4 cups 1½-inch pieces assorted vegetables, such as onion wedges, bell pepper strips, broccoli flowerets or mushrooms

Sour cream, if desired

1 Pour oil into 3-quart saucepan until 1 inch deep. Heat over medium-high heat to 375°F.

2 Mix Bisquick mix, paprika and dressing mix (dry) in resealable plastic food-storage bag. Mix water and egg in large bowl. Add vegetables to egg mixture; stir well to coat. Transfer vegetables to plastic bag with slotted spoon. Seal bag and shake to coat with Bisquick mixture.

3 Fry batches of vegetables in oil 1 to 2 minutes or until light golden brown. Remove from oil with slotted spoon; drain on paper towels. Serve immediately with sour cream.

High Altitude (3500–6500 ft): Heat oil to 350°F to 365°F.

1 SERVING: Calories 305 (Calories from Fat 25); Total Fat 25g (Saturated Fat 4g); Cholesterol 35mg; Sodium 570mg; Total Carbohydrate 16g (Dietary Fiber 1g; Sugars 2g); Protein 4g **% DAILY VALUE:** Vitamin A 10%; Vitamin C 22%; Calcium 6%; Iron 6% **EXCHANGES:** ½ Starch, 1½ Vegetable, 5 Fat **CARBOHYDRATE CHOICES:** 1

Quick Tip These battered, deep-fried bites will convince even the most reluctant kids to eat their veggies! Dip them into reduced-fat ranch or Caesar dressing instead of sour cream for a little flavor variation.

Olive and Ham Appetizer Stacks

PREP TIME: 35 MINUTES ● START TO FINISH: 35 MINUTES
48 APPETIZERS

1 cup Original Bisquick mix

1 teaspoon dried basil leaves

⅓ cup spicy hot vegetable juice

1 package (8 oz) deli ham slices (8 thin slices)

48 pimiento-stuffed green olives

1 Heat oven to 400°F. In medium bowl, stir Bisquick mix, basil and vegetable juice until soft dough forms; beat vigorously 20 strokes. Place dough on surface sprinkled with Bisquick mix; roll in Bisquick mix to coat. Shape into a ball; knead 5 times.

2 Press or roll dough about ¼ inch thick. With 1¼-inch round cutter, cut into rounds. Gather dough scraps together and reroll; cut to make 48 rounds. On ungreased cookie sheets, place dough rounds 1 inch apart.

3 Bake 6 to 8 minutes or until edges begin to turn golden brown. Remove from cookie sheet to cooling rack. Cool 10 minutes.

4 Cut each ham slice into 6 wedge-shaped pieces; roll up each wedge. For each appetizer, spear toothpick into olive, 1 piece of rolled-up ham and baked round.

High Altitude (3500–6500 ft): No change.

1 APPETIZER: Calories 25 (Calories from Fat 10); Total Fat 1g (Saturated Fat 0g); Cholesterol 0mg; Sodium 150mg; Total Carbohydrate 2g (Dietary Fiber 0g; Sugars 0g); Protein 1g **% DAILY VALUE:** Vitamin A 0%; Vitamin C 0%; Calcium 0%; Iron 0% **EXCHANGES:** ½ Other Carbohydrate **CARBOHYDRATE CHOICES:** 0

Quick Tip For a meatless treat, substitute other foods like cheese cubes, quartered artichoke hearts and roasted red pepper strips for the ham.

Bisquick hams it up in this 1993 ad, showing the easy way to party—with minimal time in the kitchen.

Sausage Twists

PREP TIME: 15 MINUTES ● **START TO FINISH: 45 MINUTES**
36 APPETIZERS

2½ cups Original Bisquick mix

⅔ cup milk

½ cup shredded American-
Cheddar cheese blend
(2 oz)

2 tablespoons barbecue sauce

36 cocktail-size smoked
sausages (from 14-oz
package)

1 Heat oven to 400°F. Spray cookie sheets with cooking spray. In large bowl, stir Bisquick mix, milk and cheese until soft dough forms.

2 Divide dough in half. On surface lightly sprinkled with Bisquick mix, roll 1 half into 9 × 6-inch rectangle. Brush 1 tablespoon of the barbecue sauce over dough rectangle. Cut dough lengthwise into 18 (½-inch) strips. Roll each dough strip around 1 sausage; place about 1 inch apart on cookie sheets.

3 Repeat with remaining dough, barbecue sauce and sausages.

4 Bake 8 to 11 minutes or until dough begins to turn golden brown.

High Altitude (3500–6500 ft): Bake 10 to 12 minutes.

1 APPETIZER: Calories 70 (Calories from Fat 40); Total Fat 4.5g (Saturated Fat 2g); Cholesterol 5mg; Sodium 250mg; Total Carbohydrate 6g (Dietary Fiber 0g; Sugars 0g); Protein 2g **% DAILY VALUE:** Vitamin A 0%; Vitamin C 0%; Calcium 2%; Iron 2% **EXCHANGES:** ½ Starch, 1 Fat **CARBOHYDRATE CHOICES:** ½

Pepperoni Rounds

PREP TIME: 15 MINUTES ● START TO FINISH: 35 MINUTES
36 APPETIZERS

1½ cups Original Bisquick mix

½ cup milk

1 egg

1 stick (6 oz) pepperoni, diced

1 cup shredded mozzarella cheese (4 oz)

¾ cup tomato pasta sauce, heated

1 Heat oven to 400°F. Spray cookie sheets with cooking spray. In medium bowl, stir Bisquick mix, milk and egg until blended. Stir in pepperoni and cheese.

2 Drop dough by rounded teaspoonfuls about 2 inches apart on cookie sheets.

3 Bake 8 to 10 minutes or until light golden brown. Immediately remove from cookie sheet to cooling rack. Serve with pasta sauce.

High Altitude (3500–6500 ft): Bake 7 to 9 minutes.

1 APPETIZER (WITH 1 TEASPOON SAUCE): Calories 60 (Calories from Fat 30); Total Fat 3.5g (Saturated Fat 1.5g); Cholesterol 15mg; Sodium 190mg; Total Carbohydrate 5g (Dietary Fiber 0g; Sugars 0g); Protein 3g **% DAILY VALUE:** Vitamin A 0%; Vitamin C 0%; Calcium 4%; Iron 0% **EXCHANGES:** ½ Starch, ½ Fat **CARBOHYDRATE CHOICES:** ½

Sausage-Stuffed Mushrooms

PREP TIME: 20 MINUTES ● **START TO FINISH: 35 MINUTES**
36 APPETIZERS

36 large fresh mushrooms
(about 2 lb)

1 lb bulk pork sausage

¼ cup freeze-dried chopped
chives

2 tablespoons chopped onion

1 clove garlic, finely chopped

¾ cup Original Bisquick mix

¼ cup Italian-style dry bread
crumbs

¼ cup grated Parmesan cheese

1 Heat oven to 350°F. Remove stems from mushrooms; finely chop stems.

2 In 10-inch skillet, cook sausage, chopped mushroom stems, chives, onion and garlic until sausage is no longer pink; drain, reserving drippings. Stir Bisquick mix and bread crumbs into sausage mixture until mixture holds together. (If mixture is dry, add 1 to 2 tablespoons reserved drippings.)

3 Spoon about 1 rounded tablespoon sausage mixture into each mushroom cap. In ungreased 15 × 10 × 1-inch pan, place filled mushrooms; sprinkle with cheese.

4 Bake about 15 minutes or until hot. Serve immediately.

High Altitude (3500–6500 ft): No change.

1 APPETIZER: Calories 45 (Calories from Fat 20); Total Fat 2.5g (Saturated Fat 1g); Cholesterol 5mg; Sodium 100mg; Total Carbohydrate 3g (Dietary Fiber 0g; Sugars 0g); Protein 2g **% DAILY VALUE:** Vitamin A 0%; Vitamin C 0%; Calcium 0%; Iron 0% **EXCHANGES:** ½ High-Fat Meat **CARBOHYDRATE CHOICES:** 0

Beef Empanaditas

PREP TIME: 25 MINUTES ● START TO FINISH: 55 MINUTES
20 APPETIZERS

2 cups Original Bisquick mix

½ cup hot water

¼ lb lean (at least 80%) ground beef

½ cup chunky-style salsa

1 tablespoon raisins

8 pimiento-stuffed green olives, sliced

½ teaspoon ground cumin

⅛ teaspoon ground cinnamon

1 egg

1 tablespoon water

1 Heat oven to 350°F. Line cookie sheet with cooking parchment paper. In medium bowl, stir Bisquick mix and hot water until stiff dough forms. Let stand 10 minutes.

2 Meanwhile, in 8-inch skillet, cook beef over medium-high heat 5 to 7 minutes, stirring occasionally, until thoroughly cooked; drain. Stir in salsa, raisins, olives, cumin and cinnamon; set aside.

3 Place dough on surface sprinkled with Bisquick mix; gently roll in Bisquick mix to coat. Shape into a ball; knead 10 times. Roll dough into 13-inch round. With 3-inch round cutter, cut dough into rounds. Gather dough scraps together and reroll to ⅛-inch thickness. Cut to make 20 rounds.

4 Spoon 2 to 3 teaspoons beef mixture onto center of each dough round. Fold dough in half over filling; press edges firmly with fork to seal. Place 1 inch apart on cookie sheet.

5 In small bowl, stir egg and 1 tablespoon water to combine; brush mixture over tops of each empanadita. Bake 14 to 16 minutes or until golden brown.

High Altitude (3500–6500 ft): Bake 20 to 22 minutes.

1 APPETIZER: Calories 70 (Calories from Fat 2.5); Total Fat 2.5g (Saturated Fat 1g); Cholesterol 15mg; Sodium 220mg; Total Carbohydrate 9g (Dietary Fiber 0g; Sugars 0g); Protein 2g **% DAILY VALUE:** Vitamin A 0%; Vitamin C 0%; Calcium 0%; Iron 4% **EXCHANGES:** ½ Starch, ½ Fat **CARBOHYDRATE CHOICES:** ½

Taco Pinwheels

PREP TIME: 20 MINUTES ● START TO FINISH: 40 MINUTES
26 APPETIZERS

½ lb lean (at least 80%) ground beef

⅓ cup water

2 teaspoons taco seasoning mix (from 1.25-oz package)

2¼ cups Original Bisquick mix

2 cups taco sauce

1 In 8-inch skillet, cook beef over medium-high heat 5 to 7 minutes, stirring occasionally, until thoroughly cooked; drain. Stir in water and taco seasoning mix. Cook uncovered over medium heat 2 to 4 minutes, stirring occasionally, until most of liquid is absorbed. Set aside to cool.

2 Heat oven to 375°F. Spray cookie sheets with cooking spray. In medium bowl, stir Bisquick mix and ½ cup of the taco sauce until soft dough forms. Place dough on surface generously sprinkled with Bisquick mix; gently roll in Bisquick mix to coat. Shape into a ball; knead 10 times.

3 Roll dough into 13 × 10-inch rectangle. Spoon beef mixture over rectangle to within 1 inch of long sides. Starting with 13-inch side, roll up tightly; pinch edge to seal. Cut roll crosswise into ½-inch slices, using serrated knife. Place slices 1 inch apart on cookie sheets.

4 Bake 8 to 10 minutes or until light golden brown. Serve warm with remaining 1½ cups taco sauce.

High Altitude (3500–6500 ft): No change.

1 APPETIZER (WITH ABOUT 1 TABLESPOON SAUCE): Calories 60 (Calories from Fat 20); Total Fat 2.5g (Saturated Fat 1g); Cholesterol 5mg; Sodium 260mg; Total Carbohydrate 8g (Dietary Fiber 0g; Sugars 1g); Protein 3g **% DAILY VALUE:** Vitamin A 0%; Vitamin C 0%; Calcium 0%; Iron 4% **EXCHANGES:** ½ Other Carbohydrate, ½ Medium-Fat Meat **CARBOHYDRATE CHOICES:** ½

Quick Tip Keep the slices round by turning the dough roll a quarter turn after cutting each slice.

Apricot-Glazed Coconut-Chicken Bites

PREP TIME: 15 MINUTES ● START TO FINISH: 50 MINUTES
ABOUT 3 DOZEN APPETIZERS

APRICOT GLAZE

½ cup apricot spreadable fruit

2 tablespoons honey

2 tablespoons Dijon mustard

1 tablespoon white vinegar

COCONUT-CHICKEN BITES

½ cup sweetened condensed milk

2 tablespoons Dijon mustard

1½ cups Original Bisquick mix

⅔ cup flaked coconut

½ teaspoon salt

½ teaspoon paprika

1 pound boneless skinless chicken breast halves, cut into 1-inch pieces

¼ cup margarine or butter, melted

Hot mustard, if desired

1 Stir together all ingredients for Apricot Glaze until blended. Set aside.

2 Heat oven to 425°F. Mix milk and Dijon mustard. In a separate bowl, stir Bisquick mix, coconut, salt and paprika. Dip chicken into milk mixture, then coat with Bisquick mixture.

3 Pour 2 tablespoons of the melted margarine in jelly roll pan, 15½ × 10½ × 1 inch. Place coated chicken in pan. Drizzle remaining margarine over chicken.

4 Bake uncovered 20 minutes. Turn chicken; brush with glaze. Bake 10 to 15 minutes longer or until chicken is no longer pink in center and glaze is bubbly. Serve with hot mustard.

High Altitude (3500–6500 ft): No change.

1 APPETIZER: Calories 80 (Calories from Fat 25); Total Fat 3g (Saturated Fat 1g); Cholesterol 5mg; Sodium 160mg; Carbohydrate 10g (Dietary Fiber 0g; Sugars 6g); Protein 3g **% DAILY VALUE:** Vitamin A 2%; Vitamin C 0%; Calcium 2%; Iron 2% **EXCHANGES:** ½ Starch, ½ Fat, ½ Lean Meat **CARBOHYDRATE CHOICES:** 1

Quick Tip In 1986, Coconut Chicken Breasts took first place in the Bisquick Invitational recipe contest for professional chefs and cooks. We've taken this winning combination, added a fruity twist and scaled it down to snack size—it's a winner for everyone!

Chicken Dippers with Peanut Sauce

PREP TIME: 10 MINUTES ● START TO FINISH: 35 MINUTES
ABOUT 36 APPETIZERS

CHICKEN

1½ cups Country Corn Flakes cereal, crushed (½ cup)

½ cup Bisquick Heart Smart mix

¾ teaspoon paprika

¼ teaspoon salt

¼ teaspoon pepper

3 boneless skinless chicken breasts, cut into 1-inch pieces

Cooking spray

PEANUT SAUCE

½ cup plain fat-free yogurt

¼ cup reduced-fat peanut butter spread

½ cup fat-free (skim) milk

1 tablespoon soy sauce

⅛ teaspoon ground red pepper (cayenne), if desired

1 Heat oven to 400°F. Line 15 × 10 × 1-inch pan with foil. In 2-quart resealable food-storage plastic bag, place cereal, Bisquick mix, paprika, salt and pepper. Seal bag; shake to mix. Shake about 6 chicken pieces at a time in bag until coated. Shake off any extra crumbs. Place chicken pieces in pan. Spray chicken with cooking spray.

2 Bake 20 to 25 minutes or until coating is crisp and chicken is no longer pink in center.

3 Meanwhile, in 10-inch nonstick skillet, cook all sauce ingredients over medium heat 3 to 4 minutes, stirring occasionally, until mixture begins to thicken. Serve sauce with chicken.

High Altitude (3500–6500 ft): No change.

1 APPETIZER (WITH ABOUT 2 TEASPOONS SAUCE): Calories 40 (Calories from Fat 10); Total Fat 1.5g (Saturated Fat 0g); Cholesterol 10mg; Sodium 95mg; Total Carbohydrate 4g (Dietary Fiber 0g; Sugars 0g); Protein 4g **% DAILY VALUE:** Vitamin A 0%; Vitamin C 0%; Calcium 2%; Iron 4% **EXCHANGES:** ½ Medium-Fat Meat **CARBOHYDRATE CHOICES:** 0

Cornmeal-Coated Chicken Bites

PREP TIME: 15 MINUTES ● START TO FINISH: 35 MINUTES
ABOUT 48 APPETIZERS

1 cup Original Bisquick mix

½ cup cornmeal

1 teaspoon seasoned salt

¼ cup milk

1 egg

4 boneless skinless chicken breasts, cut into 1-inch pieces

¼ cup butter or margarine, melted

1 cup barbecue sauce, heated

1 Heat oven to 425°F. In resealable 1-gallon food-storage plastic bag, place Bisquick mix, cornmeal and seasoned salt.

2 In medium bowl, beat milk and egg until blended. Dip chicken pieces in milk mixture, then shake about 6 pieces at a time in bag of Bisquick mixture.

3 In 15 × 10 × 1-inch pan, pour 2 tablespoons of the melted butter. Arrange coated chicken pieces in pan. Drizzle remaining 2 tablespoons melted butter over chicken pieces.

4 Bake 12 minutes. Turn chicken pieces over. Bake 7 to 8 minutes longer or until chicken pieces are golden brown. Serve with barbecue sauce.

High Altitude (3500–6500 ft): No change.

1 APPETIZER (WITH ABOUT 1 TEASPOON SAUCE): Calories 45 (Calories from Fat 15); Total Fat 2g (Saturated Fat 1g); Cholesterol 15mg; Sodium 130mg; Total Carbohydrate 5g (Dietary Fiber 0g; Sugars 2g); Protein 3g **% DAILY VALUE:** Vitamin A 0%; Vitamin C 0%; Calcium 0%; Iron 0% **EXCHANGES:** ½ Very Lean Meat, ½ Fat **CARBOHYDRATE CHOICES:** ½

Ham and String Cheese Roll-Ups

PREP TIME: 15 MINUTES ● START TO FINISH: 45 MINUTES
4 SANDWICHES

2 cups Original Bisquick mix

¼ cup water

1 egg

2 teaspoons honey mustard

4 sticks (1 oz each) mozzarella string cheese

8 slices (about 1 oz each) thinly sliced cooked ham (from deli)

1 tablespoon milk

1 Heat oven to 375°F. In medium bowl, stir Bisquick mix, water and egg until dough forms. On surface sprinkled with Bisquick mix, knead dough about 10 times. Divide dough in fourths.

2 For each sandwich, place piece of dough on surface sprinkled with Bisquick mix; roll in Bisquick mix to coat. Press or roll into 6½ × 4½-inch rectangle, ¼ inch thick.

3 Spread each dough rectangle with ½ teaspoon mustard. Wrap each cheese stick with 2 slices ham. Place ham and cheese bundle lengthwise in center of dough. Bring dough up over bundle; pinch to seal. Pinch ends and tuck under. On ungreased cookie sheet, place rolls seam side down. Brush with milk.

4 Bake 18 to 23 minutes or until crust is golden brown. Let stand 5 minutes before serving.

High Altitude (3500–6500 ft): Bake 23 to 28 minutes.

1 SANDWICH: Calories 320 (Calories from Fat 90); Total Fat 10g (Saturated Fat 3g); Cholesterol 75mg; Sodium 1080mg; Total Carbohydrate 42g (Dietary Fiber 0g; Sugars 5g); Protein 16g **% DAILY VALUE:** Vitamin A 4%; Vitamin C 0%; Calcium 35%; Iron 15% **EXCHANGES:** 2 Starch, 1 Other Carbohydrate, 1½ Medium-Fat Meat **CARBOHYDRATE CHOICES:** 3

Triple Cheese Flatbread

PREP TIME: 10 MINUTES ● START TO FINISH: 25 MINUTES
16 SERVINGS

2 cups Original Bisquick mix

½ cup hot water

2 tablespoons margarine or butter, melted

¼ cup shredded Cheddar cheese (1 oz)

¼ cup shredded Monterey Jack cheese (1 oz)

¼ cup grated Parmesan cheese

½ teaspoon garlic powder

½ teaspoon Italian seasoning, if desired

1 Heat oven to 450°F. Stir Bisquick mix and hot water until stiff dough forms. Let stand 10 minutes. Place dough on surface sprinkled with Bisquick; gently roll in Bisquick to coat. Shape into a ball; knead 60 times.

2 Roll or pat dough into 12-inch square on ungreased cookie sheet. Spread margarine over dough. Mix remaining ingredients; sprinkle over dough.

3 Bake 10 to 12 minutes or until edges are golden brown. Serve warm.

High Altitude (3500–6500 ft): No change.

1 SERVING: Calories 90 (Calories from Fat 45); Total Fat 5g (Saturated Fat 2g); Cholesterol 5mg; Sodium 280mg; Carbohydrate 9g (Dietary Fiber 0g; Sugars 0g); Protein 2g **% DAILY VALUE:** Vitamin A 2%; Vitamin C 0%; Calcium 6%; Iron 2% **EXCHANGES:** ½ Starch, 1 Fat **CARBOHYDRATE CHOICES:** 1

Pepperoni-Cheese Sticks

PREP TIME: 15 MINUTES ● START TO FINISH: 35 MINUTES
6 BREADSTICKS

1 cup Original Bisquick mix

2 tablespoons grated Parmesan cheese

¼ cup water

¼ teaspoon Italian seasoning

1 oz sliced pepperoni (from 3.25-oz package), cut in half

¼ cup shredded mozzarella cheese (1 oz)

Sliced ripe olives, if desired

Pizza sauce, heated, if desired

1 Heat oven to 400°F. Generously grease bottom and sides of 8 × 4-inch loaf pan with shortening or cooking spray.

2 In medium bowl, stir Bisquick mix, Parmesan cheese, water, Italian seasoning and pepperoni until moistened; spread on bottom of pan. Sprinkle with mozzarella cheese. Top with olives.

3 Bake uncovered 18 to 20 minutes or until edges are light golden brown and cheese is melted. Cool 5 minutes. Run knife around edges; remove bread from pan. Cut loaf crosswise into 6 sticks. Serve warm with pizza sauce.

High Altitude (3500–6500 ft): No change.

1 BREADSTICK: Calories 190 (Calories from Fat 50); Total Fat 6g (Saturated Fat 2g); Cholesterol 10mg; Sodium 580mg; Total Carbohydrate 27g (Dietary Fiber 0g; Sugars 3g); Protein 6g **% DAILY VALUE:** Vitamin A 0%; Vitamin C 0%; Calcium 20%; Iron 8% **EXCHANGES:** 2 Starch, 1 Fat **CARBOHYDRATE CHOICES:** 2

This ad appeared in 1961, Bisquick's 30-year anniversary. Time to look back on the biscuits and pancakes that started it all.

Parmesan-Sesame Breadsticks

PREP TIME: 15 MINUTES ● START TO FINISH: 30 MINUTES
12 BREADSTICKS

2 cups Original Bisquick mix

¼ cup shredded Parmesan cheese

2 tablespoons sesame seed

½ cup cold water

1 tablespoon butter or margarine, melted

1 Heat oven to 450°F. Spray large cookie sheet with cooking spray. In medium bowl, stir Bisquick mix, 2 tablespoons of the cheese, 1 tablespoon of the sesame seed and the water with spoon until soft dough forms.

2 Place dough on surface sprinkled with Bisquick mix; roll in Bisquick mix to coat. Press or roll into 10 × 8-inch rectangle. Brush with butter. Sprinkle with remaining cheese and sesame seed; press in gently. Cut crosswise into 12 strips. Gently twist each strip. On cookie sheet, place strips ½ inch apart.

3 Bake 10 to 12 minutes until light golden brown. Serve warm.

High Altitude (3500–6500 ft): No change.

1 BREADSTICK: Calories 110 (Calories from Fat 45); Total Fat 5g (Saturated Fat 2g); Cholesterol 0mg; Sodium 290mg; Total Carbohydrate 13g (Dietary Fiber 0g; Sugars 0g); Protein 3g **% DAILY VALUE:** Vitamin A 0%; Vitamin C 0%; Calcium 4%; Iron 4% **EXCHANGES:** 1 Starch, 1 Fat **CARBOHYDRATE CHOICES:** 1

Quick Cornbread Sticks

PREP TIME: 10 MINUTES ● START TO FINISH: 25 MINUTES
8 BREADSTICKS

1 egg
½ cup Bisquick Heart Smart mix
½ cup yellow cornmeal
¾ cup buttermilk
1 tablespoon vegetable oil
Yellow cornmeal

1 Heat oven to 450°F. Grease bottom and sides of 9-inch loaf pan with shortening. In large bowl, beat egg with wire whisk or fork until fluffy. Beat in Bisquick mix, ½ cup cornmeal, the buttermilk and oil just until smooth (do not overbeat). Pour into pan. Sprinkle lightly with cornmeal.

2 Bake about 15 minutes or until toothpick inserted in center comes out clean. Remove from pan. Cut loaf crosswise into 8 sticks. Serve warm.

High Altitude (3500–6500 ft): Bake about 20 minutes.

1 BREADSTICK: Calories 100 (Calories from Fat 30); Total Fat 3.5g (Saturated Fat 1g); Cholesterol 30mg; Sodium 110mg; Total Carbohydrate 13g (Dietary Fiber 0g; Sugars 2g); Protein 3g **% DAILY VALUE:** Vitamin A 0%; Vitamin C 0%; Calcium 6%; Iron 4% **EXCHANGES:** 1 Starch, ½ Fat **CARBOHYDRATE CHOICES:** 1

Quick Tip No buttermilk on hand? Use 2 teaspoons plus ¼ teaspoon lemon juice or white vinegar plus enough milk to equal ¾ cup. Let stand a few minutes until it thickens slightly.

Garlic and Parmesan Churros

PREP TIME: 35 MINUTES ● START TO FINISH: 35 MINUTES
26 APPETIZERS

Vegetable oil for deep frying
1⅔ cups Original Bisquick mix
1 teaspoon garlic powder
⅔ cup hot water
½ cup grated Parmesan cheese

1 In 3-quart saucepan, heat 2 to 3 inches oil over medium-high heat to 350°F.

2 In medium bowl, stir Bisquick mix, garlic powder and hot water until soft dough forms. Spoon mixture into decorating bag fitted with star tip #4.

3 Squeeze 5 or 6 (2½-inch) strips of dough at a time into hot oil. If necessary, cut dough with knife or scissors between each churro. Fry 30 seconds to 1 minute 30 seconds, turning frequently, until golden brown. Remove from oil; drain on paper towels. Immediately roll in cheese. Serve warm.

High Altitude (3500–6500 ft): No change.

1 APPETIZER: Calories 160 (Calories from Fat 130); Total Fat 14g (Saturated Fat 2.5g); Cholesterol 0mg; Sodium 125mg; Total Carbohydrate 5g (Dietary Fiber 0g; Sugars 0g); Protein 1g **% DAILY VALUE:** Vitamin A 0%; Vitamin C 0%; Calcium 2%; Iron 0% **EXCHANGES:** ½ Starch, 2½ Fat **CARBOHYDRATE CHOICES:** ½

Canadian Bacon–Pineapple Pinwheels

PREP TIME: 15 MINUTES ● START TO FINISH: 35 MINUTES
12 PINWHEELS

2 cups Original Bisquick mix

½ cup milk

1 can (8 oz) crushed pineapple, well drained

1 package (6 oz) Canadian-style bacon, chopped

¾ cup shredded mozzarella cheese (3 oz)

2 tablespoons butter or margarine, melted

¼ teaspoon garlic powder

1 cup spaghetti sauce, heated

1 Heat oven to 375°F. Spray cookie sheet with cooking spray. Stir Bisquick mix and milk until soft dough forms. Place dough on surface generously dusted with Bisquick mix; gently roll in Bisquick mix to coat. Shape into a ball; knead 10 times.

2 Roll dough into 15 × 10-inch rectangle. Layer pineapple, bacon and cheese on rectangle to within 1 inch of edges. Fold in each 10-inch side of rectangle 1 inch. Beginning at 15-inch side, tightly roll up rectangle; pinch edge into roll to seal. Cut into 12 slices. Place on cookie sheet.

3 Bake 16 to 18 minutes or until light golden and cheese is melted. Mix butter and garlic powder; brush over warm pinwheels. Serve with spaghetti sauce.

High Altitude (3500–6500 ft): Bake 17 to 20 minutes.

1 APPETIZER: Calories 170 (Calories from Fat 74); Total Fat 8g (Saturated Fat 3.5g); Cholesterol 19mg; Sodium 600mg; Total Carbohydrate 18g (Dietary Fiber 1g; Sugars 3g); Protein 7g **% DAILY VALUE:** Vitamin A 6%; Vitamin C 4%; Calcium 10%; Iron 4% **EXCHANGES:** 1 Starch, ½ Lean Meat, 1 Fat **CARBOHYDRATE CHOICES:** 1

Quick Tip Dipped in spaghetti sauce, these yummy little pinwheels have all the flavors of pizza. If your family loves pepperoni, you can substitute 1 package (35 ounces) sliced pepperoni for the Canadian bacon.

Sesame Wedges

PREP TIME: 10 MINUTES ● **START TO FINISH: 30 MINUTES**
12 APPETIZERS

2 cups Original Bisquick mix
½ cup water
2 tablespoons butter or margarine, melted
2 tablespoons sesame seed

1 Heat oven to 400°F. Spray cookie sheet with cooking spray. In medium bowl, stir Bisquick mix and water until soft dough forms.

2 On cookie sheet, press dough into 10-inch round. Brush with butter. Sprinkle with sesame seed; press firmly into dough with rubber spatula. Cut dough round into 12 wedges, but do not separate.

3 Bake 15 to 20 minutes or until golden brown. Carefully separate wedges. Serve warm.

High Altitude (3500–6500 ft): No change.

1 APPETIZER: Calories 110 (Calories from Fat 50); Total Fat 5g (Saturated Fat 2g); Cholesterol 5mg; Sodium 260mg; Total Carbohydrate 13g (Dietary Fiber 0g; Sugars 0g); Protein 2g **% DAILY VALUE:** Vitamin A 0%; Vitamin C 0%; Calcium 2%; Iron 4% **EXCHANGES:** 1 Starch, 1 Fat **CARBOHYDRATE CHOICES:** 1

Quick Tip Sprinkle 2 tablespoons chopped fresh or 2 teaspoons dried basil or sage leaves on the top before baking to create irresistible aroma and flavor.

Quick French Onion Biscuits

PREP TIME: 10 MINUTES ● START TO FINISH: 20 MINUTES
12 BISCUITS

2 cups Original Bisquick mix
¼ cup milk
1 container (8 oz)
    refrigerated French onion dip

1 Heat oven to 450°F. In medium bowl, stir all ingredients until soft dough forms.

2 On ungreased cookie sheet, drop dough by heaping tablespoonfuls into 12 mounds.

3 Bake 7 to 9 minutes or until light golden brown. Serve warm.

High Altitude (3500–6500 ft): Increase Bisquick mix to 2¼ cups. Bake 12 to 14 minutes.

1 BISCUIT: Calories 120 (Calories from Fat 50); Total Fat 6g (Saturated Fat 2.5g); Cholesterol 5mg; Sodium 380mg; Total Carbohydrate 14g (Dietary Fiber 0g; Sugars 2g); Protein 2g **% DAILY VALUE:** Vitamin A 2%; Vitamin C 0%; Calcium 4%; Iron 4% **EXCHANGES:** 1 Starch, 1 Fat **CARBOHYDRATE CHOICES:** 1

Quick Tip If you'd prefer, pick your favorite flavored sour cream and use it instead of the French onion dip.

Green Chile Cornbread

PREP TIME: 10 MINUTES ● START TO FINISH: 45 MINUTES
16 SERVINGS

1 cup Original Bisquick mix

1 cup cornmeal

2 tablespoons sugar, if desired

½ teaspoon salt

1 cup milk

¼ cup vegetable oil

2 eggs

1 cup shredded sharp Cheddar cheese (4 oz)

⅔ cup frozen whole kernel corn, thawed, drained

2 tablespoons chopped green chiles (from 4.5-oz can)

1 Heat oven to 400°F. Spray bottom only of 9-inch square pan with cooking spray. In medium bowl, stir Bisquick mix, cornmeal, sugar, salt, milk, oil and eggs with wire whisk or fork just until moistened. Gently stir in remaining ingredients. Pour into pan.

2 Bake 28 to 32 minutes or until light golden brown. Serve warm.

High Altitude (3500–6500 ft): No change.

1 SERVING: Calories 140 (Calories from Fat 70); Total Fat 8g (Saturated Fat 2.5g); Cholesterol 35mg; Sodium 230mg; Total Carbohydrate 14g (Dietary Fiber 0g; Sugars 1g); Protein 5g **% DAILY VALUE:** Vitamin A 4%; Vitamin C 0%; Calcium 6%; Iron 4% **EXCHANGES:** 1 Starch, 1½ Fat **CARBOHYDRATE CHOICES:** 1

Quick Tip For a full flavor kick, substitute jalapeño chile peppers for the green chiles and use an equal amount of pepper Jack cheese for the Cheddar.

Easy Greek-Style Bread

PREP TIME: 15 MINUTES ● START TO FINISH: 30 MINUTES
24 SERVINGS

½ cup Original Bisquick mix

½ cup crumbled feta cheese

1 teaspoon dried basil leaves

1 teaspoon dried oregano leaves

3 cups Original Bisquick mix

¾ cup sun-dried tomatoes in oil, drained and chopped

½ cup chopped ripe olives

1 cup hot water

3 tablespoons vegetable oil

1 egg

1 Heat oven to 425°F. Grease bottom and sides of 13 × 9-inch pan with shortening or spray with cooking spray. Stir together ½ cup Bisquick mix, the cheese, basil and oregano; set aside.

2 Stir remaining ingredients until moistened. Spread batter in pan; sprinkle with cheese mixture.

3 Bake 13 to 15 minutes or until golden brown. To serve, cut into 4 rows by 6 rows. Serve warm.

High Altitude (3500–6500 ft): No change.

1 SERVING: Calories 110 (Calories from Fat 50); Total Fat 3g (Saturated Fat 2g); Cholesterol 10mg; Sodium 320mg; Total Carbohydrate 12g (Dietary Fiber 0g; Sugars 0.5g); Protein 2g **% DAILY VALUE:** Vitamin A 0%; Vitamin C 0%; Calcium 4%; Iron 4% **EXCHANGES:** 1 Starch, 1 Fat **CARBOHYDRATE CHOICES:** 1

Quick Tip Homemade bread in 30 minutes? It's easy with Bisquick! This flavorful bread is a great one to serve with a special dinner, eat as a snack or enjoy for breakfast or brunch.

CHAPTER 4

Comforting
Casseroles
and Oven Meals

Cheesy Italian Beef Bake

PREP TIME: 10 MINUTES ● START TO FINISH: 55 MINUTES
10 SERVINGS

1½ lb lean (at least 80%) ground beef

1 jar (26 oz) chunky garden-style tomato pasta sauce

1 package (8 oz) cream cheese, softened

⅓ cup sour cream

2 cups shredded Parmesan cheese (8 oz)

¾ teaspoon Italian seasoning

2 cups Original Bisquick mix

1½ cups milk

1 Heat oven to 375°F. Spray 13 × 9-inch (3-quart) glass baking dish with cooking spray. In 10-inch skillet, cook beef over medium-high heat 5 to 7 minutes, stirring frequently, until thoroughly cooked; drain. Stir in pasta sauce.

2 In small bowl, mix cream cheese, sour cream, ½ cup of the Parmesan cheese and ¼ teaspoon of the Italian seasoning until smooth and creamy. Spoon half of beef mixture (about 2 cups) into baking dish. Drop spoonfuls of cream cheese mixture evenly onto beef mixture. Spoon remaining beef mixture over cream cheese mixture.

3 In medium bowl, stir 1 cup of the Parmesan cheese, the Bisquick mix and milk with wire whisk or fork until blended. Pour over beef mixture.

4 Bake uncovered 30 to 35 minutes or until light golden brown. Sprinkle with remaining ½ cup Parmesan cheese and ½ teaspoon Italian seasoning. Bake 5 minutes. Let stand at least 10 minutes before serving.

High Altitude (3500–6500 ft): Heat oven to 400°F.

1 SERVING: Calories 500 (Calories from Fat 260); Total Fat 29g (Saturated Fat 14g); Cholesterol 90mg; Sodium 1130mg; Total Carbohydrate 33g (Dietary Fiber 1g; Sugars 11g); Protein 26g **% DAILY VALUE:** Vitamin A 15%; Vitamin C 6%; Calcium 40%; Iron 15% **EXCHANGES:** 1 Starch, 1 Other Carbohydrate, 3½ High-Fat Meat **CARBOHYDRATE CHOICES:** 2

Cheesy Italian Turkey Bake: Substitute 1½ pounds ground turkey for the ground beef.

Skillet Tomato Mac with Cheese Biscuits

PREP TIME: 15 MINUTES ● START TO FINISH: 45 MINUTES
5 SERVINGS

½ cup Original Bisquick mix

½ cup grated Parmesan cheese

¼ teaspoon garlic powder, if desired

¼ cup water

1 egg

1 lb lean (at least 80%) ground beef

2 cups tomato pasta sauce

¾ cup water

1 cup uncooked elbow macaroni (4 oz)

1 Heat oven to 375°F. In small bowl, stir Bisquick mix, cheese, garlic powder, ¼ cup water and the egg with wire whisk or fork until blended; set aside.

2 In 10-inch ovenproof skillet, cook beef over medium-high heat 5 to 7 minutes, stirring frequently, until thoroughly cooked; drain. Stir in pasta sauce, ¾ cup water and the macaroni. Heat to boiling, about 5 minutes, stirring constantly. Spoon Bisquick mixture around edge of mixture in skillet, leaving center open.

3 Bake uncovered 20 to 25 minutes or until top is golden brown. Sprinkle with additional Parmesan cheese if desired.

High Altitude (3500–6500 ft): Increase water for beef mixture to 1 cup. Bake 22 to 27 minutes.

1 SERVING: Calories 470 (Calories from Fat 180); Total Fat 20g (Saturated Fat 7g); Cholesterol 110mg; Sodium 840mg; Total Carbohydrate 46g (Dietary Fiber 3g; Sugars 10g); Protein 27g **% DAILY VALUE:** Vitamin A 10%; Vitamin C 8%; Calcium 15%; Iron 20% **EXCHANGES:** 2 Starch, 1 Other Carbohydrate, 3 Medium-Fat Meat, ½ Fat **CARBOHYDRATE CHOICES:** 3

Quick Tip No ovenproof skillet? Cook the beef mixture in a 10-inch skillet and pour it into a 2-quart casserole. Spoon the Bisquick mixture on top and bake.

Quick Cheeseburger and Vegetable Bake

PREP TIME: 15 MINUTES ● START TO FINISH: 50 MINUTES
16 TO 20 SERVINGS

1½ lb extra lean (at least 90%) ground beef

1¼ cups chopped onions (about 2 medium)

1 can (10.75 oz) condensed Cheddar cheese soup

1¼ cups frozen mixed vegetables (from 1-lb bag), if desired

½ cup milk

2⅓ cups Original Bisquick mix

⅔ cup water

1⅓ cups shredded Cheddar cheese (about 5 oz)

1 Heat oven to 375°F. Generously spray bottom and sides of jelly roll pan, 15½ × 10½ × 1 inch, with cooking spray. Cook beef and onions in 12-inch skillet over medium heat, about 10 minutes, stirring occasionally, until beef is brown; drain. Stir in soup, vegetables and milk.

2 Stir Bisquick mix and water until moistened. Spread evenly in pan. Spread beef mixture over batter. Sprinkle with cheese.

3 Bake uncovered 35 minutes.

High Altitude (3500–6500 ft): Do not add cheese before baking. Bake 35 minutes. Sprinkle with cheese. Bake about 5 minutes longer or until cheese is melted.

1 SERVING: Calories 215 (Calories from Fat 98); Total Fat 11g (Saturated Fat 5g); Cholesterol 38mg; Sodium 446mg; Total Carbohydrate 14g (Dietary Fiber 0g; Sugars 5g); Protein 13g **% DAILY VALUE:** Vitamin A 10%; Vitamin C 2%; Calcium 10%; Iron 10% **EXCHANGES:** 1 Starch, 1 Lean Meat, 1 Fat **CARBOHYDRATE CHOICES:** 1

Quick Tip Mushroom-lovers can use 1½ cups of sliced fresh mushrooms in place of the onions. For an easy meal with lots of crowd appeal, put together a fresh-vegetable tray and a purchased dip while this recipe is in the oven. For dessert, top brownie squares with butter pecan or butter brickle ice cream and drizzle with chocolate sauce.

Cheesy Chicken Casserole

PREP TIME: 10 MINUTES ● START TO FINISH: 35 MINUTES
6 SERVINGS

2 cups cut-up cooked chicken

1 jar (16 oz) Cheddar cheese pasta sauce

1 bag (1 lb) frozen broccoli, carrots and cauliflower, thawed and drained

1¼ cups Original Bisquick mix

¼ cup grated Parmesan cheese

¼ cup firm butter or margarine

1 egg, slightly beaten

1 Heat oven to 400°F. Mix chicken, pasta sauce and vegetables. Pour into ungreased square pan, 9 × 9 × 2 inches.

2 Mix Bisquick mix, Parmesan cheese and butter with fork or pastry blender until crumbly. Stir in egg. Sprinkle over chicken mixture.

3 Bake uncovered 20 to 22 minutes or until topping is light golden brown.

High Altitude (3500–6500 ft): Heat chicken, pasta sauce and vegetables in 3-quart saucepan over medium heat, stirring occasionally, until hot and bubbly before pouring into square pan.

1 SERVING: Calories 420 (Calories from Fat 230); Total Fat 26g (Saturated Fat 11g); Cholesterol 72mg; Sodium 1072mg; Total Carbohydrate 24g (Dietary Fiber 2g; Sugars 4g); Protein 22g **% DAILY VALUE:** Vitamin A 25%; Vitamin C 25%; Calcium 20%; Iron 10% **EXCHANGES:** 1 Starch, 2 Medium-Fat Meat, 4 Fat, 1 Vegetable **CARBOHYDRATE CHOICES:** 1½

Quick Tip Using frozen cooked chicken, thawed, or two 5-oz cans of chunk chicken, drained, will give you a head start on this casserole. A 16-oz jar of purchased Alfredo pasta sauce can be used in place of the Cheddar cheese sauce for a change of flavor.

Baked Chili with Cornmeal Crust

PREP TIME: 20 MINUTES ● START TO FINISH: 1 HOUR
8 SERVINGS

1 lb lean (at least 80%) round beef

1 small onion, chopped (¼ cup)

1 tablespoon chili powder

1 tablespoon Original Bisquick mix

3 tablespoons water

1 can (14.5 oz) whole tomatoes, undrained

1 can (15.25 oz) whole kernel corn, drained

1 teaspoon salt

¾ cup Original Bisquick mix

¾ cup yellow cornmeal

⅔ cup milk

1 egg

1 Heat oven to 350°F. In 2-quart saucepan, cook beef and onion over medium-high heat 5 to 7 minutes, stirring frequently, until beef is thoroughly cooked; drain.

2 In small bowl, mix chili powder, 1 tablespoon Bisquick mix and the water; add to beef mixture. Stir in tomatoes, corn and salt; break up tomatoes. Heat to boiling, stirring frequently. Pour into ungreased 8-inch square (2-quart) glass baking dish or 2-quart casserole.

3 In medium bowl, stir all remaining ingredients with wire whisk or fork until blended. Pour over beef mixture.

4 Bake uncovered 35 to 40 minutes or until golden brown.

High Altitude (3500–6500 ft): Heat oven to 375°F.

1 SERVING: Calories 280 (Calories from Fat 90); Total Fat 10g (Saturated Fat 3.5g); Cholesterol 65mg; Sodium 680mg; Total Carbohydrate 32g (Dietary Fiber 3g; Sugars 5g); Protein 15g **% DAILY VALUE:** Vitamin A 10%; Vitamin C 8%; Calcium 8%; Iron 15% **EXCHANGES:** 2 Starch, 1½ Lean Meat, 1 Fat **CARBOHYDRATE CHOICES:** 2

Beef and Potato Biscuit Casserole

PREP TIME: 15 MINUTES ● **START TO FINISH: 45 MINUTES**
6 SERVINGS

1 lb lean (at least 80%) ground beef

1 large onion, chopped (1 cup)

1 package (8 oz) sliced fresh mushrooms

1 teaspoon salt

¾ cup water

2 tablespoons butter or margarine

1 cup plain mashed potato mix (dry)

¾ cup sour cream

⅔ cup Original Bisquick mix

2 teaspoons chopped fresh chives

1 egg

1 can (18 oz) creamy mushroom soup

3 tablespoons Original Bisquick mix

1 bag (1 lb) frozen broccoli cuts, thawed, drained

¼ cup ketchup

1 Heat oven to 400°F. In 12-inch skillet, cook beef, onion, mushrooms and salt over medium-high heat 5 to 7 minutes, stirring frequently, until beef is thoroughly cooked; drain.

2 While beef is cooking, in 2-quart saucepan, heat water and butter to boiling; remove from heat. Stir in potato mix and sour cream. Let stand 1 minute. Stir vigorously until smooth. Stir in ⅔ cup Bisquick mix, the chives and egg.

3 In small bowl, mix soup and 3 tablespoons Bisquick mix. Stir soup mixture, broccoli and ketchup into beef mixture. Heat to boiling. Boil uncovered 1 minute. Pour mixture into ungreased 3-quart casserole. Spoon potato mixture around edge of mixture in casserole.

4 Bake uncovered 25 to 30 minutes or until biscuits are light golden brown.

High Altitude (3500–6500 ft): In step 1, cook over high heat. Bake 30 to 35 minutes.

1 SERVING: Calories 460 (Calories from Fat 240); Total Fat 26g (Saturated Fat 11g); Cholesterol 115mg; Sodium 1410mg; Total Carbohydrate 35g (Dietary Fiber 4g; Sugars 8g); Protein 22g **% DAILY VALUE:** Vitamin A 25%; Vitamin C 30%; Calcium 15%; Iron 15% **EXCHANGES:** 1½ Starch, ½ Other Carbohydrate, 1 Vegetable, 2 Medium-Fat Meat, 3 Fat **CARBOHYDRATE CHOICES:** 2

Steak Bake

PREP TIME: 15 MINUTES ● **START TO FINISH: 35 MINUTES**
6 SERVINGS

1 lb beef sirloin steak, about
   ½ inch thick

¼ cup Original Bisquick mix

¼ teaspoon pepper

2 tablespoons vegetable oil

1 bag (16 oz) frozen green
   beans, potatoes, onions and
   red peppers (or other
   combination), thawed

1 can (14.5 oz) diced
   tomatoes, undrained

¼ cup water

1½ tablespoons soy sauce

1½ tablespoons molasses

1 cup Original Bisquick mix

⅓ cup milk

¼ teaspoon ground mustard

1 egg

1 tablespoon sesame seed,
   if desired

1 Heat oven to 400°F. Cut beef into 1-inch pieces. Mix beef, ¼ cup Bisquick mix and the pepper until beef is coated. Heat oil in 10-inch nonstick skillet over medium heat. Cook beef in oil, stirring occasionally, until brown.

2 Mix beef, vegetables, tomatoes, water, soy sauce and molasses in ungreased rectangular baking dish, 13 × 9 × 2 inches. Bake uncovered 15 minutes; stir.

3 Stir 1 cup Bisquick mix, the milk, mustard and egg until blended. Drop dough by 6 spoonfuls onto beef mixture. Sprinkle sesame seed over dough. Bake uncovered 20 to 25 minutes or until biscuits are golden brown.

High Altitude (3500–6500 ft): No change.

1 SERVING: Calories 340 (Calories from Fat 120); Total Fat 13.5g (Saturated Fat 3.5g); Cholesterol 70mg; Sodium 810mg; Total Carbohydrate 32g (Dietary Fiber 3g; Sugars 10g); Protein 22g. **% DAILY VALUE:** Vitamin A 8%; Vitamin C 30%; Calcium 10%; Iron 20% **EXCHANGES:** 1½ Starch, 2 Lean Meat, 1 Vegetable, 1 Fat **CARBOHYDRATE CHOICES:** 2

Quick Tip You'll find beef is easier to cut if it's partially frozen. Just pop it in the freezer about 1½ hours before you plan to slice it up for this recipe.

Italian Beef Bake

PREP TIME: 15 MINUTES ● START TO FINISH: 40 MINUTES
6 SERVINGS

1 lb lean (at least 80%) ground beef

1¼ cups tomato pasta sauce

1 cup shredded mozzarella cheese (4 oz)

2 cups Original Bisquick mix

¾ cup milk

¼ cup grated Parmesan cheese

Additional tomato pasta sauce, heated, if desired

1 Heat oven to 400°F. Spray 8-inch square (2-quart) glass baking dish with cooking spray. In 10-inch skillet, cook beef over medium-high heat 5 to 7 minutes, stirring frequently, until thoroughly cooked; drain.

2 Stir in 1¼ cups pasta sauce. Heat to boiling; spoon into baking dish. Sprinkle with mozzarella cheese.

3 Meanwhile, in medium bowl, stir Bisquick mix, milk and Parmesan cheese until soft dough forms. Drop dough by 12 tablespoonfuls onto beef mixture.

4 Bake uncovered 20 to 24 minutes or until topping is golden brown and toothpick inserted in topping comes out clean. Serve with pasta sauce.

High Altitude (3500–6500 ft): In step 2, stir in ¼ cup water with the pasta sauce.

1 SERVING: Calories 440 (Calories from Fat 190); Total Fat 21g (Saturated Fat 8g); Cholesterol 65mg; Sodium 960mg; Total Carbohydrate 38g (Dietary Fiber 2g; Sugars 8g); Protein 24g **% DAILY VALUE:** Vitamin A 8%; Vitamin C 4%; Calcium 30%; Iron 15% **EXCHANGES:** 2 Starch, ½ Other Carbohydrate, 2½ Medium-Fat Meat, 1½ Fat **CARBOHYDRATE CHOICES:** 2½

Quick Tip Add flavor to the topping by stirring in either 1 teaspoon Italian seasoning or ½ teaspoon onion or garlic powder with the Bisquick mix.

In 1952, Bisquick showed that one-dish meals were not only economical but also easy and satisfying. If only everything were this convenient!

Black-Eyed Pea Casserole

PREP TIME: 20 MINUTES ● **START TO FINISH: 1 HOUR 10 MINUTES**
12 SERVINGS

1½ lb lean (at least 80%) ground beef

2½ teaspoons seasoned salt

½ teaspoon pepper

1 medium green bell pepper, chopped (1 cup)

1 small jalapeño chile, finely chopped

⅔ cup chopped onion

1¼ teaspoons ground cumin

1 teaspoon garlic powder

¾ teaspoon chili powder

2 cans (15 to 16 oz each) black-eyed peas, drained, rinsed

1 can (14.5 oz) stewed tomatoes, undrained

1 cup Original Bisquick mix

1 cup yellow cornmeal

½ cup milk

½ cup water

1 Heat oven to 375°F. In 10-inch skillet, cook beef, seasoned salt, pepper, bell pepper, jalapeño chile and onion over medium-high heat 5 to 7 minutes, stirring occasionally, until beef is thoroughly cooked; drain.

2 Stir in cumin, garlic powder, chili powder, black-eyed peas and tomatoes. Spoon into ungreased 13 × 9-inch (3-quart) glass baking dish.

3 In medium bowl, stir all remaining ingredients with wire whisk or fork until blended. Pour evenly over beef mixture.

4 Bake uncovered 40 to 50 minutes or until light golden brown.

High Altitude (3500–6500 ft): No change.

1 SERVING: Calories 280 (Calories from Fat 80); Total Fat 8g (Saturated Fat 3g); Cholesterol 35mg; Sodium 690mg; Total Carbohydrate 33g (Dietary Fiber 4g; Sugars 4g); Protein 17g **% DAILY VALUE:** Vitamin A 4%; Vitamin C 10%; Calcium 6%; Iron 20% **EXCHANGES:** 2 Starch, 1½ Medium-Fat Meat **CARBOHYDRATE CHOICES:** 2

Hidden Sloppy Joes

PREP TIME: 15 MINUTES ● **START TO FINISH: 55 MINUTES**
8 SERVINGS

1 lb lean (at least 80%) ground beef

1 jar (14.5 oz) sloppy joe sauce

3½ cups Original Bisquick mix

⅔ cup milk

2 tablespoons butter or margarine, softened

2 eggs

1 Heat oven to 350°F. Generously spray 12-cup fluted tube cake pan with cooking spray. In 10-inch skillet, cook beef over medium-high heat 5 to 7 minutes, stirring frequently, until thoroughly cooked; drain. Stir in sloppy joe sauce.

2 In large bowl, stir Bisquick mix, milk, butter and eggs with wire whisk or fork until blended. Spoon about two-thirds of Bisquick mixture onto bottom and halfway up side of pan. Spoon beef mixture over Bisquick mixture. Drop remaining Bisquick mixture by spoonfuls to cover beef.

3 Bake 30 to 35 minutes or until light golden brown. Cool 5 minutes. Turn pan upside down onto heatproof plate; remove pan.

High Altitude (3500–6500 ft): No change.

1 SERVING: Calories 390 (Calories from Fat 160); Total Fat 17g (Saturated Fat 7g); Cholesterol 95mg; Sodium 1020mg; Total Carbohydrate 40g (Dietary Fiber 2g; Sugars 6g); Protein 17g **% DAILY VALUE:** Vitamin A 8%; Vitamin C 0%; Calcium 10%; Iron 20% **EXCHANGES:** 2 Starch, ½ Other Carbohydrate, 1½ Medium-Fat Meat, 2 Fat **CARBOHYDRATE CHOICES:** 2½

Quick Tip Like a little spice? Use bulk hot Italian sausage, cooked and well drained, for the ground beef.

Cowboy Casserole

**PREP TIME: 15 MINUTES ● START TO FINISH: 45 MINUTES
6 SERVINGS**

1 lb lean (at least 80%) ground beef

1 can (16 oz) baked beans

½ cup barbecue sauce

2 cups Original Bisquick mix

⅔ cup milk

1 tablespoon butter or margarine, softened

½ cup shredded Cheddar cheese (2 oz)

1 Heat oven to 425°F. In 10-inch skillet, cook beef over medium-high heat 5 to 7 minutes, stirring frequently, until thoroughly cooked; drain. Stir in baked beans and barbecue sauce. Heat to boiling, stirring occasionally. Pour into ungreased 2-quart casserole.

2 Meanwhile, in medium bowl, stir Bisquick mix, milk and butter until soft dough forms. Drop dough by 12 spoonfuls onto beef mixture.

3 Bake uncovered 18 to 22 minutes or until topping is golden brown. Sprinkle with cheese. Bake about 3 minutes longer or until cheese is melted.

High Altitude (3500–6500 ft): No change.

1 SERVING: Calories 470 (Calories from Fat 180); Total Fat 20g (Saturated Fat 8g); Cholesterol 70mg; Sodium 1160mg; Total Carbohydrate 50g (Dietary Fiber 5g; Sugars 14g); Protein 23g **% DAILY VALUE:** Vitamin A 6%; Vitamin C 2%; Calcium 20%; Iron 30% **EXCHANGES:** 2 Starch, 1½ Other Carbohydrate, 2½ Lean Meat, 2 Fat **CARBOHYDRATE CHOICES:** 3

Quick Tip Swing by the deli to pick up some creamy coleslaw to serve with this hearty casserole.

Beef and Bean Pot Pie

PREP TIME: 25 MINUTES ● **START TO FINISH: 50 MINUTES**
4 SERVINGS

1 lb lean (at least 80%)
ground beef

3 tablespoons packed brown
sugar

2 teaspoons dried minced
onion

1 can (16 oz) pork and beans,
undrained

1 can (8 oz) tomato sauce

1 cup Original Bisquick mix

3 tablespoons boiling water

1 tablespoon ketchup

1 Heat oven to 375°F. Spray 1½-quart round casserole with cooking spray. In 10-inch skillet, cook beef over medium-high heat 5 to 7 minutes, stirring frequently, until thoroughly cooked; drain. Stir in brown sugar, onion, pork and beans and tomato sauce. Pour into casserole; set aside.

2 In medium bowl, stir remaining ingredients until soft dough forms; beat vigorously 20 strokes. Place dough on surface sprinkled with Bisquick mix; gently roll in Bisquick mix to coat. Shape into a ball; knead about 10 times or until smooth. Press or roll into 7½-inch round or round the size of top of casserole. Place on beef mixture in casserole.

3 Bake uncovered 20 to 25 minutes or until crust is light golden brown.

High Altitude (3500–6500 ft): In step 1, heat beef and bean mixture to boiling before pouring into casserole.

1 SERVING: Calories 500 (Calories from Fat 160); Total Fat 18g (Saturated Fat 6g); Cholesterol 80mg; Sodium 1260mg; Total Carbohydrate 57g (Dietary Fiber 8g; Sugars 21g); Protein 29g **% DAILY VALUE:** Vitamin A 6%; Vitamin C 8%; Calcium 15%; Iron 40% **EXCHANGES:** 2 Starch, 2 Other Carbohydrate, 3 Medium-Fat Meat **CARBOHYDRATE CHOICES:** 4

Hot Dog and Bean Pot Pie: Substitute 1 pound of hot dogs, cut into ¼-inch slices, for the ground beef. Heat hot dogs with pork and beans mixture.

California Taco Chili Bake

PREP TIME: 10 MINUTES ● START TO FINISH: 35 MINUTES
6 SERVINGS

1 can (15 oz) chili with beans

1½ cups Original Bisquick mix

½ cup milk

¾ cup shredded Cheddar cheese (3 oz)

Paprika

1 cup shredded lettuce

2 medium tomatoes, chopped (1½ cups)

Additional shredded Cheddar cheese, if desired

1 Heat oven to 400°F. In 2-quart saucepan, heat chili, stirring occasionally, until hot.

2 In medium bowl, stir Bisquick mix and milk until soft dough forms. In ungreased 9- or 8-inch square (2-quart) glass baking dish, spread half of dough. Top with chili. Sprinkle with ¾ cup cheese. Drop remaining dough by 6 spoonfuls onto top. Sprinkle with paprika.

3 Bake uncovered about 25 minutes or until topping is light golden brown. Top with lettuce, tomatoes and additional cheese.

High Altitude (3500–6500 ft): Bake 25 to 28 minutes.

1 SERVING: Calories 280 (Calories from Fat 100); Total Fat 11g (Saturated Fat 5g); Cholesterol 25mg; Sodium 820mg; Total Carbohydrate 32g (Dietary Fiber 3g; Sugars 4g); Protein 12g **% DAILY VALUE:** Vitamin A 15%; Vitamin C 15%; Calcium 15%; Iron 10% **EXCHANGES:** 2 Starch, 1 Medium-Fat Meat, 1 Fat **CARBOHYDRATE CHOICES:** 2

Who is the "Hostess with the Mostest" in this 1957 cookbook? You are, with Betty and a box of Bisquick!

Roast Beef Pot Pie

PREP TIME: 15 MINUTES ● **START TO FINISH: 45 MINUTES**
12 SERVINGS

2 cups cubed cooked
    roast beef

2 jars (12 oz each) beef gravy

2 bags (1 lb each) frozen
    potatoes, carrots, celery
    and onions

1 teaspoon seasoned salt

2 cups Original Bisquick mix

1½ cups milk

1 Heat oven to 400°F. Heat beef, gravy, frozen vegetables and seasoned salt to boiling in 4-quart Dutch oven, stirring constantly. Boil and stir 1 minute. Spread in ungreased 3-quart casserole.

2 Stir Bisquick mix and milk until blended. Pour evenly over beef mixture.

3 Bake uncovered about 30 minutes or until light brown.

High Altitude (3500–6500 ft): Bake uncovered about 35 minutes.

1 SERVING: Calories 215 (Calories from Fat 70); Total Fat 8g (Saturated Fat 3g); Cholesterol 20mg; Sodium 860mg; Carbohydrate 25g (Dietary Fiber 2g; Sugars 5g); Protein 11g **% DAILY VALUE:** Vitamin A 78%; Vitamin C 2%; Calcium 8%; Iron 10% **EXCHANGES:** 1½ Starch, 1 High-Fat Meat **CARBOHYDRATE CHOICES:** 1½

Quick Tip Love herbs? Add extra flavor to the topping by stirring in either 1 teaspoon Italian seasoning, 1 teaspoon dried dill weed or ½ teaspoon garlic or onion powder with the Bisquick mix. At Thanksgiving, turn leftovers into Turkey Pot Pie by using 2 cups cubed roasted turkey and leftover gravy or jarred chicken gravy instead of the roast beef and beef gravy.

Roast Beef and Swiss Sandwich Bake

PREP TIME: 10 MINUTES ● **START TO FINISH: 1 HOUR 5 MINUTES**
6 SERVINGS

2 cups Original Bisquick mix

1 cup milk

2 tablespoons yellow
   mustard

1 egg

1 package (6 oz) thinly sliced
   cooked roast beef, chopped

1 cup shredded Swiss cheese
   (4 oz)

Freshly ground pepper,
   if desired

1 Heat oven to 350°F. Grease square baking dish, 8 × 8 × 2 inches.

2 Stir Bisquick mix, milk, mustard and egg until blended. Pour half of the batter into baking dish. Top with half of the roast beef and ½ cup of the cheese. Top with remaining roast beef. Pour remaining batter over roast beef.

3 Bake uncovered 45 to 50 minutes or until golden brown and center is set. Sprinkle with remaining ½ cup cheese and the pepper. Let stand 5 minutes before serving.

High Altitude (3500–6500 ft): Sprinkle with cheese to within ¼ inch of edges of baking dish. Bake 47 to 52 minutes.

1 SERVING: Calories 330 (Calories from Fat 155); Total Fat 17g (Saturated Fat 7g); Cholesterol 75mg; Sodium 730mg; Carbohydrate 27g (Dietary Fiber 1g; Sugars 3g); Protein 18g **% DAILY VALUE:** Vitamin A 6%; Vitamin C 4%; Calcium 22%; Iron 10% **EXCHANGES:** 1 Starch, 1½ High-Fat Meat, 2 Vegetable, 1 Fat **CARBOHYDRATE CHOICES:** 2

Quick Tip Vary this dish by using thinly sliced cooked turkey or chicken instead of roast beef and shredded Cheddar cheese instead of Swiss.

Beef Pot Pie with Potato Crust

PREP TIME: 20 MINUTES ● **START TO FINISH: 55 MINUTES**
6 SERVINGS

1 slice (½ lb) deli roast beef, cubed (1½ cups)

2 cups frozen mixed vegetables

1 medium onion, chopped (½ cup)

1 jar (12 oz) beef gravy

⅔ cup plain mashed potato mix (dry)

⅔ cup hot water

1½ cups Original Bisquick mix

3 tablespoons milk

1 tablespoon freeze-dried chopped chives

1 Heat oven to 375°F. In 2-quart saucepan, heat beef, frozen vegetables, onion and gravy to boiling over medium heat, stirring frequently. Boil and stir 1 minute. Keep warm.

2 In medium bowl, stir potato mix and hot water until well mixed; let stand until water is absorbed. Stir in Bisquick mix, milk and chives until dough forms.

3 Place dough on surface sprinkled with Bisquick mix; gently roll in Bisquick mix to coat. Shape into a ball; knead 10 times. Press into 11 × 7-inch rectangle. Fold dough cross-wise into thirds.

4 Pour beef mixture into ungreased 11 × 7-inch (2-quart) glass baking dish. Carefully unfold dough onto beef mixture.

5 Bake uncovered 30 to 35 minutes or until crust is golden brown.

High Altitude (3500–6500 ft): Bake uncovered 35 to 40 minutes.

1 SERVING: Calories 260 (Calories from Fat 60); Total Fat 6g (Saturated Fat 2.5g); Cholesterol 20mg; Sodium 1100mg; Total Carbohydrate 37g (Dietary Fiber 4g; Sugars 5g); Protein 14g **% DAILY VALUE:** Vitamin A 50%; Vitamin C 6%; Calcium 6%; Iron 15% **EXCHANGES:** 2 Starch, 1 Vegetable, 1 Lean Meat, ½ Fat **CARBOHYDRATE CHOICES:** 2½

Chicken Pot Pie with Potato Crust: Substitute 1½ cups cooked cubed chicken for the beef and chicken gravy for beef gravy.

Quick Tip It's important that the beef mixture is warm when the crust is placed on top. The heat from below helps cook the topping evenly and it won't be soggy on the bottom.

Italian Meatball and Biscuit Bake

PREP TIME: 20 MINUTES ● **START TO FINISH: 55 MINUTES**
8 SERVINGS

1 bag (16 oz) frozen cooked Italian meatballs, thawed

1 jar (26 oz) tomato pasta sauce

2¼ cups Original Bisquick mix

½ cup milk

1 tablespoon olive or vegetable oil

1½ cups shredded Italian-style five-cheese blend or mozzarella cheese (6 oz)

1 Heat oven to 350°F. Spray 13 × 9-inch (3-quart) glass baking dish with cooking spray. Place meatballs in baking dish. Pour pasta sauce over meatballs; stir to coat.

2 In medium bowl, stir Bisquick mix and milk until soft dough forms. Place dough on surface sprinkled with Bisquick mix; knead 10 times. Roll dough into 12 × 9-inch rectangle. Brush oil over dough; sprinkle with 1 cup of the cheese. Roll up jelly-roll style, starting with 12-inch side. Cut crosswise into 16 (¾-inch) pinwheel slices.

3 Push meatballs to center of dish; place 5 dough pinwheels along each side of dish and 3 on each end.

4 Bake 25 to 30 minutes or until biscuits are golden brown. Sprinkle with remaining ½ cup cheese. Bake about 5 minutes longer or until cheese is melted.

High Altitude (3500–6500 ft): No change.

1 SERVING: Calories 480 (Calories from Fat 210); Total Fat 23g (Saturated Fat 9g); Cholesterol 75mg; Sodium 1380mg; Total Carbohydrate 46g (Dietary Fiber 2g; Sugars 12g); Protein 21g **% DAILY VALUE:** Vitamin A 15%; Vitamin C 8%; Calcium 25%; Iron 20% **EXCHANGES:** 2 Starch, 1 Other Carbohydrate, 2 High-Fat Meat, 1 Fat **CARBOHYDRATE CHOICES:** 3

During World War II, Bisquick helped out on the home front, extending precious supplies of meat, sugar, and other goods. Truly one of Bisquick's finest hours!

Easy Hamburger Pot Pie

PREP TIME: 15 MINUTES ● START TO FINISH: 50 MINUTES
6 SERVINGS (1 CUP EACH)

1 lb lean (at least 80%) ground beef

1½ teaspoons onion powder

½ teaspoon salt

¾ teaspoon pepper

1 bag (1 lb) frozen mixed vegetables, thawed, drained

1 can (10.75 oz) condensed tomato soup

1 cup Original Bisquick mix

½ cup milk

1 egg

1 Heat oven to 375°F. In 12-inch skillet, cook beef, onion powder, salt and pepper over medium-high heat 5 to 7 minutes, stirring frequently, until beef is thoroughly cooked; drain.

2 Stir vegetables and soup into beef; heat to boiling. Spoon into ungreased 2-quart casserole.

3 In small bowl, stir remaining ingredients with wire whisk or fork until blended. Pour over hot beef mixture.

4 Bake 28 to 33 minutes or until crust is golden brown.

High Altitude (3500–6500 ft): No change.

1 SERVING: Calories 320 (Calories from Fat 120); Total Fat 13g (Saturated Fat 4.5g); Cholesterol 85mg; Sodium 820mg; Total Carbohydrate 32g (Dietary Fiber 4g; Sugars 8g); Protein 19g **% DAILY VALUE:** Vitamin A 70%; Vitamin C 6%; Calcium 8%; Iron 15% **EXCHANGES:** ½ Starch, 1½ Other Carbohydrate, 1 Vegetable, 2 Medium-Fat Meat, ½ Fat **CARBOHYDRATE CHOICES:** 2

Easy Turkey Pot Pie: Substitute 1 pound ground turkey breast for the ground beef.

Heart Smart Chicken Pot Pie

PREP TIME: 10 MINUTES ● START TO FINISH: 30 MINUTES
3 SERVINGS

½ cup canned condensed reduced-fat reduced-sodium cream of chicken soup

¼ cup fat-free (skim) milk

1 cup frozen mixed vegetables

½ cup diced cooked chicken breast

½ cup Bisquick Heart Smart mix

¼ cup fat-free (skim) milk

2 tablespoons fat-free egg product or 1 egg white

1 Heat oven to 400°F. In ungreased microwavable 1-quart casserole, mix soup and ¼ cup milk; stir in vegetables and chicken. Microwave uncovered on High 3 minutes; stir.

2 In small bowl, stir remaining ingredients with wire whisk or fork until blended. Pour over chicken mixture.

3 Bake uncovered about 20 minutes or until crust is golden brown.

High Altitude (3500–6500 ft): In step 1, increase milk to ⅓ cup. Bake 25 minutes.

1 SERVING: Calories 190 (Calories from Fat 30); Total Fat 3.5g (Saturated Fat 0.5g); Cholesterol 20mg; Sodium 450mg; Total Carbohydrate 27g (Dietary Fiber 3g; Sugars 6g); Protein 14g **% DAILY VALUE:** Vitamin A 60%; Vitamin C 0%; Calcium 15%; Iron 10% **EXCHANGES:** 1½ Starch, ½ Other Carbohydrate, 1½ Very Lean Meat **CARBOHYDRATE CHOICES:** 2

Quick Tip If you are a broccoli lover, use frozen broccoli cuts for the mixed vegetables.

Slow Cooker
Chicken Stroganoff Pot Pie

PREP TIME: 20 MINUTES ● **START TO FINISH: 5 HOURS 30 MINUTES**
4 SERVINGS

1 envelope (0.87 to 1.2 oz) chicken gravy mix

1 can (10.5 oz) condensed chicken broth

1 lb boneless skinless chicken breasts, cut into 1-inch pieces

1 bag (1 lb) frozen stew vegetables, thawed, drained

1 jar (4.5 oz) sliced mushrooms, drained

1 cup frozen sweet peas, thawed, drained

½ cup sour cream

1 tablespoon all-purpose flour

1½ cups Original Bisquick mix

4 medium green onions, chopped (¼ cup)

½ cup milk

1 In 3½- to 6-quart slow cooker, stir gravy mix and broth until smooth. Stir in chicken, stew vegetables and mushrooms.

2 Cover; cook on Low heat setting about 4 hours or until chicken is tender.

3 Stir in peas. In small bowl, mix sour cream and flour until blended. Stir into chicken mixture. Increase heat setting to High. Cover; cook 20 minutes.

4 In small bowl, stir Bisquick mix and onions; stir in milk just until moistened. Drop dough by rounded tablespoonfuls onto hot chicken mixture. Cover; cook on High heat setting 45 to 50 minutes or until toothpick inserted in center of topping comes out clean. Serve immediately.

High Altitude (3500–6500 ft): After adding Bisquick dough, cover and cook on High heat setting 55 to 60 minutes.

1 SERVING: Calories 550 (Calories from Fat 160); Total Fat 17g (Saturated Fat 7g); Cholesterol 90mg; Sodium 1660mg; Total Carbohydrate 59g (Dietary Fiber 8g; Sugars 10g); Protein 40g **% DAILY VALUE:** Vitamin A 110%; Vitamin C 6%; Calcium 20%; Iron 25% **EXCHANGES:** 2½ Starch, 1 Other Carbohydrate, 1 Vegetable, 4½ Very Lean Meat, 2½ Fat **CARBOHYDRATE CHOICES:** 4

Quick Tip If you like more sour cream flavor, use a 1-ounce envelope of beef stroganoff mix instead of chicken gravy.

Apple-Cranberry-Sage Chicken

PREP TIME: 20 MINUTES ● **START TO FINISH: 1 HOUR 5 MINUTES**
4 SERVINGS

⅔ cup grape jelly

2 tablespoons butter or margarine

1 large unpeeled red cooking apple, cut into 2-inch chunks

1 medium stalk celery, sliced (½ cup)

½ cup fresh or frozen (thawed) cranberries

¾ cup Original Bisquick mix

½ teaspoon ground sage

¾ teaspoon chopped fresh or ¼ teaspoon dried thyme leaves

4 boneless skinless chicken breasts (about 1¼ lb)

2 tablespoons water

1 Heat oven to 350°F. In 1½-quart saucepan, melt jelly and butter over medium heat, stirring occasionally. Stir in apple, celery and cranberries; remove from heat.

2 In small bowl, stir Bisquick mix, sage and thyme. Dip chicken into water, then coat with Bisquick mixture.

3 Spray 10-inch skillet with cooking spray; heat over medium-high heat. Cook chicken in skillet 6 to 8 minutes, turning once, until coating is brown.

4 In ungreased 13 × 9-inch (3-quart) glass baking dish, place chicken. Spoon cranberry mixture over chicken.

5 Bake 40 to 45 minutes or until juice of chicken is clear when center of thickest part is cut (170°F).

High Altitude (3500–6500 ft): No change.

1 SERVING: Calories 490 (Calories from Fat 120); Total Fat 13g (Saturated Fat 6g); Cholesterol 100mg; Sodium 420mg; Total Carbohydrate 58g (Dietary Fiber 3g; Sugars 31g); Protein 33g **% DAILY VALUE:** Vitamin A 6%; Vitamin C 8%; Calcium 6%; Iron 10% **EXCHANGES:** 2 Starch, 2 Other Carbohydrate, 3½ Very Lean Meat, 2 Fat **CARBOHYDRATE CHOICES:** 4

Alfredo Chicken Bake

PREP TIME: 15 MINUTES ● START TO FINISH: 40 MINUTES
4 SERVINGS

1 package (9 oz) frozen diced cooked chicken, thawed

½ cup frozen baby sweet peas

½ cup shredded Swiss cheese (2 oz)

¾ cup Alfredo pasta sauce

2 tablespoons slivered almonds

1 cup Original Bisquick mix

⅓ cup milk

1 Heat oven to 425°F. In 1 ½-quart saucepan, heat chicken, peas, cheese, Alfredo sauce and almonds to boiling over medium-high heat. Pour into ungreased 1 ½-quart casserole.

2 In small bowl, stir Bisquick mix and milk until soft dough forms. Drop dough by about 12 spoonfuls onto chicken mixture.

3 Bake uncovered 20 to 25 minutes or until golden brown.

High Altitude (3500-6500 ft): In step 1, stir ¼ cup water into chicken mixture. In step 3, bake uncovered 25 to 30 minutes.

1 SERVING: Calories 490 (Calories from Fat 260); Total Fat 29g (Saturated Fat 14g); Cholesterol 115mg; Sodium 850mg, Total Carbohydrate 27g (Dietary Fiber 2g; Sugars 3g); Protein 30g **% DAILY VALUE:** Vitamin A 20%; Vitamin C 0%, Calcium 30%; Iron 10% **EXCHANGES:** 1½ starch, ½ Other Carbohydrate, 3½ Lean Meat, 3½ Fat **CARBOHYDRATE CHOICES:** 2

Thai Chicken with Spicy Peanut Sauce

PREP TIME: 10 MINUTES ● **START TO FINISH: 40 MINUTES**
4 SERVINGS

CHICKEN

3 tablespoons margarine or butter

1 cup Original Bisquick mix

1½ teaspoons curry powder

1½ teaspoons garlic powder

1 teaspoon ground ginger

4 boneless skinless chicken breast halves (about 1¼ lb)

⅓ cup milk

SPICY PEANUT SAUCE

½ cup plain yogurt

¼ cup creamy peanut butter

½ cup milk

1 tablespoon soy sauce

⅛ teaspoon ground red pepper (cayenne)

2 tablespoons cocktail peanuts, finely chopped

1 Heat oven to 425°F. Melt margarine in rectangular baking dish, 13 × 9 × 2 inches, in oven.

2 Stir Bisquick mix, curry powder, garlic powder and ginger. Dip chicken into milk, then coat with Bisquick mixture. Place in dish.

3 Bake uncovered 20 minutes; turn chicken. Bake about 10 minutes longer or until juice of chicken is no longer pink when centers of thickest pieces are cut. While chicken is baking, make Spicy Peanut Sauce. To make the sauce, mix all ingredients except peanuts in 10-inch nonstick skillet. Cook over medium heat 3 to 4 minutes, stirring occasionally, until mixture begins to thicken. Serve it over chicken. Sprinkle with peanuts.

High Altitude (3500–6500 ft): No change.

1 SERVING: Calories 540 (Calories from Fat 245); Total Fat 27g (Saturated Fat 6g); Cholesterol 90mg; Sodium 1021mg; Total Carbohydrate 29g (Dietary Fiber 2g; Sugars 7g); Protein 44g **% DAILY VALUE:** Vitamin A 10%; Vitamin C 4%; Calcium 20%; Iron 15% **EXCHANGES:** 1½ Starch, 3½ Lean Meat, 4 Fat **CARBOHYDRATE CHOICES:** 2

Quick Tip Entertaining? Serve this spicy chicken over hot cooked jasmine rice with steamed carrots and broccoli or broccolini a new kind of broccoli with sparse flowerets.

Barbecue Crispy Chicken Melts

PREP TIME: 10 MINUTES ● **START TO FINISH: 45 MINUTES**
4 SERVINGS

3 tablespoons butter or margarine

½ cup Original Bisquick mix

¼ teaspoon pepper

¼ cup milk

4 boneless skinless chicken breasts (about 1¼ lb)

¼ cup barbecue sauce

½ cup shredded Cheddar cheese (2 oz)

1 Heat oven to 425°F. In 13 × 9-inch pan, heat butter in oven 2 to 3 minutes or until melted.

2 In shallow dish, stir Bisquick mix and pepper. Pour milk into small bowl. Coat chicken with Bisquick mixture, then dip in milk; coat again with Bisquick mixture. Place in pan.

3 Bake about 30 minutes or until juice of chicken is clear when center of thickest part is cut (170°F).

4 In small microwavable bowl, microwave barbecue sauce uncovered on High about 30 seconds or until warm. Spoon sauce evenly over chicken; top with cheese.

High Altitude (3500–6500 ft): No change.

1 SERVING: Calories 400 (Calories from Fat 180); Total Fat 20g (Saturated Fat 10g); Cholesterol 125mg; Sodium 580mg; Total Carbohydrate 17g (Dietary Fiber 0g; Sugars 6g); Protein 36g **% DAILY VALUE:** Vitamin A 10%; Vitamin C 0%; Calcium 15%; Iron 10% **EXCHANGES:** ½ Starch, ½ Other Carbohydrate, 5 Very Lean Meat, 3½ Fat **CARBOHYDRATE CHOICES:** 1

Lemon-Ginger Chicken

PREP TIME: 15 MINUTES ● **START TO FINISH: 15 MINUTES**
4 SERVINGS

CHICKEN

4 boneless skinless chicken
   breast halves (about 1¼ lb)

½ cup Original Bisquick mix

¼ cup plain bread crumbs

1 tablespoon grated lemon
   peel

½ teaspoon grated
   gingerroot

½ cup water

3 tablespoons vegetable oil

LEMON SAUCE

¼ cup lemon juice

¼ cup water

3 tablespoons sugar

1 tablespoon cornstarch

¼ teaspoon grated gingerroot

1 drop yellow food color,
   if desired

Lemon slices, if desired

1 Flatten each chicken breast half to about ¼-inch thickness between sheets of waxed paper or plastic wrap.

2 Mix Bisquick mix, bread crumbs, lemon peel and gingerroot. Pour water into shallow glass or plastic bowl. Dip chicken into water, then coat with Bisquick mixture.

3 Heat oil in 12-inch nonstick skillet over medium heat. Cook chicken in oil 8 to 10 minutes, turning once, until no longer pink in center.

4 While chicken is cooking, make sauce. To make Lemon Sauce, mix all ingredients except lemon slices in 1-quart saucepan. Heat over medium heat, stirring occasionally, until thickened and bubbly. Pour it over chicken. Garnish with lemon slices.

High Altitude (3500–6500 ft): Cook chicken in oil 11 to 13 minutes or until meat thermometer inserted in center of chicken reads 170°F.

1 SERVING: Calories 375 (Calories from Fat 130); Total Fat 15g (Saturated Fat 3g); Cholesterol 82mg; Sodium 332mg; Total Carbohydrate 25g (Dietary Fiber 1g; Sugars 11g); Protein 35g **% DAILY VALUE:** Vitamin A 0%; Vitamin C 4%; Calcium 6%; Iron 10% **EXCHANGES:** 2 Starch, 3½ Lean Meat, 2 Fat **CARBOHYDRATE CHOICES:** 2

Quick Tip Flatten chicken breasts by pounding with a meat mallet, rolling pin or even the heel of your hand. Thinner chicken breasts cook more evenly and quickly, so it's a good step to take time to flatten them, even when you're short on time.

Chicken Tenders and Broccoli Bake

PREP TIME: 15 MINUTES ● **START TO FINISH: 50 MINUTES**
5 SERVINGS

1 can (10¾ oz) condensed
cream of chicken soup

1 can (14.75 oz) cream-style
corn

6 cups frozen broccoli florets

¾ cup Original Bisquick mix

1 teaspoon paprika

¼ cup butter or margarine

1 package (about 14 oz)
uncooked chicken breast
tenders (not breaded)

1 can (2.8 oz) French-fried
onions

1 Heat oven to 400°F. In ungreased 13 × 9-inch (3-quart) glass baking dish, mix soup, corn and frozen broccoli.

2 In 1-gallon resealable food-storage plastic bag, mix Bisquick mix and paprika. In medium microwavable bowl, microwave butter on High 1 to 2 minutes or until melted. Dip chicken in butter, then place in bag with Bisquick mixture. Seal bag; shake until chicken is coated. Place chicken on corn mixture.

3 Bake 25 to 30 minutes or until chicken is no longer pink in center. Sprinkle with onions. Bake 2 to 3 minutes longer or until onions are golden.

High Altitude (3500–6500 ft): Heat oven to 425°F. In step 3, bake 30 to 35 minutes. Sprinkle with onions. Bake 2 to 3 minutes longer.

1 SERVING: Calories 530 (Calories from Fat 220); Total Fat 25g (Saturated Fat 10g); Cholesterol 65mg; Sodium 1140mg; Total Carbohydrate 48g (Dietary Fiber 7g; Sugars 6g); Protein 28g **% DAILY VALUE:** Vitamin A 50%; Vitamin C 60%; Calcium 8%; Iron 15% **EXCHANGES:** 2 Starch, 1 Other Carbohydrate, 1 Vegetable, 3 Very Lean Meat, 4 Fat **CARBOHYDRATE CHOICES:** 3

Quick Tip For a cheesy version of this hearty dinner, use a 10¾-ounce can of condensed Cheddar cheese soup instead of the cream of chicken soup.

Fajita Chicken Pot Pie

PREP TIME: 15 MINUTES ● **START TO FINISH: 45 MINUTES**
4 SERVINGS

1 teaspoon vegetable oil

½ medium bell pepper, cut into ½-inch strips

2 cups cut-up cooked chicken

1¾ cups chunky-style salsa

¼ cup water

1 cup Original Bisquick mix

⅓ cup shredded Monterey Jack cheese

½ cup milk

1 Heat oven to 400°F. In 10-inch skillet, heat oil over medium heat. Cook bell pepper in oil, stirring occasionally, until crisp-tender. Stir in chicken, salsa and water. Cook 1 to 2 minutes, stirring occasionally, until bubbly. Pour into ungreased 1½-quart casserole.

2 In small bowl, stir remaining ingredients with wire whisk or fork until blended. Pour over chicken mixture; carefully spread almost to edge of casserole.

3 Bake uncovered about 30 minutes or until light golden brown.

High Altitude (3500–6500 ft): Bake 33 to 35 minutes.

1 SERVING: Calories 340 (Calories from Fat 120); Total Fat 14g (Saturated Fat 5g); Cholesterol 70mg; Sodium 1170mg; Total Carbohydrate 29g (Dietary Fiber 3g; Sugars 6g); Protein 27g **% DAILY VALUE:** Vitamin A 10%; Vitamin C 10%; Calcium 20%; Iron 15% **EXCHANGES:** 1 Starch, 1 Other Carbohydrate, 3½ Lean Meat, ½ Fat **CARBOHYDRATE CHOICES:** 2

Italian Chicken Fingers

PREP TIME: 20 MINUTES ● **START TO FINISH: 40 MINUTES**
4 SERVINGS

1 egg

1 package (14 oz) uncooked chicken breast tenders (not breaded)

1¼ cups Original Bisquick mix

1 teaspoon Italian seasoning

3 tablespoons butter or margarine, melted

1 cup tomato pasta sauce, heated

1 Heat oven to 450°F. Spray 15 × 10 × 1-inch pan with cooking spray. In medium bowl, beat egg slightly. Add chicken; toss to coat.

2 In resealable food-storage plastic bag, place Bisquick mix and Italian seasoning; seal bag and shake to mix. Add chicken; seal bag and shake to coat chicken with Bisquick mixture. Place chicken in single layer in pan. Drizzle with butter.

3 Bake 14 to 16 minutes, turning chicken after 6 minutes, until chicken is brown and crisp on the outside and no longer pink in center. Serve with pasta sauce for dipping.

High Altitude (3500–6500 ft): No change.

1 SERVING: Calories 410 (Calories from Fat 160); Total Fat 17g (Saturated Fat 8g); Cholesterol 120mg; Sodium 950mg; Total Carbohydrate 36g (Dietary Fiber 2g; Sugars 7g); Protein 26g **% DAILY VALUE:** Vitamin A 15%; Vitamin C 6%; Calcium 6%; Iron 10% **EXCHANGES:** 1½ Starch, 1 Other Carbohydrate, 3 Lean Meat, 1½ Fat **CARBOHYDRATE CHOICES:** 2½

Ultimate Oven-Fried Chicken

PREP TIME: 10 MINUTES ● START TO FINISH: 1 HOUR 5 MINUTES
12 SERVINGS

1 cup buttermilk

12 boneless skinless chicken breast halves (3¾ lb)

1½ cups cornflakes cereal

1½ cups Original Bisquick mix

2 envelopes (1 oz each) ranch dressing mix

Cooking spray

1 Heat oven to 400°F. Spray jelly roll pan, 15½ × 10½ × 1 inch, with cooking spray; set aside. Pour buttermilk into rectangular baking dish, 13 × 9 ×2 inches. Add chicken; turn to coat. Let stand 5 minutes.

2 Divide cereal between two 1-gallon resealable plastic food-storage bags, placing ¾ cup cereal in each bag; crush with rolling pin. Add ¾ cup of the Bisquick mix and 1 envelope dressing mix (dry) to cereal in each bag. Remove chicken from buttermilk; discard buttermilk. Add a few pieces of chicken at a time to cereal mixture. Seal bag; shake to coat.

3 Place chicken in jelly roll pan. Spray with cooking spray. Bake uncovered 40 to 50 minutes or until juice of chicken is no longer pink when centers of thickest pieces are cut.

High Altitude (3500–6500 ft): No change.

1 SERVING: Calories 344 (Calories from Fat 34); Total Fat 4g (Saturated Fat 1g); Cholesterol 83mg; Sodium 855mg; Total Carbohydrate 16g (Dietary Fiber 0g; Sugars 1g); Protein 35g **% DAILY VALUE:** Vitamin A 8%; Vitamin C 4%; Calcium 15%; Iron 10% **EXCHANGES:** 1 Starch, 4 Very Lean Meat **CARBOHYDRATE CHOICES:** 1

Quick Tip Did you know that buttermilk, with its thick consistency and slightly tangy flavor, has long been a cook's "secret" for making fried chicken? You can enjoy this chicken hot or cold—if you'd like to make and take, bake it the night before, and then pack it up for a picnic in the park the next day!

Easy Italian Chicken Pie

**PREP TIME: 10 MINUTES ● START TO FINISH: 45 MINUTES
5 SERVINGS**

2 cups cubed cooked chicken

⅓ cup thinly sliced green or red bell pepper

½ cup pizza sauce

1 cup shredded Italian-style cheese blend, pizza cheese blend or mozzarella cheese (4 oz)

½ cup Original Bisquick mix

1 cup milk

1 egg

1 Heat oven to 400°F. Spray 9-inch glass pie plate with cooking spray. In pie plate, stir chicken, bell pepper and pizza sauce; spread evenly. Sprinkle with cheese.

2 In small bowl, stir remaining ingredients with wire whisk or fork until blended. Pour into pie plate.

3 Bake 25 to 30 minutes or until knife inserted in center comes out clean. Let stand 5 minutes before serving.

High Altitude (3500–6500 ft): Increase Bisquick to ¾ cup. Bake 30 to 35 minutes.

1 SERVING: Calories 270 (Calories from Fat 120); Total Fat 13g (Saturated Fat 6g); Cholesterol 115mg; Sodium 500mg; Total Carbohydrate 13g (Dietary Fiber 0g; Sugars 5g); Protein 25g **% DAILY VALUE:** Vitamin A 8%; Vitamin C 6%; Calcium 20%; Iron 8% **EXCHANGES:** 1 Other Carbohydrate, 3½ Lean Meat, ½ Fat **CARBOHYDRATE CHOICES:** 1

Quick Tip This easy pie is a great way to use leftover cooked meat. Use 2 cups cooked turkey, pork or beef instead of the chicken.

Curry Chicken Pie

PREP TIME: 10 MINUTES ● START TO FINISH: 45 MINUTES
2 SERVINGS

CHICKEN MIXTURE

1 cup cubed cooked chicken breast

1½ cups frozen mixed vegetables, thawed, drained

½ to 1 teaspoon curry powder

1 can (18.5 oz) ready-to-serve creamy chicken corn chowder

TOPPING

⅔ cup Original Bisquick mix

⅓ cup milk

1 tablespoon chopped fresh parsley

1 Heat oven to 425°F. Spray 1½-quart round casserole with cooking spray. In casserole, stir together chicken mixture ingredients; spread evenly.

2 In small bowl, stir topping ingredients with wire whisk or fork until blended. Pour over chicken mixture.

3 Bake uncovered 30 to 35 minutes or until top is golden brown.

High Altitude (3500–6500 ft): Use 1½-quart round microwavable casserole. In step 1, after spreading chicken mixture in casserole, cover and microwave on High about 3 minutes. Uncover; stir. Then, pour topping over hot chicken mixture and bake as directed.

1 SERVING: Calories 740 (Calories from Fat 270); Total Fat 30g (Saturated Fat 8g); Cholesterol 55mg; Sodium 2040mg; Total Carbohydrate 87g (Dietary Fiber 11g; Sugars 13g); Protein 31g **% DAILY VALUE:** Vitamin A 160%; Vitamin C 4%; Calcium 20%; Iron 25% **EXCHANGES:** 4 Starch, 1½ Other Carbohydrate, 1 Vegetable, 2½ Lean Meat, 4 Fat **CARBOHYDRATE CHOICES:** 6

A hint to all wives in the 1940s—be kind to your husband with great Bisquick meals, and he'll be sure to return the favor.

Chicken-Veggie Casserole

PREP TIME: 20 MINUTES ● **START TO FINISH: 45 MINUTES**
6 SERVINGS

1 can (10.75 oz) condensed Cheddar cheese soup

1 cup milk

2 tablespoons dried minced onion

2 cups frozen mixed vegetables, thawed, drained

1½ cups cut-up cooked chicken

2 cups Original Bisquick mix

¼ cup sliced green onions

2 tablespoons mayonnaise or salad dressing

1 egg

1 Heat oven to 400°F. In 3-quart saucepan, heat soup, milk and dried minced onion to boiling, stirring constantly. Stir in vegetables and chicken. Pour into ungreased 11 × 7-inch (2-quart) glass baking dish.

2 In medium bowl, mix all remaining ingredients with fork until crumbly. Sprinkle over chicken mixture.

3 Bake uncovered about 25 minutes or until topping is golden brown and soup is bubbly.

High Altitude (3500–6500 ft): Use 13 x 9-inch (3-quart) glass baking dish.

1 SERVING: Calories 400 (Calories from Fat 150); Total Fat 17g (Saturated Fat 5g); Cholesterol 80mg; Sodium 1050mg; Total Carbohydrate 42g (Dietary Fiber 4g; Sugars 7g); Protein 19g **% DAILY VALUE:** Vitamin A 80%; Vitamin C 4%; Calcium 15%; Iron 15% **EXCHANGES:** 2½ Starch, ½ Other Carbohydrate, 1½ Lean Meat, 2 Fat **CARBOHYDRATE CHOICES:** 3

Quick Tip For extra crunch and flavor, sprinkle the top with toasted almonds or a can of French-fried onions after baking.

Easy Chicken Pot Pie

PREP TIME: 10 MINUTES ● **START TO FINISH: 40 MINUTES**
6 SERVINGS

1 bag (1 lb) frozen mixed
vegetables, thawed, drained

1 cup diced cooked chicken

1 can (10.75 oz) condensed
cream of chicken soup

1 cup Original Bisquick mix

½ cup milk

1 egg

1 Heat oven to 400°F. In ungreased 2-quart casserole, mix vegetables, chicken and soup until blended.

2 In medium bowl, stir all remaining ingredients with wire whisk or fork until blended. Pour over chicken mixture.

3 Bake uncovered about 30 minutes or until crust is golden brown.

High Altitude (3500–6500 ft): Heat oven to 425°F.

1 SERVING: Calories 240 (Calories from Fat 80); Total Fat 9g (Saturated Fat 3g); Cholesterol 60mg; Sodium 670mg; Total Carbohydrate 28g (Dietary Fiber 4g; Sugars 4g); Protein 13g **% DAILY VALUE:** Vitamin A 70%; Vitamin C 0%; Calcium 8%; Iron 10% **EXCHANGES:** 1½ Starch, 1 Vegetable, 1 Lean Meat, 1 Fat **CARBOHYDRATE CHOICES:** 2

Quick Tip Thaw frozen vegetables quickly by placing them in a colander and rinsing them with cold water until they are thawed.

In 1996, Bisquick makes light work of cooking, and ushers in great taste without all the work.

Biscuit-Topped Chicken and Cheese Casserole

PREP TIME: 15 MINUTES ● **START TO FINISH: 40 MINUTES**
6 SERVINGS

2 cups cut-up cooked chicken

1 can (11 oz) whole kernel corn with red and green peppers, drained

1 can (10.75 oz) condensed cream of chicken soup

2 cups shredded Monterey Jack cheese (8 oz)

1⅔ cups Original Bisquick mix

½ cup milk

1 Heat oven to 375°F. In 8-inch square (2-quart) glass baking dish, mix chicken, corn, soup and cheese.

2 In medium bowl, stir Bisquick mix and milk with wire whisk or fork until soft dough forms. Place dough on surface sprinkled with Bisquick mix. Shape into a ball; knead 10 times. Press or roll into 7½-inch round, ½ inch thick. Cut 6 biscuits with 2½-inch round cutter. Place biscuits on chicken mixture.

3 Bake uncovered 20 to 25 minutes or until biscuits are golden brown.

High Altitude (3500–6500 ft): Heat oven to 400°F. In 2-quart saucepan, heat chicken, corn, soup and cheese to boiling. Make biscuits. Pour chicken mixture into 8-inch square (2-quart) glass baking dish. Top with biscuits. Bake 30 to 35 minutes.

1 SERVING: Calories 470 (Calories from Fat 210); Total Fat 23g (Saturated Fat 11g); Cholesterol 80mg; Sodium 1020mg; Total Carbohydrate 37g (Dietary Fiber 2g; Sugars 4g); Protein 28g **% DAILY VALUE:** Vitamin A 15%; Vitamin C 4%; Calcium 35%; Iron 10% **EXCHANGES:** 2½ Starch, 3 Lean Meat, 2½ Fat **CARBOHYDRATE CHOICES:** 2½

Quick Tip Add a little color to this comfort-food casserole with a dash of chili powder sprinkled on top of each serving.

Layered Biscuit Chicken Divan

PREP TIME: 15 MINUTES ● START TO FINISH: 50 MINUTES
10 SERVINGS

1 package (9 oz) frozen chicken breast strips, thawed and cut in half if necessary

1 jar (1 lb) roasted garlic Parmesan pasta sauce (white sauce)

1 bag (1 lb) frozen broccoli cuts, thawed, drained and patted dry

2 cups Original Bisquick mix

1 cup milk

½ cup sour cream

¼ cup grated Parmesan cheese

1 Heat oven to 375°F. Heat chicken, pasta sauce and broccoli to boiling in 3-quart saucepan, stirring frequently. Spread half of the mixture in ungreased square pan, 9 × 9 × 2 inches.

2 Stir Bisquick mix, milk and sour cream until blended. Pour half of the batter over chicken mixture in pan. Spread with remaining chicken mixture; top with remaining batter. Sprinkle with cheese.

3 Bake uncovered about 35 minutes or until toothpick inserted in center comes out clean.

High Altitude (3500–6500 ft): Bake about 40 minutes.

1 SERVING: Calories 267 (Calories from Fat 135); Total Fat 15g (Saturated Fat 7g); Cholesterol 48mg; Sodium 839mg; Total Carbohydrate 21g (Dietary Fiber 2g; Sugars 3g); Protein 12g **% DAILY VALUE:** Vitamin A 10%; Vitamin C 30%; Calcium 15%; Iron 8% **EXCHANGES:** 1½ Starch, ½ Vegetable, 1 Lean Meat, 2 Fat **CARBOHYDRATE CHOICES:** 1½

Quick Tip Create fun family moments by letting the kids help with dinner; they can stir the Bisquick mixture and sprinkle cheese over the top. While you're waiting for dinner to bake, have them set the table and help you mix up a quick salad.

Chicken Enchilada Pie

PREP TIME: 15 MINUTES ● **START TO FINISH: 50 MINUTES**
6 SERVINGS

1 package (9 oz) frozen diced
   cooked chicken, thawed

1 can (4.5 oz) chopped green
   chiles, undrained

½ cup enchilada sauce
   (from 10-oz can)

½ cup Original Bisquick mix

½ cup cornmeal

½ cup milk

1 egg

1 can (11 oz) whole kernel corn
   with red and green peppers,
   drained

1 cup shredded Mexican
   cheese blend (4 oz)

1 medium tomato, chopped
   (¾ cup)

1 Place sheet of foil on lower oven rack to catch any drips. Heat oven to 400°F. In 10-inch skillet, cook chicken, chiles and enchilada sauce over medium-high heat 3 to 4 minutes, stirring occasionally, until hot and bubbly. Pour into ungreased 9-inch glass pie plate.

2 In medium bowl, stir Bisquick mix, cornmeal, milk and egg with wire whisk or fork until blended. Stir in corn. Spoon over chicken mixture.

3 Place pie plate on rack above foil. Bake 22 to 27 minutes or until toothpick inserted in topping comes out clean. Top with cheese and tomato. Let stand 5 minutes before serving.

High Altitude (3500–6500 ft): Bake 27 to 32 minutes.

1 SERVING: Calories 320 (Calories from Fat 110); Total Fat 12g (Saturated Fat 6g); Cholesterol 90mg; Sodium 680mg; Total Carbohydrate 30g (Dietary Fiber 3g; Sugars 6g); Protein 22g **% DAILY VALUE:** Vitamin A 15%; Vitamin C 15%; Calcium 20%; Iron 10% **EXCHANGES:** 1 Starch, 1 Other Carbohydrate, 2½ Very Lean Meat, 2 Fat **CARBOHYDRATE CHOICES:** 2

Chicken Tamale Pie

PREP TIME: 10 MINUTES ● **START TO FINISH: 40 MINUTES**
6 SERVINGS

1 package (9 oz) frozen diced cooked chicken, thawed

1 can (4.5 oz) chopped green chiles, drained

2 teaspoons taco seasoning mix (from 1.25-oz package)

1 cup shredded Mexican cheese blend (4 oz)

½ cup Original Bisquick mix

½ cup cornmeal

¾ cup milk

1 egg

1 can (11 oz) whole kernel corn with red and green peppers, drained

Chunky-style salsa, if desired

1 Heat oven to 400°F. In 9-inch glass pie plate, stir chicken, chiles and taco seasoning mix until combined. Sprinkle with cheese.

2 In medium bowl, stir Bisquick mix, cornmeal, milk, egg and corn with wire whisk or fork until blended. Pour over chicken.

3 Bake 25 to 30 minutes or until toothpick inserted in topping comes out clean. Serve with salsa.

High Altitude (3500–6500 ft): Bake 33 to 38 minutes.

1 SERVING: Calories 330 (Calories from Fat 120); Total Fat 14g (Saturated Fat 6g); Cholesterol 95mg; Sodium 600mg; Total Carbohydrate 29g (Dietary Fiber 2g; Sugars 6g); Protein 22g **% DAILY VALUE:** Vitamin A 15%; Vitamin C 10%; Calcium 20%; Iron 10% **EXCHANGES:** 1½ Starch, ½ Other Carbohydrate, 2½ Lean Meat, 1 Fat **CARBOHYDRATE CHOICES:** 2

Beef Tamale Pie: Substitute 1 pound ground beef for the chicken. Cook the beef over medium heat 8 to 10 minutes, stirring occasionally, until brown; drain.

Quick Tip Like things spicy? Add a chopped canned chipotle chile to the chicken mixture.

Chicken Chile Verde

PREP TIME: 10 MINUTES ● **START TO FINISH: 45 MINUTES**
6 SERVINGS

1 cup sour cream

1 teaspoon ground cumin or chili powder

1 can (10.75 oz) condensed cream of chicken soup

1 can (15 to 16 oz) black beans, drained, rinsed

1 can (14.5 oz) diced tomatoes with green chiles, drained

1 package (9 oz) frozen cooked southwestern-seasoned chicken breast strips, thawed, cut in half

1 can (4.5 oz) chopped green chiles, drained

2¼ cups Original Bisquick mix

⅔ cup milk

½ cup shredded Cheddar cheese (2 oz)

1 Heat oven to 400°F. In ungreased 9-inch square pan, mix sour cream, cumin and soup until blended. Stir in beans, tomatoes, chicken and chiles; spread evenly. Bake 15 minutes.

2 In medium bowl, stir Bisquick mix, milk and cheese until soft dough forms. Drop dough by 12 spoonfuls onto hot chicken mixture.

3 Bake uncovered 18 to 20 minutes or until biscuits are golden brown.

High Altitude (3500–6500 ft): In step 1, increase bake time to 25 minutes. In step 3, increase bake time to 20 to 22 minutes.

1 SERVING: Calories 530 (Calories from Fat 200); Total Fat 22g (Saturated Fat 10g); Cholesterol 70mg; Sodium 1670mg; Total Carbohydrate 58g (Dietary Fiber 9g; Sugars 8g); Protein 25g **% DAILY VALUE:** Vitamin A 15%; Vitamin C 10%; Calcium 25%; Iron 25% **EXCHANGES:** 3½ Starch, ½ Other Carbohydrate, 2 Very Lean Meat, 3½ Fat **CARBOHYDRATE CHOICES:** 4

Everybody needs something warm and comforting on a cold night.

Wild Rice–Turkey Pot Pie

PREP TIME: 10 MINUTES ● **START TO FINISH: 45 MINUTES**
6 SERVINGS

TURKEY FILLING

1 can (15 oz) cooked wild rice, drained

2 cups cubed cooked turkey (about 1 lb)

1 bag (1 lb) frozen mixed vegetables, thawed, drained

1 can (10.75 oz) condensed 98% fat-free cream of mushroom soup with 30% less sodium

¼ cup fat-free (skim) milk

2 tablespoons dried minced onion

TOPPING

1½ cups Original Bisquick mix

¾ cup fat-free (skim) milk

1 egg or ¼ cup fat-free egg product

1 Heat oven to 400°F. Reserve ½ cup of the wild rice. In ungreased 2-quart casserole, stir remaining wild rice and remaining filling ingredients until mixed.

2 In medium bowl, stir reserved ½ cup wild rice and the topping ingredients with wire whisk or fork just until blended. Pour over turkey mixture.

3 Bake uncovered 25 to 35 minutes or until crust is golden brown.

High Altitude (3500–6500 ft): Increase milk to ¾ cup. In step 1, in 3-quart saucepan, mix remaining wild rice and remaining filling ingredients. Heat over medium heat, stirring constantly, until filling is very hot. Pour into 2-quart casserole; add topping. In step 3, bake uncovered 30 to 35 minutes.

1 SERVING: Calories 440 (Calories from Fat 110); Total Fat 12g (Saturated Fat 3.5g); Cholesterol 105mg; Sodium 920mg; Total Carbohydrate 52g (Dietary Fiber 6g; Sugars 8g); Protein 32g **% DAILY VALUE:** Vitamin A 70%; Vitamin C 4%; Calcium 15%; Iron 20% **EXCHANGES:** 3 Starch, 1 Vegetable, 3 Lean Meat **CARBOHYDRATE CHOICES:** 3½

Quick Tip You can use regular or brown cooked rice instead of wild rice if you prefer. A 15-ounce can contains about 2 cups of wild rice.

Turkey and Corn Bread Stuffing Casserole

PREP TIME: 15 MINUTES ● START TO FINISH: 55 MINUTES
6 SERVINGS

1 can (10¾ oz) condensed cream of chicken or celery soup

1¼ cups milk

1 cup frozen green peas

½ cup dried cranberries

4 medium green onions, sliced (¼ cup)

2 cups cut-up cooked turkey or chicken

1½ cups corn bread stuffing mix

1 cup Original Bisquick mix

¼ cup milk

2 eggs

1 Heat oven to 400°F. Grease 3-quart casserole. Heat soup and milk to boiling in 3-quart saucepan, stirring frequently; remove from heat. Stir in turkey and stuffing mix. Spoon into casserole.

2 Stir remaining ingredients until blended. Pour over stuffing mixture.

3 Bake uncovered 35 to 40 minutes or until knife inserted in center comes out clean.

High Altitude (3500-6500 ft): In step 1, stir 1 ½ cup water into soup.

1 SERVING: Calories 380 (Calories from Fat 120); Total Fat 13g (Saturated Fat 4g); Cholesterol 120mg; Sodium 870mg; Total Carbohydrate 43g (Dietary Fiber 2g, Sugars 13g); Protein 22g **% DAILY VALUE:** Vitamin A 20%; Vitamin C 2%; Calcium 15%; Iron 15% **EXCHANGES:** 2 Starch; 1 Other Carbohydrate; 0 Vegetable; 2 Lean Meat; 1 Fat Carbohydrate Choices: 3

Gravy Pork Chops
with Stuffing Biscuits

PREP TIME: 20 MINUTES ● **START TO FINISH: 45 MINUTES**
4 SERVINGS

1 tablespoon butter or
  margarine

4 bone-in pork loin chops,
  about ½ inch thick (about
  1¾ lb)

1 jar (12 oz) home-style pork
  gravy

1 medium stalk celery, thinly
  sliced (½ cup)

¼ cup chopped onion

1 cup Original Bisquick mix

½ teaspoon dried sage leaves

⅓ cup milk

1 Heat oven to 375°F. Spray 13 × 9-inch (3-quart) glass baking dish with cooking spray.

2 In 12-inch nonstick skillet, melt butter over medium-high heat. Add pork chops; cook 8 to 10 minutes, turning once, until browned. Place pork chops in baking dish. Pour gravy over top.

3 In same skillet, cook celery and onion over medium-high heat 3 to 5 minutes, stirring frequently, until tender; remove from heat.

4 In small bowl, stir Bisquick mix, sage and milk until blended. Stir in celery and onion mixture. Drop large spoonful of dough onto each pork chop.

5 Bake 20 to 25 minutes or until biscuits are golden brown and pork chops are no longer pink in center.

High Altitude (3500–6500 ft): Bake 23 to 28 minutes.

1 SERVING: Calories 430 (Calories from Fat 180); Total Fat 20g (Saturated Fat 8g); Cholesterol 100mg; Sodium 940mg; Total Carbohydrate 26g (Dietary Fiber 1g; Sugars 3g); Protein 37g **% DAILY VALUE:** Vitamin A 4%; Vitamin C 0%; Calcium 8%; Iron 15% **EXCHANGES:** 1½ Starch, 4½ Lean Meat, 1 Fat **CARBOHYDRATE CHOICES:** 2

Breaded Pork Chops

PREP TIME: 15 MINUTES ● **START TO FINISH: 15 MINUTES**
8 SERVINGS

½ cup Original Bisquick mix

12 saltine crackers, crushed (½ cup)

1 teaspoon seasoned salt

¼ teaspoon pepper

1 egg

2 tablespoons water

8 pork boneless loin chops, ½ inch thick (about 2 lb)

1 Stir Bisquick mix, cracker crumbs, seasoned salt and pepper. Mix egg and water.

2 Dip pork into egg mixture, then coat with Bisquick mixture.

3 Spray 12-inch nonstick skillet with cooking spray; heat over medium-high heat. Cook pork in skillet 8 to 10 minutes, turning once, until slightly pink in center.

High Altitude (3500–6500 ft): No change.

1 SERVING: Calories 215 (Calories from Fat 90); Total Fat 10g (Saturated Fat 3g); Cholesterol 90mg; Sodium 370mg; Total Carbohydrate 7g (Dietary Fiber 0g; Sugars 0g); Protein 24g **% DAILY VALUE:** Vitamin A 0%; Vitamin C 0%; Calcium 2%; Iron 6% **EXCHANGES:** ½ Starch, 3 Lean Meat **CARBOHYDRATE CHOICES:** ½

Polish Sausage Supper

PREP TIME: 15 MINUTES ● START TO FINISH: 1 HOUR 5 MINUTES
4 SERVINGS (1 CUP SAUSAGE MIXTURE AND 2 BISCUITS EACH)

1 ring (1 lb) fully cooked smoked sausage, cut into 1-inch pieces

1 large Granny Smith apple, peeled, cut into eighths

1 can (14 to 15 oz) sauerkraut, drained

1 cup apple cider or apple juice

1½ cups Original Bisquick mix

½ cup milk

½ cup shredded Cheddar cheese (2 oz)

1 tablespoon chopped fresh parsley

1 egg, slightly beaten

1 Heat oven to 425°F. In ungreased 11 × 7-inch (2-quart) glass baking dish, layer sausage and apple; top with sauerkraut. Pour apple cider into baking dish.

2 Cover with foil; bake 30 to 40 minutes or until mixture is hot and apple pieces can be pierced with fork. Remove baking dish from oven.

3 In medium bowl, stir remaining ingredients until soft dough forms. Drop dough by 8 spoonfuls onto sausage mixture.

4 Bake uncovered 10 to 12 minutes or until biscuits are cooked and golden brown on top.

High Altitude (3500–6500 ft): In step 4, bake uncovered 14 to 16 minutes.

1 SERVING: Calories 690 (Calories from Fat 400); Total Fat 45g (Saturated Fat 17g); Cholesterol 140mg; Sodium 2420mg; Total Carbohydrate 50g (Dietary Fiber 4g; Sugars 20g); Protein 23g **% DAILY VALUE:** Vitamin A 8%; Vitamin C 15%; Calcium 25%; Iron 25% **EXCHANGES:** 1½ Starch, 1½ Other Carbohydrate, 1 Vegetable, 2½ High-Fat Meat, 5 Fat **CARBOHYDRATE CHOICES:** 3

Quick Tip Add 1 teaspoon caraway seed to the biscuit topping for an authentic German-inspired dish.

Lasagna-Style Casserole

PREP TIME: 15 MINUTES ● **START TO FINISH: 55 MINUTES**
6 SERVINGS

1 lb bulk Italian pork
   sausage

1 cup tomato pasta sauce

1 cup ricotta cheese

⅓ cup grated Parmesan cheese

1 egg

1 cup Original Bisquick mix

½ cup milk

1 egg

1 cup shredded mozzarella
   cheese (4 oz)

1 Heat oven to 400°F. In 10-inch skillet, cook sausage over medium-high heat 5 to 7 minutes, stirring frequently, until thoroughly cooked; drain. Stir in pasta sauce. Spoon into 8-inch square (2-quart) glass baking dish.

2 In small bowl, stir ricotta cheese, Parmesan cheese and 1 egg until mixed. Drop by heaping tablespoonfuls onto sausage mixture.

3 In small bowl, stir Bisquick mix, milk and 1 egg with wire whisk or fork until blended. Pour over cheese and sausage mixtures.

4 Spray sheet of foil large enough to cover baking dish with cooking spray. Place sprayed side down on dish; seal tightly. Bake 23 to 28 minutes or until light golden brown. Sprinkle with mozzarella cheese. Bake uncovered 5 to 10 minutes longer or until cheese is melted.

High Altitude (3500–6500 ft): Increase first bake time to 33 to 38 minutes. For frozen casserole, bake 1 hour 10 minutes to 1 hour 20 minutes.

1 SERVING: Calories 490 (Calories from Fat 270); Total Fat 30g (Saturated Fat 12g); Cholesterol 130mg; Sodium 1380mg; Total Carbohydrate 27g (Dietary Fiber 1g; Sugars 8g); Protein 27g **% DAILY VALUE:** Vitamin A 10%; Vitamin C 4%; Calcium 40%; Iron 10% **EXCHANGES:** 1 Starch, 1 Other Carbohydrate, 3½ High-Fat Meat **CARBOHYDRATE CHOICES:** 2

Trust Bisquick to outdo itself—this 1980s ad shows a lasagna easier to make than pie. Everything should be this simple.

Quick Tip To make ahead, spray sheet of foil large enough to cover baking dish with cooking spray. Place sprayed piece of foil sprayed side down on unbaked casserole; seal tightly. Freeze up to 2 months. Bake covered at 400°F 1 hour to 1 hour 15 minutes or until golden brown. Sprinkle with mozzarella cheese. Bake uncovered 5 to 10 minutes longer or until cheese is melted.

Sausage Chili Bake

PREP TIME: 15 MINUTES ● **START TO FINISH: 55 MINUTES**
10 SERVINGS

1 lb smoked sausage, cut into
½-inch slices

1 small onion, chopped
(¼ cup)

1 teaspoon garlic salt

1 to 2 tablespoons chili powder

1 can (14.5 oz) stewed
tomatoes, undrained

1 can (15 to 16 oz) kidney
beans, undrained

2 cups Original Bisquick mix

½ cup cornmeal

1 cup milk

2 eggs

1 Heat oven to 350°F. Spray 10-inch skillet with cooking spray; heat over medium-high heat. Cook sausage and onion in skillet 4 to 5 minutes, stirring occasionally, until onion is tender.

2 Spoon mixture into ungreased 13 × 9-inch (3-quart) glass baking dish. Stir in garlic salt, chili powder, tomatoes and beans. In medium bowl, stir remaining ingredients with wire whisk or fork until blended. Pour over sausage mixture.

3 Bake uncovered 35 to 40 minutes or until crust is light golden brown.

High Altitude (3500–6500 ft): No change.

1 SERVING: Calories 350 (Calories from Fat 160); Total Fat 18g (Saturated Fat 6g); Cholesterol 70mg; Sodium 1050mg; Total Carbohydrate 36g (Dietary Fiber 4g; Sugars 6g); Protein 13g **% DAILY VALUE:** Vitamin A 8%; Vitamin C 4%; Calcium 10%; Iron 15% **EXCHANGES:** 1½ Starch, 1 Other Carbohydrate, 1 High-Fat Meat, 2 Fat **CARBOHYDRATE CHOICES:** 2½

Quick Tip If you love garlic you may want to use kielbasa in place of the smoked sausage to punch up the garlic flavor.

Salsa Beef Biscuit Bake

PREP TIME: 15 MINUTES ● **START TO FINISH: 40 MINUTES**
6 SERVINGS

1 lb ground beef

1 jar (16 oz) thick 'n' chunky salsa

2 cups Original Bisquick mix

¾ cup milk

1 medium green onion, chopped (1 tablespoon)

1 cup shredded Cheddar cheese (4 oz)

1 Heat oven to 400°F. Spray bottom and sides of square pan, 9 × 9 × 2 inches, with cooking spray. Cook beef in 10-inch skillet over medium-high heat, about 8 minutes, stirring occasionally, until brown; drain. Stir in salsa. Spread beef mixture in pan.

2 Stir Bisquick mix, milk, onion and cheese until soft dough forms. Drop dough by 12 tablespoonfuls over beef mixture.

3 Bake uncovered about 20 minutes or until golden brown and toothpick inserted in biscuits comes out clean.

High Altitude (3500–6500 ft): Use 2¼ cups Bisquick mix. Bake about 27 minutes.

1 SERVING: Calories 420 (Calories from Fat 205); Total Fat 23g (Saturated Fat 10g); Cholesterol 65mg; Sodium 1060mg; Total Carbohydrate 30g (Dietary Fiber 2g; Sugars 5g); Protein 23g **% DAILY VALUE:** Vitamin A 16%; Vitamin C 8%; Calcium 22%; Iron 18% **EXCHANGES:** 2 Starch, 2 High-Fat Meat, 1 Fat **CARBOHYDRATE CHOICES:** 2

Quick Tip Ground turkey can be used instead of beef in this quick and easy bake. Garnish with the works—chopped tomatoes, chopped avocado and sour cream!

Italian Sausage Pot Pies

PREP TIME: 15 MINUTES ● **START TO FINISH: 35 MINUTES**
4 SERVINGS

1 lb bulk Italian sausage
  or ground beef

1 medium onion, chopped
  (½ cup)

1 small green bell pepper,
  chopped (½ cup)

½ cup sliced mushrooms

1 can (8 oz) pizza sauce

1 cup shredded mozzarella
  cheese (4 oz)

1 cup Original Bisquick mix

¼ cup boiling water

1 Heat oven to 375°F. Grease four 10- to 12-ounce casseroles. Cook sausage, onion and bell pepper in 10-inch skillet over medium heat, stirring frequently, until sausage is no longer pink; drain. Stir in mushrooms and pizza sauce. Heat to boiling; reduce heat. Simmer uncovered 5 minutes, stirring occasionally. Spoon sausage mixture into casseroles. Sprinkle ¼ cup of the cheese over each.

2 Stir Bisquick mix and boiling water; beat vigorously 20 strokes. Place dough on surface sprinkled with Bisquick mix; gently roll in Bisquick mix to coat. Shape into a ball; knead about 10 times or until smooth.

3 Divide dough into 4 balls. Pat each ball into circle the size of the diameter of the casseroles. Make cut in each circle with knife to vent steam. Place circles on sausage mixture in casseroles. Bake 15 to 20 minutes or until light golden brown.

High Altitude (3500–6500 ft): Bake 22 to 25 minutes.

1 SERVING: Calories 520 (Calories from Fat 295); Total Fat 33g (Saturated Fat 12g); Cholesterol 80mg; Sodium 1540mg; Total Carbohydrate 29g (Dietary Fiber 2g; Sugars 7g); Protein 28g **% DAILY VALUE:** Vitamin A 8%; Vitamin C 28%; Calcium 28%; Iron 16% **EXCHANGES:** 2 Starch, 3 High-Fat Meat, 1½ Fat **CARBOHYDRATE CHOICES:** 2

Quick Tip For a special holiday treat, use a small cookie cutter to cut a festive shape out of the dough circle before putting it on the sausage mixture. For itty-bitty pastry treats, place the cut-outs on a cookie sheet and bake in a 375°F oven about 15 minutes or until light golden brown.

Louisiana-Style Shrimp Casserole

PREP TIME: 20 MINUTES ● **START TO FINISH: 50 MINUTES**
4 SERVINGS

2 tablespoons butter or margarine

1 clove garlic, finely chopped

2 cups frozen stir-fry bell peppers and onions (from 1-lb bag)

¼ cup finely chopped celery

2 tablespoons Original Bisquick mix

1 can (14.5 oz) diced tomatoes, undrained

¼ teaspoon salt

¼ teaspoon red pepper sauce

12 oz cooked peeled deveined medium shrimp, thawed if frozen and tails removed

¾ cup Original Bisquick mix

¼ cup milk

1 egg

1 Heat oven to 400°F. In 10-inch skillet, melt butter over medium-high heat. Cook garlic, stir-fry vegetables and celery in butter about 5 minutes, stirring frequently, until vegetables are crisp-tender.

2 Stir 2 tablespoons Bisquick mix into vegetable mixture until blended. Stir in tomatoes, salt, pepper sauce and shrimp. Reduce heat to medium-low. Cook about 7 minutes, stirring occasionally, until bubbling and thickened. Pour shrimp mixture into ungreased 8-inch square (2-quart) glass baking dish.

3 In small bowl, stir ¾ cup Bisquick mix, the milk and egg with wire whisk or fork until blended. Pour over shrimp mixture.

4 Bake uncovered 20 to 30 minutes or until crust is golden brown.

High Altitude (3500–6500 ft): No change.

1 SERVING: Calories 320 (Calories from Fat 110); Total Fat 12g (Saturated Fat 6g); Cholesterol 235mg; Sodium 870mg; Total Carbohydrate 29g (Dietary Fiber 2g; Sugars 7g); Protein 24g **% DAILY VALUE:** Vitamin A 15%; Vitamin C 30%; Calcium 15%; Iron 25% **EXCHANGES:** 1 Starch, 2 Vegetable, 2½ Very Lean Meat, 2 Fat **CARBOHYDRATE CHOICES:** 2

Louisiana-Style Chicken Casserole: Substitute 2 cups diced cooked chicken for the shrimp.

Quick Tip You can make the shrimp filling ahead, spoon it into the baking dish, then cover and refrigerate up to 24 hours. When ready to bake, just stir up the Bisquick topping and bake as directed.

Easy Salmon Puff

PREP TIME: 15 MINUTES ● **START TO FINISH: 55 MINUTES**
6 SERVINGS

1 cup Original Bisquick mix

1 teaspoon dried dill weed

1 cup milk

½ cup sour cream

4 eggs

2 cans (6 oz each) boneless skinless salmon, drained, flaked

1 cup shredded Havarti or Swiss cheese (4 oz)

1 Heat oven to 375°F. Spray 9-inch glass pie plate with cooking spray. In medium bowl, stir Bisquick mix, dill weed, milk, sour cream and eggs with wire whisk or fork until blended. Gently stir in salmon and cheese. Pour into pie plate.

2 Bake uncovered 35 to 40 minutes or until knife inserted in center comes out clean.

High Altitude (3500–6500 ft): Bake uncovered 38 to 43 minutes.

1 SERVING: Calories 350 (Calories from Fat 180); Total Fat 20g (Saturated Fat 10g); Cholesterol 225mg; Sodium 680mg; Total Carbohydrate 17g (Dietary Fiber 1g; Sugars 4g); Protein 25g **% DAILY VALUE:** Vitamin A 15%; Vitamin C 0%; Calcium 35%; Iron 8% **EXCHANGES:** 1 Starch, 3 Medium-Fat Meat, 1 Fat **CARBOHYDRATE CHOICES:** 1

Easy Tuna Puff: Substitute 2 cans (6 ounces each) tuna, drained, for the salmon.

Quick Tip Dill Havarti cheese is also available and would be a nice flavor addition to this salmon puff.

Sausage Casserole
with Cheesy Corn Bread

PREP TIME: 10 MINUTES ● **START TO FINISH: 40 MINUTES**
10 SERVINGS

1 ring (1 lb) fully cooked
  smoked sausage or kielbasa,
  cut into ¼-inch slices

1 bag (1 lb) frozen broccoli,
  carrots and cauliflower,
  thawed and drained

2 cans (10¾ oz each)
  condensed Cheddar cheese
  soup

1¼ cups Original Bisquick mix

1½ cups milk

¾ cup cornmeal

2 eggs

1 cup shredded Cheddar
  cheese (4 oz)

1 Heat oven to 450°F. Spray bottom and sides of rectangular pan, 13 × 9 × 2 inches, with cooking spray. Mix sausage, vegetables and soup in pan.

2 Stir Bisquick mix, milk, cornmeal, eggs and ½ cup of the cheese until blended. Pour over sausage mixture.

3 Bake uncovered 25 to 30 minutes; sprinkle with remaining ½ cup cheese and continue to bake 1 or 2 minutes more, until light brown.

High Altitude (3500–6500 ft): Bake about 30 minutes.

1 SERVING: Calories 400 (Calories from Fat 225); Total Fat 25g (Saturated Fat 11g); Cholesterol 95mg; Sodium 1340mg; Total Carbohydrate 28g (Dietary Fiber 2g; Sugars 5g); Protein 16g **% DAILY VALUE:** Vitamin A 60%; Vitamin C 35%; Calcium 20%; Iron 10% **EXCHANGES:** 2 Starch, 1½ High-Fat Meat, 2 Fat **CARBOHYDRATE CHOICES:** 2

Quick Tip Check out your freezer and pantry—you can use a 1-pound bag of frozen mixed vegetables or an equal amount of any of your favorite frozen vegetable combinations (thawed and drained) in this casserole. You can also substitute condensed nacho cheese soup or a 16-ounce jar of double Cheddar cheese pasta sauce for the Cheddar cheese soup.

CHAPTER 5

30-Minute
Weeknight Dinners

Beef and Onion Soup
with Cheesy Biscuit Croutons

PREP TIME: 25 MINUTES ● **START TO FINISH: 30 MINUTES**
4 SERVINGS

SOUP

1 lb lean (at least 80%) ground beef

1 envelope onion soup and dip mix (from 2-oz box)

¼ teaspoon pepper

1 can (14 oz) beef broth

3 cups water

1 tablespoon packed brown sugar

1 tablespoon Worcestershire sauce

CROUTONS

1 cup Original Bisquick mix

3 tablespoons grated Parmesan cheese

¼ cup water

¾ cup finely shredded Swiss cheese (3 oz)

1 In 3-quart saucepan, cook beef, onion soup mix and pepper over medium-high heat 5 to 7 minutes, stirring occasionally, until beef is thoroughly cooked; drain. Add broth, water, brown sugar and Worcestershire sauce. Heat to boiling. Reduce heat to medium-low; cook uncovered 10 minutes. Cover; remove from heat.

2 Meanwhile, heat oven to 425°F. Spray cookie sheet with cooking spray. In medium bowl, stir Bisquick mix, Parmesan cheese and water until soft dough forms. Place dough on surface sprinkled with Bisquick mix; roll in Bisquick mix to coat. Shape into a ball; knead 10 times. Press or roll dough into 12 × 6-inch rectangle, ¼ inch thick, on cookie sheet. Cut into 8 squares, but do not separate. Bake 6 to 8 minutes or until golden brown. Remove from oven.

3 Set oven control to broil. Sprinkle croutons with Swiss cheese. Cut and separate squares slightly. Broil with tops 4 to 6 inches from heat 2 to 3 minutes or until cheese is bubbly and slightly browned.

4 Float 1 or 2 croutons in individual bowls of soup. Serve any remaining croutons with soup.

High Altitude (3500–6500 ft): No change.

1 SERVING: Calories 460 (Calories from Fat 220); Total Fat 24g (Saturated Fat 11g); Cholesterol 95mg; Sodium 1630mg; Total Carbohydrate 30g (Dietary Fiber 1g; Sugars 7g); Protein 31g **% DAILY VALUE:** Vitamin A 4%; Vitamin C 2%; Calcium 30%; Iron 20% **EXCHANGES:** 1½ Starch, ½ Other Carbohydrate, 3½ Medium-Fat Meat, 1 Fat **CARBOHYDRATE CHOICES:** 2

Salisbury Steak
with Mushroom Gravy

PREP TIME: 30 MINUTES ● START TO FINISH: 30 MINUTES
6 SERVINGS

1 lb lean (at least 80%) ground beef

1 egg

½ cup Original Bisquick mix

⅛ teaspoon pepper

1 tablespoon vegetable oil

1 medium onion, cut in half, sliced

1 jar (4.5 oz) sliced mushrooms, drained

1 jar (12 oz) beef gravy

1 In large bowl, mix beef, egg, ¼ cup of the Bisquick mix and the pepper. With wet hands, shape beef mixture into 6 oval patties, about ½ inch thick. Lightly coat patties with remaining ¼ cup Bisquick mix.

2 In 12-inch nonstick skillet, heat oil over medium heat. Arrange patties in a single layer in skillet. Add onion slices around and on top of patties. Cook 12 to 16 minutes, turning patties once and stirring onions occasionally, until meat thermometer inserted in center of patties reads 160°F.

3 Spoon fat from skillet if necessary; discard. Add mushrooms and gravy to skillet. Turn patties to coat with gravy. Heat to boiling.

High Altitude (3500–6500 ft): No change.

1 SERVING: Calories 250 (Calories from Fat 130); Total Fat 14g (Saturated Fat 5g); Cholesterol 85mg; Sodium 580mg; Total Carbohydrate 12g (Dietary Fiber 1g; Sugars 1g); Protein 18g **% DAILY VALUE:** Vitamin A 0%; Vitamin C 0%; Calcium 4%; Iron 15% **EXCHANGES:** 1 Starch, 2 Medium-Fat Meat, ½ Fat **CARBOHYDRATE CHOICES:** 1

In the 1930s, Bisquick rides the radio airwaves. Betty and Bob have hundreds of fans and help make Bisquick a household word.

Crunchy-Crust Southwestern Cube Steaks

PREP TIME: 15 MINUTES ● **START TO FINISH: 30 MINUTES**
4 SERVINGS

1 lb beef cube steaks

2 eggs

½ cup water

3 cups nacho cheese–flavored tortilla chips (3 oz), finely crushed

1 cup Original Bisquick mix

3 tablespoons vegetable oil

½ cup chunky-style salsa

¼ cup shredded Mexican cheese blend (1 oz)

1 Cut beef into 4 serving pieces if necessary. In medium bowl, beat eggs and water with wire whisk. In shallow dish, mix crushed tortilla chips and Bisquick mix. Dip beef into egg mixture, then coat with Bisquick mixture, pressing to coat.

2 In 12-inch nonstick skillet, heat 2 tablespoons of the oil over medium heat. Add beef; cook 10 to 12 minutes, turning once and adding remaining 1 tablespoon oil, until beef is no longer pink in center.

3 Top each serving with 2 tablespoons salsa and 1 tablespoon cheese.

High Altitude (3500–6500 ft): In step 2, heat 2 tablespoons oil over medium-high heat. Cook beef as directed, adding 2 tablespoons oil when turning beef.

1 SERVING: Calories 570 (Calories from Fat 290); Total Fat 32g (Saturated Fat 8g); Cholesterol 160mg; Sodium 810mg; Total Carbohydrate 36g (Dietary Fiber 2g; Sugars 3g); Protein 35g **% DAILY VALUE:** Vitamin A 8%; Vitamin C 0%; Calcium 10%; Iron 25% **EXCHANGES:** 2 Starch, ½ Other Carbohydrate, 4 Medium-Fat Meat, 2 Fat **CARBOHYDRATE CHOICES:** 2½

Beef and Peppers
with Cheese Biscuits

PREP TIME: 20 MINUTES ● START TO FINISH: 30 MINUTES
6 SERVINGS

1¾ cups Original Bisquick mix

½ cup milk

½ cup shredded Swiss or provolone cheese (2 oz)

1 can (10.75 oz) condensed French onion soup

2 packages (5 oz each) deli-style sliced cooked beef, cut into thin strips

2 small bell peppers, sliced

½ teaspoon garlic-pepper blend

1⅓ cups water

⅓ cup all-purpose flour

1 Heat oven to 450°F. In medium bowl, stir Bisquick mix, milk and cheese until soft dough forms; beat 20 strokes. Place dough on surface generously sprinkled with Bisquick mix; gently roll in Bisquick mix to coat. Shape into a ball; knead 10 times.

2 Press or roll dough until ¼ inch thick. With 3-inch round cutter, cut into 6 biscuits. On ungreased cookie sheet, place biscuits.

3 Bake 6 to 8 minutes or until golden brown.

4 Meanwhile, in 2-quart saucepan, mix soup, beef, bell peppers, garlic-pepper blend and 1 cup of the water. Heat to boiling over medium-high heat. Reduce heat to medium-low. In small bowl, stir remaining ⅓ cup water and the flour until mixed; stir into beef mixture. Heat to boiling, stirring frequently, until thickened.

5 Split biscuits. Serve beef mixture over biscuits.

High Altitude (3500–6500 ft): No change.

1 SERVING: Calories 300 (Calories from Fat 90); Total Fat 10g (Saturated Fat 4g); Cholesterol 35mg; Sodium 1340mg; Total Carbohydrate 36g (Dietary Fiber 2g; Sugars 5g); Protein 17g **% DAILY VALUE:** Vitamin A 4%; Vitamin C 20%; Calcium 15%; Iron 15% **EXCHANGES:** 1½ Starch, 1 Other Carbohydrate, 2 Lean Meat, ½ Fat **CARBOHYDRATE CHOICES:** 2½

Quick Tip If you want to reduce the fat in this hearty fork-and-knife meal, make the biscuits with Bisquick Heart Smart mix and fat-free (skim) milk.

Barbecue Beef Cheese Melts

PREP TIME: 15 MINUTES ● **START TO FINISH: 30 MINUTES**
8 SERVINGS

2 cups Original Bisquick mix

½ teaspoon ground mustard

1 cup milk

1 egg, beaten

1 teaspoon vegetable oil

½ cup chopped green bell pepper

¼ cup chopped onion

1 cup barbecue sauce

¾ lb cooked roast beef (from deli), chopped

2 cups shredded Cheddar cheese (8 oz)

1 Heat oven to 350°F. Spray 13 × 9-inch pan with cooking spray. In large bowl, stir Bisquick mix, mustard, milk and egg until mixed. Pour and spread in pan.

2 Bake 15 to 17 minutes or until toothpick inserted in center comes out clean. (Top will not brown.) Remove from oven.

3 Meanwhile, in 10-inch nonstick skillet, heat oil over medium heat. Add bell pepper and onion. Cook 3 to 4 minutes, stirring occasionally, until crisp-tender. Stir in barbecue sauce and beef. Cook until hot. Spread over baked bread base. Top with cheese.

4 Bake 4 to 5 minutes longer or until cheese is melted. Cut into squares.

High Altitude (3500–6500 ft): No change.

1 SERVING: Calories 400 (Calories from Fat 180); Total Fat 20g (Saturated Fat 10g); Cholesterol 85mg; Sodium 920mg; Total Carbohydrate 35g (Dietary Fiber 1g; Sugars 13g); Protein 19g **% DAILY VALUE:** Vitamin A 10%; Vitamin C 8%; Calcium 25%; Iron 15% **EXCHANGES:** 1½ Starch, 1 Other Carbohydrate, 2 Lean Meat, 2½ Fat **CARBOHYDRATE CHOICES:** 2

Quick Tip For a beef cheese melt with more kick, substitute pepper Jack cheese for the Cheddar cheese.

Easy Chili Skillet Bake

PREP TIME: 10 MINUTES ● **START TO FINISH: 30 MINUTES**
6 SERVINGS

2 cans (15 oz each) chili
  with beans

½ cup Original Bisquick mix

¼ cup milk

1 egg, beaten

1 cup shredded Cheddar
  cheese (4 oz)

1 Heat oven to 400°F. Spray 10-inch ovenproof skillet with cooking spray. In skillet, heat chili over medium heat, stirring occasionally, just until simmering. Remove from heat.

2 In small bowl, stir Bisquick mix, milk and egg with wire whisk or fork until blended. Spoon batter in ring around outer edge of chili. Sprinkle ½ cup of the cheese over batter.

3 Bake about 20 minutes or until crust is golden brown and knife inserted in center of crust comes out clean. Immediately sprinkle remaining ½ cup cheese over center.

High Altitude (3500–6500 ft): No change.

1 SERVING: Calories 290 (Calories from Fat 120); Total Fat 13g (Saturated Fat 6g); Cholesterol 75mg; Sodium 960mg; Total Carbohydrate 26g (Dietary Fiber 4g; Sugars 3g); Protein 16g **% DAILY VALUE:** Vitamin A 15%; Vitamin C 6%; Calcium 15%; Iron 15% **EXCHANGES:** 2 Starch, 1½ Very Lean Meat, 2 Fat **CARBOHYDRATE CHOICES:** 2

Quick Tip If you don't have an ovenproof skillet, use a 2-quart casserole dish. Cover and microwave chili in a microwavable dish on High 2 to 3 minutes, stirring after 1 minute, until hot. Pour into the casserole and continue as directed in step 2.

Cajun Chicken

**PREP TIME: 20 MINUTES ● START TO FINISH: 20 MINUTES
4 SERVINGS**

4 boneless skinless chicken breast halves (about 1¼ lb)

1½ cups cornflakes cereal, crushed (½ cup)

½ cup Original Bisquick mix

2 teaspoons Cajun seasoning

½ cup water

2 tablespoons margarine or butter

1 Flatten each chicken breast half to about ¼-inch thickness between sheets of waxed paper or plastic wrap.

2 Stir cereal, Bisquick mix and Cajun seasoning. Dip chicken into water, then coat with cereal mixture.

3 Melt margarine in 12-inch nonstick skillet over medium heat. Cook chicken in margarine 8 to 10 minutes, turning once, until juice is no longer pink when centers of thickest pieces are cut.

High Altitude (3500–6500 ft): Cook chicken 10 to 12 minutes.

1 SERVING: Calories 275 (Calories from Fat 90); Total Fat 10g (Saturated Fat 2g); Cholesterol 75mg; Sodium 450mg; Total Carbohydrate 18g (Dietary Fiber 1g; Sugars 1g); Protein 28g **% DAILY VALUE:** Vitamin A 18%; Vitamin C 2%; Calcium 4%; Iron 26% **EXCHANGES:** 1 Starch, 4 Lean Meat **CARBOHYDRATE CHOICES:** 1

Quick Tip For a southern-style chicken sandwich, serve in toasted sesame buns with barbecue sauce, lettuce, red onion and tomato slices.

Skillet Chicken Parmesan

PREP TIME: 25 MINUTES ● **START TO FINISH: 25 MINUTES**
4 SERVINGS

¾ cup Original Bisquick mix

1 teaspoon Italian seasoning

2 tablespoons grated Parmesan cheese

1 egg

4 boneless skinless chicken breasts (4 oz each)

3 tablespoons olive or vegetable oil

2 cups tomato pasta sauce (from 26-oz jar)

1 cup shredded Italian cheese blend (4 oz)

1 In shallow dish or pie plate, mix Bisquick mix, Italian seasoning and Parmesan cheese. In another shallow dish or pie plate, beat egg. Coat chicken with Bisquick mixture, then dip into egg, and coat again with Bisquick mixture.

2 In 12-inch nonstick skillet, heat oil over medium heat. Add chicken; cook 4 to 6 minutes, turning once, until golden brown. Cover; cook 8 to 10 minutes longer, turning once, until juice of chicken is clear when center of thickest part is cut (170°F). Remove from skillet to plate.

3 Add pasta sauce to skillet. Place chicken on top of sauce. Sprinkle with Italian cheese blend. Cover; cook 2 to 3 minutes or until bubbly and cheese is melted.

High Altitude (3500–6500 ft): No change.

1 SERVING: Calories 580 (Calories from Fat 270); Total Fat 30g (Saturated Fat 9g); Cholesterol 150mg; Sodium 1400mg; Total Carbohydrate 39g (Dietary Fiber 2g; Sugars 13g); Protein 38g **% DAILY VALUE:** Vitamin A 20%; Vitamin C 10%; Calcium 35%; Iron 20% **EXCHANGES:** 1 Starch, 1½ Other Carbohydrate, 5 Lean Meat, 3 Fat **CARBOHYDRATE CHOICES:** 2½

Quick Tip For a classic chicken Parmesan meal, serve this easy chicken dish with cooked spaghetti, broccoli and a tossed salad. Your family will love it.

Chicken Cutlets
with Creamy Mushroom Gravy

PREP TIME: 30 MINUTES ● **START TO FINISH: 30 MINUTES**
4 SERVINGS

4 boneless skinless chicken breasts (4 oz each)

½ cup Original Bisquick mix

½ teaspoon garlic powder

1 egg

3 tablespoons vegetable oil

1½ cups sliced fresh mushrooms

3 tablespoons Original Bisquick mix

2 medium green onions, sliced (2 tablespoons)

1 cup milk

1½ teaspoons soy sauce

1 Between pieces of plastic wrap or waxed paper, place each chicken breast smooth side down; gently pound with flat side of meat mallet or rolling pin until about ¼ inch thick.

2 In shallow dish, stir ½ cup Bisquick mix and the garlic powder. In another shallow dish, beat egg. Dip chicken in egg, then coat with Bisquick mixture.

3 In 12-inch nonstick skillet, heat 2 tablespoons of the oil over medium heat. Add chicken. Cook about 3 minutes or until golden brown. Turn chicken; cover and cook 4 to 6 minutes longer or until chicken is no longer pink in center. Remove to serving platter; cover to keep warm.

4 In same skillet, heat remaining 1 tablespoon oil over medium heat. Add mushrooms; cook 3 to 4 minutes, stirring frequently, until browned. Add 3 tablespoons Bisquick mix and the onions; cook and stir until mixed. Stir in milk and soy sauce. Cook until mixture is thick and bubbly. Serve over chicken.

High Altitude (3500–6500 ft): For gravy, add an additional 2 tablespoons milk and cook 3 to 4 minutes.

1 SERVING: Calories 370 (Calories from Fat 170); Total Fat 19g (Saturated Fat 4.5g); Cholesterol 125mg; Sodium 470mg; Total Carbohydrate 18g (Dietary Fiber 0g; Sugars 4g); Protein 31g **% DAILY VALUE:** Vitamin A 4%; Vitamin C 0%; Calcium 10%; Iron 10% **EXCHANGES:** ½ Starch, ½ Other Carbohydrate, 4 Very Lean Meat, 3½ Fat **CARBOHYDRATE CHOICES:** 1

Crispy Chicken Caesar Salad

PREP TIME: 15 MINUTES ● START TO FINISH: 30 MINUTES
4 SERVINGS

½ cup Original Bisquick mix

¼ teaspoon pepper

1 egg

4 boneless skinless chicken breasts (about 1¼ lb)

3 tablespoons vegetable oil

2 packages (7.5 oz each) Caesar salad kit with lettuce, dressing, Parmesan cheese and croutons

1 tomato, cut into 8 wedges

1 In shallow dish, stir Bisquick mix and pepper. In another shallow dish, beat egg. Dip chicken in egg, then coat with Bisquick mixture.

2 In 10-inch nonstick skillet, heat oil over medium heat. Cook chicken in oil 12 to 14 minutes, turning once, until juice of chicken is clear when thickest part is cut (170°F).

3 In large serving bowl, toss salad ingredients; divide evenly onto individual plates. Cut chicken crosswise into ½-inch slices; place on top of salads. Top with tomato.

High Altitude (3500–6500 ft): No change.

1 SERVING: Calories 520 (Calories from Fat 300); Total Fat 33g (Saturated Fat 6g); Cholesterol 150mg; Sodium 680mg; Total Carbohydrate 20g (Dietary Fiber 2g; Sugars 3g); Protein 37g **% DAILY VALUE:** Vitamin A 45%; Vitamin C 35%; Calcium 10%; Iron 15% **EXCHANGES:** 1 Starch, 1 Vegetable, 4½ Very Lean Meat, 6 Fat **CARBOHYDRATE CHOICES:** 1

Quick Tip Coat the chicken up to 4 hours ahead of time to cut down on last-minute preparation. Keep the chicken in the fridge.

Mandarin Chicken Salad

PREP TIME: 10 MINUTES ● **START TO FINISH: 30 MINUTES**
5 SERVINGS

½ cup Original Bisquick mix

2 tablespoons sesame seed

1 teaspoon ground ginger

2 tablespoons teriyaki sauce

1 tablespoon olive or canola oil

1 lb boneless skinless chicken breasts, cut into 1-inch pieces

1 bag (10 oz) European-style or romaine salad mix

1 can (11 oz) mandarin orange segments, drained

1 cup fresh snow (Chinese) pea pods, strings removed, cut in half if necessary

½ cup reduced-fat honey mustard dressing

1 Heat oven to 425°F. Spray cookie sheet with cooking spray. In 1-gallon resealable food-storage plastic bag, place Bisquick mix, sesame seed and ginger. Seal bag; shake to mix.

2 In small bowl, mix teriyaki sauce and oil. Coat chicken pieces with oil mixture. Shake about 6 chicken pieces at a time in bag of Bisquick mixture until coated. Shake off any extra mixture. On cookie sheet, place chicken pieces in single layer.

3 Bake 10 to 15 minutes or until chicken is no longer pink in center. Cool 5 minutes.

4 Meanwhile, in large bowl, mix salad mix, orange segments and pea pods. Top with warm chicken pieces and drizzle with dressing; toss to coat.

High Altitude (3500–6500 ft): No change.

1 SERVING: Calories 300 (Calories from Fat 100); Total Fat 11g (Saturated Fat 2g); Cholesterol 55mg; Sodium 730mg; Total Carbohydrate 26g (Dietary Fiber 3g; Sugars 13g); Protein 24g **% DAILY VALUE:** Vitamin A 80%; Vitamin C 60%; Calcium 6%; Iron 15% **EXCHANGES:** ½ Starch, 1 Other Carbohydrate, 1 Vegetable, 3 Very Lean Meat, 1½ Fat **CARBOHYDRATE CHOICES:** 2

Quick Tip For added crunch, toss some crispy chow mein noodles with the salad greens and sprinkle the top of the salad with sliced toasted almonds.

Sweet-and-Sour Chicken Crepes

PREP TIME: 25 MINUTES ● **START TO FINISH: 25 MINUTES**
4 SERVINGS (2 CREPES EACH)

CREPES

1 cup Original Bisquick mix

¾ cup milk

1 teaspoon soy sauce

1 egg

CHICKEN

2 cups frozen stir-fry bell
peppers and onions
(from 1-lb bag), thawed
and drained

1 cup cut-up cooked chicken

1 can (8 oz) pineapple tidbits
or chunks, drained

⅔ cup sweet-and-sour sauce

1 Stir all ingredients for crepes until blended. Lightly spray 6- or 7-inch skillet with cooking spray; heat over medium-high heat. For each crepe, pour 2 tablespoons batter into hot skillet; rotate skillet until batter covers bottom. Cook until golden brown. Gently loosen edge with metal spatula; turn and cook other side until golden brown. Stack crepes as you remove them from skillet, placing waxed paper between them. Keep crepes covered to prevent them from drying out.

2 Heat stir-fry vegetables, chicken, pineapple and ⅓ cup of the sweet-and-sour sauce in 2-quart saucepan over medium-high heat, stirring constantly, until hot.

3 Spoon about 2 tablespoons filling onto each crepe. Roll up; carefully place seam side down. Heat remaining ⅓ cup sweet-and-sour sauce until hot. Serve over crepes.

High Altitude (3500–6500 ft): No change.

1 SERVING: Calories 325 (Calories from Fat 90); Total Fat 10g (Saturated Fat 3g); Cholesterol 85mg; Sodium 730mg; Total Carbohydrate 43g (Dietary Fiber 3g; Sugars 8g); Protein 16g **% DAILY VALUE:** Vitamin A 8%; Vitamin C 38%; Calcium 14%; Iron 12% **EXCHANGES:** 2 Starch, ½ Fruit, 1 Vegetable, 1 Medium-Fat Meat, 1 Fat **CARBOHYDRATE CHOICES:** 3

Quick Tip Make the crepes ahead of time. Stack crepes with waxed paper between them, place them in a plastic bag (so they won't dry out) and refrigerate. At suppertime, make the filling and quickly reheat the crepes in the microwave on High for 30 seconds. Assemble and serve.

Chicken Chili
with Cornbread Dumplings

PREP TIME: 10 MINUTES ● **START TO FINISH: 30 MINUTES**
6 SERVINGS

CHILI

3 cups cubed cooked chicken

1½ cups water

1 can (10.75 oz) condensed
cream of chicken soup

1 can (15 oz) navy beans,
drained, rinsed

1 can (11 oz) whole kernel corn
with red and green peppers,
undrained

1 can (4.5 oz) chopped green
chiles

1 teaspoon ground cumin

DUMPLINGS

1⅓ cups Original Bisquick mix

⅔ cup yellow cornmeal

⅔ cup milk

1 teaspoon chili powder

1 In 5-quart nonstick Dutch oven, heat all chili ingredients over medium-high heat, stirring occasionally, until bubbly.

2 Meanwhile, in medium bowl, stir all dumpling ingredients until soft dough forms.

3 Drop dough by 6 rounded spoonfuls onto simmering chili. Reduce heat to medium-low. Cover; cook 13 to 15 minutes or until dumplings are dry.

High Altitude (3500–6500 ft): After adding dumplings, simmer covered 14 to 16 minutes.

1 SERVING: Calories 490 (Calories from Fat 120); Total Fat 13g (Saturated Fat 4g); Cholesterol 65mg; Sodium 1250mg; Total Carbohydrate 60g (Dietary Fiber 9g; Sugars 6g); Protein 31g **% DAILY VALUE:** Vitamin A 15%; Vitamin C 4%; Calcium 10%; Iron 25% **EXCHANGES:** 3 Starch, 1 Other Carbohydrate, 3 Very Lean Meat, 2 Fat **CARBOHYDRATE CHOICES:** 4

Turkey à la King

PREP TIME: 30 MINUTES ● START TO FINISH: 30 MINUTES
6 SERVINGS

2½ cups Original Bisquick mix

⅓ cup grated Parmesan cheese

¼ teaspoon dried thyme leaves

2⅔ cups milk

1 package (20 oz) lean ground turkey

1 small clove garlic, finely chopped

1 cup sliced fresh mushrooms (3 oz)

½ cup chopped red bell pepper

1 cup frozen sweet peas

½ teaspoon salt

¼ teaspoon pepper

1 Heat oven to 425°F. Spray cookie sheet with cooking spray. In medium bowl, mix 2¼ cups of the Bisquick mix, 2 tablespoons of the Parmesan cheese, the thyme and ⅔ cup of the milk until soft dough forms. Drop dough by 6 large spoonfuls onto cookie sheet.

2 Bake 8 to 10 minutes or until golden brown.

3 Meanwhile, in 12-inch nonstick skillet, cook turkey over medium-high heat 5 to 7 minutes, stirring occasionally, until no longer pink. Add garlic, mushrooms and bell pepper. Cook 3 to 4 minutes, stirring occasionally, until vegetables are crisp-tender. Stir in remaining ¼ cup Bisquick mix until blended. Stir in peas, salt, pepper and remaining 2 cups milk. Cook until mixture bubbles and thickens. Stir in remaining Parmesan cheese.

4 Split biscuits and place bottoms on individual serving plates. Spoon ⅓ cup turkey mixture over each biscuit bottom. Top with biscuit tops and remaining turkey mixture.

High Altitude (3500–6500 ft): No change.

1 SERVING: Calories 430 (Calories from Fat 140); Total Fat 15g (Saturated Fat 6g); Cholesterol 75mg; Sodium 1020mg; Total Carbohydrate 42g (Dietary Fiber 2g; Sugars 9g); Protein 32g **% DAILY VALUE:** Vitamin A 20%; Vitamin C 20%; Calcium 25%; Iron 15% **EXCHANGES:** 2 Starch, 1 Other Carbohydrate, 3½ Lean Meat, ½ Fat **CARBOHYDRATE CHOICES:** 3

Ah 1952, when families ate together at the same time each day—or so we like to remember! Whatever time you like to eat, Bisquick helps you get there on time.

Quick Tip For a richer sauce, use 1 cup half-and-half and 1⅔ cups milk. Fat-free half-and-half will give you the same great richness as regular but with less fat and fewer calories.

Turkey Cornbread Tostadas

PREP TIME: 25 MINUTES ● START TO FINISH: 25 MINUTES
4 SERVINGS

1¼ cups Original Bisquick mix

½ cup cornmeal

½ cup milk

1 lb lean ground turkey

1 package (1.25 oz) 40%-less-sodium taco seasoning mix

⅔ cup water

½ cup finely shredded Mexican cheese blend (2 oz)

1 cup shredded lettuce

¼ cup sour cream

¼ cup taco sauce

1 Heat oven to 425°F. Spray cookie sheet with cooking spray. In medium bowl, stir Bisquick mix, cornmeal and milk until soft dough forms. Drop dough into 4 mounds on cookie sheet. With fingers coated in Bisquick mix, pat each mound into 5-inch round; pinch edges to form ¼-inch rim. Prick bottoms with fork.

2 Bake 8 to 10 minutes or until golden brown. Place on individual serving plates.

3 Meanwhile, in 10-inch nonstick skillet, cook turkey over medium-high heat 5 to 7 minutes, stirring occasionally, until no longer pink. Stir in taco seasoning mix and water. Cook uncovered about 5 minutes, stirring occasionally, until thick and bubbly. Spoon mixture onto baked rounds. Top with cheese, lettuce, sour cream and taco sauce.

High Altitude (3500–6500 ft): Bake 10 to 12 minutes.

1 SERVING: Calories 500 (Calories from Fat 170); Total Fat 19g (Saturated Fat 8g); Cholesterol 100mg; Sodium 1230mg; Total Carbohydrate 47g (Dietary Fiber 2g; Sugars 4g); Protein 34g **% DAILY VALUE:** Vitamin A 15%; Vitamin C 0%; Calcium 20%; Iron 20% **EXCHANGES:** 2 Starch, 1 Other Carbohydrate, 4 Lean Meat, 1½ Fat **CARBOHYDRATE CHOICES:** 3

Crispy Turkey Divan

PREP TIME: 25 MINUTES ● START TO FINISH: 25 MINUTES
6 SERVINGS

1 package (20 oz) uncooked turkey breast tenderloins

1 cup Original Bisquick mix

1 cup Country Corn Flakes cereal, crushed

¼ teaspoon pepper

2 eggs

3 tablespoons vegetable oil

1 bag (24 oz) frozen broccoli and three-cheese sauce

½ cup cheese dip (from 15-oz jar)

1 Cut turkey crosswise and at an angle into ½-inch-thick slices. In shallow dish, mix Bisquick mix, crushed cereal and pepper. In small bowl, beat eggs. Dip turkey into eggs, then coat with Bisquick mixture.

2 In 12-inch nonstick skillet, heat 1 tablespoon of the oil over medium heat. Cooking in batches, cook turkey in oil in single layer 5 to 8 minutes, turning once, until golden brown on outside and no longer pink in center. Remove cooked turkey from skillet; cover to keep warm. Add remaining 2 tablespoons oil as needed to cook remaining turkey.

3 Meanwhile, cook broccoli in microwave as directed on bag. Stir in cheese dip. Cover and microwave on High about 2 minutes or until thoroughly heated. Spoon broccoli and cheese mixture over turkey.

High Altitude (3500–6500 ft): No change.

1 SERVING: Calories 370 (Calories from Fat 150); Total Fat 16g (Saturated Fat 4.5g); Cholesterol 145mg; Sodium 900mg; Total Carbohydrate 26g (Dietary Fiber 3g; Sugars 5g); Protein 31g **% DAILY VALUE:** Vitamin A 6%; Vitamin C 30%; Calcium 15%; Iron 20% **EXCHANGES:** 1 Starch, ½ Other Carbohydrate, 1 Vegetable, 3½ Lean Meat, 1 Fat **CARBOHYDRATE CHOICES:** 2

Crispy Chicken Divan: Substitute 4 boneless skinless chicken breasts (about 1¼ pounds) for the turkey.

Easy Turkey Club Bake

PREP TIME: 10 MINUTES ● **START TO FINISH: 30 MINUTES**
6 SERVINGS

2 cups Original Bisquick mix

⅓ cup mayonnaise or salad dressing

⅓ cup milk

2 cups cubed cooked turkey

2 tablespoons sliced green onions (2 medium)

6 slices bacon, crisply cooked, crumbled

¼ cup mayonnaise or salad dressing

1 large tomato, chopped (1 cup)

1 cup shredded Colby-Monterey Jack cheese (4 oz)

1 Heat oven to 450°F. Spray cookie sheet with cooking spray. In medium bowl, stir Bisquick mix, ⅓ cup mayonnaise and the milk until soft dough forms. On cookie sheet, press dough into 12 × 8-inch rectangle.

2 Bake 8 to 10 minutes or until crust is golden brown.

3. In medium bowl, mix turkey, onions, bacon and ¼ cup mayonnaise. Spoon over crust to within ¼ inch of edges. Sprinkle with tomato and cheese.

4 Bake about 5 minutes or until mixture is hot and cheese is melted.

High Altitude (3500–6500 ft): In step 2, bake crust about 10 minutes. In step 4, bake 6 to 8 minutes.

1 SERVING: Calories 530 (Calories from Fat 310); Total Fat 35g (Saturated Fat 10g); Cholesterol 75mg; Sodium 950mg; Total Carbohydrate 29g (Dietary Fiber 1g; Sugars 4g); Protein 25g **% DAILY VALUE:** Vitamin A 10%; Vitamin C 4%; Calcium 20%; Iron 10% **EXCHANGES:** 1 Starch, 1 Other Carbohydrate, 3 Lean Meat, 5 Fat **CARBOHYDRATE CHOICES:** 2

Quick Tip Like to trim the fat from this dish? Use fat-free (skim) milk, reduced-fat mayonnaise and turkey bacon. You'll save 11 grams of fat and over 85 calories per serving.

California Pork Tenderloin Sandwiches

PREP TIME: 25 MINUTES ● **START TO FINISH: 25 MINUTES**
4 SANDWICHES

¾ lb pork tenderloin, cut into 4 pieces

½ cup Original Bisquick mix

¼ teaspoon ground mustard

1 egg

2 to 3 tablespoons vegetable oil

4 large hamburger buns, split

4 lettuce leaves

4 slices tomato

2 tablespoons mayonnaise or salad dressing

1 Between pieces of plastic wrap, place 1 pork tenderloin piece, cut side down. Gently pound with meat mallet or rolling pin, beginning in center, until ¼ inch thick. Repeat with remaining pork pieces.

2 In shallow dish or pie plate, stir Bisquick mix and mustard until mixed. In another shallow dish or pie plate, beat egg. Dip pork pieces in egg, then coat in Bisquick mixture.

3 In 12-inch nonstick skillet, heat 2 tablespoons of the oil over medium heat. Add pork. Cook 6 to 8 minutes, turning once and adding remaining 1 tablespoon oil if needed, until golden brown on outside and no longer pink in center.

4 Place pork on bottom halves of buns. Top with lettuce and tomato. Spread cut sides of bun tops with mayonnaise; add to sandwiches.

High Altitude (3500–6500 ft): No change.

1 SANDWICH: Calories 460 (Calories from Fat 190); Total Fat 21g (Saturated Fat 4.5g); Cholesterol 110mg; Sodium 550mg; Total Carbohydrate 39g (Dietary Fiber 2g; Sugars 5g); Protein 28g **% DAILY VALUE:** Vitamin A 6%; Vitamin C 6%; Calcium 10%; Iron 20% **EXCHANGES:** 2 Starch, ½ Other Carbohydrate, 3 Lean Meat, 2½ Fat **CARBOHYDRATE CHOICES:** 2½

Quick Tip Thin pork cutlets are sometimes available at the meat counter. To save a few minutes, substitute 4 cutlets for the tenderloin.

Black Beans and Ham

PREP TIME: 15 MINUTES ● **START TO FINISH: 40 MINUTES**
6 SERVINGS

1 tablespoon vegetable oil

1 large onion, chopped
(1 cup)

½ cup chopped red or green
bell pepper

2 cans (15 oz each) black
beans, undrained

2 cups cubed fully cooked ham
(12 oz)

2 teaspoons chili powder

1½ cups Original Bisquick mix

⅓ cup cornmeal

⅔ cup milk

½ cup shredded Cheddar
cheese (2 oz)

1 Heat oil in 4-quart Dutch oven over medium heat. Cook onion and bell pepper in oil, stirring occasionally, until tender. Stir in beans, ham and 1 teaspoon of the chili powder. Heat to boiling; reduce heat to low.

2 Stir remaining 1 teaspoon chili powder, the Bisquick mix, cornmeal and milk until soft dough forms. Drop by 6 spoonfuls onto simmering bean mixture.

3 Cook uncovered 10 minutes. Cover and cook 5 minutes longer. Sprinkle with cheese. Cover and let stand until cheese is melted.

High Altitude (3500–6500 ft): After dropping dough onto bean mixture, cook uncovered over medium-low heat 12 minutes. Cover and cook 10 minutes longer. Sprinkle with cheese. Cover and cook 2 minutes.

1 SERVING: Calories 470 (Calories from Fat 135); Total Fat 15g (Saturated Fat 5g); Cholesterol 40mg; Sodium 1720mg; Total Carbohydrate 66g (Dietary Fiber 11g; Sugars 7g); Protein 29g **% DAILY VALUE:** Vitamin A 24%; Vitamin C 22%; Calcium 24%; Iron 30% **EXCHANGES:** 4½ Starch, 1½ Medium-Fat Meat **CARBOHYDRATE CHOICES:** 4½

Quick Tip Pinto beans or a combination of black and pinto beans will give a slightly different twist to this dish. A southern-inspired meal, this ham and black bean casserole has a subtle spicy taste and cornmeal dumplings. Serve with cooked greens or okra and iced tea for a complete southern theme.

Barbecue Pork Shortcakes

PREP TIME: 10 MINUTES ● **START TO FINISH: 20 MINUTES**

4 SANDWICHES

½ cup milk

2 teaspoons maple extract

1¾ cups Original Bisquick mix

1 container (18 oz) refrigerated fully cooked original barbecue sauce with shredded pork

1 cup frozen mixed vegetables, thawed, drained

2 tablespoons maple-flavored syrup

1 Heat oven to 450°F. In large bowl, mix milk and maple extract. Stir in Bisquick mix until soft dough forms; beat 20 strokes.

2 Place dough on surface generously sprinkled with Bisquick mix; gently roll in Bisquick mix to coat. Shape into a ball; knead 10 times. Press or roll into 6-inch square, about ½ inch thick. Cut into 4 square biscuits. On ungreased cookie sheet, place biscuits.

3 Bake 7 to 9 minutes or until lightly browned.

4 Meanwhile, place pork in 1½-quart microwavable bowl. Cover with microwavable plastic wrap, folding back one edge ¼ inch to vent steam. Microwave on High 2 minutes; stir. If not hot, cover and microwave up to 4 minutes longer, stirring every minute. Stir in vegetables and maple syrup. Cover and microwave on High 1 minute.

5 To serve, split biscuits in half. Fill with pork mixture.

High Altitude (3500–6500 ft): No change.

1 SANDWICH: Calories 490 (Calories from Fat 110); Total Fat 12g (Saturated Fat 3.5g); Cholesterol 35mg; Sodium 1530mg; Total Carbohydrate 74g (Dietary Fiber 3g; Sugars 28g); Protein 20g **% DAILY VALUE:** Vitamin A 50%; Vitamin C 0%; Calcium 10%; Iron 20% **EXCHANGES:** 2 Starch, 3 Other Carbohydrate, 2 Medium-Fat Meat **CARBOHYDRATE CHOICES:** 5

Barbecue Pork Chops

PREP TIME: 10 MINUTES ● **START TO FINISH: 30 MINUTES**
6 SERVINGS

1 cup barbecue-flavored potato chips (about 1 oz)

½ cup Original Bisquick mix

1 egg, beaten

2 tablespoons barbecue sauce

6 boneless pork loin chops, ½ inch thick (about 1½ lb)

1 tablespoon canola or soybean oil

¾ cup barbecue sauce

1 Place potato chips in 1-gallon resealable food storage plastic bag; crush with rolling pin. Add Bisquick mix to chips; mix well.

2 In small shallow dish, mix egg and 2 tablespoons barbecue sauce. Dip pork chops into egg mixture, then shake in bag to coat with Bisquick mixture.

3 In 12-inch nonstick skillet, heat oil over medium-low heat. Cook pork chops in oil 15 to 18 minutes, turning once, until golden brown on outside and no longer pink in center. Serve with ¾ cup barbecue sauce.

High Altitude (3500–6500 ft): No change.

1 SERVING: Calories 330 (Calories from Fat 130); Total Fat 15g (Saturated Fat 4g); Cholesterol 105mg; Sodium 590mg; Total Carbohydrate 24g (Dietary Fiber 0g; Sugars 12g); Protein 26g **% DAILY VALUE:** Vitamin A 2%; Vitamin C 2%; Calcium 4%; Iron 10% **EXCHANGES:** ½ Starch, 1 Other Carbohydrate, 3½ Lean Meat, 1 Fat **CARBOHYDRATE CHOICES:** 1½

Quick Tip After coating pork chops with potato chip mixture, don't cook them. Instead, wrap each pork chop in heavy-duty foil. Freeze up to 2 months. Place in refrigerator 8 hours or overnight until thawed and then cook as directed.

Twisted Pizza Dogs

PREP TIME: 15 MINUTES ● **START TO FINISH: 30 MINUTES**
8 SERVINGS

1¾ cups Original Bisquick mix

⅓ cup milk

1 can (8 oz) pizza sauce

8 hot dogs

1 tablespoon milk

2 tablespoons grated Parmesan cheese

1 Heat oven to 425°F. Spray cookie sheet with cooking spray. In medium bowl, stir Bisquick mix, ⅓ cup milk and 2 tablespoons of the pizza sauce until soft dough forms; beat 30 seconds.

2 Place dough on surface sprinkled with Bisquick mix; roll in Bisquick mix to coat. Shape into a ball; knead 10 times.

3 Press or roll dough into 12 × 8-inch rectangle. Cut dough lengthwise into eight 1-inch strips. Shape 1 piece of dough around each hot dog in a spiral design; seal ends if necessary. Place on cookie sheet. Brush 1 tablespoon milk over dough; sprinkle with cheese.

4 Bake 10 to 12 minutes or until golden brown. Serve with remaining pizza sauce, heated if desired.

High Altitude (3500–6500 ft): Bake 11 to 13 minutes.

1 SERVING: Calories 270 (Calories from Fat 150); Total Fat 17g (Saturated Fat 6g); Cholesterol 25mg; Sodium 1000mg; Total Carbohydrate 22g (Dietary Fiber 1g; Sugars 4g); Protein 8g **% DAILY VALUE:** Vitamin A 0%; Vitamin C 0%; Calcium 6%; Iron 8% **EXCHANGES:** 1 Starch, ½ Other Carbohydrate, ½ High-Fat Meat, 2½ Fat **CARBOHYDRATE CHOICES:** 1½

The days of rationing recalled in this 1943 ad are long gone, but these delightful dogs are popular as ever.

Muffuletta Sandwiches

PREP TIME: 20 MINUTES ● START TO FINISH: 30 MINUTES
4 SANDWICHES

2 cups Original Bisquick mix

½ teaspoon dried basil leaves

¼ cup grated Parmesan cheese

½ cup water

¼ cup finely chopped pimiento-stuffed green olives

¼ cup Italian dressing

4 thin slices (about 4 oz) cooked ham (from deli)

12 thin slices (about 4 oz) hard salami

4 slices (about 3 oz) provolone cheese

1 Heat oven to 425°F. In medium bowl, stir Bisquick mix, basil, Parmesan cheese and water until soft dough forms. Place dough on surface dusted with Bisquick mix; roll in Bisquick mix to form ball. Knead 10 times. On ungreased cookie sheet, pat dough into 8-inch square. Cut into 4 squares; separate slightly.

2 Bake 8 to 10 minutes or until golden brown. Remove from cookie sheet to cooling rack; cool 5 minutes.

3 Meanwhile, in small bowl, mix olives and Italian dressing.

4 With serrated knife, split biscuits. On bottom halves, spread olive mixture. Layer ham, salami and provolone cheese on olive mixture. Top with biscuit tops.

High Altitude (3500–6500 ft): Bake 10 to 12 minutes.

1 SANDWICH: Calories 530 (Calories from Fat 260); Total Fat 29g (Saturated Fat 11g); Cholesterol 65mg; Sodium 2220mg; Total Carbohydrate 43g (Dietary Fiber 2g; Sugars 4g); Protein 25g **% DAILY VALUE:** Vitamin A 6%; Vitamin C 0%; Calcium 30%; Iron 15% **EXCHANGES:** 2 Starch, 1 Other Carbohydrate, 2½ High-Fat Meat, 1½ Fat **CARBOHYDRATE CHOICES:** 3

Quick Tip Here's a fun to way serve these sandwiches. For each sandwich, spear additional pitted olives with a colorful cellophane-topped toothpick and poke into top of sandwich.

Beer-Battered Shrimp

PREP TIME: 25 MINUTES ● **START TO FINISH: 25 MINUTES**
4 SERVINGS

1 cup Original Bisquick mix

½ teaspoon garlic powder

½ cup regular or nonalcoholic beer

1 egg

1 lb uncooked peeled deveined large (16 to 20 count) shrimp, thawed if frozen, tail shells removed

¼ cup Original Bisquick mix

Vegetable oil for frying

½ cup sweet-and-sour sauce

1 In deep 10-inch skillet, heat 1½ inches oil over medium heat to 375°F.

2 In medium bowl, stir 1 cup Bisquick mix, the garlic powder, beer and egg with wire whisk or fork until smooth. (If batter is too thick, stir in additional beer, 1 tablespoon at a time, until desired consistency.)

3 Lightly coat 6 shrimp in the ¼ cup Bisquick mix. Dip shrimp into batter, letting excess drip into bowl. Fry in oil about 2 minutes on each side or until golden brown; drain on paper towels. Repeat with remaining shrimp. Serve hot with sweet-and-sour sauce.

High Altitude (3500–6500 ft): No change.

1 SERVING: Calories 610 (Calories from Fat 390); Total Fat 44g (Saturated Fat 7g); Cholesterol 215mg; Sodium 750mg; Total Carbohydrate 32g (Dietary Fiber 1g; Sugars 7g); Protein 22g **% DAILY VALUE:** Vitamin A 6%; Vitamin C 0%; Calcium 8%; Iron 20% **EXCHANGES:** 1 Starch, 1 Other Carbohydrate, 2½ Very Lean Meat, 8½ Fat **CARBOHYDRATE CHOICES:** 2

Coconut Shrimp

PREP TIME: 30 MINUTES ● **START TO FINISH: 30 MINUTES**
6 SERVINGS

1 lb uncooked deveined peeled medium shrimp (31 to 35), thawed if frozen, tail shells removed

1 cup Original Bisquick mix

¾ cup milk

1 egg

1 cup vegetable oil

2½ cups flaked coconut

½ cup chili sauce

½ cup apricot preserves

1 Pat shrimp dry with paper towels. In medium bowl, stir Bisquick mix, milk and egg with wire whisk or fork until blended. Add shrimp; gently stir to coat well.

2 In 10-inch skillet, heat oil over medium heat to 375°F. In shallow dish, place half of the coconut (add remaining coconut after coating half of the shrimp). Cooking in batches, remove shrimp one at a time from batter and coat with coconut; place in oil in single layer.

3 Cook 3 to 4 minutes, turning once, until coating is crispy and golden brown and shrimp are pink (cut 1 shrimp open to check doneness). Drain on paper towels.

4 In small bowl, mix chili sauce and apricot preserves. Serve shrimp with sauce for dipping.

High Altitude (3500–6500 ft): Cook shrimp 4 to 5 minutes, turning every minute.

1 SERVING: Calories 440 (Calories from Fat 190); Total Fat 21g (Saturated Fat 11g); Cholesterol 110mg; Sodium 520mg; Total Carbohydrate 50g (Dietary Fiber 3g; Sugars 27g); Protein 15g **% DAILY VALUE:** Vitamin A 6%; Vitamin C 6%; Calcium 4%; Iron 20% **EXCHANGES:** 1 Starch, 2 Other Carbohydrate, 1½ Very Lean Meat, 4 Fat **CARBOHYDRATE CHOICES:** 3

Quick Tip For a great supper salad, serve these crispy shrimp on a bed of mixed salad greens. Add enough water to the dipping sauce so you can drizzle it over the salad.

Crab Cake Sandwiches

PREP TIME: 20 MINUTES ● **START TO FINISH: 20 MINUTES**
4 SANDWICHES

1 cup soft bread crumbs
(about 1½ slices bread)

½ cup Original Bisquick mix

2 teaspoons seafood seasoning
(from 6-oz container)

2 medium green onions, finely
chopped (2 tablespoons)

2 eggs, slightly beaten

2 cans (6 oz each) lump
crabmeat, drained

2 tablespoons butter or
margarine

4 whole wheat burger buns,
split

½ cup shredded lettuce

4 slices tomato

4 tablespoons tartar sauce

1 In medium bowl, mix bread crumbs, Bisquick mix, seafood seasoning, onions, eggs and crabmeat until well blended. Shape mixture into 4 (¾-inch-thick) patties.

2 In 12-inch nonstick skillet, melt 1 tablespoon of the butter over medium heat. Add patties; cook 4 minutes. Turn patties; add remaining 1 tablespoon butter to skillet. Cook about 4 minutes longer or until golden brown.

3 Fill buns with lettuce, patties, tomato and tartar sauce.

High Altitude (3500–6500 ft): No change.

1 SANDWICH: Calories 430 (Calories from Fat 180); Total Fat 20g (Saturated Fat 7g); Cholesterol 185mg; Sodium 1220mg; Total Carbohydrate 39g (Dietary Fiber 4g; Sugars 7g); Protein 24g **% DAILY VALUE:** Vitamin A 10%; Vitamin C 4%; Calcium 15%; Iron 20% **EXCHANGES:** 2 Starch, ½ Other Carbohydrate, 2½ Very Lean Meat, 3½ Fat **CARBOHYDRATE CHOICES:** 2½

Seafood à la King

PREP TIME: 15 MINUTES ● START TO FINISH: 20 MINUTES
6 SERVINGS

2¼ cups Original or Reduced Fat Bisquick mix

¾ cup fat-free (skim) milk

1 can (18.5 oz) ready-to-serve New England clam chowder

1 cup frozen mixed vegetables (from 1-lb bag)

1 package (5 oz) frozen cooked salad shrimp, thawed and drained

1 tablespoon Original Bisquick mix

1 teaspoon dried dill weed

⅛ teaspoon pepper

1 Heat oven to 450°F. Stir 2¼ cups Bisquick mix and the milk until soft dough forms. Drop by 6 spoonfuls onto ungreased cookie sheet. Bake about 10 minutes or until golden brown.

2 While biscuits are baking, mix remaining ingredients in 2-quart saucepan. Heat to boiling over medium heat, stirring occasionally.

3 To serve, split biscuits in half. Spoon generous ¼ cup hot chowder mixture over bottom of each biscuit. Top with remaining biscuit halves. Spoon ¼ cup chowder mixture over top of each biscuit.

High Altitude (3500–6500 ft): No change.

1 SERVING: Calories 315 (Calories from Fat 110); Total Fat 12g (Saturated Fat 3g); Cholesterol 50mg; Sodium 1140mg; Total Carbohydrate 39g (Dietary Fiber 3g; Sugars 4g); Protein 13g **% DAILY VALUE:** Vitamin A 30%; Vitamin C 4%; Calcium 10%; Iron 26% **EXCHANGES:** 3 Starch, 1 Medium-Fat Meat **CARBOHYDRATE CHOICES:** 2½

Quick Tip You can make both the biscuits and the seafood chowder ahead. Store baked biscuits at room temperature, then warm in the oven or microwave. Refrigerate chowder until serving time, then reheat. If you don't like shrimp, use instead a 6-ounce can of skinless boneless salmon or tuna, drained.

Ranch Tuna Melt Pizza

PREP TIME: 15 MINUTES ● **START TO FINISH: 25 MINUTES**
6 SERVINGS

1½ cups Original Bisquick mix

⅓ cup boiling water

1 can (12 oz) chunk light tuna in water, well drained

¼ cup ranch dressing

3 tablespoons finely chopped green onions (3 medium)

1 small tomato, cut into 6 slices

3 slices American cheese, cut in half diagonally

1 Heat oven to 450°F. In medium bowl, stir Bisquick mix and boiling water until soft dough forms. Gather dough into a ball.

2 Place dough on surface sprinkled with Bisquick mix. Roll dough into 13-inch round. Place on ungreased 12-inch pizza pan; pinch edge to form ½-inch rim.

3 Bake 6 to 8 minutes or until light golden brown.

4 Meanwhile, in medium bowl, mix tuna, dressing and onions. Spread tuna mixture over crust. Arrange tomato and cheese slices alternately in a pinwheel pattern on tuna mixture. Bake 1 to 2 minutes or until cheese is melted. Cut into wedges.

High Altitude (3500–6500 ft): In step 3, bake 8 to 10 minutes.

1 SERVING: Calories 270 (Calories from Fat 110); Total Fat 13g (Saturated Fat 4g); Cholesterol 30mg; Sodium 780mg; Total Carbohydrate 21g (Dietary Fiber 1g; Sugars 2g); Protein 18g **% DAILY VALUE:** Vitamin A 6%; Vitamin C 2%; Calcium 10%; Iron 10% **EXCHANGES:** 1½ Starch, 2 Very Lean Meat, 2 Fat **CARBOHYDRATE CHOICES:** 1½

Quick Tip The easiest way to move the rolled-out pizza dough to the pan is to fold the round into quarters, then gently unfold into the pan.

Lemon-Dill Breaded Fish

PREP TIME: 20 MINUTES ● START TO FINISH: 20 MINUTES
4 SERVINGS

½ cup Original Bisquick mix

¼ cup unseasoned dry bread crumbs

2 teaspoons grated lemon peel

1 teaspoon dried dill weed

½ teaspoon salt

1 egg

4 tilapia or other mild-flavored fish fillets, about ½ inch thick (about 1 lb)

2 tablespoons vegetable oil

1 In shallow dish, stir Bisquick mix, bread crumbs, lemon peel, dill weed and salt until blended. In another shallow dish, beat egg. Dip fish into egg, then coat with Bisquick mixture.

2 In 12-inch nonstick skillet, heat oil over medium-low heat. Add fish. Cook 8 to 10 minutes, turning once, until fish flakes easily with fork and is brown on both sides.

High Altitude (3500–6500 ft): No change.

1 SERVING: Calories 270 (Calories from Fat 110); Total Fat 12g (Saturated Fat 2.5g); Cholesterol 115mg; Sodium 640mg; Total Carbohydrate 15g (Dietary Fiber 0g; Sugars 1g); Protein 25g **% DAILY VALUE:** Vitamin A 2%; Vitamin C 0%; Calcium 6%; Iron 8% **EXCHANGES:** 1 Starch, 3 Very Lean Meat, 2 Fat **CARBOHYDRATE CHOICES:** 1

Potato Patties with Black Bean Salsa

PREP TIME: 10 MINUTES ● **START TO FINISH: 25 MINUTES**
6 SERVINGS

1 bag (1 lb 4 oz) refrigerated Southwest-style shredded hash brown potatoes

1 cup shredded reduced-fat Cheddar cheese (4 oz)

½ cup Original Bisquick mix

3 eggs, beaten, or ¾ cup fat-free egg product

¼ cup canola or olive oil

1 can (11 oz) whole kernel corn with red and green peppers, drained

1 can (15 oz) black beans, drained, rinsed

¼ cup chunky-style salsa

1 In large bowl, mix potatoes, cheese, Bisquick mix and eggs until blended.

2 In 12-inch skillet, heat 2 tablespoons of the oil over medium heat. For each patty, spoon about ½ cup potato mixture into oil in skillet. Flatten with back of spatula.

3 Cook patties about 4 minutes, turning once, until golden brown. Remove from skillet; cover to keep warm while cooking remaining patties. Add remaining 2 tablespoons oil as needed to prevent sticking.

4 In 2-quart saucepan, heat corn, beans and salsa over medium heat 2 to 3 minutes, stirring occasionally, until hot. Serve over patties.

High Altitude (3500–6500 ft): In step 4, increase cook time to 4 to 5 minutes.

1 SERVING: Calories 400 (Calories from Fat 140); Total Fat 15g (Saturated Fat 3g); Cholesterol 110mg; Sodium 430mg; Total Carbohydrate 50g (Dietary Fiber 10g; Sugars 3g); Protein 17g **% DAILY VALUE:** Vitamin A 10%; Vitamin C 15%; Calcium 20%; Iron 20% **EXCHANGES:** 3 Starch, 1 Very Lean Meat, 2½ Fat **CARBOHYDRATE CHOICES:** 3

Cooking
for Two

Beef Sloppy Joe Supreme

PREP TIME: 15 MINUTES ● **START TO FINISH: 40 MINUTES**
3 SERVINGS

½ cup Bisquick Heart Smart mix

¾ cup shredded reduced-fat Cheddar cheese (3 oz)

¼ cup water

2 tablespoons fat-free egg product or 1 egg white

½ lb extra-lean (at least 90%) ground beef

½ cup canned tomato sauce

¼ cup ketchup

¼ teaspoon salt

1 Heat oven to 400°F. In small bowl, stir Bisquick mix, ½ cup of the cheese, the water and egg product; set aside.

2 In ovenproof 8-inch skillet, cook beef over medium-high heat 5 to 7 minutes, stirring frequently, until thoroughly cooked; drain. Stir in tomato sauce, ketchup and salt. Cook, stirring occasionally, until hot. Pour Bisquick mixture over top.

3 Bake about 25 minutes or until golden brown. Sprinkle with remaining ¼ cup cheese.

High Altitude (3500–6500 ft): No change.

1 SERVING: Calories 270 (Calories from Fat 90); Total Fat 9g (Saturated Fat 3.5g); Cholesterol 55mg; Sodium 1170mg; Total Carbohydrate 22g (Dietary Fiber 0g; Sugars 8g); Protein 25g **% DAILY VALUE:** Vitamin A 8%; Vitamin C 4%; Calcium 30%; Iron 15% **EXCHANGES:** 1 Starch, ½ Other Carbohydrate, 3 Lean Meat **CARBOHYDRATE CHOICES:** 1½

Turkey Sloppy Joe Supreme: Substitute ½ pound ground turkey breast for the ground beef.

Quick Tip No ovenproof 8-inch skillet? Cook the beef in your favorite skillet, then place the hot cooked beef mixture in an 8-inch round pan. Top with the Bisquick mixture and bake.

Bisquick is a number-one hit in the musical scene evoked in this 1950s ad.

Italian Chicken

PREP TIME: 20 MINUTES ● START TO FINISH: 20 MINUTES
2 SERVINGS

2 boneless skinless chicken breasts (about 4 oz each)

¾ cup Wheaties® cereal, finely crushed

¼ cup Bisquick Heart Smart mix

¾ teaspoon Italian seasoning

¼ teaspoon garlic powder

¼ cup fat-free egg product

1 tablespoon vegetable oil

1 Between pieces of plastic wrap or waxed paper, place each chicken breast smooth side down; gently pound with flat side of meat mallet or rolling pin until about ¼ inch thick.

2 In shallow dish, stir cereal, Bisquick mix, Italian seasoning and garlic powder. In another shallow dish, place egg product. Dip chicken in egg product, then coat with cereal mixture.

3 In 10-inch nonstick skillet, heat 1½ teaspoons of the oil over medium-low heat. Add chicken; cook 4 minutes. Turn chicken; add remaining 1½ teaspoons oil to skillet. Cook 5 to 6 minutes longer or until chicken is no longer pink in center.

High Altitude (3500–6500 ft): In step 3, cook over medium-high heat.

1 SERVING: Calories 320 (Calories from Fat 110); Total Fat 12g (Saturated Fat 2g); Cholesterol 70mg; Sodium 380mg; Total Carbohydrate 22g (Dietary Fiber 2g; Sugars 3g); Protein 31g **% DAILY VALUE:** Vitamin A 8%; Vitamin C 2%; Calcium 10%; Iron 35% **EXCHANGES:** 1½ Starch, 4 Very Lean Meat, 1½ Fat **CARBOHYDRATE CHOICES:** 1½

Quick Tip Top each serving with chopped fresh tomato and chopped cilantro or heat some low-sodium tomato sauce and spoon over each serving and sprinkle with chopped cilantro.

Curried Country Chicken

PREP TIME: 15 MINUTES ● START TO FINISH: 30 MINUTES
2 SERVINGS

2 boneless skinless chicken breasts (about ½ lb), cut into 1-inch pieces

¼ cup chopped onion (½ medium)

¼ cup chopped green bell pepper

1 can (14.5 oz) diced tomatoes, undrained

¼ cup golden raisins

½ to 1 teaspoon curry powder

⅛ teaspoon salt

⅛ teaspoon ground nutmeg

⅔ cup Bisquick Heart Smart mix

3 tablespoons cornmeal

⅓ cup fat-free (skim) milk

1 In 3-quart nonstick saucepan, cook chicken over medium-high heat 3 minutes, stirring occasionally, until no longer pink in center. Stir in onion and bell pepper. Cook about 2 minutes, stirring occasionally, until vegetables are tender.

2 Stir in tomatoes, raisins, curry powder, salt and nutmeg. Heat to boiling.

3 Meanwhile, in small bowl, stir Bisquick mix, cornmeal and milk until soft dough forms.

4 Drop dough by 4 spoonfuls onto hot chicken mixture. Reduce heat to medium-low. Cover; cook 10 to 12 minutes or until dumplings are dry.

High Altitude (3500–6500 ft): In step 2, add ¼ cup water with tomatoes. In step 4, cook covered 11 to 13 minutes.

1 SERVING: Calories 450 (Calories from Fat 60); Total Fat 7g (Saturated Fat 1g); Cholesterol 70mg; Sodium 920mg; Total Carbohydrate 65g (Dietary Fiber 4g; Sugars 22g); Protein 33g **% DAILY VALUE:** Vitamin A 8%; Vitamin C 30%; Calcium 30%; Iron 30% **EXCHANGES:** 2 Starch, 2 Other Carbohydrate, 1 Vegetable, 3½ Very Lean Meat, ½ Fat **CARBOHYDRATE CHOICES:** 4

Southwest Country Chicken: Omit raisins, curry powder and nutmeg. Add 1 to 2 teaspoons chili powder with the tomatoes.

Cajun Country Chicken: Omit raisins, curry powder and nutmeg. Add 1 teaspoon Cajun seasoning and ¼ teaspoon dried oregano leaves with the tomatoes.

Lemon-Apricot Chicken

PREP TIME: 20 MINUTES ● **START TO FINISH: 50 MINUTES**
3 SERVINGS

CHICKEN

2 tablespoons fat-free egg
    product or 1 egg white

1 tablespoon water

½ cup Bisquick Heart Smart mix

1½ teaspoons grated lemon
    peel

⅛ teaspoon garlic powder

3 small boneless skinless
    chicken breasts (½ lb)

Cooking spray

Lemon slices, if desired

SAUCE

⅓ cup apricot preserves

1 tablespoon lemon juice

¼ teaspoon soy sauce

⅛ teaspoon ground ginger

1 Heat oven to 425°F. Spray 13 × 9-inch pan with cooking spray. In shallow dish, beat egg product and water slightly. In another shallow dish, stir Bisquick mix, lemon peel and garlic powder.

2 Between pieces of plastic wrap or waxed paper, place each chicken breast smooth side down; gently pound with flat side of meat mallet or rolling pin until about ½ inch thick. Dip chicken into egg mixture, then coat with Bisquick mixture. In pan, place chicken breasts. Spray chicken with cooking spray.

3 Bake uncovered 20 minutes. Turn; bake 10 minutes longer or until juice of chicken is clear when thickest part is cut (170°F).

4 In small microwavable bowl, stir all sauce ingredients. Microwave on High 1 minute; stir. Cut chicken crosswise into ½-inch slices. Pour sauce over chicken. Garnish with lemon slices.

High Altitude (3500–6500 ft): No change.

1 SERVING: Calories 270 (Calories from Fat 40); Total Fat 4.5g (Saturated Fat 0.5g); Cholesterol 40mg; Sodium 310mg; Total Carbohydrate 39g (Dietary Fiber 0g; Sugars 19g); Protein 18g **% DAILY VALUE:** Vitamin A 0%; Vitamin C 4%; Calcium 10%; Iron 10% **EXCHANGES:** 1 Starch, 1½ Other Carbohydrate, 2 Very Lean Meat, ½ Fat **CARBOHYDRATE CHOICES:** 2½

Southwest Tamale Tart

PREP TIME: 15 MINUTES ● START TO FINISH: 40 MINUTES
2 SERVINGS

½ cup Bisquick Heart Smart mix

¼ cup cornmeal

¾ cup shredded reduced-fat Cheddar cheese (3 oz)

1 tablespoon canned chopped green chiles, drained

3 tablespoons condensed beef broth

1 cup canned black beans, drained, rinsed

¼ cup chopped fresh cilantro

1 small tomato, seeded, chopped (½ cup)

Salsa (any variety), if desired

Reduced-fat sour cream, if desired

Guacamole, if desired

1 Heat oven to 350°F. Spray cooking sheet with cooking spray.

2 In small bowl, stir Bisquick mix, cornmeal, ½ cup of the cheese and the chiles thoroughly. Stir in broth. Spread mixture in 7-inch circle on cookie sheet. In small bowl, mix beans and cilantro; spoon over cornmeal mixture to within ½ inch of edge. Sprinkle with remaining ¼ cup cheese.

3 Bake 23 to 25 minutes or until edge is golden brown. Arrange tomatoes around edge of tart. Cut tart into wedges; serve with salsa, sour cream and guacamole.

High Altitude (3500–6500 ft): Increase beef broth by 1 to 2 tablespoons and bake time to 25 to 27 minutes.

1 SERVING: Calories 380 (Calories from Fat 50); Total Fat 6g (Saturated Fat 2g); Cholesterol 10mg; Sodium 920mg; Total Carbohydrate 59g (Dietary Fiber 7g; Sugars 7g); Protein 23g **% DAILY VALUE:** Vitamin A 15%; Vitamin C 6%; Calcium 50%; Iron 25% **EXCHANGES:** 3½ Starch, ½ Other Carbohydrate, 1½ Very Lean Meat, ½ Fat **CARBOHYDRATE CHOICES:** 4

Quick Tip If you have beef broth remaining, freeze it in a clean ice-cube tray. Store the frozen broth cubes in a plastic freezer bag, and use in soups and stews. Pull one out to add extra flavor to meat dishes.

Savory Baked Chicken and Potato Dinner

PREP TIME: 15 MINUTES ● **START TO FINISH: 50 MINUTES**
2 SERVINGS

2 tablespoons grated Parmesan cheese

½ teaspoon paprika

3 tablespoons water

2 tablespoons Dijon mustard

½ lb small red potatoes, cut into ½-inch cubes (1½ cups)

½ medium bell pepper, cut into bite-size strips (½ cup)

½ medium onion, cut into 16 wedges (1 cup)

Cooking spray

2 boneless skinless chicken breasts (about ½ lb)

3 tablespoons Bisquick Heart Smart mix

1 Heat oven to 400°F. Spray 13 × 9-inch pan with cooking spray. In small bowl, mix Parmesan cheese and paprika; set aside. In medium bowl, mix water and 1 tablespoon of the mustard. Stir potatoes, bell pepper and onion into mustard mixture. Spoon vegetable mixture in single layer onto half of the pan. Spray cooking spray over top; sprinkle with half of the cheese mixture. Bake 15 minutes.

2 Meanwhile, brush chicken breasts with remaining 1 tablespoon mustard; coat with Bisquick mix. Add chicken to pan. Spray chicken with cooking spray; sprinkle with remaining cheese mixture.

3 Bake 15 to 18 minutes longer or until potatoes are tender and juice of chicken is clear when center of thickest part is cut (170°F).

High Altitude (3500–6500 ft): Heat oven to 425°F.

1 SERVING: Calories 330 (Calories from Fat 80); Total Fat 8g (Saturated Fat 2.5g); Cholesterol 75mg; Sodium 660mg; Total Carbohydrate 33g (Dietary Fiber 4g; Sugars 4g); Protein 31g **% DAILY VALUE:** Vitamin A 10%; Vitamin C 35%; Calcium 15%; Iron 20% **EXCHANGES:** 1½ Starch, ½ Other Carbohydrate, 4 Very Lean Meat, 1 Fat **CARBOHYDRATE CHOICES:** 2

Savory Baked Pork and Potato Dinner: Substitute 2 boneless pork chops, ½ inch thick (about ½ pound) for the chicken.

Chicken Caesar Salad in Bread Bowls

PREP TIME: 35 MINUTES ● **START TO FINISH: 45 MINUTES**
2 SERVINGS

1 teaspoon regular active dry yeast

1 tablespoon sugar

¼ cup plus 2 tablespoons warm water (105°F to 115°F)

1½ cups Bisquick Heart Smart mix

½ teaspoon garlic powder

2 boneless skinless chicken breasts (about ½ lb)

¼ cup reduced-fat Caesar dressing

3 cups bite-size pieces romaine lettuce

½ cup Caesar or garlic-flavored croutons

2 tablespoons shredded Parmesan cheese

Freshly ground black pepper

1 In large bowl, dissolve yeast and sugar in warm water. Stir in Bisquick mix and garlic powder until dough leaves side of bowl and forms a ball. On surface sprinkled with Bisquick mix, gently roll dough in Bisquick mix to coat. Knead about 1 minute or until smooth. Cover; let rise 10 minutes.

2 Heat oven to 375°F. Grease outsides of two 10-ounce (large) custard cups. On ungreased cookie sheet, place cups upside down. Divide dough in half. Press or roll each half into 7-inch round. Shape rounds over outsides of custard cups. (Do not curl dough under edges of cups.)

3 Bake 12 to 15 minutes or until golden brown. Tap custard cups to loosen bread bowls; cool 3 minutes. Carefully lift bread bowls from custard cups (custard cups and bread will be hot). Cool bread bowls upright on cooling rack.

4 Meanwhile, heat gas or charcoal grill. Place chicken on grill. Cover grill; cook over medium heat 15 to 20 minutes, turning once, until juice of chicken is clear when center of thickest part is cut (170°F).

5 Cut chicken diagonally into ½-inch slices. Pour dressing into large bowl. Add romaine; toss to coat. Sprinkle with croutons, cheese and pepper; toss. Divide salad among bread bowls. Top each with chicken.

High Altitude (3500–6500 ft): No change.

1 SERVING: Calories 610 (Calories from Fat 130); Total Fat 15g (Saturated Fat 3g); Cholesterol 75mg; Sodium 1600mg; Total Carbohydrate 83g (Dietary Fiber 2g; Sugars 18g); Protein 37g **% DAILY VALUE:** Vitamin A 80%; Vitamin C 30%; Calcium 50%; Iron 30% **EXCHANGES:** 3½ Starch, 1½ Other Carbohydrate, 1 Vegetable, 3½ Very Lean Meat, 2 Fat **CARBOHYDRATE CHOICES:** 5½

Chicken Chowder
with Dijon Dumplings

PREP TIME: 15 MINUTES ● START TO FINISH: 30 MINUTES
2 SERVINGS

CHOWDER

1 teaspoon vegetable oil

¼ cup chopped onion
(½ medium)

2 cups cubed cooked chicken
breast

1 cup fat-free (skim) milk

1 cup frozen mixed
vegetables

½ cup less sodium chicken
broth

⅛ teaspoon dried thyme leaves

DUMPLINGS

⅔ cup Bisquick Heart Smart mix

¼ cup skim milk

2 teaspoons Dijon mustard

1 In 2-quart saucepan, heat oil over medium-high heat. Add onion; cook 2 to 4 minutes, stirring occasionally, until tender.

2 Stir in remaining chowder ingredients; heat to boiling.

3 In small bowl, stir Bisquick mix, milk and mustard until soft dough forms. Drop dough by 4 spoonfuls onto chicken mixture. Reduce heat to low. Cover; cook 10 to 12 minutes or until dumplings are dry.

High Altitude (3500–6500 ft): Increase chicken broth to ¾ cup. In step 3, reduce heat to medium-low. Cover; cook 12 to 14 minutes.

1 SERVING: Calories 510 (Calories from Fat 100); Total Fat 11g (Saturated Fat 2.5g); Cholesterol 120mg; Sodium 890mg; Total Carbohydrate 49g (Dietary Fiber 5g; Sugars 15g); Protein 54g **% DAILY VALUE:** Vitamin A 90%; Vitamin C 4%; Calcium 40%; Iron 20% **EXCHANGES:** 2 Starch, 1 Other Carbohydrate, 1 Vegetable, 6½ Very Lean Meat, 1 Fat **CARBOHYDRATE CHOICES:** 3

Quick Tip If you like corn chowder, use a cup of frozen corn instead of the mixed vegetables.

Easy Mexican Bake

PREP TIME: 15 MINUTES ● **START TO FINISH: 45 MINUTES**
3 SERVINGS

1 tablespoon Bisquick Heart Smart mix

½ cup canned Mexican-style stewed tomatoes, drained, liquid reserved

1 cup kidney beans (from 15-oz can), drained, rinsed

½ cup cut-up cooked chicken breast

½ cup frozen whole kernel corn

⅔ cup Bisquick Heart Smart mix

¼ cup fat-free (skim) milk

2 tablespoons fat-free egg product or 1 egg white

1 Heat oven to 400°F. Spray 1-quart microwavable casserole with cooking spray. In casserole, stir 1 tablespoon Bisquick mix and the reserved liquid from tomatoes with wire whisk or fork until blended. Stir in beans, chicken, corn and tomatoes; cut up large tomato chunks. Microwave on High 3 minutes; stir.

2 In small bowl, stir ⅔ cup Bisquick mix, the milk and egg product with wire whisk or fork until blended. Pour over mixture in casserole.

3 Bake uncovered 23 to 28 minutes or until golden brown.

High Altitude (3500–6500 ft): No change.

1 SERVING: Calories 270 (Calories from Fat 30); Total Fat 3.5g (Saturated Fat 0g); Cholesterol 20mg; Sodium 370mg; Total Carbohydrate 42g (Dietary Fiber 5g; Sugars 7g); Protein 17g **% DAILY VALUE:** Vitamin A 6%; Vitamin C 4%; Calcium 20%; Iron 20% **EXCHANGES:** 2 Starch, 1 Other Carbohydrate, 1½ Very Lean Meat **CARBOHYDRATE CHOICES:** 3

Hearty Chicken-Vegetable Stew with Dumplings

PREP TIME: 10 MINUTES ● **START TO FINISH: 30 MINUTES**
3 SERVINGS

STEW

2 cups frozen broccoli florets

2 medium carrots, thinly sliced (about 1 cup)

1 cup diced cooked chicken breast

½ teaspoon Italian seasoning

⅛ teaspoon garlic salt

⅛ teaspoon pepper

¾ cup water

1 tablespoon ketchup

1 can (14.5 oz) stewed tomatoes, undrained

DUMPLINGS

1 cup Bisquick Heart Smart mix

½ teaspoon parsley flakes

⅛ teaspoon garlic salt

⅓ cup milk

1 In 2-quart saucepan, heat all stew ingredients to boiling, stirring occasionally.

2 In medium bowl, stir all dumpling ingredients until soft dough forms. Drop by 6 spoonfuls onto boiling stew.

3 Reduce heat; simmer uncovered 10 minutes. Cover; simmer 10 minutes longer.

High Altitude (3500–6500 ft): No change.

1 SERVING: Calories 330 (Calories from Fat 50); Total Fat 5g (Saturated Fat 1g); Cholesterol 40mg; Sodium 1040mg; Total Carbohydrate 48g (Dietary Fiber 5g; Sugars 16g); Protein 22g **% DAILY VALUE:** Vitamin A 160%; Vitamin C 45%; Calcium 30%; Iron 20% **EXCHANGES:** 1½ Starch, 1 Other Carbohydrate, 2 Vegetable, 2 Very Lean Meat, ½ Fat **CARBOHYDRATE CHOICES:** 3

Deluxe Turkey Cheeseburger Melt

PREP TIME: 10 MINUTES ● START TO FINISH: 30 MINUTES
2 SERVINGS

⅓ cup Bisquick Heart Smart mix

1 tablespoon water

2 tablespoons fat-free egg product or 1 egg white

¼ cup plus 2 tablespoons shredded reduced-fat Cheddar cheese (1½ oz)

¼ lb lean ground turkey

½ cup canned condensed 98% fat-free cream of mushroom soup with 30% less sodium

¾ cup frozen mixed vegetables

1 Heat oven to 400°F. Spray 8 × 4-inch loaf pan with cooking spray. In small bowl, stir Bisquick mix, water, egg product and ¼ cup of the cheese until blended; spread in pan.

2 In 10-inch skillet, cook turkey over medium-high heat, stirring occasionally, until thoroughly cooked; drain. Stir in soup and vegetables; heat until hot. Spoon turkey mixture over batter in pan. Sprinkle with remaining 2 tablespoons cheese.

3 Bake about 20 minutes or until edges are light golden brown.

High Altitude (3500–6500 ft): No change.

1 SERVING: Calories 250 (Calories from Fat 70); Total Fat 7g (Saturated Fat 2g); Cholesterol 45mg; Sodium 740mg; Total Carbohydrate 24g (Dietary Fiber 1g; Sugars 5g); Protein 22g **% DAILY VALUE:** Vitamin A 15%; Vitamin C 2%; Calcium 25%; Iron 10% **EXCHANGES:** 1 Starch, ½ Other Carbohydrate, 2½ Lean Meat **CARBOHYDRATE CHOICES:** 1½

Deluxe Beef Cheeseburger Melt: Substitute ¼ pound extra-lean ground beef for the turkey.

Easy Ham Bake

PREP TIME: 10 MINUTES ● **START TO FINISH: 40 MINUTES**
3 SERVINGS

1½ cups frozen broccoli cuts

¼ cup canned condensed 98% fat-free cream of mushroom soup

¼ cup canned condensed Cheddar cheese soup

¼ cup fat-free (skim) milk

¾ cup cut-up cooked ham

½ cup Bisquick Heart Smart mix

⅓ cup fat-free (skim) milk

1 Heat oven to 425°F. Spray 1-quart microwavable casserole with cooking spray. In casserole, mix broccoli, soups, ¼ cup milk and the ham. Microwave on High 3 minutes; stir.

2 In small bowl, stir Bisquick mix and ⅓ cup milk with wire whisk or fork until blended. Pour evenly over soup mixture.

3 Bake uncovered 20 to 23 minutes or until crust is light golden brown. Let stand 5 minutes before serving.

High Altitude (3500–6500 ft): Bake 25 to 28 minutes.

1 SERVING: Calories 210 (Calories from Fat 60); Total Fat 7g (Saturated Fat 2g); Cholesterol 25mg; Sodium 1090mg; Total Carbohydrate 23g (Dietary Fiber 2g; Sugars 5g); Protein 14g **% DAILY VALUE:** Vitamin A 25%; Vitamin C 25%; Calcium 20%; Iron 10% **EXCHANGES:** ½ Starch, ½ Other Carbohydrate, 1 Vegetable, 1½ Medium-Fat Meat **CARBOHYDRATE CHOICES:** 1½

Easy Turkey Bake: Substitute ¾ cup cut-up cooked turkey or chicken for the ham.

Easy Beef Bake: Substitute ¾ cup cut-up cooked beef for the ham.

Baked Monte Cristo Sandwiches

PREP TIME: 10 MINUTES ● **START TO FINISH: 35 MINUTES**
3 SERVINGS

1 cup Bisquick Heart Smart mix

⅓ cup fat-free (skim) milk

2 tablespoons fat-free egg product or 1 egg white

2 oz reduced-fat Swiss cheese, thinly sliced

3 oz deli-style lean or fat-free ham or turkey ham, very thinly sliced

3 oz deli-style lean or fat-free turkey, very thinly sliced

2 tablespoons strawberry or raspberry fruit spread

Powdered sugar

1 Heat oven to 400°F. Spray 8 × 4-inch loaf pan with cooking spray. In small bowl, stir Bisquick mix, milk and egg product until blended.

2 Spread half of dough in bottom of pan. Top with half each of the cheese, ham and turkey. Spread fruit spread over turkey to within ½ inch of sides of pan. Top with remaining ham, turkey and cheese. Spread remaining dough over cheese to sides of pan.

3 Bake uncovered about 25 minutes or until golden brown. Let stand 5 minutes before serving. Sprinkle generously with powdered sugar. Serve warm.

High Altitude (3500–6500 ft): Bake uncovered about 30 minutes.

1 SERVING: Calories 290 (Calories from Fat 50); Total Fat 6g (Saturated Fat 1.5g); Cholesterol 35mg; Sodium 1320mg; Total Carbohydrate 40g (Dietary Fiber 0g; Sugars 13g); Protein 21g **% DAILY VALUE:** Vitamin A 0%; Vitamin C 0%; Calcium 30%; Iron 15% **EXCHANGES:** 1½ Starch, 1 Other Carbohydrate, 2 Lean Meat **CARBOHYDRATE CHOICES:** 2½

Quick Tip This is a great sandwich for using holiday leftovers. Use very thinly sliced turkey or ham—or both if you have them—and use leftover cranberry sauce for the strawberry preserves.

Fall Pork Dinner

PREP TIME: 20 MINUTES ● **START TO FINISH: 1 HOUR 5 MINUTES**
3 SERVINGS

¼ cup packed brown sugar

½ teaspoon ground
    cinnamon

1 tablespoon firm butter or
    margarine, cut up

½ small acorn squash

1 small unpeeled red
    cooking apple

⅓ cup Bisquick Heart Smart mix

½ teaspoon seasoned salt

⅛ teaspoon pepper

5 saltine crackers, crushed

1 egg white or 2 tablespoons
    fat-free egg product

1 tablespoon water

3 boneless pork loin chops,
    ½ inch thick (3–4 lb)

1 Heat oven to 350°F. In small bowl, mix brown sugar, cinnamon and butter until crumbly; set aside. Cut squash into ½-inch rings; remove seeds. Cut apple into chunks.

2 In shallow dish, stir Bisquick mix, seasoned salt, pepper and cracker crumbs. In another shallow dish, mix egg white and water. Dip pork into egg mixture, then coat with Bisquick mixture.

3 Spray 10-inch skillet with cooking spray; heat over medium-high heat. Cook pork in skillet 6 to 8 minutes, turning once, until coating is brown. Place pork in ungreased 8-inch square or 11 × 7-inch (2-quart) glass baking dish. Arrange squash and apples around pork. Sprinkle with brown sugar mixture.

4 Bake uncovered 40 to 45 minutes or until squash is tender and pork is no longer pink in center.

High Altitude (3500–6500 ft): No change.

1 SERVING: Calories 410 (Calories from Fat 130); Total Fat 14g (Saturated Fat 6g); Cholesterol 80mg; Sodium 530mg; Total Carbohydrate 43g (Dietary Fiber 3g; Sugars 24g); Protein 28g **% DAILY VALUE:** Vitamin A 8%; Vitamin C 6%; Calcium 10%; Iron 15% **EXCHANGES:** 1 Starch, 1½ Other Carbohydrate, 1 Vegetable, 3 Lean Meat, 1 Fat **CARBOHYDRATE CHOICES:** 3

Quick Tip If you don't have seasoned salt, use ½ teaspoon regular salt and a dash of paprika instead.

Spicy Orange Pork Chops with Sweet Potatoes

PREP TIME: 25 MINUTES ● **START TO FINISH: 55 MINUTES**
2 SERVINGS

⅓ cup orange marmalade

1 tablespoon butter or margarine, melted

¼ teaspoon ground cinnamon

¼ teaspoon ground ginger

1 tablespoon dried cranberries

1 medium sweet potato, peeled, cut into ½-inch slices

¼ cup Bisquick Heart Smart mix

⅛ teaspoon ground red pepper (cayenne)

2 boneless pork loin chops, ½ inch thick (½ lb)

1 tablespoon soy sauce or water

1 teaspoon vegetable oil

1 Heat oven to 350°F. In small bowl, mix marmalade, butter, cinnamon and ginger. Stir in cranberries and sweet potato. In ungreased 8-inch square (2-quart) glass baking dish, spoon potato mixture diagonally. Bake 10 minutes.

2 Meanwhile, in medium bowl, stir Bisquick mix and red pepper. Dip pork into soy sauce, then coat with Bisquick mixture. In 10-inch nonstick skillet, heat oil over medium-high heat. Add pork; cook 5 to 7 minutes, turning once, until coating is brown.

3 Place 1 pork chop on each side of potato mixture. Bake uncovered 30 to 35 minutes or until sweet potatoes are tender and pork is no longer pink in center.

High Altitude (3500–6500 ft): Increase Bisquick mix to ¼ cup plus 2 tablespoons. In step 1, bake potatoes 20 minutes. In step 2, cook pork 4 to 6 minutes.

1 SERVING: Calories 520 (Calories from Fat 160); Total Fat 18g (Saturated Fat 7g); Cholesterol 85mg; Sodium 730mg; Total Carbohydrate 63g (Dietary Fiber 3g; Sugars 35g); Protein 27g **% DAILY VALUE:** Vitamin A 220%; Vitamin C 15%; Calcium 10%; Iron 15% **EXCHANGES:** 2 Starch, 2 Other Carbohydrate, 3 Lean Meat, 1½ Fat **CARBOHYDRATE CHOICES:** 4

Quick Tip Looking for a shortcut? Substitute an 18-ounce can of vacuum-packed sweet potatoes, cut crosswise in half, for the fresh sweet potatoes.

Easy Garden Bake

PREP TIME: 15 MINUTES ● **START TO FINISH: 55 MINUTES**
2 SERVINGS

1 small zucchini, chopped
(½ cup)

1 large tomato, chopped
(1 cup)

¼ cup chopped onion

⅓ cup grated Parmesan cheese

¼ cup Bisquick Heart Smart mix

½ cup fat-free (skim) milk

½ cup fat-free egg product or
2 eggs

¼ teaspoon salt

Dash pepper

1 Heat oven to 400°F. Lightly spray 9 × 5-inch (1½-quart) glass loaf dish with cooking spray. Sprinkle zucchini, tomato, onion and cheese in dish.

2 In medium bowl, stir remaining ingredients until blended. Pour over vegetables and cheese.

3 Bake 30 to 35 minutes or until knife inserted in center comes out clean. Cool 5 minutes before serving.

High Altitude (3500–6500 ft): Increase Bisquick mix to ⅓ cup.

1 SERVING: Calories 210 (Calories from Fat 50); Total Fat 6g (Saturated Fat 3g); Cholesterol 15mg; Sodium 860mg; Total Carbohydrate 21g (Dietary Fiber 2g; Sugars 9g); Protein 18g **% DAILY VALUE:** Vitamin A 25%; Vitamin C 15%; Calcium 35%; Iron 10% **EXCHANGES:** ½ Starch, ½ Other Carbohydrate, 1 Vegetable, 2 Very Lean Meat, 1 Fat **CARBOHYDRATE CHOICES:** 1½

Quick Tip Fat-free egg products are sold in the refrigerator and freezer sections of your grocery store.

Hash Browns and Egg Bake

PREP TIME: 10 MINUTES ● **START TO FINISH: 35 MINUTES**
2 SERVINGS

1½ cups frozen potatoes O'Brien with onions and peppers (from 28-oz bag), thawed

¼ cup fat-free egg product

½ cup fat-free (skim) milk

¼ cup Bisquick Heart Smart mix

1 teaspoon salt-free original seasoning blend

⅓ cup shredded reduced-fat Cheddar cheese

1 Heat oven to 375°F. Spray bottom and side of 8- or 9-inch glass pie plate with cooking spray. Spread uncooked potatoes in bottom of pie plate.

2 In medium bowl, mix remaining ingredients except cheese with wire whisk or fork until well blended. Pour over potatoes. Sprinkle cheese over top.

3 Bake 20 to 22 minutes or until eggs in center are set.

High Altitude (3500–6500 ft): Bake 22 to 24 minutes.

1 SERVING: Calories 250 (Calories from Fat 25); Total Fat 2.5g (Saturated Fat 1g); Cholesterol 5mg; Sodium 480mg; Total Carbohydrate 42g (Dietary Fiber 3g; Sugars 5g); Protein 14g **% DAILY VALUE:** Vitamin A 10%; Vitamin C 15%; Calcium 30%; Iron 15% **EXCHANGES:** 2 Starch, 1 Other Carbohydrate, 1 Very Lean Meat **CARBOHYDRATE CHOICES:** 3

Quick Tip Like bacon with your eggs and hash browns? Add 1 tablespoon of bacon-flavor bits to the egg mixture.

Chili-Bean Bake

PREP TIME: 15 MINUTES ● **START TO FINISH: 40 MINUTES**
3 SERVINGS

1 cup kidney beans (from 15-oz can), drained, rinsed

1 can (14.5 oz) no-salt-added stewed tomatoes

⅓ cup water

¼ cup chunky-style salsa

2 tablespoons ketchup

2 teaspoons chili powder

¾ cup Bisquick Heart Smart mix

3 tablespoons yellow cornmeal

⅓ cup fat-free (skim) milk

1 teaspoon butter or margarine, softened

2 tablespoons sliced green onions (2 medium)

1 Heat oven to 425°F. In 1½-quart microwavable casserole, mix beans, tomatoes, water, salsa, ketchup and chili powder. Microwave uncovered on High 4 minutes; stir.

2 In small bowl, stir remaining ingredients until blended. Drop by 6 spoonfuls onto hot bean mixture.

3 Bake uncovered 20 to 23 minutes or until golden brown.

High Altitude (3500–6500 ft): No change.

1 SERVING: Calories 310 (Calories from Fat 35); Total Fat 4g (Saturated Fat 1g); Cholesterol 0mg; Sodium 640mg; Total Carbohydrate 57g (Dietary Fiber 6g; Sugars 14g); Protein 12g **% DAILY VALUE:** Vitamin A 25%; Vitamin C 10%; Calcium 25%; Iron 20% **EXCHANGES:** 2 Starch, 1½ Other Carbohydrate, 1 Very Lean Meat, ½ Fat **CARBOHYDRATE CHOICES:** 4

A 1931 ad promises to banish "muss and fuss" from biscuit making and introduces housewives to some of the first exciting recipes made with Bisquick.

Mexican Corn Cakes

PREP TIME: 20 MINUTES ● **START TO FINISH: 20 MINUTES**
3 SERVINGS

¾ cup Bisquick Heart Smart mix

¼ cup cornmeal

½ cup fat-free (skim) milk

2 egg whites

1 cup chunky-style salsa

¼ cup frozen whole kernel corn, cooked, drained

1 tablespoon chopped ripe olives

½ cup fat-free refried beans (from 16-oz can)

¼ cup shredded reduced-fat Cheddar cheese (1 oz)

Fat-free sour cream, if desired

1 In small bowl, stir Bisquick mix, cornmeal, milk and egg whites with wire whisk or fork until blended.

2 Brush griddle or skillet with vegetable oil or spray with cooking spray; heat griddle to 375°F or heat skillet over medium heat. For each pancake, pour slightly less than ¼ cup batter onto hot griddle. Cook until edges are dry. Turn; cook other sides until golden brown.

3 In small bowl, mix salsa, corn and olives. On each of 3 microwavable serving plates, place 1 corn cake; spread each cake with generous 2 tablespoons beans. Top each with additional corn cake. Spread ⅓ cup salsa mixture over top of each cake stack. Sprinkle each serving with generous 1 tablespoon cheese.

4 Microwave each serving uncovered on High about 1 minute or until heated through and cheese is melted. Serve with additional salsa and sour cream if desired.

High Altitude (3500–6500 ft): No change.

1 SERVING: Calories 270 (Calories from Fat 30); Total Fat 3.5g (Saturated Fat 0.5g); Cholesterol 0mg; Sodium 1270mg; Total Carbohydrate 49g (Dietary Fiber 3g; Sugars 8g); Protein 12g **% DAILY VALUE:** Vitamin A 8%; Vitamin C 0%; Calcium 25%; Iron 15% **EXCHANGES:** 2 Starch, 1 Other Carbohydrate, 1 Very Lean Meat, ½ Fat **CARBOHYDRATE CHOICES:** 3

Quick Tip Yellow cornmeal will give these corn cakes a nice golden color, but white cornmeal can also be used. You may want to sprinkle some fresh chopped cilantro on top of each stack for added flavor and color.

Santa Fe Foldover

PREP TIME: 15 MINUTES ● **START TO FINISH: 45 MINUTES**
3 SERVINGS

1 cup Bisquick Heart Smart mix

2 tablespoons cornmeal

¼ cup very hot water

1 cup canned no-salt-added
    black beans, drained, rinsed

⅓ cup chunky-style salsa

2 tablespoons sliced green
    onions (2 medium)

¼ cup shredded reduced-fat
    Colby–Monterey Jack cheese
    blend (1 oz)

½ cup shredded lettuce

⅓ cup chopped tomato

3 tablespoons fat-free sour
    cream

1 Move oven rack to lowest position. Heat oven to 375°F. Spray 12-inch pizza pan with cooking spray. In small bowl, stir Bisquick mix, cornmeal and very hot water until soft dough forms.

2 Place dough on surface sprinkled with Bisquick mix and gently roll in Bisquick mix to coat. Shape into a ball; knead about 5 times or until smooth. Press or roll dough into 10-inch round; fold into fourths. Unfold in pizza pan.

3 In small bowl, mix beans and salsa; spread over dough to within 2 inches of edge. Sprinkle with onions. Fold edge over. Sprinkle cheese over beans.

4 Bake 25 to 28 minutes or until crust is golden brown and cheese is melted. Top with remaining ingredients.

High Altitude (3500–6500 ft): Bake 28 to 31 minutes.

1 SERVING: Calories 300 (Calories from Fat 45); Total Fat 5g (Saturated Fat 1g); Cholesterol 5mg; Sodium 730mg; Total Carbohydrate 53g (Dietary Fiber 6g; Sugars 6g); Protein 11g **% DAILY VALUE:** Vitamin A 10%; Vitamin C 4%; Calcium 30%; Iron 20% **EXCHANGES:** 3½ Starch, ½ Very Lean Meat, ½ Fat **CARBOHYDRATE CHOICES:** 3½

Vegetable Stew with Herb Dumplings

PREP TIME: 25 MINUTES ● **START TO FINISH: 45 MINUTES**
4 SERVINGS

STEW

1 small onion, chopped (¼ cup)

2 teaspoons vegetable oil

¼ cup uncooked orzo or rosamarina pasta

2 cups vegetable or chicken broth

½ teaspoon ground mustard

½ cup frozen sweet peas

½ cup diced peeled potatoes

½ cup thinly sliced carrots (1 medium)

½ can (15 to 16 oz) great northern beans, drained, rinsed

DUMPLINGS

½ cup Bisquick Heart Smart mix

⅓ cup cornmeal

¼ teaspoon dried oregano leaves

¼ teaspoon dried basil leaves

⅓ cup fat-free (skim) milk

1 In 3-quart saucepan, cook onion in oil over medium heat, stirring occasionally, until onion is crisp-tender. Stir in pasta, broth, mustard, peas, potatoes, carrots and beans. Heat to boiling, stirring occasionally.

2 Meanwhile, in medium bowl, mix Bisquick mix, cornmeal, oregano and basil. Stir in milk just until dry ingredients are moistened.

3 Drop dough by 4 rounded tablespoonfuls onto boiling stew; reduce heat to low. Cover; cook 18 to 20 minutes or until dumplings are dry.

High Altitude (3500–6500 ft): No change.

1 SERVING: Calories 530 (Calories from Fat 60); Total Fat 7g (Saturated Fat 1g); Cholesterol 0mg; Sodium 1390mg; Total Carbohydrate 97g (Dietary Fiber 11g; Sugars 12g); Protein 20g **% DAILY VALUE:** Vitamin A 140%; Vitamin C 8%; Calcium 30%; Iron 40% **EXCHANGES:** 5 Starch, 1 Other Carbohydrate, 1 Vegetable, 1 Fat **CARBOHYDRATE CHOICES:** 6½

Quick Tip For light, fluffy dumplings, avoid overmixing and overcooking. Mix the ingredients just until a soft dough forms, and follow the cooking times in the recipe.

Herbed Fish

PREP TIME: 15 MINUTES ● **START TO FINISH: 15 MINUTES**
2 SERVINGS

½ lb cod or other mild-flavored fish fillets, about ½ inch thick

¼ cup Bisquick Heart Smart mix

2 tablespoons garlic herb dry bread crumbs

1½ teaspoons chopped fresh or ½ teaspoon dried basil leaves

⅛ teaspoon salt

2 tablespoons fat-free egg product or 1 egg white

1 tablespoon olive or vegetable oil

1 Cut fish into 2 serving pieces. In small shallow dish, stir Bisquick mix, bread crumbs, basil and salt. In another shallow dish, beat egg product.

2 In 8-inch skillet, heat oil over medium heat. Dip fish into egg product, then coat with Bisquick mixture.

3 Reduce heat to medium-low. Cook fish in oil 8 to 10 minutes, turning once, until fish flakes easily with fork and is brown on both sides.

High Altitude (3500–6500 ft): No change.

1 SERVING: Calories 250 (Calories from Fat 90); Total Fat 9g (Saturated Fat 1.5g); Cholesterol 60mg; Sodium 560mg; Total Carbohydrate 15g (Dietary Fiber 0g; Sugars 1g); Protein 25g **% DAILY VALUE:** Vitamin A 2%; Vitamin C 0%; Calcium 8%; Iron 8% **EXCHANGES:** 1 Starch, 3 Lean Meat **CARBOHYDRATE CHOICES:** 1

Quick Tip Top the fish with an easy basil sauce. Mix ¼ cup fat-free mayonnaise and a tablespoon or two of basil pesto. For added zest, serve with lemon wedges.

Lemon-Pepper Baked Orange Roughy

PREP TIME: 5 MINUTES ● **START TO FINISH: 30 MINUTES**
2 SERVINGS

1 tablespoon butter or margarine

⅓ cup Bisquick Heart Smart mix

2 tablespoons yellow cornmeal

¼ teaspoon lemon-pepper seasoning

¼ teaspoon salt

2 tablespoons fat-free egg product or 1 egg white

1 tablespoon water

½ lb orange roughy or other mild-flavored fish fillets

1 Heat oven to 425°F. In 9-inch square pan, melt butter in oven.

2 In shallow dish, stir Bisquick mix, cornmeal, lemon-pepper seasoning and salt. In another shallow dish, mix egg product and water. Dip fish into egg mixture, then coat with Bisquick mixture. Place in pan.

3 Bake uncovered 10 minutes. Turn fish with spatula; bake about 15 minutes longer or until fish flakes easily with fork.

High Altitude (3500–6500 ft): No change.

1 SERVING: Calories 270 (Calories from Fat 80); Total Fat 9g (Saturated Fat 4g); Cholesterol 80mg; Sodium 750mg; Total Carbohydrate 21g (Dietary Fiber 0g; Sugars 2g); Protein 28g **% DAILY VALUE:** Vitamin A 8%; Vitamin C 0%; Calcium 10%; Iron 10% **EXCHANGES:** 1½ Starch, 3 Lean Meat **CARBOHYDRATE CHOICES:** 1½

Quick Tip Heating the butter and pan in the oven before adding the fish helps to create a crisp bottom crust.

Italian Pizza Bake

PREP TIME: 15 MINUTES ● START TO FINISH: 40 MINUTES
2 SERVINGS

⅓ cup Bisquick Heart Smart mix

1 egg white

1 tablespoon water

⅛ teaspoon garlic powder

¼ cup diced green or yellow bell pepper

¼ cup chopped onion

½ cup cut-up cooked chicken breast

½ cup drained diced tomatoes with Italian herbs (from 14.5-oz can)

¼ teaspoon Italian seasoning

¼ cup shredded mozzarella cheese (1 oz)

1 Heat oven to 400°F. Spray 8 × 4-inch loaf pan with cooking spray. In small bowl, mix Bisquick mix, egg white, water and garlic powder; spread in pan.

2 In 10-inch nonstick skillet, cook bell pepper and onion over medium-high heat, stirring frequently, until onion is tender. Stir in chicken, tomatoes and Italian seasoning; cook until thoroughly heated. Spoon over batter in pan. Sprinkle with cheese.

3 Bake 20 to 23 minutes or until golden brown; loosen from sides of pan.

High Altitude (3500–6500 ft): Increase water by 1 tablespoon and increase bake time to 23–25 minutes.

1 SERVING: Calories 200 (Calories from Fat 50); Total Fat 6g (Saturated Fat 2.5g); Cholesterol 35mg; Sodium 420mg; Total Carbohydrate 20g (Dietary Fiber 1g; Sugars 5g); Protein 18g **% DAILY VALUE:** Vitamin A 4%; Vitamin C 20%; Calcium 20%; Iron 10% **EXCHANGES:** ½ Starch, ½ Other Carbohydrate, 1 Vegetable, 2 Very Lean Meat, 1 Fat **CARBOHYDRATE CHOICES:** 1

Quick Tip When you need only a small amount of cooked chicken breast, it's handy to just purchase one piece of cooked chicken from the grocery store deli. Remove the skin and bone, and you will have about 1 cup of chicken.

Southwestern Corn Cakes

PREP TIME: 10 MINUTES ● **START TO FINISH: 45 MINUTES**
2 SERVINGS

½ cup frozen corn, broccoli and red pepper mixture, thawed

1 tablespoon sliced ripe olives

2 cooked pork sausage links (2 ounces), chopped

1 cup low-fat (skim) milk

¼ cup fat-free cholesterol-free egg product or 1 egg white

⅓ cup Original Bisquick mix

2 tablespoons yellow cornmeal

½ teaspoon chili powder

¼ cup chunky salsa, if desired

Cilantro, if desired

1 Heat oven to 425°F. Spray two 10- to 12-ounce individual casseroles or custard cups with cooking spray.

2 Spoon half the corn mixture, olives and sausage into each casserole. Place milk, egg product, Bisquick mix, cornmeal and chili powder in blender. Cover and blend on high speed 15 seconds or until smooth. (Or beat on high speed 1 minute.) Pour evenly over sausage mixture.

3 Bake uncovered 20 to 25 minutes or until knife inserted in center comes out clean. Cool 10 minutes. Top with salsa and cilantro.

High Altitude (3500–6500 ft): Increase bake time to 25–30 minutes.

1 SERVING: Calories 301 (Calories from Fat 110); Total Fat 12g (Saturated Fat 4g); Cholesterol 24mg; Sodium 856mg; Total Carbohydrate 32g (Dietary Fiber 2g; Sugars 10g); Protein 15g **% DAILY VALUE:** Vitamin A 15%; Vitamin C 10%; Calcium 20%; Iron 10% **EXCHANGES:** 2 Starch, 1 Lean Meat, 1 Fat **CARBOHYDRATE CHOICES:** 2

Warm Biscuits

PREP TIME: 5 MINUTES ● START TO FINISH: 15 MINUTES
5 BISCUITS

1¼ cups Original Bisquick mix
½ cup milk

1 Heat oven to 450°F. Stir ingredients until soft dough forms.

2 Turn onto surface dusted with Bisquick mix. Knead 10 times. Roll ½ inch thick. Cut with 2½-inch cutter. Place on ungreased cookie sheet.

3 Bake 8 to 10 minutes or until golden brown.

High Altitude (3500–6500 ft): Add 1 to 2 tablespoons milk—follow directions for drop biscuits.

1 BISCUIT: Calories 135 (Calories from Fat 45); Total Fat 5g (Saturated Fat 2g); Cholesterol 2mg; Sodium 338mg; Total Carbohydrate 20g (Dietary Fiber 1g; Sugars 2g); Protein 3g **% DAILY VALUE:** Vitamin A 0%; Vitamin C 0%; Calcium 8%; Iron 6% **EXCHANGES:** 1 Starch; ½ Fat **CARBOHYDRATE CHOICES:** 1

Easy Garlic-Cheese Biscuits

PREP TIME: 10 MINUTES ● **START TO FINISH: 20 MINUTES**
5 BISCUITS

1 cup Bisquick Heart Smart mix

⅓ cup fat-free (skim) milk

¼ cup shredded reduced-fat Cheddar cheese (1 oz)

1 tablespoon butter, melted (do not use margarine)

⅛ teaspoon garlic powder

1 Heat oven to 450°F. In small bowl, stir Bisquick mix, milk and cheese with wire whisk or fork until soft dough forms; beat vigorously 30 seconds.

2 Onto ungreased cookie sheet, drop dough by 5 spoonfuls about 2 inches apart.

3 Bake 8 to 10 minutes or until golden brown. In small bowl, stir butter and garlic powder until well mixed; brush on warm biscuits before removing from cookie sheet. Serve warm.

High Altitude (3500–6500 ft): Add 1 to 2 tablespoons milk.

1 BISCUIT: Calories 120 (Calories from Fat 40); Total Fat 4g (Saturated Fat 1.5g); Cholesterol 10mg; Sodium 340mg; Total Carbohydrate 17g (Dietary Fiber 0g; Sugars 3g); Protein 4g **% DAILY VALUE:** Vitamin A 2%; Vitamin C 0%; Calcium 15%; Iron 6% **EXCHANGES:** 1 Starch, 1 Fat **CARBOHYDRATE CHOICES:** 1

Quick Tip To make Easy Herb-Cheese Biscuits, stir in ¼ to ½ teaspoon dried dill weed, dried rosemary leaves (crushed) or Italian seasoning with the Bisquick mix.

Small-Batch Lemon-Blueberry Muffins

PREP TIME: 10 MINUTES ● **START TO FINISH: 25 MINUTES**
4 MUFFINS

½ cup Bisquick Heart Smart mix

¼ cup fat-free egg product

1 tablespoon sugar

2 tablespoons fat-free
    sour cream

1 teaspoon grated lemon peel

2 teaspoons vegetable oil

¼ teaspoon vanilla

¼ cup fresh or frozen
    (do not thaw) blueberries

1 teaspoon sugar

1 Heat oven to 400°F. Line 4 regular-size muffin cups with paper baking cups; spray inside of baking cups with cooking spray.

2 In small bowl, stir all ingredients except blueberries and 1 teaspoon sugar just until moistened. Stir in blueberries. Spoon batter into muffin cups. Sprinkle 1 teaspoon sugar over tops.

3 Bake 12 to 13 minutes or until toothpick inserted in center comes out clean.

High Altitude (3500–6500 ft): Bake 13 to 14 minutes.

1 MUFFIN: Calories 90 (Calories from Fat 10); Total Fat 1.5g (Saturated Fat 0g); Cholesterol 0mg; Sodium 200mg; Total Carbohydrate 17g (Dietary Fiber 0g; Sugars 7g); Protein 3g **% DAILY VALUE:** Vitamin A 0%; Vitamin C 0%; Calcium 8%; Iron 4% **EXCHANGES:** 1 Starch **CARBOHYDRATE CHOICES:** 1

Quick Tip For more texture and interesting tops, sprinkle muffins with coarse sugar instead of granulated sugar.

Buttermilk Cornbread Wedges

PREP TIME: 10 MINUTES ● START TO FINISH: 20 MINUTES
4 WEDGES

¼ cup Bisquick Heart Smart mix

¼ cup yellow cornmeal

⅓ cup buttermilk

2 tablespoons fat-free egg product

1 tablespoon sugar

1 teaspoon vegetable oil

1 teaspoon yellow cornmeal

1 Heat oven to 450°F. Spray bottom only of 8 × 4- or 9 × 5-inch loaf pan with cooking spray.

2 In small bowl, beat Bisquick mix, ¼ cup cornmeal, the buttermilk, egg product, sugar and oil just until smooth (do not overbeat). Pour into pan. Sprinkle with 1 teaspoon cornmeal.

3 Bake 6 to 8 minutes or until toothpick inserted in center comes out clean. Remove from pan. Cut loaf crosswise in half, then cut each square in half diagonally. Serve warm.

High Altitude (3500–6500 ft): Bake 8 to 10 minutes.

1 WEDGE: Calories 100 (Calories from Fat 20); Total Fat 2g (Saturated Fat 0g); Cholesterol 0mg; Sodium 115mg; Total Carbohydrate 17g (Dietary Fiber 0g; Sugars 5g); Protein 3g **% DAILY VALUE:** Vitamin A 0%; Vitamin C 0%; Calcium 6%; Iron 4% **EXCHANGES:** 1 Starch, ½ Fat **CARBOHYDRATE CHOICES:** 1

Cherry Cobbler for Two

PREP TIME: 5 MINUTES ● **START TO FINISH: 25 MINUTES**
2 SERVINGS

1 cup cherry pie filling
   (from 21-oz. can)

½ cup Bisquick Heart Smart mix

3 tablespoons fat-free milk

1 tablespoon sugar

1 teaspoon butter or
   margarine, softened

1 Heat oven to 400° F. Divide pie filling between 2 ungreased 10-ounce custard cups.

2 In small bowl, stir remaining ingredients until thick batter forms. Pour and spread half onto pie filling in each custard cup. Sprinkle with additional sugar, if desired.

3 Bake 15 to 18 minutes or until topping is light brown.

1 SERVING: Calories 315 (Calories from Fat 35); Total Fat 4 g (Saturated Fat 1½); Cholesterol 6 mg; Sodium 396 mg; Total Carbohydrate 66 g (Dietary Fiber 1 g; Sugars 9 g); Protein 4 g **% DAILY VALUE:** Vitamin A 8 %; Vitamin C 8 %; Calcium 8 %; Iron 8 % **EXCHANGES:** 1½ Starch, 2½ Other Carbohydrate; ½ Fat **CARBOHYDRATE CHOICES:** 4½

Quick Tip Extra pie filling? It makes a great topper for ice cream, pancakes, waffles and French toast.

Peach Cobbler

PREP TIME: 10 MINUTES • **START TO FINISH: 30 MINUTES**
2 SERVINGS

1 cup peach pie filling
(from 21-oz can)

½ cup Bisquick Heart Smart mix

3 tablespoons fat-free (skim)
milk

1 tablespoon sugar

1 teaspoon butter or
margarine, softened

1 teaspoon sugar

1 Heat oven to 400°F. In 1-quart saucepan, heat pie filling to boiling. Spoon into 2 ungreased 10-ounce custard cups.

2 In small bowl, stir Bisquick mix, milk, 1 tablespoon sugar and the butter until thick batter forms. Pour and spread half of batter onto pie filling in each custard cup. Sprinkle top of each dessert with ½ teaspoon sugar. On cookie sheet, place filled custard cups.

3 Bake 16 to 18 minutes or until topping is light golden brown.

High Altitude (3500–6500 ft): Bake 17 to 19 minutes.

1 SERVING: Calories 310 (Calories from Fat 35); Total Fat 4g (Saturated Fat 1.5g); Cholesterol 5mg; Sodium 350mg; Total Carbohydrate 65g (Dietary Fiber 1g; Sugars 42g); Protein 3g **% DAILY VALUE:** Vitamin A 2%; Vitamin C 0%; Calcium 15%; Iron 8% **EXCHANGES:** 1 Starch, 3½ Other Carbohydrate, ½ Fat **CARBOHYDRATE CHOICES:** 4

Blueberry Cobbler: Substitute 1 cup blueberry pie filling (from 21-oz can) for the peach pie filling.

Quick Tip What to do with the leftover pie filling? It makes a great topper for pancakes, waffles, French toast or ice cream.

This 1952 ad was a foreshadowing of an even peachier proposition—the World's Largest Peach Shortcake! With four tons of Bisquick and nine tons of peaches, the five-layer shortcake was created in 1981 at the South Carolina Peach Festival. Plenty for even the hungriest spouse!

Mango-Lime Shortcakes

PREP TIME: 10 MINUTES ● **START TO FINISH: 35 MINUTES**
2 SERVINGS

⅔ cup Bisquick Heart Smart mix

1 tablespoon sugar

1 teaspoon grated lime peel

2 tablespoons fat-free (skim) milk

2 teaspoons vegetable oil

1 snack-size container (4 oz) refrigerated vanilla pudding snack (from 6-snack package)

1 tablespoon lime juice

½ teaspoon grated lime peel

½ cup refrigerated mango in light syrup (from 1-lb 8-oz jar), drained, cubed

Whipped topping, if desired

1 Heat oven to 375°F. Spray cookie sheet with cooking spray. In medium bowl, stir Bisquick mix, sugar, 1 teaspoon lime peel, the milk and oil until soft dough forms. Drop dough by 2 spoonfuls on cookie sheet.

2 Bake 9 to 12 minutes or until golden brown. Cool 10 minutes.

3 Meanwhile, in small bowl, mix pudding, lime juice and ½ teaspoon lime peel until well blended.

4 Split warm shortcakes. Fill and top with mango and pudding mixture. Top with whipped topping.

High Altitude (3500–6500 ft): Add up to 2 teaspoons more milk if necessary to make a soft dough. Bake 12 to 15 minutes.

1 SERVING: Calories 330 (Calories from Fat 80); Total Fat 9g (Saturated Fat 1.5g); Cholesterol 0mg; Sodium 520mg; Total Carbohydrate 57g (Dietary Fiber 0g; Sugars 29g); Protein 5g **% DAILY VALUE:** Vitamin A 8%; Vitamin C 60%; Calcium 20%; Iron 8% **EXCHANGES:** 1 Starch, 1 Fruit, 1 Other Carbohydrate, 1½ Fat **CARBOHYDRATE CHOICES:** 4

Quick Tip Look for the jar of mango in the produce section of the supermarket.

Caramel-Pecan Coffee Cake

PREP TIME: 5 MINUTES ● START TO FINISH: 8 MINUTES
2 SERVINGS

3 tablespoons butter or margarine

¼ cup packed brown sugar

2 tablespoons chopped pecans

2 tablespoons light corn syrup

¼ teaspoon ground cinnamon

1 cup Original Bisquick mix

¼ cup cold water

1 Place butter in 1-quart casserole. Microwave on High (100%) until melted, 20 to 30 seconds. Stir in brown sugar, pecans, corn syrup and cinnamon; spread evenly in casserole. Microwave uncovered until bubbly, 45 to 60 seconds. Tilt casserole so brown sugar mixture runs to side; place 6-ounce juice glass in center of casserole.

2 Mix bisquick and water until soft dough forms. Drop dough by 6 spoonfuls onto brown sugar mixture. Place casserole on inverted plate in microwave oven. Microwave uncovered on Medium-High (70%) 2 minutes; rotate casserole ½ turn. Microwave uncovered until wooden toothpick inserted in center comes out clean, 2 to 2½ minutes longer.

3 Remove glass. Immediately invert on heatproof serving plate; let casserole stand 1 minute so caramel can drizzle over coffee cake. Serve warm.

High Altitude (3500–6500 ft): Please provide the wording for this.

1 SERVING: Calories 616 (Calories from Fat 283); Total Fat 32g (Saturated Fat 14g); Cholesterol 46mg; Sodium 900mg; Total Carbohydrate 82g (Dietary Fiber 2g; Sugars 34g); Protein 5g
% DAILY VALUE: Vitamin A 10%; Vitamin C 0%; Calcium 15%; Iron 15% **EXCHANGES:** 2½ Starch, 2½ Other Starch, 5 Fat **CARBOHYDRATE CHOICES:** 5

Impossibly Easy
Pies and Pizzas

Impossibly Easy Taco Pie

PREP TIME: 15 MINUTES ● **START TO FINISH: 45 MINUTES**
6 SERVINGS

1 lb ground beef

1 medium onion, chopped
(½ cup)

1 envelope (1.25 oz) taco
seasoning mix

1 can (4 oz) chopped green
chiles, drained

½ cup Original Bisquick mix

1 cup milk

2 eggs

¾ cup shredded Monterey Jack
or Cheddar cheese (3 oz)

Salsa, if desired

Sour cream, if desired

1 Heat oven to 400°F. Spray 9-inch glass pie plate with cooking spray. Cook beef and onion in 10-inch skillet over medium heat, stirring occasionally, until beef is brown; drain. Stir in seasoning mix (dry). Spread in pie plate. Top with chiles.

2 Stir Bisquick mix, milk and eggs until blended. Pour into pie plate.

3 Bake about 25 minutes or until knife inserted in center comes out clean. Sprinkle with cheese. Bake 2 to 3 minutes or until cheese is melted. Let stand 5 minutes before serving. Serve with salsa and sour cream.

High Altitude (3500–6500 ft): Increase first bake time to about 28 minutes.

1 SERVING: Calories 315 (Calories from Fat 170); Total Fat 19g (Saturated Fat 8g); Cholesterol 130mg; Sodium 590mg; Total Carbohydrate 15g (Dietary Fiber 1g; Sugars 3g); Protein 22g **% DAILY VALUE:** Vitamin A 16%; Vitamin C 14%; Calcium 20%; Iron 12% **EXCHANGES:** 1 Starch, 3 Medium-Fat Meat **CARBOHYDRATE CHOICES:** 1

Quick Tip In addition to the salsa and sour cream, try serving this zesty pie with shredded lettuce, chopped jalapeño chile peppers and sliced green onions.

Impossibly Easy Barbecue Beef Pie

PREP TIME: 20 MINUTES ● **START TO FINISH: 50 MINUTES**
6 SERVINGS

1 lb lean (at least 80%)
  ground beef

1 small bell pepper, chopped
  (½ cup)

1 medium onion, chopped
  (½ cup)

⅓ cup barbecue sauce

1½ cups shredded Cheddar
  cheese (6 oz)

1 cup Original Bisquick mix

1 cup milk

2 eggs

Additional barbecue sauce,
  heated, if desired

1 Heat oven to 400°F. Spray 9-inch glass pie plate with cooking spray. In 10-inch skillet, cook beef, bell pepper and onion over medium-high heat 5 to 7 minutes, stirring frequently, until beef is thoroughly cooked; drain. Stir in ⅓ cup barbecue sauce. Spread in pie plate. Sprinkle with ¾ cup of the cheese.

2 In medium bowl, stir Bisquick mix, milk and eggs with wire whisk or fork until blended. Pour into pie plate.

3 Bake 25 minutes. Sprinkle with remaining ¾ cup cheese. Bake about 5 minutes longer or until knife inserted in center comes out clean. Serve with additional barbecue sauce.

High Altitude (3500–6500 ft): No change.

1 SERVING: Calories 400 (Calories from Fat 210); Total Fat 23g (Saturated Fat 11g); Cholesterol 150mg; Sodium 640mg; Total Carbohydrate 23g (Dietary Fiber 1g; Sugars 9g); Protein 25g **% DAILY VALUE:** Vitamin A 10%; Vitamin C 10%; Calcium 25%; Iron 15% **EXCHANGES:** 1 Starch, ½ Other Carbohydrate, 3 Medium-Fat Meat, 1½ Fat **CARBOHYDRATE CHOICES:** 1½

Quick Tip If you are lucky enough to have leftovers, cover and refrigerate any Impossibly Easy Pie up to 24 hours. To reheat a slice, cover and microwave on Medium (50%) 2 to 3 minutes or until hot. Let stand 2 minutes before serving.

Impossibly Easy Sloppy Joe Pie

PREP TIME: 15 MINUTES ● **START TO FINISH: 50 MINUTES**
6 SERVINGS

1 lb lean (at least 80%) ground beef

½ teaspoon salt

¼ teaspoon pepper

1 medium onion, finely chopped (½ cup)

¼ cup chopped green bell pepper

3 tablespoons ketchup

½ cup Original Bisquick mix

1 cup milk

2 eggs

Additional ketchup, if desired

1 Heat oven to 400°F. Spray 9-inch glass pie plate with cooking spray. In 10-inch skillet, cook beef, salt, pepper, onion and bell pepper over medium-high heat 5 to 7 minutes, stirring frequently, until beef is thoroughly cooked; drain. Stir in ketchup. Spread in pie plate.

2 In medium bowl, stir remaining ingredients with wire whisk or fork until blended. Pour into pie plate.

3 Bake 25 to 30 minutes or until knife inserted in center comes out clean. Let stand 5 minutes before serving. Top each serving with additional ketchup.

High Altitude (3500–6500 ft): Bake 27 to 32 minutes.

1 SERVING: Calories 170 (Calories from Fat 70); Total Fat 8g (Saturated Fat 3g); Cholesterol 95mg; Sodium 460mg; Total Carbohydrate 12g (Dietary Fiber 0g; Sugars 5g); Protein 11g **% DAILY VALUE:** Vitamin A 6%; Vitamin C 10%; Calcium 8%; Iron 8% **EXCHANGES:** 1 Starch, 1 Medium-Fat Meat, ½ Fat **CARBOHYDRATE CHOICES:** 1

Quick Tip Speed things up by using ¾ cup of the frozen chopped onion and bell pepper mixture for the fresh onion and bell pepper.

Impossibly Easy Cheesy Meatball Pie

PREP TIME: 10 MINUTES ● START TO FINISH: 55 MINUTES
6 SERVINGS

1½ cups refrigerated shredded hash brown potatoes

½ teaspoon salt

¼ teaspoon pepper

¾ cup frozen sweet peas, thawed, drained

12 frozen meatballs (from 16-oz bag), thawed, cut in half

1 cup shredded Cheddar cheese (4 oz)

½ cup Original Bisquick mix

1 cup milk

2 eggs

1 Heat oven to 400°F. Spray 9-inch glass pie plate with cooking spray. In small bowl, toss potatoes with salt and pepper.

2 In pie plate, layer potatoes, peas, meatballs and cheese.

3 In medium bowl, stir Bisquick mix, milk and eggs with wire whisk or fork until blended. Pour into pie plate.

4 Bake 30 to 40 minutes or until center is set and top is golden brown. Let stand 5 minutes before serving.

High Altitude (3500–6500 ft): Bake 32 to 37 minutes.

1 SERVING: Calories 360 (Calories from Fat 160); Total Fat 17g (Saturated Fat 8g); Cholesterol 155mg; Sodium 800mg; Total Carbohydrate 28g (Dietary Fiber 2g; Sugars 6g); Protein 22g **% DAILY VALUE:** Vitamin A 15%; Vitamin C 4%; Calcium 25%; Iron 15% **EXCHANGES:** 1½ Starch, ½ Other Carbohydrate, 2½ Medium-Fat Meat, ½ Fat **CARBOHYDRATE CHOICES:** 2

"It takes the impossible to please your family. Here's the recipe," reads this ad from 1995.

Quick Tip Frozen meatballs come in a variety of flavors. Try Swedish meatballs for a subtle spicy flavor or Italian meatballs for a heartier flavor.

Impossibly Easy Ham and Swiss Pie

PREP TIME: 10 MINUTES ● **START TO FINISH: 55 MINUTES**
6 SERVINGS

1½ cups cut-up fully cooked ham

1 cup shredded Swiss cheese (4 oz)

4 medium green onions, sliced (¼ cup)

½ cup Original Bisquick mix

1 cup milk

¼ teaspoon salt

⅛ teaspoon pepper

2 eggs

1 Heat oven to 400°F. Spray 9-inch glass pie plate with cooking spray. Sprinkle ham, cheese and onions in pie plate.

2 Stir remaining ingredients until blended. Pour into pie plate.

3 Bake 35 to 40 minutes or until knife inserted in center comes out clean. Let stand 5 minutes before serving.

High Altitude (3500–6500 ft): Bake about 45 minutes.

1 SERVING: Calories 215 (Calories from Fat 110); Total Fat 12g (Saturated Fat 6g); Cholesterol 110mg; Sodium 830mg; Total Carbohydrate 10g (Dietary Fiber 0g; Sugars 3g); Protein 17g **% DAILY VALUE:** Vitamin A 8%; Vitamin C 2%; Calcium 26%; Iron 6% **EXCHANGES:** ½ Starch, 2 Lean Meat, 1 Fat **CARBOHYDRATE CHOICES:** 1

Quick Tip Impossibly Easy Pies are as easy to reheat as they are to make. To reheat in the microwave, arrange slices evenly spaced and with points toward the center on a large microwavable plate. Cover with waxed paper (except those with a cheese topping) and microwave on Medium 2 to 3 minutes per slice. Rotate ½ turn after 3 minutes. Let stand 2 minutes before serving.

Impossibly Easy Turkey Taco Pie

PREP TIME: 20 MINUTES ● START TO FINISH: 55 MINUTES
6 SERVINGS

1 lb ground turkey breast

1 medium onion, chopped (½ cup)

1 package (1.25 oz) taco seasoning mix

1 can (4.5 oz) chopped green chiles, undrained

½ cup Original Bisquick mix

1 cup milk

2 eggs

½ cup shredded Colby–Monterey Jack cheese blend (2 oz)

1 medium tomato, chopped (¾ cup)

1½ cups shredded lettuce

2 medium green onions, sliced (2 tablespoons)

1 Heat oven to 400°F. Spray 9-inch glass pie plate with cooking spray. In 10-inch skillet, cook turkey and onion over medium-high heat, stirring occasionally, until turkey is no longer pink. Sprinkle taco seasoning mix over turkey mixture; mix well. Spread in pie plate. Top evenly with chiles.

2 In medium bowl, stir Bisquick mix, milk and eggs with wire whisk or fork until blended. Pour into pie plate.

3 Bake 25 minutes. Top with cheese and tomato. Bake 2 to 3 minutes longer or until cheese is melted. Let stand 5 minutes before serving. Place ¼ cup lettuce on each plate; place wedge of pie on top of lettuce. Sprinkle with green onions.

High Altitude (3500–6500 ft): No change.

1 SERVING: Calories 240 (Calories from Fat 70); Total Fat 8g (Saturated Fat 3.5g); Cholesterol 130mg; Sodium 810mg; Total Carbohydrate 16g (Dietary Fiber 2g; Sugars 8g); Protein 25g **% DAILY VALUE:** Vitamin A 25%; Vitamin C 8%; Calcium 15%; Iron 10% **EXCHANGES:** ½ Starch, ½ Other Carbohydrate, 3½ Very Lean Meat, 1 Fat **CARBOHYDRATE CHOICES:** 1

Impossibly Easy Turkey Ranch Pie

PREP TIME: 10 MINUTES ● **START TO FINISH: 55 MINUTES**
6 SERVINGS

1½ cups cut-up cooked turkey

1½ cups frozen mixed vegetables

½ cup shredded Monterey Jack cheese (2 oz)

½ cup Original Bisquick mix

1 package (1 oz) ranch dressing mix

1 cup milk

2 eggs

1 Heat oven to 400°F. Spray 9-inch glass pie plate with cooking spray. Spread turkey and vegetables in pie plate. Sprinkle with cheese.

2 In small bowl, stir remaining ingredients with wire whisk or fork until blended. Pour into pie plate.

3 Bake 33 to 38 minutes or until knife inserted in center comes out clean. Let stand 5 minutes before serving.

High Altitude (3500–6500 ft): Bake 35 to 40 minutes.

1 SERVING: Calories 230 (Calories from Fat 80); Total Fat 9g (Saturated Fat 4g); Cholesterol 115mg; Sodium 600mg; Total Carbohydrate 17g (Dietary Fiber 2g; Sugars 5g); Protein 18g **% DAILY VALUE:** Vitamin A 45%; Vitamin C 0%; Calcium 20%; Iron 8% **EXCHANGES:** 1 Starch, 2 Medium-Fat Meat **CARBOHYDRATE CHOICES:** 1

Impossibly Easy Ham Ranch Pie: Substitute 1½ cups cut-up cooked ham for the turkey and ½ cup Swiss cheese for the Monterey Jack cheese.

Quick Tip It is important to let the pie stand before cutting because it will continue to cook and set up.

Impossibly Easy Turkey Club Pie

PREP TIME: 15 MINUTES ● **START TO FINISH: 55 MINUTES**
6 SERVINGS

1½ cups cut-up cooked turkey

8 slices bacon, crisply cooked
and crumbled

1 cup shredded Cheddar
cheese (4 oz)

½ cup Original or Reduced Fat
Bisquick mix

1 cup milk

2 eggs

1 Heat oven to 400°F. Spray 9-inch glass pie plate with cooking spray. Sprinkle turkey, bacon and cheese in pie plate.

2 Stir remaining ingredients until blended. Pour into pie plate.

3 Bake 30 to 35 minutes or until knife inserted in center comes out clean. Let stand 5 minutes before serving.

High Altitude (3500–6500 ft): No changes.

1 SERVING: Calories 275 (Calories from Fat 155); Total Fat 17g (Saturated Fat 8g); Cholesterol 130mg; Sodium 460mg; Carbohydrate 8g (Dietary Fiber 0g; Sugars 2g); Protein 21g **% DAILY VALUE:** Vitamin A 8%; Vitamin C 0%; Calcium 18%; Iron 6% **EXCHANGES:** ½ Starch, 3 Medium-Fat Meat **CARBOHYDRATE CHOICES:** ½

Quick Tip Get a head start on your dinner by cooking the bacon, cutting up the turkey and shredding the cheese the night before. Enjoy an easy one-dish meal by topping the pie with shredded lettuce and sliced tomatoes. For dessert, serve fruit-yogurt smoothies.

Impossibly Easy Cheesy Italian Chicken Pie

PREP TIME: 20 MINUTES ● **START TO FINISH: 1 HOUR 10 MINUTES**
6 SERVINGS

1½ cups cut-up cooked chicken

1¼ cups shredded
 mozzarella cheese (5 oz)

⅓ cup grated Parmesan cheese

½ teaspoon dried oregano
 leaves

½ teaspoon dried basil leaves

½ teaspoon garlic powder

1 can (8 oz) tomato sauce

½ cup Original Bisquick mix

¼ teaspoon pepper

1 cup milk

2 eggs

1 Heat oven to 400°F. Spray 9-inch glass pie plate with cooking spray. In medium bowl, mix chicken, ½ cup of the mozzarella cheese, the Parmesan cheese, oregano, basil, garlic powder and ½ cup of the tomato sauce; spoon into pie plate.

2 In small bowl, stir Bisquick mix, pepper, milk and eggs with wire whisk or fork until blended. Pour into pie plate.

3 Bake 35 minutes. Sprinkle with remaining ¾ cup mozzarella cheese. Bake 5 to 8 minutes longer or until knife inserted in center comes out clean. Let stand 5 minutes before serving. Serve with remaining tomato sauce, heated if desired.

High Altitude (3500–6500 ft): No change.

1 SERVING: Calories 250 (Calories from Fat 110); Total Fat 12g (Saturated Fat 6g); Cholesterol 120mg; Sodium 600mg; Total Carbohydrate 13g (Dietary Fiber 0g; Sugars 5g); Protein 23g **% DAILY VALUE:** Vitamin A 10%; Vitamin C 2%; Calcium 35%; Iron 8% **EXCHANGES:** ½ Starch, ½ Other Carbohydrate, 3 Lean Meat, ½ Fat **CARBOHYDRATE CHOICES:** 1

Quick Tip Doubling an Impossibly Easy Pie recipe is a breeze. Just double the ingredients and bake in either two 9-inch glass pie plates or in a 13 × 9-inch (3-quart) glass baking dish. If you use the baking dish, bake the pie for 10 minutes longer than the recipe indicates.

This 1964 ad depicts Bisquick as the building block to all sorts of meals. The possibilities stack higher and higher.

Impossibly Easy
Chicken Primavera Pie

PREP TIME: 10 MINUTES ● START TO FINISH: 50 MINUTES
6 SERVINGS

1½ cups cut-up cooked chicken

1 package (10 oz) frozen asparagus cuts, thawed and well drained

1 cup frozen stir-fry bell peppers and onions (from 16-oz bag), thawed and well drained

⅓ cup grated Parmesan cheese

½ cup Original Bisquick mix

1 cup milk

½ teaspoon salt

2 eggs

1 Heat oven to 400°F. Spray 9-inch glass pie plate with cooking spray. Layer chicken, asparagus, stir-fry mixture and cheese in pie plate.

2 Stir remaining ingredients until blended. Pour into pie plate.

3 Bake 30 to 35 minutes or until knife inserted in center comes out clean. Let stand 5 minutes before serving.

High Altitude (3500–6500 ft): Bake 38 to 40 minutes.

1 SERVING: Calories 185 (Calories from Fat 70); Total Fat 8g (Saturated Fat 3g); Cholesterol 105mg; Sodium 490mg; Total Carbohydrate 12g (Dietary Fiber 1g; Sugars 4g); Protein 17g **% DAILY VALUE:** Vitamin A 8%; Vitamin C 14%; Calcium 14%; Iron 8% **EXCHANGES:** ½ Starch, 2 Lean Meat, 1 Vegetable **CARBOHYDRATE CHOICES:** 1

Quick Tip Is company coming? Garnish each serving of this pie with a spoonful of warmed marinara or spaghetti sauce and a sprinkle of freshly shredded Parmesan cheese on top.

Impossibly Easy Italian Sausage Pie

PREP TIME: 15 MINUTES ● **START TO FINISH: 50 MINUTES**
6 SERVINGS

½ lb bulk Italian pork sausage

2 cups frozen mixed
    vegetables, thawed, drained

½ cup Original Bisquick mix

1 cup milk

½ teaspoon salt

¼ teaspoon pepper

2 eggs

1 Heat oven to 400°F. Spray 9-inch glass pie plate with cooking spray. In 10-inch skillet, cook sausage over medium heat 8 to 10 minutes, stirring occasionally, until thoroughly cooked; drain. Spread sausage in pie plate. Sprinkle with vegetables.

2 In medium bowl, stir remaining ingredients with wire whisk or fork until blended. Pour into pie plate.

3 Bake 30 to 35 minutes or until top is golden brown and knife inserted in center comes out clean. Let stand 5 minutes before serving.

High Altitude (3500–6500 ft): Bake 33 to 38 minutes.

1 SERVING: Calories 180 (Calories from Fat 80); Total Fat 9g (Saturated Fat 3g); Cholesterol 90mg; Sodium 510mg; Total Carbohydrate 17g (Dietary Fiber 3g; Sugars 5g); Protein 9g **% DAILY VALUE:** Vitamin A 60%; Vitamin C 0%; Calcium 8%; Iron 6% **EXCHANGES:** 1 Other Carbohydrate, 1 Vegetable, 1 High-Fat Meat **CARBOHYDRATE CHOICES:** 1

Quick Tip Try substituting 2 cups frozen corn, thawed and drained, or frozen cut green beans, thawed and drained, for the mixed vegetables.

Impossibly Easy Pepperoni Pie

PREP TIME: 10 MINUTES ● START TO FINISH: 50 MINUTES
6 SERVINGS

½ package (3.5 oz size) sliced pepperoni

1 small onion, chopped

1 tomato, chopped

¼ cup chopped green bell pepper

¾ cup shredded mozzarella cheese (3 oz)

⅓ cup grated Parmesan cheese

¾ cup Original Bisquick mix

1 teaspoon Italian seasoning

1 cup milk

3 eggs

¾ cup marinara or pizza sauce

1 Heat oven to 400°F. Spray 9-inch glass pie plate with cooking spray. In pie plate, layer pepperoni, onion, tomato and bell pepper. Sprinkle with cheeses.

2 In large bowl, stir Bisquick mix, Italian seasoning, milk and eggs with wire whisk or fork until blended. Pour into pie plate.

3 Bake 30 to 35 minutes or until knife inserted in center comes out clean. Cool 5 minutes. Top servings with marinara sauce.

High Altitude (3500–6500 ft): No change.

1 SERVING: Calories 270 (Calories from Fat 130); Total Fat 14g (Saturated Fat 6g); Cholesterol 130mg; Sodium 710mg; Total Carbohydrate 21g (Dietary Fiber 1g; Sugars 7g); Protein 14g **% DAILY VALUE:** Vitamin A 15%; Vitamin C 10%; Calcium 25%; Iron 8% **EXCHANGES:** 1 Starch, ½ Other Carbohydrate, 1½ Medium-Fat Meat, 1 Fat **CARBOHYDRATE CHOICES:** 1½

Quick Tip Pie plates vary in size and using too small a pan will cause the filling to run over while baking. If your pie plate isn't marked with the size on the bottom, measure from inside rim to inside rim to determine the pie size.

Impossibly Easy BLT Pie

PREP TIME: 15 MINUTES ● **START TO FINISH: 50 MINUTES**
6 SERVINGS

12 slices bacon, crisply cooked, crumbled

1 cup shredded Swiss cheese (4 oz)

½ cup Original Bisquick mix

⅛ teaspoon pepper

¾ cup milk

⅓ cup mayonnaise or salad dressing

2 eggs

2 tablespoons mayonnaise or salad dressing

1 cup shredded lettuce

6 thin slices tomato

1 Heat oven to 400°F. Spray 9-inch glass pie plate with cooking spray. Layer bacon and cheese in pie plate.

2 In medium bowl, stir Bisquick mix, pepper, milk, ⅓ cup mayonnaise and the eggs with wire whisk or fork until blended. Pour into pie plate.

3 Bake 25 to 30 minutes or until top is golden brown and knife inserted in center comes out clean. Let stand 5 minutes before serving. Spread 2 tablespoons mayonnaise over top of pie. Sprinkle with lettuce. Place tomato slices on lettuce.

High Altitude (3500–6500 ft): Bake 30 to 35 minutes.

1 SERVING: Calories 360 (Calories from Fat 260); Total Fat 29g (Saturated Fat 9g); Cholesterol 115mg; Sodium 660mg; Total Carbohydrate 11g (Dietary Fiber 0g; Sugars 3g); Protein 15g **% DAILY VALUE:** Vitamin A 10%; Vitamin C 4%; Calcium 20%; Iron 6% **EXCHANGES:** ½ Starch, 2 High-Fat Meat, 2½ Fat **CARBOHYDRATE CHOICES:** 1

Quick Tip In a hurry? Try using precooked bacon. Just heat it in the microwave for a few seconds so it will crumble more easily.

Impossibly Easy Oktoberfest Pie

PREP TIME: 10 MINUTES ● **START TO FINISH: 50 MINUTES**
6 SERVINGS

½ lb fully cooked bratwurst (about 3), cut into ¾-inch pieces

1 can (8 oz) sauerkraut, drained (1⅓ cups)

1 cup shredded Swiss cheese (4 oz)

¾ cup Original or Reduced Fat Bisquick mix

½ cup milk

½ cup regular or nonalcoholic beer

2 eggs

1 Heat oven to 400°F. Spray 9-inch glass pie plate with cooking spray. Sprinkle bratwurst, sauerkraut and cheese in pie plate.

2 Stir remaining ingredients until blended. Pour into pie plate.

3 Bake 30 to 35 minutes or until knife inserted in center comes out clean. Let stand 5 minutes before serving.

High Altitude (3500–6500 ft): No change.

1 SERVING: Calories 285 (Calories from Fat 180); Total Fat 20g (Saturated Fat 8g); Cholesterol 110mg; Sodium 930mg; Carbohydrate 15g (Dietary Fiber 1g; Sugars 2g); Protein 14g **% DAILY VALUE:** Vitamin A 6%; Vitamin C 4%; Calcium 24%; Iron 8% **EXCHANGES:** ½ Starch, 1 Vegetable, 2 Medium-Fat Meat, 2 Fat **CARBOHYDRATE CHOICES:** 1

Quick Tip Serve this pie with sliced apples on a bed of greens drizzled with poppy seed dressing and rye rolls or bread.

Impossibly Easy Calico Corn and Bacon Pie

PREP TIME: 15 MINUTES ● **START TO FINISH: 50 MINUTES**
6 SERVINGS

8 slices bacon, crisply cooked and crumbled (½ cup)

1 small onion, chopped (¼ cup)

¼ cup chopped green bell pepper

1 can (about 8 oz) whole kernel corn, drained

1 jar (2 oz) diced pimientos, drained

⅔ cup Original or Reduced Fat Bisquick mix

1 cup milk

⅛ teaspoon pepper

2 eggs

Sour cream, if desired

1 Heat oven to 400°F. Spray 9-inch glass pie plate with cooking spray. Reserve 2 tablespoons of the bacon. Sprinkle remaining bacon, the onion, bell pepper, corn and pimientos in pie plate.

2 Stir remaining ingredients, except sour cream, until blended. Pour into pie plate.

3 Bake uncovered about 30 minutes or until knife inserted in center comes out clean. Let stand 5 minutes before serving. Garnish with sour cream and reserved bacon.

High Altitude (3500–6500 ft): No change.

1 SERVING: Calories 185 (Calories from Fat 80); Total Fat 9g (Saturated Fat 3g); Cholesterol 80mg; Sodium 440mg; Total Carbohydrate 18g (Dietary Fiber 1g, Sugars 5g); Protein 8g **% DAILY VALUE:** Vitamin A 10%; Vitamin C 14%; Calcium 8%; Iron 6% **EXCHANGES:** 1 Starch, 1 Vegetable, ½ High-Fat Meat, 1 Fat **CARBOHYDRATE CHOICES:** 1

Quick Tip Get a jump start on dinner. Mix up this tasty pie the night or morning before, then pop it in the oven when you get home from work! After adding all ingredients to the pie plate, cover and refrigerate up to 24 hours. Uncover and bake 30 to 35 minutes (33 to 38 minutes at high altitude).

Impossibly Easy Bacon Cheeseburger Pie

PREP TIME: 25 MINUTES ● **START TO FINISH: 50 MINUTES**
6 SERVINGS

6 slices bacon

1 lb lean (at least 80%) ground beef

¼ teaspoon pepper

1 large onion, chopped (1 cup)

¼ cup ketchup

1 cup shredded Cheddar cheese (4 oz)

½ cup Original Bisquick mix

1 cup milk

2 eggs

1 Heat oven to 400°F. Spray 9-inch glass pie plate with cooking spray. In 10-inch skillet, cook bacon over medium-high heat 5 to 7 minutes, turning once, until crisp; drain on paper towels. Crumble bacon; set aside.

2 In same skillet, cook beef, pepper and onion over medium-high heat 5 to 7 minutes, stirring occasionally, until beef is thoroughly cooked; drain. Stir in ketchup. Spread in pie plate; sprinkle with cheese and bacon.

3 In medium bowl, stir remaining ingredients with wire whisk or fork until blended. Pour into pie plate.

4 Bake 20 to 25 minutes or until knife inserted in center comes out clean. Serve with additional ketchup if desired.

High Altitude (3500–6500 ft): Increase Bisquick mix to ¾ cup.

1 SERVING: Calories 360 (Calories from Fat 200); Total Fat 22g (Saturated Fat 10g); Cholesterol 150mg; Sodium 610mg; Total Carbohydrate 14g (Dietary Fiber 0g; Sugars 6g); Protein 25g **% DAILY VALUE:** Vitamin A 10%; Vitamin C 2%; Calcium 20%; Iron 10% **EXCHANGES:** ½ Starch, ½ Other Carbohydrate, 3 Medium-Fat Meat, 1½ Fat **CARBOHYDRATE CHOICES:** 1

Impossibly Easy Chef's Salad Pie

PREP TIME: 15 MINUTES ● **START TO FINISH: 50 MINUTES**
6 SERVINGS

½ cup diced smoked ham

½ cup diced smoked turkey

½ cup shredded Swiss cheese (2 oz)

½ cup shredded Cheddar cheese (2 oz)

3 eggs

1½ cups milk

1 tablespoon dry ranch dressing mix (about half of 1-oz package)

¾ cup Original Bisquick mix

2 cups shredded lettuce

1 cup grape tomatoes, halved

1 Heat oven to 400°F. Spray 9-inch deep-dish glass pie plate or 8-inch square (2-quart) baking dish with cooking spray. Sprinkle ham, turkey and cheeses in pie plate.

2 In medium bowl, stir eggs, milk, dressing mix and Bisquick mix with fork or whisk until blended. Pour into pie plate.

3 Bake 30 to 35 minutes or until knife inserted in center comes out clean. Let stand 5 minutes before serving. Top each serving with lettuce and tomatoes.

High Altitude (3500–6500 ft): Bake 35 to 40 minutes.

1 SERVING: Calories 250 (Calories from Fat 120); Total Fat 14g (Saturated Fat 6g); Cholesterol 145mg; Sodium 710mg; Total Carbohydrate 16g (Dietary Fiber 0g; Sugars 6g); Protein 18g **% DAILY VALUE:** Vitamin A 15%; Vitamin C 6%; Calcium 25%; Iron 8% **EXCHANGES:** ½ Starch, ½ Other Carbohydrate, 2½ Lean Meat, 1 Fat **CARBOHYDRATE CHOICES:** 1

Quick Tip For an added touch, drizzle ranch dressing over each serving.

Impossibly Easy Ham, Cheddar and Apple Pie

PREP TIME: 10 MINUTES ● **START TO FINISH: 55 MINUTES**
6 SERVINGS

1½ cups cut-up cooked ham

1 cup shredded Cheddar cheese (4 oz)

4 medium green onions, sliced (¼ cup)

1 small cooking apple, peeled, chopped (½ cup)

½ cup Original Bisquick mix

1 cup milk

⅛ teaspoon pepper

2 eggs

1 Heat oven to 400°F. Spray 9-inch glass pie plate with cooking spray. Sprinkle ham, cheese, onions and apple in pie plate.

2 In medium bowl, stir together remaining ingredients until blended. Pour over ham mixture.

3 Bake uncovered 35 to 40 minutes or until knife inserted in center comes out clean. Let stand 5 minutes before serving.

High Altitude (3500–6500 ft): Bake uncovered about 45 minutes.

1 SERVING: Calories 240 (Calories from Fat 140); Total Fat 15g (Saturated Fat 7g); Cholesterol 115mg; Sodium 590mg; Total Carbohydrate 11g (Dietary Fiber 0g; Sugars 4g); Protein 16g **% DAILY VALUE:** Vitamin A 8%; Vitamin C 0%; Calcium 15%; Iron 6% **EXCHANGES:** ½ Starch, 2 Medium-Fat Meat, 1 Fat **CARBOHYDRATE CHOICES:** 1

Impossibly Easy Bacon, Swiss and Apple Pie: Substitute 12 slices bacon, crisply cooked and crumbled, for the ham and 1 cup Swiss cheese for the Cheddar cheese.

Impossibly Easy Quesadilla Pie

PREP TIME: 20 MINUTES ● **START TO FINISH: 1 HOUR 5 MINUTES**
6 SERVINGS

1 tablespoon butter or
  margarine

1 large onion, chopped (1 cup)

1 large tomato, chopped
  (1 cup)

1 can (4.5 oz) chopped green
  chiles, drained

1 can (4 oz) sliced ripe olives,
  drained

2 cups shredded Colby–
  Monterey Jack cheese
  (8 oz)

½ teaspoon ground cumin

¼ teaspoon salt, if desired

½ cup Original Bisquick mix

1 cup milk

2 eggs

1 Heat oven to 400°F. Spray 9-inch glass pie plate with cooking spray. In 10-inch skillet, melt butter over medium heat. Cook onion in butter, stirring occasionally, until tender; remove from heat. Stir in tomato, chiles, olives, 1 cup of the cheese, the cumin and salt. Spread in pie plate.

2 In small bowl, stir Bisquick mix, milk and eggs with wire whisk or fork until blended. Pour over vegetable mixture.

3 Bake 30 minutes. Sprinkle with remaining 1 cup cheese. Bake 3 to 5 minutes longer or until knife inserted in center comes out clean. Let stand 10 minutes before serving.

High Altitude (3500–6500 ft): Increase first bake time to about 33 minutes.

1 SERVING: Calories 300 (Calories from Fat 180); Total Fat 20g (Saturated Fat 10g); Cholesterol 115mg; Sodium 870mg; Total Carbohydrate 15g (Dietary Fiber 2g; Sugars 6g); Protein 14g **% DAILY VALUE:** Vitamin A 25%; Vitamin C 6%; Calcium 35%; Iron 10% **EXCHANGES:** ½ Starch, ½ Other Carbohydrate, 1½ Medium-Fat Meat, 2½ Fat **CARBOHYDRATE CHOICES:** 1

Quick Tip Green chiles are milder than jalapeños, yet they add nice flavor to this quesadilla pie. For a spicier dish, use canned jalapeño chiles.

Impossibly Easy Shrimp Pie

PREP TIME: 10 MINUTES ● **START TO FINISH: 45 MINUTES**
6 SERVINGS

1 bag (12 oz) frozen cooked medium shrimp, tails removed

⅓ cup chopped celery

¼ cup chopped green bell pepper

½ teaspoon seafood seasoning

1 cup Original Bisquick mix

1 teaspoon dried basil leaves

½ cup milk

2 eggs

¾ cup tomato pasta sauce, heated

1 Heat oven to 350°F. Spray 9-inch glass pie plate with cooking spray. In medium bowl, mix frozen shrimp, celery, bell pepper and seafood seasoning. Pour into pie plate.

2 In medium bowl, stir Bisquick mix, basil, milk and eggs with wire whisk or fork until blended. Pour over shrimp mixture.

3 Bake 30 to 35 minutes or until knife inserted in center comes out clean. Spoon pasta sauce over each serving.

High Altitude (3500–6500 ft): Heat oven to 375°F. Bake 38 to 42 minutes.

1 SERVING: Calories 210 (Calories from Fat 60); Total Fat 6g (Saturated Fat 2g); Cholesterol 185mg; Sodium 610mg; Total Carbohydrate 20g (Dietary Fiber 1g; Sugars 5g); Protein 17g **% DAILY VALUE:** Vitamin A 10%; Vitamin C 8%; Calcium 8%; Iron 15% **EXCHANGES:** 1 Starch, ½ Other Carbohydrate, 2 Very Lean Meat, 1 Fat **CARBOHYDRATE CHOICES:** 1

Quick Tip For a special lunch, serve this shrimp pie with ¾ cup heated Alfredo pasta sauce instead of tomato pasta sauce. Spoon the sauce over each serving and sprinkle with shredded Parmesan cheese and toasted sliced almonds.

Impossibly Easy Mac 'n' Cheese Pie

PREP TIME: 10 MINUTES ● **START TO FINISH: 50 MINUTES**
6 SERVINGS

1 cup uncooked elbow
    macaroni (3.5 oz)

2 cups shredded Cheddar
    cheese (8 oz)

½ cup Original Bisquick

1½ cups milk

¼ teaspoon red pepper sauce

2 eggs

1 Heat oven to 400°F. Grease 9-inch glass pie plate. Place uncooked macaroni in pie plate. Sprinkle with 1¾ cups of the cheese.

2 Stir remaining ingredients until blended. Pour into pie plate.

3 Bake 25 to 30 minutes or until knife inserted in center comes out clean. Sprinkle with remaining ¼ cup cheese. Bake 1 to 2 minutes or until cheese is melted. Let stand 5 minutes before serving.

High Altitude (3500–6500 ft): Cook macaroni in boiling water 5 minutes (add 1 tablespoon vegetable oil to prevent boilover). Drain thoroughly; cool completely.

1 SERVING: Calories 320 (Calories from Fat 155); Total Fat 17g (Saturated Fat 10g); Cholesterol 115mg; Sodium 430mg; Total Carbohydrate 26g (Dietary Fiber 1g; Sugars 4g); Protein 17g **% DAILY VALUE:** Vitamin A 12%; Vitamin C 0%; Calcium 30%; Iron 8% **EXCHANGES:** 1 Starch, 1 High-Fat Meat, ½ Medium-Fat Meat, ½ Fat **CARBOHYDRATE CHOICES:** 2

Quick Tip Add some color to this comfort-food classic with a dash of paprika and a little chopped fresh parsley. If you're craving something crunchy, sprinkle crushed seasoned croutons over the top.

Stuffed Pizza

PREP TIME: 30 MINUTES ● START TO FINISH: 55 MINUTES
8 SERVINGS

½ lb bulk Italian pork sausage

½ lb lean (at least 80%) ground beef

3⅓ cups Original Bisquick mix

¾ cup cold water

3 cups shredded mozzarella cheese (12 oz)

1 jar (14 to 15 oz) pizza sauce

1 cup sliced fresh mushrooms (3 oz)

¼ cup chopped green bell pepper

1 Heat oven to 450°F. Spray 13 × 9-inch (3-quart) glass baking dish with cooking spray. In 10-inch skillet, cook sausage and ground beef over medium-high heat 5 to 7 minutes, stirring frequently, until thoroughly cooked; drain. Set aside.

2 In large bowl, stir Bisquick mix and cold water until dough forms. Divide dough into 2 parts, 1 part slightly larger. Press or roll larger part of dough into 16 × 14-inch rectangle on surface sprinkled with Bisquick mix. Fold crosswise into thirds. Place in center of baking dish; unfold. Press on bottom and up sides of dish. Sprinkle with 1 cup of the cheese; top with ¾ cup of the pizza sauce, the meat mixture, mushrooms and bell pepper and 1½ cups of the cheese.

3 Press or roll remaining part of dough into 13 × 9-inch rectangle. Fold crosswise into thirds. Place on cheese in center of baking dish; unfold. Press bottom and top crust edges together to seal. Make small slits in top crust. Spread remaining pizza sauce over crust; sprinkle with remaining cheese.

4 Bake uncovered 22 to 25 minutes or until edges of crust are golden brown.

High Altitude (3500–6500 ft): In step 3, do not sprinkle remaining cheese on pizza before baking. Bake pizza uncovered 25 minutes. Sprinkle with remaining cheese; bake 3 to 5 minutes longer to melt cheese.

1 SERVING: Calories 450 (Calories from Fat 200); Total Fat 22g (Saturated Fat 10g); Cholesterol 50mg; Sodium 1190mg; Total Carbohydrate 39g (Dietary Fiber 2g; Sugars 5g); Protein 24g **% DAILY VALUE:** Vitamin A 6%; Vitamin C 6%; Calcium 35%; Iron 20% **EXCHANGES:** 2 Starch, ½ Other Carbohydrate, 2½ High-Fat Meat **CARBOHYDRATE CHOICES:** 2½

Cheesy Beef Sloppy Joe Pizza

PREP TIME: 15 MINUTES ● START TO FINISH: 30 MINUTES
8 SERVINGS

1½ cups Original Bisquick mix

⅓ cup very hot water

1 lb lean (at least 80%) ground beef

1 can (15.5 oz) sloppy joe sauce

1 cup shredded Cheddar cheese (4 oz)

2 plum (Roma) tomatoes, thinly sliced

2 tablespoons sliced green onions (2 medium)

1 Move oven rack to lowest position. Heat oven to 450°F. Spray cookie sheet or 12-inch pizza pan with cooking spray. In medium bowl, stir Bisquick mix and water until soft dough forms. On cookie sheet, press dough into 12-inch round or press in pizza pan, using fingers coated with Bisquick mix; pinch edge to form ½-inch rim.

2 In 10-inch skillet, cook beef over medium-high heat 5 to 7 minutes, stirring frequently, until thoroughly cooked; drain. Stir in sloppy joe sauce. Spoon beef mixture over dough. Sprinkle with cheese.

3 Bake 12 to 15 minutes or until crust is golden brown and cheese is bubbly. Top with tomatoes and onions.

High Altitude (3500–6500 ft): Heat oven to 475°F. In step 1, bake crust 8 minutes before topping with beef mixture. In step 3, bake 6 to 8 minutes.

1 SERVING: Calories 270 (Calories from Fat 120); Total Fat 14g (Saturated Fat 6g); Cholesterol 50mg; Sodium 720mg; Total Carbohydrate 21g (Dietary Fiber 1g; Sugars 5g); Protein 16g **% DAILY VALUE:** Vitamin A 10%; Vitamin C 4%; Calcium 10%; Iron 15% **EXCHANGES:** 1 Starch, ½ Other Carbohydrate, 2 Medium-Fat Meat, ½ Fat **CARBOHYDRATE CHOICES:** 1½

Cheesy Turkey Sloppy Joe Pizza: Substitute 1 pound ground turkey for the ground beef.

Cheesy Meatball Pizza

PREP TIME: 15 MINUTES ● **START TO FINISH: 40 MINUTES**
8 SERVINGS

1½ cups Original Bisquick mix

⅓ cup hot water

½ cup tomato pasta sauce (from 26-oz jar)

¼ cup grated Parmesan cheese

16 frozen Italian-style meatballs (½ oz each; from 16-oz package), thawed, cut in half

1½ cups shredded Italian cheese blend (6 oz)

½ cup diced green bell pepper

1 Heat oven to 425°F. Spray 12-inch pizza pan or cookie sheet with cooking spray. In medium bowl, stir Bisquick mix and hot water until soft dough forms. Press dough in pizza pan, using fingers dipped in Bisquick mix; pinch edge to form ½-inch rim.

2 Bake 7 to 8 minutes or until light golden brown. Remove from oven.

3 Spread pasta sauce over partially baked crust. Top with Parmesan cheese, meatball halves (place cut sides down), shredded cheese and bell pepper.

4 Bake 10 to 15 minutes longer or until crust is golden brown and cheese is melted.

High Altitude (3500–6500 ft): No change.

1 SERVING: Calories 260 (Calories from Fat 120); Total Fat 13g (Saturated Fat 6g); Cholesterol 50mg; Sodium 850mg; Total Carbohydrate 22g (Dietary Fiber 1g; Sugars 3g); Protein 14g **% DAILY VALUE:** Vitamin A 8%; Vitamin C 8%; Calcium 25%; Iron 10% **EXCHANGES:** 1 Starch, ½ Other Carbohydrate, 1½ High-Fat Meat **CARBOHYDRATE CHOICES:** 1½

Quick Tip Thaw the meatballs overnight in the refrigerator, or use the Defrost setting on your microwave to quickly thaw them.

Cowboy BBQ Chicken Pizza

PREP TIME: 15 MINUTES ● **START TO FINISH: 40 MINUTES**
8 SERVINGS

2 cups Original Bisquick mix

¼ cup sour cream

¼ cup very hot water

3 cups cubed cooked chicken

1 cup barbecue sauce

4 medium green onions, sliced (¼ cup)

¼ cup chopped packaged precooked bacon (about 4 slices from 2.2-oz package)

1½ cups shredded Colby–Monterey Jack cheese (6 oz)

1 Heat oven to 400°F. In medium bowl, stir Bisquick mix, sour cream and hot water until soft dough forms.

2 On surface sprinkled with Bisquick mix, shape dough into a ball. Knead 5 times. Roll dough into 14-inch round; fold round in half. Place dough on ungreased 14-inch pizza pan or large cookie sheet; unfold dough.

3 In medium bowl, mix chicken, barbecue sauce and onions. Spread chicken mixture over dough to within 1 inch of edge. Fold edge just to chicken mixture. Top with half of the bacon. Sprinkle with cheese and remaining bacon.

4 Bake 20 to 25 minutes or until crust is light golden brown and cheese is melted.

High Altitude (3500–6500 ft): Bake 18 to 23 minutes.

1 SERVING: Calories 380 (Calories from Fat 160); Total Fat 17g (Saturated Fat 8g); Cholesterol 75mg; Sodium 920mg; Total Carbohydrate 33g (Dietary Fiber 0g; Sugars 13g); Protein 23g **% DAILY VALUE:** Vitamin A 8%; Vitamin C 0%; Calcium 20%; Iron 10% **EXCHANGES:** 1 Starch, 1 Other Carbohydrate, 3 Lean Meat, 1½ Fat **CARBOHYDRATE CHOICES:** 2

Chicken Cordon Bleu Pizza

PREP TIME: 10 MINUTES ● **START TO FINISH: 35 MINUTES**
8 SERVINGS

1½ cups Original Bisquick mix

2 tablespoons grated Parmesan cheese

⅓ cup hot water

½ cup Alfredo pasta sauce (from 16-oz jar)

2 cups chopped cooked chicken

½ cup chopped cooked ham

1½ cups finely shredded Swiss cheese (6 oz)

3 medium green onions, sliced (3 tablespoons)

1 Heat oven to 425°F. Spray 12-inch pizza pan or cookie sheet with cooking spray. In medium bowl, stir Bisquick mix, Parmesan cheese and hot water until soft dough forms. Press dough in pizza pan, using fingers dipped in Bisquick mix; pinch edge to form ½-inch rim.

2 Bake 7 to 8 minutes or until light golden brown. Remove from oven.

3 Spread Alfredo sauce over partially baked crust. Top with chicken, ham, Swiss cheese and onions.

4 Bake 10 to 15 minutes longer or until crust is golden brown and cheese is melted.

High Altitude (3500–6500 ft): No change.

1 SERVING: Calories 310 (Calories from Fat 150); Total Fat 17g (Saturated Fat 9g); Cholesterol 70mg; Sodium 550mg; Total Carbohydrate 17g (Dietary Fiber 0g; Sugars 1g); Protein 21g **% DAILY VALUE:** Vitamin A 8%; Vitamin C 0%; Calcium 25%; Iron 6% **EXCHANGES:** 1 Starch, 2½ Lean Meat, 2 Fat **CARBOHYDRATE CHOICES:** 1

Quick Tip Why use hot water? It helps keep the crust from rising too high during baking and keeps it chewy on the inside and crisp on the outside.

Chicken and Veggie Pizza

PREP TIME: 20 MINUTES ● **START TO FINISH: 35 MINUTES**
8 SERVINGS

2 cups Original Bisquick mix

⅓ cup very hot water

¾ cup spinach dip

1 cup chopped cooked chicken

1 medium tomato, seeded and chopped (¾ cup)

1 package (8 oz) sliced fresh mushrooms

1½ cups shredded mozzarella cheese (6 oz)

1 Move oven rack to lowest position. Heat oven to 450°F. Spray 12-inch pizza pan with cooking spray. In medium bowl, stir Bisquick mix, hot water and ¼ cup of the spinach dip until soft dough forms; beat vigorously 20 strokes.

2 Press dough in pizza pan, using fingers dipped in Bisquick mix; pinch edge to form ½-inch rim. Bake 7 minutes. Remove from oven.

3 Spread remaining ½ cup spinach dip over partially baked crust. Sprinkle with chicken, tomato and mushrooms. Sprinkle with cheese.

4 Bake 12 to 15 minutes or until crust is brown and cheese is melted.

High Altitude (3500–6500 ft): No change.

1 SERVING: Calories 280 (Calories from Fat 130); Total Fat 14g (Saturated Fat 5g); Cholesterol 30mg; Sodium 620mg; Total Carbohydrate 24g (Dietary Fiber 1g; Sugars 2g); Protein 14g **% DAILY VALUE:** Vitamin A 20%; Vitamin C 2%; Calcium 20%; Iron 8% **EXCHANGES:** 1½ Starch, 1½ Lean Meat, 1½ Fat **CARBOHYDRATE CHOICES:** 1½

Quick Tip To keep your pizza crust nice and crisp, seed the tomato before adding. Just cut the tomato in half crosswise and squeeze each half to remove the seeds. This removes much of the liquid, so the tomato won't soak into the pizza crust.

It's so easy, it's scary! A 1999 Betty Crocker supermarket magazine recipe uses Bisquick to take the worry out of Halloween, and puts back the fun.

Turkey Gyro Pizza

PREP TIME: 15 MINUTES • START TO FINISH: 45 MINUTES
6 SERVINGS

2 cups Original Bisquick mix

¼ teaspoon dried oregano leaves

½ cup cold water

¼ lb sliced deli turkey breast, cut into strips

1 can (2.25 oz) sliced ripe olives, drained

½ cup crumbled feta cheese (2 oz)

1½ cups shredded mozzarella cheese (6 oz)

1 small tomato, chopped (½ cup)

½ cup chopped cucumber

1 Move oven rack to lowest position. Heat oven to 425°F. Spray 12-inch pizza pan with cooking spray. Stir Bisquick mix, oregano and water; beat vigorously with spoon 20 strokes until soft dough forms. Press dough in pizza pan, using fingers dipped in Bisquick mix; pinch edge to form ½-inch rim. Bake about 15 minutes or until golden brown.

2 Top crust with turkey and olives; sprinkle with feta and mozzarella cheeses.

3 Bake about 10 minutes or until cheese is melted. Sprinkle with tomato and cucumber.

High Altitude (3500–6500 ft): No change.

1 SERVING: Calories 300 (Calories from Fat 125); Total Fat 14g (Saturated Fat 7g); Cholesterol 35mg; Sodium 1180mg; Total Carbohydrate 28g (Dietary Fiber 1g; Sugars 2g); Protein 16g **% DAILY VALUE:** Vitamin A 8%; Vitamin C 6%; Calcium 34%; Iron 10% **EXCHANGES:** 2 Starch, 1½ Lean Meat, 1 Fat **CARBOHYDRATE CHOICES:** 2

Quick Tip The Mediterranean flavors and ingredients typical of a gyro—roasted meat with grilled vegetables and cucumber-yogurt sauce, rolled in pita bread—are transformed into a pizza the whole family will enjoy. If you prefer, mint leaves can be used in place of the oregano.

Barbecued Turkey Bake

PREP TIME: 15 MINUTES ● START TO FINISH: 45 MINUTES
6 SERVINGS

1½ cups cut-up cooked turkey

⅓ cup chili sauce

2 tablespoons honey

1 teaspoon soy sauce

¼ teaspoon red pepper sauce

1 small onion, sliced and
separated into rings

1½ cups Original Bisquick mix

⅓ cup cold water

1 cup shredded mozzarella
cheese (4 oz)

1 Heat oven to 375°F. Mix turkey, chili sauce, honey, soy sauce, pepper sauce and onion; set aside.

2 Stir Bisquick mix and cold water until dough forms; beat 20 strokes. Roll or pat dough into 12 × 6-inch rectangle on ungreased cookie sheet; pinch edge to form ½-inch rim. Spoon turkey mixture onto dough.

3 Bake 25 minutes or until edge of crust is light brown. Sprinkle with cheese. Bake about 5 minutes or until cheese is melted.

High Altitude (3500–6500 ft): Heat oven to 400°F.

1 SERVING: Calories 275 (Calories from Fat 90); Total Fat 10g (Saturated Fat 4g); Cholesterol 40mg; Sodium 790mg; Carbohydrate 30g (Dietary Fiber 1g; Sugars 10g); Protein 17g **% DAILY VALUE:** Vitamin A 4%; Vitamin C 2%; Calcium 20%; Iron 8% **EXCHANGES:** 2 Starch, 1½ Medium-Fat Meat **CARBOHYDRATE CHOICES:** 2

Quick Tip When it's refrigerated, honey crystallizes, forming a gooey, grainy mess. Instead, store honey in an airtight container in a dry place at room temperature for up to a year.

Turkey Club Squares

PREP TIME: 25 MINUTES ● START TO FINISH: 40 MINUTES
6 SERVINGS

2 cups Original Bisquick mix

⅓ cup mayonnaise or salad dressing

⅓ cup milk

2 cups cubed cooked turkey

2 medium green onions, sliced (2 tablespoons)

6 slices bacon, crisply cooked and crumbled

¼ cup mayonnaise or salad dressing

1 large tomato, chopped (1 cup)

1 cup shredded Colby-Monterey Jack cheese (4 oz)

1 Heat oven to 450°F. Grease cookie sheet. Mix Bisquick, ⅓ cup mayonnaise and the milk until soft dough forms. Roll or pat dough into 12 × 8-inch rectangle on cookie sheet. Bake 8 to 10 minutes or until golden brown.

2 Mix turkey, onions, bacon and ¼ cup mayonnaise. Spoon over crust to within ¼ inch of edges. Sprinkle with tomato and cheese.

3 Bake 5 to 6 minutes or until turkey mixture is hot and cheese is melted.

High Altitude (3500–6500 ft): Bake crust about 10 minutes in step 1. Bake 6 to 8 minutes in step 3.

1 SERVING: Calories 525 (Calories from Fat 325); Total Fat 36g (Saturated Fat 11g); Cholesterol 80mg; Sodium 960mg; Total Carbohydrate 28g (Dietary Fiber 1g; Sugars 2g); Protein 23g **% DAILY VALUE:** Vitamin A 8%; Vitamin C 4%; Calcium 20%; Iron 12%. **EXCHANGES:** 2 Starch, 1½ Lean Meat, ½ Medium-Fat Meat, 4 Fat **CARBOHYDRATE CHOICES:** 2

Quick Tip Purchase cooked turkey at the deli or prepackaged in the meat department to make this tasty brunch or supper dish in a snap.

Santa Fe Pizza

PREP TIME: 15 MINUTES ● **START TO FINISH: 45 MINUTES**
8 SERVINGS

2 cups Original Bisquick mix

¼ cup mild salsa-flavored or jalapeño-flavored process cheese sauce (room temperature)

¼ cup hot water

1 can (16 oz) refried beans

½ cup thick 'n' chunky salsa

4 medium green onions, sliced (¼ cup)

1 cup shredded Colby-Monterey Jack cheese (4 oz)

1 cup shredded lettuce

1 medium tomato, chopped (¾ cup)

1 Move oven rack to lowest position. Heat oven to 375°F. Spray 12-inch pizza pan with cooking spray. Stir Bisquick mix, cheese sauce and hot water until soft dough forms; beat vigorously with spoon 20 strokes. Place dough on surface dusted with Bisquick mix; gently roll in Bisquick mix to coat. Shape into a ball; knead about 5 times or until smooth. Roll dough into 14-inch circle; place on cookie sheet.

2 Mix beans and salsa; spread over dough to within 2 inches of edge. Sprinkle with onions. Fold edge over bean mixture. Sprinkle cheese over bean mixture.

3 Bake 25 to 28 minutes or until crust is golden brown and cheese is melted. Garnish with lettuce and tomato.

High Altitude (3500–6500 ft): No change.

1 SERVING: Calories 260 (Calories from Fat 100); Total Fat 11g (Saturated Fat 5g); Cholesterol 25mg; Sodium 800mg; Carbohydrate 30g (Dietary Fiber 4g; Sugars 3g); Protein 10g **% DAILY VALUE:** Vitamin A 10%; Vitamin C 8%; Calcium 18%; Iron 12% **EXCHANGES:** 2 Starch, 1 High-Fat Meat. ½ Vegetable **CARBOHYDRATE CHOICES:** 2

Quick Tip If you're stopping at the grocery store, swing by the salad bar and pick up shredded lettuce, sliced green onions and chopped tomato to save prep time. Canned refried beans come in a variety of types—look for traditional, fat free or vegetarian.

Pizza Biscuit Bake

PREP TIME: 15 MINUTES ● START TO FINISH: 40 MINUTES
8 SERVINGS

3⅓ cups Original Bisquick mix

1 cup milk

2 cans (8 oz each) pizza sauce (2 cups)

1 package (8 oz) sliced pepperoni

2 cups shredded mozzarella cheese (8 oz)

1 Heat oven to 375°F. Spray 13 × 9-inch (3-quart) glass baking dish with cooking spray. In medium bowl, stir Bisquick mix and milk until soft dough forms.

2 Drop half of dough by spoonfuls evenly over bottom of baking dish (dough will not completely cover bottom of dish). Drizzle 1 can pizza sauce over dough. Scatter half of the pepperoni over sauce. Top with 1 cup of the cheese. Repeat layers with remaining dough, pizza sauce, pepperoni and cheese.

3 Bake 20 to 25 minutes or until golden brown.

High Altitude (3500–6500 ft): Bake 25 to 30 minutes.

1 SERVING: Calories 450 (Calories from Fat 220); Total Fat 24g (Saturated Fat 10g); Cholesterol 50mg; Sodium 1530mg; Total Carbohydrate 41g (Dietary Fiber 2g; Sugars 6g); Protein 19g **% DAILY VALUE:** Vitamin A 6%; Vitamin C 4%; Calcium 30%; Iron 15% **EXCHANGES:** 2 Starch, ½ Other Carbohydrate, 2 High-Fat Meat, 1½ Fat **CARBOHYDRATE CHOICES:** 3

Quick Tip Add your favorite pizza toppings to the layers. Try chopped green bell pepper, chopped onion or sliced olives.

Pizza Beef Calzones

PREP TIME: 30 MINUTES ● **START TO FINISH: 55 MINUTES**
10 SERVINGS

1 lb lean (at least 80%) ground beef

¾ cup pizza sauce

5 cups Original Bisquick mix

¾ cup water

3 tablespoons vegetable oil

1⅓ cups shredded Cheddar cheese

1 Heat oven to 450°F. In 10-inch skillet, cook ground beef over medium-high heat 5 to 7 minutes, stirring frequently, until thoroughly cooked; drain. Stir in pizza sauce. Set aside.

2 In large bowl, stir Bisquick mix, water and oil until dough forms (add additional tablespoon of water if needed). Place dough on surface sprinkled with Bisquick mix; roll in Bisquick mix to coat. Shape dough into a ball; knead about 5 times or until smooth.

3 Divide dough in half. Press or roll each half into 12-inch round. On ungreased cookie sheet, place each dough round. Top half of each round with cheese and beef mixture. Fold the other half of each over filling; press with fork to seal.

4 Bake 15 to 20 minutes or until golden brown. Remove from cookie sheets to cutting boards. Cool 5 minutes. Cut each calzone into 5 wedges.

High Altitude (3500–6500 ft): No change.

1 SERVING: Calories 420 (Calories from Fat 190); Total Fat 22g (Saturated Fat 8g); Cholesterol 45mg; Sodium 930mg; Total Carbohydrate 41g (Dietary Fiber 2g; Sugars 3g); Protein 16g **% DAILY VALUE:** Vitamin A 4%; Vitamin C 0%; Calcium 15%; Iron 15% **EXCHANGES:** 2½ Starch, 1 High-Fat Meat, 2½ Fat **CARBOHYDRATE CHOICES:** 3

Pizza Turkey Calzones: Substitute 1 pound ground turkey for the ground beef.

Quick Tip If you can't fit two cookie sheets side by side in your oven, bake one calzone while you make the second one.

Barbecued Beef and Cheese Pizza

PREP TIME: 15 MINUTES ● **START TO FINISH: 35 MINUTES**
8 SERVINGS

1 lb ground beef

1½ cups barbecue sauce

1½ cups Original Bisquick mix

¼ cup very hot water

1 tablespoon vegetable oil

Dill pickle slices, if desired

5 slices (1 oz each) process
American cheese, cut
diagonally in half

1 Move oven rack to lowest position. Heat oven to 450°F. Spray 12-inch pizza pan with cooking spray. Cook beef in 10-inch skillet over medium heat, about 10 minutes, stirring occasionally, until brown; drain. Stir in ½ cup of the barbecue sauce; set aside.

2 Stir Bisquick mix, very hot water and oil until dough forms; beat vigorously with spoon 20 strokes. Press dough in pizza pan, using fingers dipped in Bisquick mix; pinch edge to form ½-inch rim.

3 Spread remaining 1 cup barbecue sauce over dough. Top with beef mixture and pickle slices. Top with cheese. Bake 12 to 15 minutes or until crust is golden brown and cheese is melted.

High Altitude (3500–6500 ft): No change.

1 SERVING: Calories 322 (Calories from Fat 133); Total Fat 15g (Saturated Fat 6g); Cholesterol 17mg; Sodium 1181mg; Carbohydrate 29g (Dietary Fiber 1g; Sugars 13g); Protein 17g **% DAILY VALUE:** Vitamin A 6%; Vitamin C 0%; Calcium 15%; Iron 15% **EXCHANGES:** 2 Starch, 2 Medium-Fat Meat, 1½ Fat **CARBOHYDRATE CHOICES:** 2

Quick Tip After you grease the pizza pan, sprinkle it with cornmeal for added crust crispness. One pound of bulk pork sausage makes a tasty variation in place of the ground beef.

Cheeseburger Calzones

PREP TIME: 20 MINUTES ● **START TO FINISH: 40 MINUTES**
5 CALZONES

½ lb lean (at least 80%) ground beef

3 tablespoons ketchup

1 teaspoon yellow mustard

1 teaspoon instant minced onion

2 cups Original Bisquick mix

½ cup boiling water

1 cup shredded reduced-fat Cheddar cheese (4 oz)

1 egg, beaten

1 teaspoon sesame seed

1 Heat oven to 375°F. In 10-inch skillet, cook beef over medium-high heat 5 to 7 minutes, stirring frequently, until thoroughly cooked; drain. Stir in ketchup, mustard and onion.

2 In medium bowl, stir Bisquick mix and boiling water until dough forms. Divide dough into 5 equal pieces. Place dough pieces on surface sprinkled with Bisquick mix; roll in Bisquick mix to coat. Press or roll each piece into 6-inch round, about ¼ inch thick.

3 Spoon beef mixture onto one side of each dough round to within ½ inch of edges. Top beef on each round with cheese. Fold dough in half, covering filling. Press edges with fork to seal. On ungreased cookie sheet, place calzones.

4 Brush calzones with egg. Sprinkle with sesame seed. Bake 15 to 20 minutes or until golden brown.

High Altitude (3500–6500 ft): In step 4, bake 20 to 25 minutes.

1 CALZONE: Calories 340 (Calories from Fat 130); Total Fat 14g (Saturated Fat 5g); Cholesterol 75mg; Sodium 950mg; Total Carbohydrate 34g (Dietary Fiber 1g; Sugars 4g); Protein 19g **% DAILY VALUE:** Vitamin A 4%; Vitamin C 0%; Calcium 25%; Iron 15% **EXCHANGES:** 2 Starch, 2 Medium-Fat Meat, ½ Fat **CARBOHYDRATE CHOICES:** 2

CHAPTER 8

Delicious
Desserts, Cookies
and Bars

Classic Strawberry Shortcakes

PREP TIME: 10 MINUTES ● START TO FINISH: 1 HOUR 40 MINUTES
6 SERVINGS

1 quart (4 cups) fresh strawberries, sliced

½ cup sugar

2⅓ cups Original Bisquick mix

3 tablespoons sugar

½ cup milk

3 tablespoons butter or margarine, melted

¾ cup whipped cream or frozen (thawed) whipped topping

1 In medium bowl, toss strawberries and ½ cup sugar until coated. Let stand 1 hour.

2 Heat oven to 425°F. In medium bowl, stir Bisquick mix, 3 tablespoons sugar, the milk and butter until soft dough forms. On ungreased cookie sheet, drop dough by 6 spoonfuls.

3 Bake 10 to 12 minutes or until golden brown. Cool 15 minutes. Using knife, split warm shortcakes. Fill and top with strawberries and whipped cream.

High Altitude (3500–6500 ft): Heat oven to 450°F. Decrease sugar in shortcakes to 1 tablespoon.

1 SERVING: Calories 400 (Calories from Fat 130); Total Fat 14g (Saturated Fat 7g); Cholesterol 15mg; Sodium 620mg; Total Carbohydrate 64g (Dietary Fiber 3g; Sugars 31g); Protein 5g **% DAILY VALUE:** Vitamin A 4%; Vitamin C 90%; Calcium 10%; Iron 10% **EXCHANGES:** 1½ Starch, ½ Fruit, 2 Other Carbohydrate, 2½ Fat **CARBOHYDRATE CHOICES:** 4

Quick Tip It's easy to make one big shortcake and cut it into 6 wedges. Just spread the dough in an ungreased 8-inch round baking pan and bake 15 to 20 minutes or until golden brown. Split each wedge and fill with strawberries and top with strawberries and whipped cream.

Chocolate-Strawberry Shortcakes

PREP TIME: 15 MINUTES ● **START TO FINISH: 1 HOUR 45 MINUTES**
6 SERVINGS

1 quart (4 cups) fresh strawberries, sliced

½ cup sugar

2 cups Original Bisquick mix

⅓ cup unsweetened baking cocoa

2 tablespoons sugar

⅔ cup milk

2 tablespoons butter or margarine, melted

⅓ cup miniature semisweet chocolate chips

1½ cups frozen (thawed) whipped topping

1 In medium bowl, toss strawberries and ½ cup sugar until coated. Let stand 1 hour.

2 Heat oven to 375°F. Spray cookie sheet with cooking spray. In medium bowl, stir Bisquick mix, cocoa, 2 tablespoons sugar, the milk and butter until soft dough forms. Stir in chocolate chips. Drop dough by about ⅓ cupfuls onto cookie sheet.

3 Bake 12 to 15 minutes or until tops of shortcakes appear dry and cracked. Cool 15 minutes. Using serrated knife, split warm shortcakes. Fill and top with strawberries and whipped topping.

High Altitude (3500–6500 ft): No change.

1 SERVING: Calories 450 (Calories from Fat 150); Total Fat 17g (Saturated Fat 9g); Cholesterol 10mg; Sodium 530mg; Total Carbohydrate 70g (Dietary Fiber 5g; Sugars 36g); Protein 6g **% DAILY VALUE:** Vitamin A 4%; Vitamin C 110%; Calcium 10%; Iron 15% **EXCHANGES:** 2 Starch, ½ Fruit, 2 Other Carbohydrate, 3 Fat **CARBOHYDRATE CHOICES:** 4½

Quick Tip For a pretty garnish, sprinkle additional miniature chocolate chips over tops of shortcakes.

Heart Smart Strawberry Shortcakes

PREP TIME: 10 MINUTES ● START TO FINISH: 1 HOUR 40 MINUTES
6 SERVINGS

1 quart (4 cups) fresh strawberries, sliced

½ cup sugar

1¾ cups Bisquick Heart Smart mix

2 tablespoons sugar

½ cup fat-free (skim) milk

2 tablespoons butter or margarine, melted

¾ cup frozen (thawed) fat-free whipped topping

1 In medium bowl, toss strawberries and ½ cup sugar until coated. Let stand 1 hour.

2 Heat oven to 425°F. In medium bowl, stir Bisquick mix, 2 tablespoons sugar, the milk and butter until soft dough forms. On ungreased cookie sheet, drop dough by 6 spoonfuls.

3 Bake 10 to 12 minutes or until golden brown. Cool 15 minutes. Using knife, split warm shortcakes. Fill and top with strawberries and whipped topping.

High Altitude (3500–6500 ft): No change.

1 SERVING: Calories 300 (Calories from Fat 60); Total Fat 7g (Saturated Fat 2.5g); Cholesterol 10mg; Sodium 420mg; Total Carbohydrate 56g (Dietary Fiber 2g; Sugars 30g); Protein 4g **% DAILY VALUE:** Vitamin A 4%; Vitamin C 90%; Calcium 15%; Iron 10% **EXCHANGES:** 1 Starch, ½ Fruit, 2 Other Carbohydrate, 1½ Fat **CARBOHYDRATE CHOICES:** 4

Peach 'n' Streusel Shortcake

PREP TIME: 15 MINUTES ● **START TO FINISH: 40 MINUTES**
6 SERVINGS

2⅓ cups Original Bisquick mix

3 tablespoons packed brown sugar

1 cup sour cream

2 tablespoons butter or margarine, melted

2 tablespoons packed brown sugar

1 tablespoon butter or margarine, softened

¼ cup chopped pecans

1 can (29 oz) sliced peaches, drained

Sweetened whipped cream

Additional chopped pecans, if desired

1 Heat oven to 400°F. In medium bowl, stir Bisquick mix, 3 tablespoons brown sugar, sour cream and 2 tablespoons butter until soft dough forms.

2 In ungreased 9-inch square pan, press dough, using fingers coated with Bisquick mix. In small bowl, mix 2 tablespoons brown sugar, 1 tablespoon butter and the pecans. Sprinkle mixture over dough.

3 Bake 20 to 25 minutes or until golden brown. Cut warm shortcake into 6 wedges. Split each wedge. Fill and top with sliced peaches. Top with whipped cream and additional chopped pecans.

High Altitude (3500–6500 ft): No change.

1 SERVING: Calories 470 (Calories from Fat 240); Total Fat 26g (Saturated Fat 13g); Cholesterol 55mg; Sodium 640mg; Total Carbohydrate 52g (Dietary Fiber 3g; Sugars 21g); Protein 6g **% DAILY VALUE:** Vitamin A 20%; Vitamin C 2%; Calcium 10%; Iron 10% **EXCHANGES:** 2 Starch, 1½ Other Carbohydrate, 5 Fat **CARBOHYDRATE CHOICES:** 3½

Quick Tip You can substitute 1 package (16 oz) frozen sliced peaches, thawed, for the canned peaches.

The time was ripe to combine the tenderness of Velvet Crumb Shortcake with the juiciness of fresh ripe peaches in this 1960s ad.

Almond Shortcake
with Strawberry-Rhubarb Sauce

PREP TIME: 10 MINUTES ● **START TO FINISH: 50 MINUTES**
8 SERVINGS

SAUCE

3 cups cut-up fresh rhubarb
(about 1¼ lb)

1 cup sugar

1 tablespoon water

2 tablespoons cornstarch

2 tablespoons cold water

1 pint (2 cups) fresh
strawberries, sliced

SHORTCAKE

2¾ cups Original Bisquick mix

3 tablespoons sugar

½ cup milk

3 tablespoons butter or
margarine, melted

1 to 2 teaspoons milk

1 teaspoon sugar

2 tablespoons slivered almonds

Whipped cream, if desired

1 Heat oven to 425°F. Spray 9-inch round cake pan with cooking spray. In 2-quart saucepan, heat rhubarb, 1 cup sugar and 1 tablespoon water to boiling over medium-high heat. In small bowl, mix cornstarch and 2 tablespoons cold water; stir into rhubarb mixture. Reduce heat to low; simmer uncovered about 5 minutes, stirring occasionally, until rhubarb is tender. Cool sauce about 30 minutes. Stir in strawberries.

2 In medium bowl, stir Bisquick mix, 3 tablespoons sugar, ½ cup milk and the butter until soft dough forms. Press in bottom of pan; brush with milk. Sprinkle with 1 teaspoon sugar and the almonds.

3 Bake 15 to 20 minutes or until light golden brown. Remove from pan; cut into wedges. Split wedges horizontally. Fill and top shortcakes with sauce; top with whipped cream.

High Altitude (3500–6500 ft): No change.

1 SERVING: Calories 370 (Calories from Fat 100); Total Fat 11g (Saturated Fat 4.5g); Cholesterol 15mg; Sodium 540mg; Total Carbohydrate 64g (Dietary Fiber 3g; Sugars 34g); Protein 5g **% DAILY VALUE:** Vitamin A 4%; Vitamin C 25%; Calcium 20%; Iron 8% **EXCHANGES:** 1½ Starch, ½ Fruit, 2 Other Carbohydrate, 2 Fat **CARBOHYDRATE CHOICES:** 4

Quick Tip If you prefer to make individual shortcakes, decrease the amount of baking mix to 2⅓ cups and drop the dough in 6 mounds onto ungreased cookie sheet. Bake 11 to 12 minutes or until golden brown. Fill and top with sauce.

Meringue-Topped Strawberry Shortcake

PREP TIME: 25 MINUTES ● **START TO FINISH: 2 HOURS 50 MINUTES**
8 SERVINGS

1 quart (4 cups) fresh
    strawberries, sliced

¼ cup granulated sugar

2⅓ cups Original Bisquick mix

3 tablespoons granulated sugar

3 tablespoons butter or
    margarine, melted

½ cup milk

2 egg whites

¼ cup powdered sugar

¼ cup granulated sugar

1 tablespoon granulated sugar

1 In medium bowl, toss strawberries with ¼ cup granulated sugar. Let stand 1 hour.

2 Meanwhile, heat oven to 375°F. In medium bowl, stir Bisquick mix, 3 tablespoons granulated sugar, the butter and milk until soft dough forms. Place on surface sprinkled with Bisquick mix. Shape into a ball; knead 8 to 10 times. Press dough in ungreased 9-inch round cake pan.

3 In medium bowl, beat egg whites until foamy. Beat in powdered sugar and ¼ cup granulated sugar, 1 tablespoon at a time, beating until stiff and glossy. Spread meringue on dough; sprinkle with 1 tablespoon granulated sugar.

4 Bake about 30 minutes or until golden brown. Cool 10 minutes. Run knife around edge of pan to loosen short-cake; turn onto cloth-covered cooling rack or plate. Turn meringue side up onto rack. Cool completely, about 1 hour. Serve with strawberries.

High Altitude (over 3500 ft): No change.

1 SERVING: Calories 310 (Calories from Fat 80); Total Fat 9g (Saturated Fat 4.5g); Cholesterol 15mg; Sodium 480mg; Total Carbohydrate 52g (Dietary Fiber 2g; Sugars 27g); Protein 5g **% DAILY VALUE:** Vitamin A 4%; Vitamin C 70%; Calcium 6%; Iron 8% **EXCHANGES:** 1½ Starch, ½ Fruit, 1½ Other Carbohydrate, 1½ Fat **CARBOHYDRATE CHOICES:** 3½

In 1942, Bisquick helped young brides win the good-natured war with their mothers-in-law! After the wedding, it was "Basic training" with Bisquick, ensuring happy hubbies and victory in the dessert arena.

White Chocolate Shortcakes with Raspberries

PREP TIME: 10 MINUTES ● **START TO FINISH: 30 MINUTES**
7 SERVINGS

4 cups fresh raspberries

¼ cup sugar

2⅓ cups Original Bisquick mix

3 tablespoons sugar

½ cup milk

2 tablespoons butter or margarine, melted

2 oz white chocolate baking bar (from 6-oz package), finely chopped

1 Heat oven to 425°F. In medium bowl, toss raspberries with ¼ cup sugar until coated. Let stand 10 minutes.

2 In medium bowl, stir all remaining ingredients until soft dough forms. Place dough on surface sprinkled with Bisquick mix. Shape into a ball; knead 10 times. Roll ½ inch thick. Cut with 3-inch round cutter. On ungreased cookie sheet, place rounds about 2 inches apart.

3 Bake 8 to 10 minutes or until golden brown. Fill and top shortcakes with raspberries.

High Altitude (3500–6500 ft): Heat oven to 450°F. Bake 10 to 12 minutes.

1 SERVING: Calories 330 (Calories from Fat 110); Total Fat 12g (Saturated Fat 5g); Cholesterol 10mg; Sodium 530mg; Total Carbohydrate 53g (Dietary Fiber 5g; Sugars 23g); Protein 5g **% DAILY VALUE:** Vitamin A 4%; Vitamin C 30%; Calcium 10%; Iron 8% **EXCHANGES:** 1 Starch, ½ Fruit, 2 Other Carbohydrate, 2 Fat **CARBOHYDRATE CHOICES:** 3½

Quick Tip You can substitute 4 cups sliced strawberries for the raspberries. Or use your favorite combination of berries—strawberries, blueberries, raspberries or blackberries.

Pumpkin Ring Cake

PREP TIME: 15 MINUTES ● START TO FINISH: 2 HOURS 15 MINUTES
12 SERVINGS

CAKE

3 cups Original Bisquick mix

1 cup granulated sugar

1 cup packed brown sugar

2½ teaspoons pumpkin pie spice

1 can (16 oz) pumpkin (not pumpkin pie mix)

¼ cup butter or margarine, softened

¼ cup milk

4 eggs

GLAZE

1 cup powdered sugar

1 tablespoon milk

½ teaspoon vanilla

1 Heat oven to 350°F. Grease and flour 12-cup fluted tube cake pan. In large bowl, beat Bisquick mix, granulated sugar, brown sugar, pumpkin pie spice, pumpkin, butter, ¼ cup milk and the eggs on low speed 30 seconds. Beat on medium speed 3 minutes. Spoon and spread in pan.

2 Bake about 50 minutes or until toothpick inserted in center comes out clean. Cool 10 minutes. Invert cake onto heatproof plate or cooling rack; carefully remove pan. Cool completely, about 1 hour.

3 In small bowl, mix all glaze ingredients until smooth and thin enough to drizzle. Drizzle over cake.

High Altitude (3500–6500 ft): Heat oven to 375°F.

1 SERVING: Calories 380 (Calories from Fat 90); Total Fat 10g (Saturated Fat 4.5g); Cholesterol 80mg; Sodium 430mg; Total Carbohydrate 68g (Dietary Fiber 2g; Sugars 46g); Protein 5g **% DAILY VALUE:** Vitamin A 120%; Vitamin C 0%; Calcium 8%; Iron 10% **EXCHANGES:** 1½ Starch, 3 Other Carbohydrate, 2 Fat **CARBOHYDRATE CHOICES:** 4½

Quick Tip For best results, do not spray fluted tube cake pans with cooking spray. Use shortening and flour or baking spray with flour.

Mango Cake

PREP TIME: 25 MINUTES ● **START TO FINISH: 1 HOUR 5 MINUTES**
8 SERVINGS

CAKE

1⅔ cups Original Bisquick mix

½ cup granulated sugar

⅓ cup milk or water

2 tablespoons vegetable oil

1 teaspoon vanilla

½ teaspoon ground nutmeg

1 egg

1 cup diced mango

TOPPING

½ cup flaked coconut

⅓ cup packed brown sugar

¼ cup chopped macadamia nuts

3 tablespoons butter or margarine, softened

2 tablespoons milk

1 Heat oven to 350°F. Grease 9-inch round cake pan or 8-inch square pan; sprinkle with Bisquick mix. In large bowl, beat all cake ingredients except mango with electric mixer on low speed 30 seconds, scraping bowl constantly. Beat on medium speed 4 minutes, scraping bowl occasionally. Fold in mango. Pour into pan.

2 Bake 30 to 35 minutes or until toothpick inserted in center comes out clean.

3 Meanwhile, in small bowl, mix all topping ingredients until well blended. Spread topping over warm cake.

4 Broil cake with top 3 inches from heat about 3 minutes or until topping is golden brown. Cool 30 minutes before serving. If desired, serve with sweetened whipped cream.

High Altitude (3500–6500 ft): Bake 32 to 37 minutes. In step 4, broil 1 to 2 minutes.

1 SERVING: Calories 340 (Calories from Fat 150); Total Fat 16g (Saturated Fat 6g); Cholesterol 40mg; Sodium 380mg; Total Carbohydrate 45g (Dietary Fiber 1g; Sugars 27g); Protein 4g **% DAILY VALUE:** Vitamin A 8%; Vitamin C 4%; Calcium 6%; Iron 6% **EXCHANGES:** 1 Starch, 2 Other Carbohydrate, 3 Fat **CARBOHYDRATE CHOICES:** 3

Pineapple Cake: Substitute ground cinnamon for the nutmeg and 1 can (20 ounces) crushed pineapple, well drained, for the mango. Substitute pecans for the macadamia nuts in the topping.

Glazed Lemon Pound Cake

PREP TIME: 15 MINUTES ● **START TO FINISH: 2 HOURS 15 MINUTES**
12 SERVINGS

CAKE

2½ cups Original Bisquick mix

⅔ cup granulated sugar

¼ cup butter or margarine, melted

3 eggs

¾ cup milk

1 teaspoon vanilla

3 tablespoons grated lemon peel

GLAZE

½ cup powdered sugar

1 tablespoon lemon juice

1 Heat oven to 325°F. Spray bottom only of 9 × 5-inch loaf pan with baking spray with flour. In large bowl, beat all cake ingredients except lemon peel with electric mixer on low speed 30 seconds, scraping bowl constantly. Beat on medium speed 2 minutes, scraping bowl occasionally. Stir in lemon peel. Pour into pan.

2 Bake 45 to 50 minutes or until toothpick inserted in center comes out clean. Cool 10 minutes. Loosen sides of cake from pan with metal spatula. Remove cake from pan to cooling rack. Cool completely, about 1 hour.

3 In small bowl, mix powdered sugar and lemon juice with spoon until smooth. Drizzle glaze over cake.

High Altitude (3500–6500 ft): Heat oven to 375°F. Increase Bisquick mix to 2¾ cups and add ¼ cup all-purpose flour.

1 SERVING: Calories 230 (Calories from Fat 80); Total Fat 9g (Saturated Fat 4g); Cholesterol 65mg; Sodium 360mg; Total Carbohydrate 34g (Dietary Fiber 0g; Sugars 18g); Protein 4g **% DAILY VALUE:** Vitamin A 4%; Vitamin C 0%; Calcium 6%; Iron 4% **EXCHANGES:** 1 Starch, 1½ Other Carbohydrate, 1½ Fat **CARBOHYDRATE CHOICES:** 2

Glazed Lime Pound Cake: Substitute 3 tablespoons grated lime peel and 1 tablespoon lime juice for the lemon.

Honey-Apple Cake

PREP TIME: 20 MINUTES ● **START TO FINISH: 2 HOURS 25 MINUTES**
12 SERVINGS

CAKE

1 cup chopped pecans

3½ cups Original Bisquick mix

1 teaspoon ground
cinnamon

¼ teaspoon ground nutmeg

1½ cups granulated sugar

½ cup vegetable oil

¼ cup honey

3 eggs

1 teaspoon vanilla

3 cups chopped medium
tart cooking apples
(Haralson or Granny Smith)

SAUCE AND TOPPING

1 cup packed brown sugar

½ cup butter or margarine

¼ cup honey

¼ cup milk

Vanilla ice cream

1 Heat oven to 350°F. Grease and flour 12-cup fluted tube cake pan. Sprinkle bottom of pan with ¼ cup of the pecans; set aside. In medium bowl, stir Bisquick mix, cinnamon and nutmeg; set aside.

2 In large bowl, beat granulated sugar, oil and ¼ cup honey with electric mixer on medium speed 30 seconds. Add eggs, one at a time, beating well after each addition. Gradually add Bisquick mixture to sugar mixture, beating at low speed just until blended. Stir in vanilla, remaining ¾ cup pecans and the apples. Spoon over pecans in pan.

3 Bake 55 to 60 minutes or until toothpick inserted in center comes out clean. Cool in pan on a cooling rack 15 minutes.

4 In 2-quart saucepan, heat brown sugar, butter, ¼ cup honey and the milk to boiling over medium-high heat, stirring constantly. Boil, stirring constantly, 2 minutes. Remove cake from pan to cooling rack. Pour ½ cup sauce over warm cake. Cool completely, about 1 hour. Serve remaining sauce with cake. Top with ice cream, if desired.

High Altitude (3500–6500 ft): Bake 60 to 65 minutes.

1 SERVING: Calories 690 (Calories from Fat 300); Total Fat 33g (Saturated Fat 11g); Cholesterol 90mg; Sodium 540mg; Total Carbohydrate 92g (Dietary Fiber 3g; Sugars 65g); Protein 7g **% DAILY VALUE:** Vitamin A 10%; Vitamin C 0%; Calcium 10%; Iron 10% **EXCHANGES:** 2 Starch, 4 Other Carbohydrate, 6½ Fat **CARBOHYDRATE CHOICES:** 6

Almond Crumb Cakes

PREP TIME: 15 MINUTES ● **START TO FINISH: 1 HOUR**
2 CAKES

TOPPING

⅓ cup Original Bisquick mix

2 tablespoons sugar

1 tablespoon butter or margarine, softened

¼ cup sliced almonds

CAKES

⅔ cup Original Bisquick mix

¼ cup sugar

⅓ cup milk

2 tablespoons fat-free egg product

1 tablespoon butter or margarine, softened

½ teaspoon almond extract

1 Heat oven to 350°F. Spray two 10-ounce custard cups with cooking spray. In small bowl, mix topping ingredients until large crumbs form; set aside.

2 In medium bowl, beat all cake ingredients with wire whisk or fork until well blended (batter will be slightly thin). Divide batter evenly among custard cups. Top each with topping mixture.

3 Bake 28 to 35 minutes or until toothpick inserted in center comes out clean. Cool 10 minutes. Remove cakes from custard cups. Serve warm or cool.

High Altitude (3500–6500 ft): For cakes, increase Bisquick mix to 1 cup.

1 CAKE: Calories 610 (Calories from Fat 240); Total Fat 26g (Saturated Fat 11g); Cholesterol 35mg; Sodium 870mg; Total Carbohydrate 81g (Dietary Fiber 3g; Sugars 42g); Protein 10g **% DAILY VALUE:** Vitamin A 10%; Vitamin C 0%; Calcium 15%; Iron 15% **EXCHANGES:** 2½ Starch, 3 Other Carbohydrate, 5 Fat **CARBOHYDRATE CHOICES:** 5½

Quick Tip Egg product is good to use when making small recipes because you can use less than a whole egg. If you don't have egg product, mix 1 egg well and use 2 tablespoons of the mixed egg.

Frosted Chocolate Malt Cupcakes

PREP TIME: 30 MINUTES ● **START TO FINISH: 1 HOUR 20 MINUTES**
16 CUPCAKES

CUPCAKES

1½ cups Original Bisquick mix

¾ cup granulated sugar

⅓ cup unsweetened baking cocoa

¼ cup chocolate-flavor malted milk powder

⅔ cup milk

¼ cup vegetable oil

1 teaspoon vanilla

2 eggs

FROSTING

2 tablespoons chocolate-flavor malted milk powder

2 tablespoons milk

2 cups powdered sugar

1 tablespoon unsweetened baking cocoa

¼ cup butter or margarine, softened

1 Heat oven to 400°F. Line 16 regular-size muffin cups with paper baking cups. In large bowl, beat all cupcake ingredients with electric mixer on low speed 30 seconds, scraping bowl constantly. Beat on medium speed 4 minutes, scraping bowl occasionally. Spoon evenly into muffin cups.

2 Bake 15 to 20 minutes or until toothpick inserted in center comes out clean. Immediately remove from pan. Cool completely, about 30 minutes.

3 In medium bowl, stir together malted milk powder and milk; let stand 5 minutes. Add remaining frosting ingredients; beat with electric mixer on medium speed 1 to 2 minutes or until smooth. Spread frosting over cupcakes.

High Altitude (3500–6500 ft): Heat oven to 375°F. Bake 13 to 18 minutes.

1 CUPCAKE: Calories 230 (Calories from Fat 80); Total Fat 9g (Saturated Fat 3.5g); Cholesterol 35mg; Sodium 180mg; Total Carbohydrate 35g (Dietary Fiber 1g; Sugars 26g); Protein 3g **% DAILY VALUE:** Vitamin A 8%; Vitamin C 2%; Calcium 4%; Iron 6% **EXCHANGES:** 1 Starch, 1½ Other Carbohydrate, 1½ Fat **CARBOHYDRATE CHOICES:** 2

Quick Tip Double your malted milk pleasure by pressing coarsely chopped malted milk balls on top of the frosted cupcakes.

Lemon Biscuit Pudding

PREP TIME: 15 MINUTES ● **START TO FINISH: 40 MINUTES**
6 SERVINGS

BISCUITS

¼ cup sugar

2½ cups Original Bisquick mix

½ cup milk

1 teaspoon grated lemon peel

PUDDING

1 cup half-and-half

½ cup sugar

1 tablespoon grated lemon peel

1 egg

1 Heat oven to 450°F. Spray 8-inch square (2-quart) glass baking dish with cooking spray.

2 Reserve 1½ teaspoons of the ¼ cup sugar. In medium bowl, stir remaining sugar and remaining biscuit ingredients until soft dough forms. Drop dough by 9 spoonfuls into dish. Sprinkle reserved 1½ teaspoons sugar over top.

3 Bake 8 to 10 minutes or until light golden brown.

4 Meanwhile, in medium bowl, beat all pudding ingredients with wire whisk or fork until well blended. Pour over hot biscuits.

5 Reduce oven temperature to 350°F. Bake 18 to 20 minutes longer or until pudding is set and knife inserted in center comes out clean. Serve warm.

High Altitude (3500–6500 ft): In step 3, bake 12 to 14 minutes. In step 5, bake 20 to 22 minutes longer.

1 SERVING: Calories 380 (Calories from Fat 110); Total Fat 12g (Saturated Fat 5g); Cholesterol 50mg; Sodium 650mg; Total Carbohydrate 60g (Dietary Fiber 1g; Sugars 29g); Protein 7g **% DAILY VALUE:** Vitamin A 4%; Vitamin C 0%; Calcium 10%; Iron 8% **EXCHANGES:** 2 Starch, 2 Other Carbohydrate, 2 Fat **CARBOHYDRATE CHOICES:** 4

Quick Tip For an autumn treat, stir ½ cup dried cranberries into the pudding mixture before pouring over the hot biscuits.

Lemon-Blueberry Crunch Dessert

PREP TIME: 15 MINUTES ● START TO FINISH: 30 MINUTES
6 SERVINGS

2⅓ cups Original Bisquick mix

3 tablespoons sugar

½ cup milk

3 tablespoons butter or margarine, melted

2 teaspoons grated lemon peel

2 tablespoons lemon juice

6 containers (6 oz each) lemon yogurt

3 cups blueberries

¾ cup crushed granola cereal

1 Heat oven to 425°F. Spray 13 × 9-inch pan with cooking spray. In medium bowl, stir Bisquick mix, sugar, milk, butter, lemon peel and lemon juice until soft dough forms. Spread in pan.

2 Bake about 15 minutes or until golden brown; cool.

3 Cut shortcake into 2-inch squares. For each serving, in tall parfait glass or dessert dish, layer shortcake, ½ container yogurt, ¼ cup blueberries and 1 tablespoon granola; repeat layers.

High Altitude (3500–6500 ft): Bake about 18 minutes.

1 SERVING: Calories 520 (Calories from Fat 130); Total Fat 15g (Saturated Fat 7g); Cholesterol 25mg; Sodium 760mg; Total Carbohydrate 82g (Dietary Fiber 4g; Sugars 42g); Protein 14g **% DAILY VALUE:** Vitamin A 10%; Vitamin C 10%; Calcium 35%; Iron 10% **EXCHANGES:** 2 Starch, 2½ Other Carbohydrate, 1 Skim Milk, 2½ Fat **CARBOHYDRATE CHOICES:** 5½

Lemon-Raspberry Crunch Dessert: Substitute 3 cups raspberries for the blueberries.

Who has time to make dessert? You do, when you rely on the speed and convenience of Bisquick!

French Apple Dessert

PREP TIME: 35 MINUTES ● START TO FINISH: 2 HOURS
12 SERVINGS

STREUSEL TOPPING

1 cup Original Bisquick mix

½ cup chopped nuts

⅓ cup packed brown sugar

3 tablespoons firm butter or margarine

FILLING

6 cups thinly sliced peeled tart apples (4 to 6 medium)

1 cup granulated sugar

¾ cup Original Bisquick mix

¾ cup milk

2 tablespoons butter or margarine, softened

1¼ teaspoons ground cinnamon

¼ teaspoon ground nutmeg

2 eggs

1 Heat oven to 350°F. Grease 13 × 9-inch (3-quart) glass baking dish with shortening or cooking spray. In small bowl, stir 1 cup Bisquick mix, the nuts and brown sugar. Cut in 3 tablespoons firm butter with pastry blender (or by pulling 2 table knives through ingredients in opposite directions) until crumbly; set aside.

2 Spread apples in baking dish. In medium bowl, stir remaining filling ingredients until blended. Pour over apples. Sprinkle with topping.

3 Bake about 55 minutes or until knife inserted in center comes out clean. Cool slightly, about 30 minutes. Serve warm or cool.

High Altitude (3500–6500 ft): Heat oven to 375°F. Bake about 50 minutes.

1 SERVING: Calories 290 (Calories from Fat 100); Total Fat 11g (Saturated Fat 4.5g); Cholesterol 50mg; Sodium 270mg; Total Carbohydrate 43g (Dietary Fiber 1g; Sugars 30g); Protein 4g **% DAILY VALUE:** Vitamin A 4%; Vitamin C 0%; Calcium 6%; Iron 6% **EXCHANGES:** 1 Starch, ½ Fruit, 1½ Other Carbohydrate, 2 Fat **CARBOHYDRATE CHOICES:** 3

Quick Tip Granny Smith or Haralson are two good tart apples for this dessert. If you prefer a slightly tart apple, use Braeburn, Jonathan, Northern Spy or Rome.

White Chocolate–Berry Bread Pudding

PREP TIME: 30 MINUTES ● **START TO FINISH: 10 HOURS 10 MINUTES**
12 SERVINGS

PUDDING

4½ cups Original Bisquick mix

1⅓ cups milk

¾ cup grated white chocolate baking bars

⅔ cup sugar

3½ cups milk

1½ cups whipping cream

2 tablespoons butter or margarine, melted

1 tablespoon vanilla

4 eggs

1 cup frozen unsweetened raspberries (do not thaw)

1 cup frozen unsweetened blueberries (do not thaw)

BERRY SAUCE

⅓ cup sugar

2 tablespoons Original Bisquick mix

1 cup frozen unsweetened raspberries (do not thaw)

1 cup frozen unsweetened blueberries (do not thaw)

½ cup water

Fresh berries, if desired

1 Heat oven to 450°F. Butter a 13 × 9-inch (3-quart) glass baking dish. In large bowl, stir 4½ cups Bisquick mix and 1⅓ cups milk until soft dough forms. On ungreased large cookie sheet, drop dough by heaping tablespoonfuls. Bake 8 to 10 minutes or until golden. Cool on cooling rack, about 30 minutes.

2 Break up biscuits into random-sized pieces; spread in baking dish. Sprinkle with grated baking bars. In large bowl, beat ⅔ cup sugar, the milk, whipping cream, butter, vanilla and eggs with electric mixer on low speed until blended. Pour over biscuits in baking dish. Cover and refrigerate at least 8 hours but no longer than 24 hours.

3 Heat oven to 350°F. Stir 1 cup frozen raspberries and 1 cup frozen blueberries into biscuit mixture. Bake uncovered about 1 hour or until top is golden brown and toothpick inserted in center comes out clean.

4 In 1-quart saucepan, place ⅓ cup sugar and 2 tablespoons Bisquick mix. Stir in 1 cup frozen raspberries, 1 cup frozen blueberries and the water. Cook over medium heat, stirring constantly, until mixture thickens and boils. Boil and stir 1 minute; remove from heat. Serve pudding warm, topped with sauce. Garnish with fresh berries. Store in refrigerator.

High Altitude (3500–6500 ft): Bake bread pudding about 1 hour 10 minutes.

1 SERVING: Calories 530 (Calories from Fat 210); Total Fat 24g (Saturated Fat 12g); Cholesterol 120mg; Sodium 660mg; Total Carbohydrate 67g (Dietary Fiber 5g; Sugars 34g); Protein 11g **% DAILY VALUE:** Vitamin A 15%; Vitamin C 10%; Calcium 20%; Iron 10% **EXCHANGES:** 3 Starch, 1½ Other Carbohydrate, 4½ Fat **CARBOHYDRATE CHOICES:** 4½

Frozen Brownie Ice Cream Pie

PREP TIME: 30 MINUTES ● **START TO FINISH: 6 HOURS 5 MINUTES**
8 SERVINGS

HOT FUDGE SAUCE

1 can (12 oz) evaporated milk

1 bag (12 oz) semisweet chocolate chips (2 cups)

½ cup granulated sugar

1 tablespoon butter or margarine

1 teaspoon vanilla

PIE

4 eggs

¼ cup butter or margarine, melted

4 oz sweet baking chocolate, melted, cooled

½ cup packed brown sugar

½ cup granulated sugar

½ cup Original Bisquick mix

¾ cup chopped nuts

½ gallon any flavor ice cream, softened

1 In 2-quart saucepan, heat milk, chocolate chips and ½ cup granulated sugar to boiling over medium heat, stirring constantly; remove from heat. Stir in 1 tablespoon butter and the vanilla.

2 Heat oven to 350°F. Spray 9-inch glass pie plate with cooking spray. In medium bowl, beat eggs, ¼ cup butter and the chocolate with electric mixer on low speed 30 seconds or until smooth. Beat in brown sugar, ½ cup granulated sugar and the Bisquick mix until well blended; beat on medium speed 1 minute or until smooth. Pour into pie plate. Sprinkle with nuts.

3 Bake about 35 minutes or until edge appears dry and top is cracked. Cool completely in pie plate on cooling rack, about 1 hour (center will sink).

4 Spread 1½ cups fudge sauce over pie. Spoon ice cream onto pie, mounding and packing firmly. Freeze at least 4 hours until firm. Heat remaining fudge sauce; serve with pie. Store pie in freezer.

High Altitude (3500–6500 ft): Decrease eggs to 3. Use 9-inch deep-dish glass pie plate. In step 2, use electric mixer.

1 SERVING: Calories 1030 (Calories from Fat 490); Total Fat 54g (Saturated Fat 28g); Cholesterol 200mg; Sodium 350mg; Total Carbohydrate 120g (Dietary Fiber 5g; Sugars 99g); Protein 16g **% DAILY VALUE:** Vitamin A 20%; Vitamin C 0%; Calcium 35%; Iron 15% **EXCHANGES:** 3 Starch, 4 Other Carbohydrate, 1 Low-Fat Milk, 9½ Fat **CARBOHYDRATE CHOICES:** 8

Quick Tip To save time, use purchased hot fudge sauce. Spread 1½ cups room-temperature sauce over the brownie. Heat additional fudge sauce to serve with the pie.

Impossibly Easy French Apple Pie

PREP TIME: 15 MINUTES ● **START TO FINISH: 1 HOUR 5 MINUTES**
8 SERVINGS

STREUSEL

½ cup Original Bisquick mix

¼ cup packed brown sugar

¼ cup chopped nuts

2 tablespoons firm butter or
   margarine

PIE

3 cups sliced peeled tart apples
   (3 medium)

1 teaspoon ground cinnamon

¼ teaspoon ground nutmeg

½ cup Original Bisquick mix

½ cup granulated sugar

½ cup milk

1 tablespoon butter or
   margarine, softened

2 eggs

1 Heat oven to 325°F. Spray 9-inch glass pie plate with cooking spray. In small bowl, stir ½ cup Bisquick mix, the brown sugar and nuts. Cut in 2 tablespoons butter, using pastry blender (or by pulling 2 table knives through ingredients in opposite directions), until crumbly; set aside.

2 In medium bowl, mix apples, cinnamon and nutmeg. Spread in pie plate.

3 In medium bowl, stir remaining ingredients with wire whisk or fork until blended. Pour into pie plate. Sprinkle with streusel.

4 Bake 40 to 45 minutes or until knife inserted in center comes out clean and top is golden brown. Cool 5 minutes. Serve warm or cool. Store in refrigerator.

High Altitude (3500–6500 ft): Heat oven to 350°F.

1 SERVING: Calories 250 (Calories from Fat 90); Total Fat 10g (Saturated Fat 4g); Cholesterol 65mg; Sodium 240mg; Total Carbohydrate 36g (Dietary Fiber 1g; Sugars 25g); Protein 4g **% DAILY VALUE:** Vitamin A 6%; Vitamin C 0%; Calcium 6%; Iron 6% **EXCHANGES:** 1 Starch, ½ Fruit, 1 Other Carbohydrate, 2 Fat **CARBOHYDRATE CHOICES:** 2½

Impossibly Easy French Peach Pie: Substitute 2 cans (16 ounces each) sliced peaches, well drained, or 4 medium peaches, peeled and sliced (3 cups), for the apples.

Quick Tip This popular apple pie is easy to double and perfect for a potluck party. Double all the ingredients. Spray a 13 × 9-inch baking pan with cooking spray. Stir apple mixture and Bisquick mixture together in a large bowl. Bake 50 to 60 minutes.

Nothing impresses like homemade apple pie. Give yourself a helping hand and use Bisquick—and don't forget the ice cream!

Impossibly Easy Pear-Custard Pie

**PREP TIME: 15 MINUTES ● START TO FINISH: 1 HOUR 25 MINUTES
8 SERVINGS**

STREUSEL

½ cup Original Bisquick mix

¼ cup old-fashioned or quick-cooking oats

¼ cup packed brown sugar

½ teaspoon ground nutmeg

1 tablespoon butter or margarine, softened

PIE

½ cup Original Bisquick mix

⅓ cup granulated sugar

½ cup milk

2 tablespoons butter or margarine, softened

2 eggs

3 medium fresh pears, peeled, sliced (about 3 cups)

1 Heat oven to 350°F. Spray 9-inch glass pie plate with cooking spray. In small bowl, stir ½ cup Bisquick mix, the oats, brown sugar and nutmeg. Cut in 1 tablespoon butter, using pastry blender (or by pulling 2 table knives through ingredients in opposite directions), until crumbly. Set aside.

2 In medium bowl, stir all pie ingredients except pears with wire whisk or fork until blended. Pour into pie plate. Arrange pears evenly over top.

3 Bake 25 minutes. Sprinkle streusel over top. Bake 12 to 15 minutes longer or until knife inserted in center comes out clean. Cool 30 minutes. Serve warm. Store in refrigerator.

High Altitude (3500–6500 ft): No change.

1 SERVING: Calories 240 (Calories from Fat 70); Total Fat 8g (Saturated Fat 4g); Cholesterol 65mg; Sodium 240mg; Total Carbohydrate 37g (Dietary Fiber 2g; Sugars 22g); Protein 4g **% DAILY VALUE:** Vitamin A 4%; Vitamin C 2%; Calcium 6%; Iron 6% **EXCHANGES:** 1 Starch, ½ Fruit, 1 Other Carbohydrate, 1½ Fat **CARBOHYDRATE CHOICES:** 2½

Impossibly Easy Chocolate-Coconut Pie

PREP TIME: 20 MINUTES ● **START TO FINISH: 3 HOURS 25 MINUTES**
8 SERVINGS

2 cups milk

¼ cup butter or margarine, softened

3 oz unsweetened baking chocolate

1 cup coconut

¾ cup sugar

½ cup Original Bisquick mix

1½ teaspoons vanilla

3 eggs, slightly beaten

1 cup frozen (thawed) whipped topping

1 Heat oven to 350°F. Spray 9-inch glass pie plate with cooking spray. In 3-quart saucepan, heat milk, butter and chocolate over medium heat 5 to 7 minutes, stirring frequently, just until chocolate is melted; remove from heat.

2 In medium bowl, stir chocolate mixture and remaining ingredients except whipped topping with wire whisk or fork until smooth. Pour into pie plate.

3 Bake 30 to 35 minutes or knife inserted in center comes out clean. Cool 30 minutes. Refrigerate at least 2 hours or until chilled. Garnish with whipped topping. Store in refrigerator.

High Altitude (3500–6500 ft): Bake 40 to 45 minutes.

1 SERVING: Calories 360 (Calories from Fat 180); Total Fat 20g (Saturated Fat 13g); Cholesterol 100mg; Sodium 210mg; Total Carbohydrate 37g (Dietary Fiber 2g; Sugars 27g); Protein 7g **% DAILY VALUE:** Vitamin A 8%; Vitamin C 0%; Calcium 10%; Iron 15% **EXCHANGES:** ½ Starch, 2 Other Carbohydrate, ½ Medium-Fat Meat, 3½ Fat **CARBOHYDRATE CHOICES:** 2½

Quick Tip Sprinkle sliced almonds over the top of the whipped topping for a classic candy bar flavor.

Heart Smart Impossibly Easy Coconut Pie

PREP TIME: 10 MINUTES ● **START TO FINISH: 6 HOURS 5 MINUTES**
8 SERVINGS

¾ cup sugar

½ cup coconut

½ cup Bisquick Heart Smart mix

1½ cups fat-free (skim) milk

¾ cup fat-free egg product

1½ teaspoons vanilla

1 cup frozen (thawed) fat-free whipped topping, if desired

1 Heat oven to 350°F. Spray 9-inch glass pie plate with cooking spray. In medium bowl, stir all ingredients except whipped topping with wire whisk or fork until blended. Pour into pie plate.

2 Bake 50 to 55 minutes or until knife inserted in center comes out clean. Cool 1 hour. Refrigerate 4 hours or until well chilled. Garnish with whipped topping. Store in refrigerator.

High Altitude (3500–6500 ft): Bake 53 to 58 minutes.

1 SERVING: Calories 160 (Calories from Fat 20); Total Fat 2g (Saturated Fat 1.5g); Cholesterol 0mg; Sodium 160mg; Total Carbohydrate 29g (Dietary Fiber 0g; Sugars 24g); Protein 5g **% DAILY VALUE:** Vitamin A 4%; Vitamin C 0%; Calcium 10%; Iron 4% **EXCHANGES:** 1 Starch, 1 Other Carbohydrate, ½ Fat **CARBOHYDRATE CHOICES:** 2

Impossibly Easy Pumpkin Pie

PREP TIME: 15 MINUTES ● **START TO FINISH: 1 HOUR 55 MINUTES**
8 SERVINGS

½ cup Original Bisquick mix

½ cup sugar

1½ teaspoons pumpkin pie spice

1 cup canned pumpkin (not pumpkin pie mix)

1 cup evaporated milk

1 tablespoon butter or margarine, softened

1 teaspoon vanilla

2 eggs

1½ cups frozen (thawed) whipped topping

¼ teaspoon pumpkin pie spice

8 pecan halves, if desired

1 Heat oven to 350°F. Spray 9-inch glass pie plate with cooking spray. In large bowl, stir Bisquick mix, sugar, 1½ teaspoons pumpkin pie spice, the pumpkin, milk, butter, vanilla and eggs with wire whisk or fork until blended. Pour into pie plate.

2 Bake 35 to 40 minutes or until knife inserted in center comes out clean. Cool completely, about 1 hour.

3 In small bowl, stir whipped topping and ¼ teaspoon pumpkin pie spice. Serve pie with topping; top with pecan halves. Store in refrigerator.

High Altitude (3500–6500 ft): Heat oven to 375°F.

1 SERVING: Calories 210 (Calories from Fat 80); Total Fat 9g (Saturated Fat 5g); Cholesterol 65mg; Sodium 150mg; Total Carbohydrate 27g (Dietary Fiber 1g; Sugars 19g); Protein 5g **% DAILY VALUE:** Vitamin A 100%; Vitamin C 0%; Calcium 10%; Iron 6% **EXCHANGES:** 1 Starch, 1 Other Carbohydrate, 1½ Fat **CARBOHYDRATE CHOICES:** 2

Impossibly Easy Sweet Potato Pie: Substitute 1 cup mashed vacuum-packed canned sweet potatoes for the pumpkin.

Quick Tip It's easy to double this pumpkin pie for the holidays. Double all ingredients. Spray a 13 × 9-inch pan with cooking spray. Stir Bisquick mixture in large bowl. Bake 36 to 46 minutes.

Nothing's impossible with Bisquick! This 1981 ad gives everyone a head start on the holidays by slashing stress and, best of all, by recommending a truly delicious pie.

Peach-Praline Tart

PREP TIME: 15 MINUTES ● **START TO FINISH: 30 MINUTES**
8 SERVINGS

2 cups Original Bisquick mix

¼ cup sugar

¼ cup butter or margarine, softened

1 can (21 oz) peach pie filling

¼ cup chopped pecans

1 teaspoon lemon juice

Ground cinnamon

Whipped topping, if desired

1 Heat oven to 375°F. In medium bowl, stir Bisquick mix and sugar. Cut in butter with pastry blender (or by pulling 2 table knives through ingredients in opposite directions), until crumbly. In ungreased 9-inch tart pan with removable bottom or 9-inch quiche pan, press mixture firmly on bottom and up sides.

2 Bake 10 to 12 minutes or until light golden brown. Cool 10 minutes.

3 In medium bowl, mix pie filling, pecans and lemon juice until blended. Spoon and spread evenly into crust. Sprinkle with cinnamon. Carefully remove side of pan. Cut tart into wedges. Serve with whipped topping.

High Altitude (3500–6500 ft): Heat oven to 400°F. Bake 12 to 14 minutes.

1 SERVING: Calories 300 (Calories from Fat 110); Total Fat 12g (Saturated Fat 5g); Cholesterol 15mg; Sodium 410mg; Total Carbohydrate 46g (Dietary Fiber 2g; Sugars 24g); Protein 3g **% DAILY VALUE:** Vitamin A 4%; Vitamin C 0%; Calcium 4%; Iron 6% **EXCHANGES:** 1 Starch, 2 Other Carbohydrate, 2½ Fat **CARBOHYDRATE CHOICES:** 3

Cherry-Praline Tart: Substitute 1 can (21 ounces) cherry pie filling for the peach. Omit the cinnamon.

Apple-Praline Tart: Substitute 1 can (21 ounces) apple pie filling for the peach.

Easy Fresh Fruit Tart

PREP TIME: 20 MINUTES ● START TO FINISH: 3 HOURS 5 MINUTES
8 SERVINGS

2 cups Original Bisquick mix

⅓ cup sugar

⅓ cup butter or margarine, softened

1 egg

1 package (3 oz) cream cheese, softened

⅓ cup sugar

1 teaspoon vanilla

¾ cup whipping cream

4 cups assorted fresh fruit (such as strawberry halves, blueberries, raspberries, blackberries, kiwifruit slices)

½ cup apple jelly, melted

1 Heat oven to 375°F. Spray cookie sheet with cooking spray; sprinkle with Bisquick mix. In medium bowl, stir Bisquick mix and ⅓ cup sugar. Cut in butter, using pastry blender (or by pulling 2 table knives through ingredients in opposite directions), until crumbly. Stir in egg until soft dough forms. Press dough into 12 × 10-inch rectangle on cookie sheet; pinch edges of rectangle to form ½-inch rim.

2 Bake 10 to 12 minutes or until edges just begin to brown. Cool crust on cookie sheet on cooling rack 2 minutes. Remove crust with spatula onto cooling rack. Cool completely, about 30 minutes.

3 In small bowl, beat cream cheese, ⅓ cup sugar and the vanilla with electric mixer on low speed until smooth. Beat in whipping cream on medium speed until stiff peaks form. Spread over crust to within ¼ inch of rim. Arrange fruits on top. Brush jelly over fruits. Refrigerate at least 2 hours. Store in refrigerator.

High Altitude (3500–6500 ft): Heat oven to 400°F.

1 SERVING: Calories 470 (Calories from Fat 210); Total Fat 23g (Saturated Fat 13g); Cholesterol 85mg; Sodium 480mg; Total Carbohydrate 59g (Dietary Fiber 3g; Sugars 32g); Protein 5g **% DAILY VALUE:** Vitamin A 15%; Vitamin C 60%; Calcium 8%; Iron 8% **EXCHANGES:** 1½ Starch, ½ Fruit, 2 Other Carbohydrate, 4½ Fat **CARBOHYDRATE CHOICES:** 4

Quick Tip No apple jelly? You can substitute apricot preserves or orange marmalade for a tasty option.

Banana Boston Cream Dessert

**PREP TIME: 15 MINUTES ● START TO FINISH: 2 HOURS 55 MINUTES
8 SERVINGS**

PUDDING

1 package (4-serving size)
   vanilla instant pudding and
   pie filling mix

1¼ cups milk

1 cup frozen (thawed) whipped
   topping

DESSERT

1½ cups Original Bisquick mix

½ cup sugar

⅓ cup milk

2 tablespoons unsweetened
   baking cocoa

2 tablespoons butter or
   margarine, melted

½ teaspoon vanilla

2 eggs

TOPPING

2 medium bananas, sliced

¼ cup chocolate or fudge
   topping

1 In medium bowl, beat pudding mix and milk with wire whisk or electric mixer on low speed about 2 minutes or until well blended. Fold in whipped topping. Cover and refrigerate 1 hour.

2 Heat oven to 350°F. Grease and flour 9-inch round cake pan. In large bowl, beat all dessert ingredients with electric mixer on low speed 30 seconds, scraping bowl constantly. Beat on medium speed 4 minutes, scraping bowl occasionally. Pour into pan.

3 Bake about 30 minutes or until toothpick inserted in center comes out clean. Cool 10 minutes; remove from pan. Cool completely, about 1 hour.

4 Serve cake topped with pudding and bananas; drizzle with chocolate topping. Store in refrigerator.

High Altitude (3500–6500 ft): No change.

1 SERVING: Calories 350 (Calories from Fat 100); Total Fat 11g (Saturated Fat 6g); Cholesterol 65mg; Sodium 540mg; Total Carbohydrate 57g (Dietary Fiber 2g; Sugars 35g); Protein 6g **% DAILY VALUE:** Vitamin A 6%; Vitamin C 2%; Calcium 10%; Iron 6% **EXCHANGES:** 2 Starch, ½ Fruit, 1 Other Carbohydrate, 2 Fat **CARBOHYDRATE CHOICES:** 4

Quick Tip To keep bananas from turning brown, dip them quickly in lemon juice just after slicing. Don't leave them in the lemon juice because they will become mushy.

Cinnamon-Apple Crisp

PREP TIME: 10 MINUTES ● START TO FINISH: 50 MINUTES
12 SERVINGS

10 medium tart apples, peeled, thinly sliced (10 cups)

2 cups Original Bisquick mix

2 cups packed brown sugar

1 teaspoon ground cinnamon

½ cup firm butter or margarine

Ice cream, if desired

1 Heat oven to 375°F. In ungreased 13 × 9-inch pan, spread apples.

2 In medium bowl, stir Bisquick mix, brown sugar and cinnamon. Cut in butter using pastry blender (or by pulling 2 table knives through ingredients in opposite directions), until crumbly. Sprinkle over apples.

3 Bake uncovered about 40 minutes or until apples are tender. Serve warm with ice cream.

High Altitude (3500–6500 ft): Heat oven to 400°F.

1 SERVING: Calories 340 (Calories from Fat 90); Total Fat 10g (Saturated Fat 6g); Cholesterol 20mg; Sodium 310mg; Total Carbohydrate 61g (Dietary Fiber 2g; Sugars 45g); Protein 2g **% DAILY VALUE:** Vitamin A 6%; Vitamin C 4%; Calcium 6%; Iron 8% **EXCHANGES:** ½ Starch, 1 Fruit, 2½ Other Carbohydrate, 2 Fat **CARBOHYDRATE CHOICES:** 4

Quick Tip The wonderful flavor and firm texture of Granny Smith, Rome Beauty or Haralson apples make them a good choice for this comfort dessert.

Peach-Toffee Crisp

PREP TIME: 10 MINUTES ● **START TO FINISH: 50 MINUTES**
6 SERVINGS

5 medium peaches (2 lb),
    peeled and sliced (5 cups) or
    5 cups frozen (thawed) sliced
    peaches
⅔ cup quick-cooking oats
½ cup packed brown sugar
½ cup Original Bisquick
¼ cup English toffee bits
¼ cup firm margarine or butter
1 teaspoon ground cinnamon

1 Heat oven to 375°F. Spread peaches in ungreased square pan, 8 × 8 × 2 inches.

2 Mix remaining ingredients until crumbly; sprinkle over peaches.

3 Bake 35 to 40 minutes or until peaches are tender and topping is golden brown. Serve warm.

High Altitude (3500–6500 ft): Heat oven to 400°F.

1 SERVING: Calories 270 (Calories from Fat 90); Total Fat 10g (Saturated Fat 2g); Cholesterol 0mg; Sodium 280mg; Total Carbohydrate 45g (Dietary Fiber 3g; Sugars 35g); Protein 3g **% DAILY VALUE:** Vitamin A 16%; Vitamin C 4%; Calcium 6%; Iron 6% **EXCHANGES:** 1 Starch, 2 Fruit, 2 Fat **CARBOHYDRATE CHOICES:** 3

Quick Tip For awesome Apple-Toffee Crisp, substitute 5 cups sliced peeled all-purpose apples for the peaches.

Apple-Cranberry Bake

PREP TIME: 20 MINUTES ● START TO FINISH: 1 HOUR
6 SERVINGS

5 cups sliced peeled apples

1 cup fresh or frozen (thawed) cranberries

⅓ cup granulated sugar

2 tablespoons Original Bisquick mix

1 teaspoon ground cinnamon

1 cup Original Bisquick mix

½ cup chopped nuts

¼ cup packed brown sugar

¼ cup butter or margarine, softened

1 Heat oven to 375°F. In medium bowl, mix apples, cranberries, granulated sugar, 2 tablespoons Bisquick mix and the cinnamon until well blended. In ungreased 8-inch square (2-quart) glass baking dish, spread mixture evenly.

2 In medium bowl, stir all remaining ingredients until crumbly; sprinkle evenly over apple mixture.

3 Bake 35 to 40 minutes or until topping is golden brown.

High Altitude (3500–6500 ft): No change.

1 SERVING: Calories 370 (Calories from Fat 150); Total Fat 17g (Saturated Fat 6g); Cholesterol 20mg; Sodium 330mg; Total Carbohydrate 50g (Dietary Fiber 3g; Sugars 31g); Protein 4g **% DAILY VALUE:** Vitamin A 6%; Vitamin C 6%; Calcium 6%; Iron 8% **EXCHANGES:** 1 Starch, 1 Fruit, 1½ Other Carbohydrate, 3 Fat **CARBOHYDRATE CHOICES:** 3

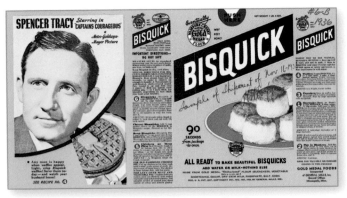

In 1936 legendary film star Spencer Tracy was enlisted to promote new Bisquick. The ideal "everyday" man and "everyday" baking mix!

Autumn Cobbler

PREP TIME: 20 MINUTES ● **START TO FINISH: 1 HOUR 5 MINUTES**
6 SERVINGS

FRUIT MIXTURE

2½ cups coarsely chopped peeled apples (2 to 3 medium)

¼ cup sugar

⅔ cup apple juice

2 tablespoons apple juice

1 tablespoon cornstarch

2 cups coarsely chopped peeled pears (2 medium)

TOPPING

1 cup Bisquick Heart Smart mix

¼ cup sugar

½ teaspoon grated orange peel

¼ cup fat-free (skim) milk

1 tablespoon sugar

1 Heat oven to 400°F. Spray 9-inch round cake pan with cooking spray. In 2-quart saucepan, heat apples, ¼ cup sugar and ⅔ cup apple juice to boiling. Cook over medium heat 5 minutes, stirring occasionally.

2 In small bowl, mix 2 tablespoons apple juice and the cornstarch until smooth. Add to apples; cook and stir until slightly thickened. Remove from heat. Stir in pears. Spoon mixture into pan.

3 In medium bowl, stir Bisquick mix, ¼ cup sugar, orange peel and milk until soft dough forms, adding additional milk if necessary. Do not overmix. Drop dough by 12 heaping teaspoonfuls onto fruit mixture. Sprinkle with 1 tablespoon sugar.

4 Bake 25 to 30 minutes or until topping is lightly browned and fruit mixture is bubbly. Cool 15 minutes before serving.

High Altitude (3500–6500 ft): Bake 28 to 33 minutes.

1 SERVING: Calories 230 (Calories from Fat 15); Total Fat 1.5g (Saturated Fat 0g); Cholesterol 0mg; Sodium 220mg; Total Carbohydrate 53g (Dietary Fiber 2g; Sugars 35g); Protein 2g **% DAILY VALUE:** Vitamin A 0%; Vitamin C 4%; Calcium 10%; Iron 6% **EXCHANGES:** 1 Starch, ½ Fruit, 2 Other Carbohydrate **CARBOHYDRATE CHOICES:** 3½

Apple-Cinnamon Cobbler

PREP TIME: 10 MINUTES ● **START TO FINISH: 30 MINUTES**
6 SERVINGS

1 can (21 oz) apple pie filling

1 cup Original Bisquick mix

¼ cup raisins

¼ cup sour cream

1 tablespoon butter or
    margarine, softened

½ teaspoon ground cinnamon

3 tablespoons sugar

1 Heat oven to 400°F. In ungreased 8-inch square pan, spread pie filling. Bake 10 minutes.

2 Meanwhile, in small bowl, stir Bisquick mix, raisins, sour cream, butter, cinnamon and 2 tablespoons of the sugar with wire whisk or fork until soft dough forms. Drop dough by 6 spoonfuls onto warm pie filling. Sprinkle tops of biscuits with remaining 1 tablespoon sugar.

3 Bake 18 to 20 minutes or until topping is light golden brown.

High Altitude (3500–6500 ft): Increase second bake time to 21 to 23 minutes.

1 SERVING: Calories 270 (Calories from Fat 60); Total Fat 6g (Saturated Fat 3g); Cholesterol 10mg; Sodium 260mg; Total Carbohydrate 51g (Dietary Fiber 2g; Sugars 34g); Protein 2g **% DAILY VALUE:** Vitamin A 2%; Vitamin C 0%; Calcium 4%; Iron 6% **EXCHANGES:** ½ Starch, 3 Other Carbohydrate, 1 Fat **CARBOHYDRATE CHOICES:** 3½

Heart Smart Blueberry Cobbler

PREP TIME: 10 MINUTES • START TO FINISH: 30 MINUTES
6 SERVINGS

1 can (21 oz) blueberry pie
   filling

1 cup Bisquick Heart Smart mix

2 tablespoons sugar

¼ cup fat-free (skim) milk

1 tablespoon butter or
   margarine, softened

1 Heat oven to 400°F. In ungreased 8-inch square (2-quart) glass baking dish, spread pie filling. Bake 10 minutes.

2 Meanwhile, in small bowl, stir Bisquick mix, 1 tablespoon of the sugar, the milk and butter with wire whisk or fork until soft dough forms. Drop dough by 6 spoonfuls onto warm pie filling. Sprinkle tops of biscuits with remaining 1 tablespoon sugar.

3 Bake 18 to 20 minutes or until topping is light golden brown.

High Altitude (3500–6500 ft): No change.

1 SERVING: Calories 220 (Calories from Fat 30); Total Fat 3g (Saturated Fat 1g); Cholesterol 5mg; Sodium 230mg; Total Carbohydrate 45g (Dietary Fiber 1g; Sugars 29g); Protein 2g **% DAILY VALUE:** Vitamin A 2%; Vitamin C 0%; Calcium 10%; Iron 6% **EXCHANGES:** ½ Starch, 2½ Other Carbohydrate, ½ Fat **CARBOHYDRATE CHOICES:** 3

Quick Tip It's a snap! Get two things done at once: Heat the pie filling while the oven heats to 400°F. Heating the blueberries before adding the biscuit topping ensures that the dough bakes through completely.

Impossibly Easy Toffee Bar Cheesecake

PREP TIME: 10 MINUTES ● **START TO FINISH: 5 HOURS 45 MINUTES**
8 SERVINGS

¼ cup milk

2 teaspoons vanilla

2 eggs

¾ cup packed brown sugar

¼ cup Original Bisquick mix

2 packages (8 oz each) cream cheese, cut into 16 pieces, softened

3 bars (1.4 oz each) chocolate-covered English toffee candy, coarsely chopped

½ cup caramel topping

1 Heat oven to 325°F. Spray bottom of 9-inch glass pie plate with cooking spray.

2 In blender, place milk, vanilla, eggs, brown sugar and Bisquick mix. Cover; blend on high speed 15 seconds. Add cream cheese. Cover; blend 2 minutes. Pour into pie plate.

3 Sprinkle candy over top; swirl gently with table knife to evenly distribute candy.

4 Bake 30 to 35 minutes or until about 2 inches of edge of pie is set and center is still soft and wiggles slightly. Cool completely, about 1 hour.

5 Refrigerate at least 4 hours. Serve with caramel topping. Store in refrigerator.

High Altitude (3500–6500 ft): No change.

1 SERVING: Calories 460 (Calories from Fat 240); Total Fat 27g (Saturated Fat 16g); Cholesterol 125mg; Sodium 360mg; Total Carbohydrate 47g (Dietary Fiber 0g; Sugars 41g); Protein 7g **% DAILY VALUE:** Vitamin A 20%; Vitamin C 0%; Calcium 10%; Iron 8% **EXCHANGES:** 3 Other Carbohydrate, 1 High-Fat Meat, 4 Fat **CARBOHYDRATE CHOICES:** 3

Impossibly Easy Raspberry Swirl Cheesecake

PREP TIME: 10 MINUTES ● **START TO FINISH: 5 HOURS 45 MINUTES**
8 SERVINGS

¼ cup milk

2 teaspoons vanilla

2 eggs

¾ cup sugar

¼ cup Original Bisquick mix

2 packages (8 oz each) cream cheese, cut into 16 pieces and softened

1 cup fresh raspberries

2 tablespoons sugar

1 Heat oven to 325°F. Spray bottom only of 9-inch glass pie plate with cooking spray. In blender, place milk, vanilla, eggs, ¾ cup sugar and the Bisquick mix. Cover; blend on high speed 15 seconds. Add cream cheese. Cover; blend 2 minutes. Pour into pie plate.

2 In same blender, place ½ cup of the raspberries and 2 tablespoons sugar. Cover; blend on high speed 15 to 20 seconds or until smooth. Drop blended raspberry sauce by teaspoonfuls on top of cream cheese mixture. With a wooden skewer or toothpick, swirl sauce into cream cheese mixture.

3 Bake 28 to 32 minutes or until about 2 inches of edge of pie is set while center is still soft and wiggles slightly. Cool completely at room temperature, about 1 hour.

4 Refrigerate at least 4 hours. Garnish with remaining ½ cup raspberries. Store in refrigerator.

High Altitude (3500–6500 ft): Bake 30 to 34 minutes.

1 SERVING: Calories 340 (Calories from Fat 200); Total Fat 22g (Saturated Fat 13g); Cholesterol 115mg; Sodium 230mg; Total Carbohydrate 28g (Dietary Fiber 1g; Sugars 24g); Protein 7g **% DAILY VALUE:** Vitamin A 15%; Vitamin C 4%; Calcium 6%; Iron 6% **EXCHANGES:** ½ Starch, 1½ Other Carbohydrate, ½ High-Fat Meat, 3½ Fat **CARBOHYDRATE CHOICES:** 2

Iced Molasses Cookies

PREP TIME: 55 MINUTES ● START TO FINISH: 1 HOUR 15 MINUTES
3 DOZEN COOKIES

COOKIES

½ cup packed brown sugar

¼ cup shortening

½ cup molasses

2 eggs

3½ cups Original Bisquick mix

1 teaspoon ground ginger

1 teaspoon ground
   cinnamon

½ teaspoon ground nutmeg

⅛ teaspoon ground cloves

ICING

1 cup powdered sugar

1 tablespoon milk

¼ teaspoon vanilla

1 Heat oven to 350°F. Spray cookie sheets with cooking spray. In large bowl, beat brown sugar, shortening and molasses with electric mixer on medium speed until well blended. Beat in eggs. Stir in remaining cookie ingredients until well blended.

2 Drop dough by rounded teaspoonfuls about 1 inch apart onto cookie sheets.

3 Bake 7 to 9 minutes or until light golden brown. Remove from cookie sheets to cooling racks. Cool completely, about 20 minutes.

4 In small bowl, mix all icing ingredients until smooth. Drizzle icing over cookies.

High Altitude (3500–6500 ft): Bake 11 to 13 minutes.

1 COOKIE: Calories 100 (Calories from Fat 30); Total Fat 3g (Saturated Fat 1g); Cholesterol 10mg; Sodium 150mg; Total Carbohydrate 18g (Dietary Fiber 0g; Sugars 9g); Protein 1g **% DAILY VALUE:** Vitamin A 0%; Vitamin C 0%; Calcium 2%; Iron 4% **EXCHANGES:** ½ Starch, ½ Other Carbohydrate, ½ Fat **CARBOHYDRATE CHOICES:** 1

Quick Tip If the icing is too thick to drizzle, stir in milk, ½ teaspoon at a time, until it is easy to drizzle.

Fudgy Frosted Brownie Cookies

PREP TIME: 1 HOUR 15 MINUTES ● **START TO FINISH: 1 HOUR 15 MINUTES**
18 COOKIES

COOKIES

1 cup Original Bisquick mix

¾ cup granulated sugar

⅔ cup chopped pecans

½ cup unsweetened baking cocoa

½ cup sour cream

1 teaspoon vanilla

1 egg

FROSTING

2 oz unsweetened baking chocolate

2 tablespoons butter or margarine

2 cups powdered sugar

3 to 4 tablespoons hot water

1 Heat oven to 350°F. Spray cookie sheets with cooking spray. In medium bowl, mix all cookie ingredients until well blended.

2 Drop dough by rounded tablespoonfuls about 2 inches apart on cookie sheets.

3 Bake 9 to 11 minutes or until set. Cool 2 minutes; remove from cookie sheets to cooling rack. Cool completely, about 30 minutes.

4 In 2-quart saucepan, melt chocolate and butter over low heat, stirring occasionally. Remove from heat. Stir in powdered sugar and 3 tablespoons of the hot water until smooth. (If frosting is too thick, add additional water, 1 teaspoon at a time.) Spread frosting over cookies.

High Altitude (3500–6500 ft): No change.

1 COOKIE: Calories 200 (Calories from Fat 80); Total Fat 9g (Saturated Fat 3.5g); Cholesterol 20mg; Sodium 100mg; Total Carbohydrate 29g (Dietary Fiber 2g; Sugars 22g); Protein 2g **% DAILY VALUE:** Vitamin A 0%; Vitamin C 0%; Calcium 2%; Iron 6% **EXCHANGES:** ½ Starch, 1½ Other Carbohydrate, 1½ Fat **CARBOHYDRATE CHOICES:** 2

Quick Tip Make these fudgy chocolate cookies a holiday favorite by frosting with your favorite vanilla frosting and sprinkling with crushed peppermint candies.

Jumbo Cashew Cookies

PREP TIME: 50 MINUTES ● **START TO FINISH: 50 MINUTES**
16 COOKIES

1¼ cups packed brown sugar

½ cup shortening

2 eggs

2½ cups Original Bisquick mix

1 cup old-fashioned or quick-
cooking oats

1 cup chopped cashews

1 Heat oven to 375°F. In large bowl, beat brown sugar, shortening and eggs with electric mixer on medium speed until blended, or mix with spoon. Stir in remaining ingredients until well blended.

2 On 2 large ungreased cookie sheets, drop dough by ¼ cupfuls about 3 inches apart. Flatten to about ½-inch thickness with bottom of glass dipped in granulated sugar.

3 Bake 8 to 10 minutes or until golden brown around edges. Cool 3 minutes; carefully remove from cookie sheets to cooling racks.

High Altitude (3500–6500 ft): Decrease shortening to ⅓ cup; increase Bisquick mix to 2¾ cups.

1 COOKIE: Calories 280 (Calories from Fat 120); Total Fat 14g (Saturated Fat 3.5g); Cholesterol 25mg; Sodium 250mg; Total Carbohydrate 35g (Dietary Fiber 1g; Sugars 18g); Protein 4g **% DAILY VALUE:** Vitamin A 0%; Vitamin C 0%; Calcium 4%; Iron 8% **EXCHANGES:** 1 Starch, 1½ Other Carbohydrate, 2½ Fat **CARBOHYDRATE CHOICES:** 2

Jumbo White Chocolate Chunk–Cashew Cookies: Stir in 1 cup white chocolate chunks or white vanilla baking chips with the cashews.

Raspberry Bars

PREP TIME: 10 MINUTES ● **START TO FINISH: 1 HOUR 40 MINUTES**
24 BARS

2 cups Original Bisquick mix

1 cup quick-cooking oats

¾ cup packed brown sugar

½ cup butter or margarine, softened

1 cup raspberry spreadable fruit, jam or preserves

1 Heat oven to 400°F. Spray 9-inch square pan with cooking spray. In large bowl, stir Bisquick mix, oats and brown sugar. Cut in butter, using pastry blender (or by pulling 2 table knives through ingredients in opposite directions), until crumbly.

2 Press half of crumb mixture in pan. Spread fruit over crumb mixture to within ¼ inch of edges. Top with remaining crumb mixture; press gently into fruit.

3 Bake 25 to 30 minutes or until light brown. Cool completely, about 1 hour. For bars, cut into 6 rows by 4 rows.

High Altitude (3500–6500 ft): Bake 27 to 32 minutes.

1 BAR: Calories 150 (Calories from Fat 50); Total Fat 5g (Saturated Fat 3g); Cholesterol 10mg; Sodium 160mg; Total Carbohydrate 25g (Dietary Fiber 0g; Sugars 13g); Protein 1g **% DAILY VALUE:** Vitamin A 2%; Vitamin C 0%; Calcium 2%; Iron 4% **EXCHANGES:** ½ Starch, 1 Other Carbohydrate, 1 Fat **CARBOHYDRATE CHOICES:** 1½

Blackberry Bars: Substitute blackberry spreadable fruit for the raspberry.

Quick Tip Brown sugar hard? Soften it in the microwave. Place the sugar in a microwavable glass bowl. Cover the bowl with a damp paper towel and then with plastic wrap. Microwave on High 1 minute and let stand covered for 2 minutes. If it is still hard, repeat microwaving for 1 minute.

Glazed Lemon-Coconut Bars

PREP TIME: 15 MINUTES ● **START TO FINISH: 1 HOUR 50 MINUTES**
16 BARS

BARS

1 cup Bisquick Heart Smart mix

2 tablespoons powdered sugar

2 tablespoons firm butter

¾ cup granulated sugar

¼ cup flaked coconut

1 tablespoon Bisquick Heart Smart mix

2 teaspoons grated lemon peel

2 tablespoons lemon juice

½ cup fat-free egg product

LEMON GLAZE

½ cup powdered sugar

1 tablespoon lemon juice

1 Heat oven to 350°F. In small bowl, stir together 1 cup Bisquick mix and 2 tablespoons powdered sugar. Cut in butter, using pastry blender or crisscrossing 2 knives, until crumbly. Press in ungreased 8-inch square pan.

2 Bake about 10 minutes or until light brown. Meanwhile, in small bowl, mix all remaining bar ingredients. Pour coconut mixture over baked layer.

3 Bake about 25 minutes or until set and golden brown. Loosen edges from sides of pan while warm. In small bowl, stir glaze ingredients until smooth; drizzle or spread over bars. Cool completely, about 1 hour. For bars, cut into 4 rows by 4 rows.

High Altitude (3500–6500 ft): In step 2, bake crust about 12 minutes.

1 BAR: Calories 110 (Calories from Fat 20); Total Fat 2g (Saturated Fat 1.5g); Cholesterol 0mg; Sodium 100mg; Total Carbohydrate 20g (Dietary Fiber 0g; Sugars 15g); Protein 1g
% DAILY VALUE: Vitamin A 0%; Vitamin C 0%; Calcium 4%; Iron 2% **EXCHANGES:** 1½ Other Carbohydrate; ½ Fat **CARBOHYDRATE CHOICES:** 1

Peanut Butter–Chocolate Chip Bars

PREP TIME: 10 MINUTES ● **START TO FINISH: 50 MINUTES**
16 BARS

¾ cup peanut butter

2 eggs

1 cup packed light brown sugar

2 cups Original Bisquick mix

1 bag (12 oz) semisweet
chocolate chips (2 cups)

1 Heat oven to 325°F. Spray 8-inch square pan with cooking spray. In large bowl, mix peanut butter and eggs until well blended. Stir in brown sugar until combined. Add Bisquick mix and chocolate chips, stirring just until moistened. Spread mixture in pan.

2 Bake 35 to 40 minutes or until golden brown. Cool completely. For bars, cut into 4 rows by 4 rows.

High Altitude (3500–6500 ft): Bake 40 to 45 minutes.

1 BAR: Calories 310 (Calories from Fat 140); Total Fat 15g (Saturated Fat 6g); Cholesterol 25mg; Sodium 250mg; Total Carbohydrate 39g (Dietary Fiber 2g; Sugars 26g); Protein 6g **% DAILY VALUE:** Vitamin A 0%; Vitamin C 0%; Calcium 4%; Iron 10% **EXCHANGES:** 1½ Starch, 1 Other Carbohydrate, 3 Fat **CARBOHYDRATE CHOICES:** 2½

Double Peanut Butter Bars: Substitute 1 bag (10 ounces) peanut butter chips for the chocolate chips.

Quick Tip For chocolate lovers, frost these bars with your favorite chocolate frosting or use a can of chocolate frosting.

Cappuccino Bars

PREP TIME: 15 MINUTES ● **START TO FINISH: 40 MINUTES**
32 BARS

BARS

1½ cups Original Bisquick mix

1 cup packed brown sugar

½ cup raisins

¼ cup chopped nuts

2 tablespoons instant coffee granules or crystals

½ teaspoon ground cinnamon

½ cup water

2 tablespoons shortening

1 egg

CAPPUCCINO GLAZE

1 cup powdered sugar

¼ teaspoon vanilla

1 to 2 tablespoons cold brewed coffee or milk

1 Heat oven to 350°F. Grease bottom and sides of 13 × 9-inch pan with shortening; lightly flour. In medium bowl, stir all bar ingredients until well blended. Spread in pan.

2 Bake 20 to 25 minutes or until toothpick inserted in center comes out clean.

3 In small bowl, mix all glaze ingredients until smooth and thin enough to drizzle. Drizzle glaze over warm bars. For bars, cut into 8 rows by 4 rows. Serve warm or cool.

High Altitude (3500–6500 ft): Heat oven to 375°F. Decrease Bisquick mix to 1¼ cups and brown sugar to ⅔ cup. Add ¼ cup all-purpose flour with the Bisquick mix.

1 BAR: Calories 90 (Calories from Fat 20); Total Fat 2.5g (Saturated Fat 0.5g); Cholesterol 5mg; Sodium 75mg; Total Carbohydrate 16g (Dietary Fiber 0g; Sugars 12g); Protein 0g **% DAILY VALUE:** Vitamin A 0%; Vitamin C 0%; Calcium 0%; Iron 2% **EXCHANGES:** 1 Other Carbohydrate, ½ Fat **CARBOHYDRATE CHOICES:** 1

Quick Tip For more coffee flavor, substitute ¼ cup chopped chocolate-covered coffee beans for the nuts.

Mississippi Mud Bars

PREP TIME: 20 MINUTES ● **START TO FINISH: 4 HOURS 35 MINUTES**
36 BARS

⅓ cup butter or margarine

5 oz unsweetened baking chocolate

¾ cup Original Bisquick mix

¾ cup plus 2 tablespoons granulated sugar

2 teaspoons vanilla

2 eggs

1½ cups miniature marshmallows

1 tablespoon butter or margarine

⅔ cup sour cream

1⅓ cups powdered sugar

1 Heat oven to 350°F. Grease and flour 9-inch square pan. In 1½-quart saucepan, melt ⅓ cup butter and 2½ ounces of the chocolate over low heat, stirring frequently. Cool slightly, about 15 minutes.

2 In medium bowl, beat chocolate mixture, Bisquick mix, granulated sugar, vanilla and eggs with electric mixer on low speed 30 seconds, scraping bowl frequently. Beat on medium speed 1 minute. Spread batter in pan.

3 Bake 20 to 25 minutes or until toothpick inserted in center comes out clean. Remove from oven; immediately sprinkle with marshmallows. Cover; let stand about 5 minutes or until marshmallows soften. Uncover; cool completely, about 1 hour.

4 In 1½-quart saucepan, melt remaining 2½ ounces chocolate and 1 tablespoon butter; cool slightly. Stir in sour cream and powdered sugar until smooth. Spread over marshmallow layer. Cover; refrigerate at least 2 hours or until firm. For bars, cut into 6 rows by 6 rows. Store in refrigerator.

High Altitude (3500–6500 ft): Heat oven to 375°F. Increase Bisquick mix to 1 cup. Bake 28 to 32 minutes.

1 BAR: Calories 110 (Calories from Fat 50); Total Fat 6g (Saturated Fat 3.5g); Cholesterol 20mg; Sodium 55mg; Total Carbohydrate 14g (Dietary Fiber 0g; Sugars 11g); Protein 1g **% DAILY VALUE:** Vitamin A 2%; Vitamin C 0%; Calcium 0%; Iron 4% **EXCHANGES:** 1 Other Carbohydrate, 1 Fat **CARBOHYDRATE CHOICES:** 1

Frosted Brownies

PREP TIME: 20 MINUTES ● **START TO FINISH: 1 HOUR 55 MINUTES**
36 BROWNIES

BROWNIES

6 oz unsweetened baking chocolate

¾ cup butter or margarine, softened

2 cups granulated sugar

1½ cups Original Bisquick mix

2 teaspoons vanilla

3 eggs

FROSTING

2 oz unsweetened baking chocolate

2 cups powdered sugar

¼ cup butter or margarine, softened

2 tablespoons milk

1 teaspoon vanilla

1 Heat oven to 350°F. Spray bottom only of 13 × 9-inch pan with cooking spray. In small microwavable bowl, microwave 6 ounces chocolate and ¾ cup butter on High 1 to 2 minutes, stirring every 30 seconds, until melted. Stir until smooth.

2 In medium bowl, stir granulated sugar, Bisquick mix, 2 teaspoons vanilla, eggs and melted chocolate mixture until well blended. Spread in pan.

3 Bake 25 to 30 minutes or until edges begin to pull away from sides of pan. Cool completely, about 1 hour.

4 In medium microwavable bowl, microwave 2 ounces chocolate on High 30 seconds to 1 minute, stirring after 30 seconds, until melted. Stir until smooth; cool 5 minutes. Stir in remaining frosting ingredients until smooth and spreadable; if necessary, add more milk, 1 teaspoon at a time. Spread frosting over brownies. Let stand until set. For brownies, cut into 6 rows by 6 rows.

High Altitude (3500–6500 ft): Decrease butter in brownies to ½ cup; decrease granulated sugar to 1½ cups.

1 BROWNIE: Calories 190 (Calories from Fat 90); Total Fat 10g (Saturated Fat 6g); Cholesterol 30mg; Sodium 105mg; Total Carbohydrate 23g (Dietary Fiber 1g; Sugars 18g); Protein 2g **% DAILY VALUE:** Vitamin A 4%; Vitamin C 0%; Calcium 0%; Iron 8% **EXCHANGES:** ½ Starch, 1 Other Carbohydrate, 2 Fat **CARBOHYDRATE CHOICES:** 1½

Helpful Nutrition
and Cooking Information

Nutrition Guidelines

We provide nutrition information for each recipe that includes calories, fat, cholesterol, sodium, carbohydrate, fiber and protein. Individual food choices can be based on this information.

Recommended intake for a daily diet of 2,000 calories as set by the Food and Drug Administration

Total Fat	Less than 65g
Saturated Fat	Less than 20g
Cholesterol	Less than 300mg
Sodium	Less than 2,400mg
Total Carbohydrate	300g
Dietary Fiber	25g

CRITERIA USED FOR CALCULATING NUTRITION INFORMATION

- The first ingredient was used wherever a choice is given (such as ⅓ cup sour cream or plain yogurt).

- The first ingredient amount was used wherever a range is given (such as 3- to 3½–pound cut-up broiler-fryer chicken).

- The first serving number was used wherever a range is given (such as 4 to 6 servings).

- "If desired" ingredients and recipe variations were not included (such as sprinkle with brown sugar, if desired).

- Only the amount of a marinade or frying oil that is estimated to be absorbed by the food during preparation or cooking was calculated.

INGREDIENTS USED IN RECIPE TESTING AND NUTRITION CALCULATIONS

- Ingredients used for testing represent those that the majority of consumers use in their homes: large eggs, 2% milk, 80%-lean ground beef, canned ready-to-use chicken broth and vegetable oil spread containing not less than 65 percent fat.

- Fat-free, low-fat or low-sodium products were not used, unless otherwise indicated.

- Solid vegetable shortening (not butter, margarine, nonstick cooking sprays or vegetable oil spread as they can cause sticking problems) was used to grease pans, unless otherwise indicated.

EQUIPMENT USED IN RECIPE TESTING

We use equipment for testing that the majority of consumers use in their homes. If a specific piece of equipment (such as a wire whisk) is necessary for recipe success, it is listed in the recipe.

- Cookware and bakeware without nonstick coatings were used, unless otherwise indicated.

- No dark-colored, black or insulated bakeware was used.

- When a pan is specified in a recipe, a metal pan was used; a baking dish or pie plate means ovenproof glass was used.

- An electric hand mixer was used for mixing only when mixer speeds are specified in the recipe directions. When a mixer speed is not given, a spoon or fork was used.

COOKING TERMS GLOSSARY

Beat: Mix ingredients vigorously with spoon, fork, wire whisk, hand beater or electric mixer until smooth and uniform.

Boil: Heat liquid until bubbles rise continuously and break on the surface and steam is given off. For rolling boil, the bubbles form rapidly.

Chop: Cut into coarse or fine irregular pieces with a knife, food chopper, blender or food processor.

Cube: Cut into squares ½ inch or larger.

Dice: Cut into squares smaller than ½ inch.

Grate: Cut into tiny particles using small rough holes of grater (citrus peel or chocolate).

Grease: Rub the inside surface of a pan with shortening, using pastry brush, piece of waxed paper or paper towel, to prevent food from sticking during baking (as for some casseroles).

Julienne: Cut into thin, matchlike strips, using knife or food processor (vegetables, fruits, meats).

Mix: Combine ingredients in any way that distributes them evenly.

Sauté: Cook foods in hot oil or margarine over medium-high heat with frequent tossing and turning motion.

Shred: Cut into long thin pieces by rubbing food across the holes of a shredder, as for cheese, or by using a knife to slice very thinly, as for cabbage.

Simmer: Cook in liquid just below the boiling point on top of the stove, usually after reducing heat from a boil. Bubbles will rise slowly and break just below the surface.

Stir: Mix ingredients until uniform consistency. Stir once in a while for stirring occasionally, often for stirring frequently and continuously for stirring constantly.

Toss: Tumble ingredients (such as green salad) lightly with a lifting motion, usually to coat evenly or mix with another food.

Index

Metric Conversion Guide

VOLUME

U.S. Units	Canadian Metric	Australian Metric
¼ teaspoon	1 mL	1 ml
½ teaspoon	2 mL	2 ml
1 teaspoon	5 mL	5 ml
1 tablespoon	15 mL	20 ml
¼ cup	50 mL	60 ml
⅓ cup	75 mL	80 ml
½ cup	125 mL	125 ml
⅔ cup	150 mL	170 ml
¾ cup	175 mL	190 ml
1 cup	250 mL	250 ml
1 quart	1 liter	1 liter
1½ quarts	1.5 liters	1.5 liters
2 quarts	2 liters	2 liters
2½ quarts	2.5 liters	2.5 liters
3 quarts	3 liters	3 liters
4 quarts	4 liters	4 liters

WEIGHT

U.S. Units	Canadian Metric	Australian Metric
1 ounce	30 grams	30 grams
2 ounces	55 grams	60 grams
3 ounces	85 grams	90 grams
4 ounces (¼ pound)	115 grams	125 grams
8 ounces (½ pound)	225 grams	225 grams
16 ounces (1 pound)	455 grams	500 grams
1 pound	455 grams	½ kilogram

MEASUREMENTS

Inches	Centimeters
1	2.5
2	5.0
3	7.5
4	10.0
5	12.5
6	15.0
7	17.5
8	20.5
9	23.0
10	25.5
11	28.0
12	30.5
13	33.0

TEMPERATURES

Fahrenheit	Celsius
32°	0°
212°	100°
250°	120°
275°	140°
300°	150°
325°	160°
350°	180°
375°	190°
400°	200°
425°	220°
450°	230°
475°	240°
500°	260°

NOTE: The recipes in this cookbook have not been developed or tested using metric measures. When converting recipes to metric, some variations in quality may be noted.